Microsoft®

Server+
Certification
Training Kit

PUBLISHED BY
Microsoft Press
A Division of Microsoft Corporation
One Microsoft Way
Redmond, Washington 98052-6399

Library of Congress Cataloging-in-Publication Data
Server+ Certification Training Kit / Microsoft Corporation.
        p. cm.
    Includes index.
    ISBN 0-7356-1272-2
      1. Electronic data processing personnel--Certification.   2. Client/server computing--Certification--Study guides.   3. Web servers--Certification--Study guides.   I. Microsoft Corporation.

QA76.3 .S463   2001
005.7'1376--dc21   2001030563

Printed and bound in the United States of America.

1 2 3 4 5 6 7 8 9   QWT   6 5 4 3 2 1

Distributed in Canada by Penguin Books Canada Limited.

A CIP catalogue record for this book is available from the British Library.

Microsoft Press books are available through booksellers and distributors worldwide. For further information about international editions, contact your local Microsoft Corporation office or contact Microsoft Press International directly at fax (425) 936-7329. Visit our Web site at mspress.microsoft.com. Send comments to *tkinput@microsoft.com.*

Special thanks to Dwight Wheeler at One Call Communications for access to One Call's co-location facilities; Christopher Pitts for his assistance with prickly details on Linux; Jim Vanne, CompTIAs Certification Program Manager for Server+; and all of the SMEs who contributed to the development of the Server+ certification, without whom this book wouldn't have been possible.

Acquisitions Editor: Thomas Pohlmann
Project Editor: Maureen Williams Zimmerman
Technical Editor: David Robinson
Author: Robert L. Bogue

Body Part No. X08-03763

Contents

Part 2   Installing and Configuring a Server

Part 3   Upgrading a Server and Peripherals

Appendix

About This Book

Welcome to the *Server+ Certification Training Kit*. This training kit will prepare you to take the CompTIA Server+ Certification exam and will help you learn techniques to better manage your servers.

You'll learn about everything from planning the environment for your server to planning the server itself to maintaining the server. Along the way, you'll find tips and tricks for server installations.

Note For more information on becoming a Server+ certified technician, see the section titled "The CompTIA Server+ Certification" later in this introduction.

Each chapter in this book is divided into lessons. Most chapters include hands-on procedures that allow you to practice or demonstrate a particular concept or skill. Each chapter ends with a short summary of the lessons and a set of review questions to test your knowledge of the chapter material.

The "Getting Started" section of this chapter provides important instructions for completing the procedures in this course. Read through this section thoroughly before you start the lessons.

Intended Audience

This book was developed for information technology (IT) professionals who need to design, plan, implement, and support server hardware or who plan to take the CompTIA Server+ Certification exam.

Prerequisites

This course recommends that students meet the following prerequisites:

- A basic understanding of PCs
- CompTIA A+ Certification (recommended)
- A basic understanding of networking technologies

- CompTIA Network+ Certification (optional)
- 18 to 24 months of experience if you wish to take the Server+ exam (recommended)

Reference Materials

You might find the following reference materials useful:

- *A+ Certification Training Kit*, Third Edition (Microsoft Press, 2001)
- *Network+ Certification Training Kit* (Microsoft Press, 2001)
- CompTIA's "Blueprint" document for the Server+ exam (available from the CompTIA Web site)
- CompTIA's "Concepts and Skills" document for the Server+ exam (also available from the CompTIA Web site)
- CompTIA's "Job Role Description" document for the Server+ exam (also available from the CompTIA Web site)

About the CD-ROM

The Supplemental Course Materials CD-ROM contains a variety of informational aids that can be used throughout this book. These aids include an electronic copy of this book, as well as worksheets you can use to record server information. (You will use these worksheets in Chapter 9.) The CD-ROM also includes an electronic copy of the *Microsoft Encyclopedia of Networking* (Microsoft Press, 2000). For more information on viewing the book on line, see the "Getting Started" section later in this introduction.

Features of This Book

After a short introduction, each chapter provides a "Before You Begin" section, which prepares you for completing the chapter. The chapters are then broken into lessons. Whenever possible, lessons contain practices that give you an opportunity to use the skills being presented. Many practices offer step-by-step procedures that are identified with a bullet symbol like the one to the left of this

▶   paragraph.

The "Review" section at the end of the chapter allows you to test what you have learned in the chapter's lessons.

The appendix, "Questions and Answers," contains all of the book's review questions and corresponding answers.

Notes

Several types of notes appear throughout the lessons:

- Notes marked **Tip** contain explanations of possible results or alternative methods.
- Notes marked **Note** contain supplemental information.
- Notes marked **Caution** contain warnings about possible safety hazards or loss of data.

Conventions

The following conventions are used throughout this book:

Notational Conventions

- Characters or commands that you type appear in **bold lowercase** type.
- *Italic* is used for book titles and for terms being introduced and defined.
- Filenames and extensions appear in uppercase when used with case-insensitive operating systems such as MS-DOS, Microsoft Windows, and Novell NetWare. They are in the correct case when used with a case-sensitive operating system, such as Linux.
- Acronyms appear in all uppercase.
- Icons represent specific sections in the book as follows:

Icon	Represents
	A hands-on practice. You should perform the practice to give yourself an opportunity to use the skills being presented in the lesson.
	Chapter review questions. These questions at the end of each chapter allow you to test what you have learned in the lessons. You will find the answers to the review questions in the "Questions and Answers" appendix at the end of the book.

Keyboard Conventions

- A plus sign (+) between two key names means that you must press those keys at the same time. For example, "Press Alt+Tab" means that you hold down Alt while you press Tab.
- A comma (,) between two or more key names means that you must press each of the keys consecutively, not together. For example, "Press Alt, F, X" means that you press and release each key in sequence. "Press Alt+W, L" means that you first press Alt and W together and then release them and press L.

- You can choose menu commands with the keyboard. Press the Alt key to activate the menu bar, and then sequentially press the keys that correspond to the highlighted or underlined letter of the menu name and the command name. For some commands, you can also press a key combination listed in the menu.

- You can select or clear check boxes or option buttons in dialog boxes with the keyboard. Press the Alt key, and then press the key that corresponds to the underlined letter of the option name. Or you can press Tab until the option is highlighted, and then press the Spacebar to select or clear the check box or option button.

- You can cancel the display of a dialog box by pressing the Esc key.

Chapter and Appendix Overview

This self-paced training course combines notes, hands-on procedures, and review questions to teach you how to plan for, maintain, and manage servers. It is designed to be completed from beginning to end, but you can also choose a customized track and complete only the sections that interest you. (See the next section, "Finding the Best Starting Point for You," for more information.) If you choose the customized track option, see the "Before You Begin" section in each chapter. Any hands-on procedures that require preliminary work from preceding chapters refer to the appropriate chapters.

The book is divided into the following parts and chapters:

The "About This Book" section contains a self-paced training overview and introduces the components of this training. Read this section thoroughly to get the greatest educational value from this self-paced training and to plan which lessons you will complete.

Part One, "Planning for a Server and Its Environment," contains Chapters 1 through 3. It covers the initial phases of server deployment and provides the framework for the rest of the book.

Chapter 1, "Laying the Groundwork," focuses on the fundamental issues that you should address before proceeding with server planning and setup. In it you learn what to read, what you can safely ignore, and what you should know before getting started with the process.

Chapter 2, "Planning a Server's Environment," discusses how to provide a good place for the server to live, including environmental issues, power issues, and the need for a disaster recovery plan.

Chapter 3, "Planning the System," gets into the real meat of selecting a system. It discusses architecture and the factors involved in choosing processors, memory, disks, and network connectivity.

Part Two, "Installing and Configuring a Server," comprises Chapters 4 through 9 and considers issues related to the configuration of a server. This part covers what you need to know to get your server operational.

Chapter 4, "Gathering and Configuring Firmware and Drivers," teaches you how to download and install firmware, as well as how to examine BIOS and RAID settings.

Chapter 5, "Installing and Configuring the Network Operating System," contains information about selecting the appropriate installation method, completing network installations, and working through the basic configuration that must be done once you've gotten the operating system running.

Chapter 6, "Installing Hardware and Peripheral Drivers," shows how to connect and configure external peripherals as well as how to update manufacturer drivers.

Chapter 7, "Performing Routine Tasks," walks you through routine tasks, such as reviewing logs and performing shutdowns.

Chapter 8, "Monitoring a Server's Performance," delves into performance monitoring and the fundamentals that you should adhere to in order to ensure meaningful data. It also teaches you how to analyze the information to identify trends.

Chapter 9, "Documenting the Installation," provides a framework for creating all of the appropriate server documentation. It explains what information is necessary for internal purposes, as well as what you may need to receive vendor support.

Part Three, "Upgrading a Server and Peripherals," consists of Chapters 10 through 13 and covers everything you'll need to know about upgrading your server once the demand has outstripped the available resources.

Chapter 10, "Upgrading Processors and Memory," discusses the issues involved in adding or replacing processors and memory, including electrostatic discharge (ESD) concerns.

Chapter 11, "Adding Hard Disks," discusses the physical steps for adding a hard disk, as well as the procedure for integrating physical storage into the logical volumes.

Chapter 12, "Adding and Replacing Add-On Cards," describes how to replace add-on cards with faster ones. It discusses issues involving interrupt request lines (IRQs), direct memory access (DMA) channels, and I/O ports.

Chapter 13, "Upgrading UPSs, Monitoring the System, and Choosing Service Tools," discusses server maintenance and monitoring issues.

Part Four, "Performing Proactive Maintenance," is made up of Chapters 14 and 15. It describes how to anticipate maintenance issues so that server problems don't sneak up on you.

Chapter 14, "Establishing a Backup Plan," discusses the different backup types and rotations and the obstacles to implementing and maintaining a backup plan.

Chapter 15, "Performing Physical Housekeeping and Verification," addresses those nagging little details that need to be checked periodically to ensure that the server is still operating correctly.

Part Five, "Troubleshooting," comprises the final two chapters in the book, Chapters 16 and 17. It describes the troubleshooting process, as well as some issues you'll need to understand to be a successful server technician.

Chapter 16, "Understanding the Troubleshooting Process," introduces the concepts behind troubleshooting, including the ways in which the troubleshooting process differs from other learning that you have accomplished in the preceding chapters.

Chapter 17, "Troubleshooting Common Problems," addresses common problems and provides background information on the components and processes involved so that you can troubleshoot problems effectively.

The appendix, "Questions and Answers," lists all of the review questions from the book, showing the page number where the question appears and giving the suggested answer.

The Glossary contains definitions of important terms used in this book.

Finding the Best Starting Point for You

Because this book is self-paced, you can skip some lessons and revisit them later. Use the following table to find the best starting point for you:

If You	Follow This Learning Path
Are preparing to take the CompTIA Server+ exam	Read through Chapter 1, "Laying the Groundwork," and then read through the review questions at the end of each chapter. Read those chapters for which the answers to the review questions aren't readily apparent to you.
Want to review information about specific topics on the exam	Use the "Where to Find Specific Skills in This Book" section that follows this table.

Where to Find Specific Skills in This Book

The following tables provide lists of the skills measured on the CompTIA Server+ Certification exam. For each skill, the table indicates where in this book you will find the lesson relating to that skill.

Note Exam skills are subject to change without prior notice and at the sole discretion of CompTIA.

1.0 Installation

Skill Being Measured	Location in Book
1.1 Conduct preinstallation planning activities	
Plan the installation	Chapter 2, Lessons 1 through 3
Verify the installation plan	Chapter 2, Lesson 3
Verify hardware compatibility with operating system	Chapter 6, Lesson 2; Chapter 12, Lesson 2
Verify power sources, space, UPS, and network availability	Chapter 2, Lesson 2
Verify that all correct components and cables have been delivered	Chapter 2, Lesson 3
1.2 Install hardware using ESD best practices (boards, drives, processors, memory, internal cable, etc.)	
Mount the rack installation	Chapter 2, Lesson 3
Cut and crimp network cabling	Chapter 13, Lesson 3.
Install UPS	Chapter 2, Lesson 2; Chapter 6, Lesson 1
Verify SCSI ID configuration and termination	Chapter 3, Lesson 3; Chapter 11, Lesson 1
Install external devices (e.g., keyboards, monitors, subsystems, modem rack, etc.)	Chapter 2, Lesson 3; Chapter 6, Lesson 1
Verify power-on via power-on sequence	Chapter 7, Lesson 2

2.0 Configuration

Skill Being Measured	Location in Book
2.1 Check/upgrade BIOS/firmware levels (system board, RAID, controller, hard disk, etc.)	Chapter 4, Lessons 1 and 2
2.2 Configure RAID	Chapter 4, Lesson 4
2.3 Install NOS	
Configure network and verify network connectivity	Chapter 3, Lesson 4; Chapter 17, Lesson 2
Verify network connectivity	Chapter 3, Lesson 4; Chapter 17, Lesson 2
2.4 Configure external peripherals (UPS, external drive subsystems, etc.)	Chapter 6, Lesson 1
2.5 Install NOS updates to design specifications	Chapter 5, Lesson 3

continued

Skill Being Measured	Location in Book
2.6 Update manufacturer-specific drivers	Chapter 6, Lesson 2
2.7 Install service tools (SNMP, backup software, system monitoring agents, event logs, etc.)	Chapter 13, Lessons 2 and 3
2.8 Perform server baseline	Chapter 8 , Lessons 1 and 2
2.9 Document the configuration	Chapter 9, Lesson 3

3.0 Upgrading

Skill Being Measured	Location in Book
3.1 Perform full backup	Chapter 14, Lesson 2
Verify backup	Chapter 14, Lesson 2
3.2 Add processors	
On single processor upgrade, verify compatibility	Chapter 1, Lesson 3; Chapter 10, Lesson 1
Verify N 1 stepping	Chapter 1, Lesson 3; Chapter 10, Lesson 1
Verify speed and cache matching	Chapter 1, Lesson 3; Chapter 10, Lesson 1
Perform BIOS upgrade	Chapter 4, Lesson 2
Perform OS upgrade to support multiprocessors	Chapter 10, Lesson 1
Perform upgrade checklist, including locate/obtain latest test drivers, OS updates, software, etc.; review FAQs, instructions, facts and issues; test and pilot; schedule downtime; implement ESD best practices; confirm that the upgrade has been recognized; review and baseline; document upgrade	Chapter 1, Lesson 1; Chapter 4, Lesson 1; Chapter 9, Lesson 1; Chapter 10, Lesson 1
3.3 Add hard disks	
Verify that disks are the appropriate types	Chapter 3, Lesson 3; Chapter 11, Lesson 1
Confirm termination and cabling	Chapter 3, Lesson 3; Chapter 11, Lesson 1
For ATA/IDE drives, confirm cabling, master/slave, and potential cross-brand compatibility	Chapter 3, Lesson 3; Chapter 11, Lesson 1
Upgrade mass storage	Chapter 11, Lesson 3
Add drives to an array	Chapter 11, Lesson 3
Replace existing drives	Chapter 11, Lesson 2

Skill Being Measured	Location in Book
Integrate into storage solution and make it available to the operating system	Chapter 11, Lesson 3
Perform upgrade checklist, including locate and obtain latest test drives, OS updates, software, etc.; review FAQs, instructions, fact and issues; test and pilot; schedule downtime; implement using ESD best practices; confirm that the upgrade has been recognized; review and baseline; document the upgrade	Chapter 1, Lesson 1; Chapter 4, Lesson 1; Chapter 8, Lesson 2; Chapter 9, Lesson 1; Chapter 10, Lesson 1; Chapter 11, Lesson 2
3.4 Increase memory	
Verify hardware and OS support for capacity increase	Chapter 10, Lesson 2
Verify memory is on hardware/vendor compatibility list	Chapter 10, Lesson 2
Verify memory compatibility (e.g., speed, brand, capacity, EDO, ECC/non-ECC, SDRAM/RDRAM)	Chapter 3, Lesson 2; Chapter 10, Lesson 2
Perform upgrade checklist, including locate and obtain latest test drivers, OS upgrades, software, etc.; review FAQs, instructions, facts and issues; test and pilot; schedule downtime; implement using ESD best practices; confirm that the upgrade has been recognized; review and baseline; document the upgrade	Chapter 1, Lesson 1; Chapter 4, Lesson 1; Chapter 8, Lesson 2; Chapter 9, Lesson 1; Chapter 10, Lesson 1
Verify that server and OS recognize the added memory	Chapter 10, Lesson 2
Perform server optimization to make use of additional RAM	Chapter 3, Lesson 2; Chapter 8, Lesson 3; Chapter 10, Lesson 2
3.5 Upgrade BIOS/firmware	Chapter 4, Lesson 2
Perform upgrade checklist, including locate and obtain latest test drivers, OS updates, software, etc.; review FAQs, instructions, facts and issues; test and pilot; schedule downtime; implement using ESD best practices; confirm that the upgrade has been recognized; review and baseline; document the upgrade	Chapter 1, Lesson 1; Chapter 4, Lesson 1; Chapter 8, Lesson 2; Chapter 9, Lesson 1; Chapter 10, Lesson 1

continued

Skill Being Measured	Location in Book
3.6 Upgrade adapters (NICs, SCSI cards, RAID, etc.)	Chapter 12
Perform upgrade checklist, including locate and obtain latest test drivers, OS upgrades, software, etc.; review FAQs, instructions, facts and issues; test and pilot; schedule downtime; implement using ESD best practices; confirm that the upgrade has been recognized; review and baseline; document the upgrade	Chapter 1, Lesson 1; Chapter 4, Lesson 1; Chapter 8, Lesson 2; Chapter 9, Lesson 1; Chapter 10, Lesson 1
3.7 Upgrade peripheral devices, internal and external	Chapter 6, Lesson 1; Chapter 11, Lessons 1 and 2; Chapter 12; Chapter 13, Lesson 1
Verify appropriate system resources (expansion slots, IRQ, DMA, etc.)	Chapter 12, Lesson 1
Perform upgrade checklist, including locate and obtain latest test drivers, OS upgrades, software, etc.; review FAQs, instructions, facts and issues; test and pilot; schedule downtime; implement using ESD best practices; confirm that the upgrade has been recognized; review and baseline; document the upgrade	Chapter 1, Lesson 1; Chapter 4, Lesson 1; Chapter 8, Lesson 2; Chapter 9, Lesson 1; Chapter 10, Lesson 1
3.8 Upgrade system monitoring agents	Chapter 13, Lesson 2
Perform upgrade checklist, including locate and obtain latest test drivers, OS upgrades, software, etc.; review FAQs, instructions, facts and issues; test and pilot; schedule downtime; implement using ESD best practices; confirm that the upgrade has been recognized; review and baseline; document the upgrade	Chapter 1, Lesson 1; Chapter 4, Lesson 1; Chapter 8, Lesson 2; Chapter 9, Lesson 1; Chapter 10, Lesson 1
3.9 Upgrade service tools (e.g., diagnostic tools, EISA configuration, diagnostic partition, SSU, etc.)	Chapter 13, Lesson 3
Perform upgrade checklist, including locate and obtain latest test drivers, OS upgrades, software, etc.; review FAQs, instructions, facts and issues; test and pilot; schedule downtime; implement using ESD best practices; confirm that the upgrade has been recognized; review and baseline; document the upgrade	Chapter 1, Lesson 1; Chapter 4, Lesson 1; Chapter 8, Lesson 2; Chapter 9, Lesson 3; Chapter 10, Lesson 1

Skill Being Measured	Location in Book
3.10 Upgrade UPS	Chapter 13, Lesson 1
Perform upgrade checklist, including locate and obtain latest test drivers, OS upgrades, software, etc.; review FAQs, instructions, facts and issues; test and pilot; schedule downtime; implement using ESD best practices; confirm that the upgrade has been recognized; review and baseline; document the upgrade	Chapter 1, Lesson 1; Chapter 4, Lesson 1; Chapter 8, Lesson 2; Chapter 9, Lesson 1; Chapter 10, Lesson 1

4.0 Proactive Maintenance

Skill Being Measured	Location in Book
4.1 Perform regular backup	Chapter 14, Lessons 2 and 3
4.2 Create baseline and compare performance	Chapter 8, Lessons 2 and 3
4.3 Set SNMP thresholds	Chapter 13, Lesson 2
4.4 Perform physical housekeeping	Chapter 15, Lesson 1
4.5 Perform hardware verification	Chapter 15, Lesson 2
4.6 Establish remote notification	Chapter 13, Lesson 2

5.0 Environment

Skill Being Measured	Location in Book
5.1 Recognize and report on physical security issues	Chapter 2, Lesson 1
Limit access to server room and backup tapes	Chapter 2, Lesson 1
Ensure physical locks exist on doors	Chapter 2, Lesson 1
Establish antitheft devices for hardware (lock server racks)	Chapter 2, Lesson 1
5.2 Recognize and report on server room environmental issues (temperature, humidity/ESD/power surges, back-up generator/fire suppression/flood considerations)	Chapter 2, Lesson 1

continued

6.0 Troubleshooting and Problem Determination

Skill Being Measured	Location in Book
6.1 Perform problem determination	Chapter 16, Lessons 1 and 2
Use questioning techniques to determine what, how, when	Chapter 16, Lesson 2
Identify contact(s) responsible for problem resolution	Chapter 16, Lesson 3
Use senses to observe problem (e.g., smell of smoke, observation of unhooked cable, etc.)	Chapter 16, Lesson 2
6.2 Use diagnostic hardware software tools and utilities	
Identify common diagnostic tools across the following OSs: Microsoft Windows NT/2000; Novell NetWare, UNIX, Linux, IBM OS/2	Chapter 13, Lesson 3
Perform shutdown across the following OSs: Microsoft Windows NT/2000, Novell NetWare, UNIX, Linux, IBM OS/2	Chapter 7, Lesson 2
Select the appropriate tool	Chapter 13, Lesson 3
Use the selected tool effectively	Chapter 13, Lesson 3
Replace defective hardware components as appropriate	Chapter 16
Identify defective FRUs and replace with correct part	Chapter 16
Interpret error logs, operating system errors, health logs, and critical events	Chapter 7, Lesson 1
Use documentation from previous technician successfully	Chapter 1, Lesson 1; Chapter 9
Locate and effectively use hot tips (e.g. fixes, OS updates, e-support, Web pages, CDs)	Chapter 1, Lesson 1
Gather resources to get problem solved	Chapter 16, Lesson 1
Identify situations requiring call for assistance	Chapter 16, Lesson 3
Acquire appropriate documentation	Chapter 9, Lesson 2
Describe how to perform remote troubleshooting for wake-on-LAN	Chapter 17, Lesson 2
Describe how to perform remote troubleshooting for a remote alert	Chapter 17, Lesson 2
6.3 Identify bottlenecks (e.g., processor, bus transfer, I/O, disk I/O, network I/O, memory)	Chapter 8, Lesson 1

Skill Being Measured	Location in Book
6.4 Identify and correct misconfigurations and/or upgrades	Chapter 16, Lesson 1
6.5 Determine if problem is hardware, software, or virus related	Chapter 16, Lesson 2

7.0 Disaster Recovery

Skill Being Measured	Location in Book
7.1 Plan for disaster recovery	
Plan for redundancy (e.g., hard disks, power supplies, fans, NICs, processors, UPSs)	Chapter 1, Lesson 3; Chapter 2, Lesson 5
Use the techniques of hot swap, warm swap, and hot spare to ensure availability	Chapter 3, Lesson 3
Use the concepts of fault tolerance/fault recovery to create a disaster recovery plan	Chapter 2, Lesson 5
Develop disaster recovery plan	Chapter 2, Lesson 5
Identify types of backup hardware	Chapter 2, Lesson 4
Identify types of backup and rotation schemes	Chapter 2, Lesson 4, and Chapter 14
Confirm and use off-site storage for backup	Chapter 14, Lesson 3
Document and test disaster recovery plan regularly, and update as needed	Chapter 2, Lesson 5; Chapter 14, Lesson 3
7.2 Restoring	
Identify hardware replacements	Chapter 2, Lesson 5
Identify hot and cold sites	Chapter 2, Lesson 5
Implement disaster recovery plan	Chapter 2, Lesson 5

Getting Started

This self-paced training course contains hands-on procedures to help you learn about CompTIA's Server+ Certification. Most of the procedures require little more than Internet access to complete, although some require a machine on which you can update firmware or change the network configuration.

The Online Book

The Supplemental Course Materials CD-ROM includes an online version of the book that you can view on-screen using Microsoft Internet Explorer 4.01 or later.

▶ **To use the online version of this book**

1. Insert the Supplemental Course Materials CD-ROM into your CD-ROM drive.

2. Select Run from the Start menu on your desktop, and type
   D:\Ebook\Setup.exe (where D is the name of your CD-ROM drive).

   This will install an icon for the online book on your Start menu.

3. Click OK to exit the Installation wizard.

Note You must have the Supplemental Course Materials CD-ROM inserted in your CD-ROM drive to use the online book.

CompTIA Certifications

The Computing Technology Industry Association (CompTIA) is a nonprofit organization that operates as a trade association for the purpose of helping shape the standards that drive the industry. CompTIA currently manages the development of five certification programs, with a sixth (and more) coming soon. The certification programs that CompTIA offers are as follows:

- **CDIA (Certified Document Imaging Architect)**   A certification focused solely on the document imaging industry. This certification is used within that industry to show competence with imaging technologies.

- **A+**   A hardware certification designed to show basic proficiency with hardware components. This entry-level certification is designed for candidates who have six months of experience in the industry. More than 250,000 people have taken and passed the A+ exams to become A+ certified. A+ certified technicians are required for a service center to become an A+ Authorized Service Center. This certification is also a prerequisite for some vendor-sponsored training programs and is required for promotions within certain organizations.

- **Network+**   A networking certification for individuals with 18 to 24 months of experience in the industry. The exam itself focuses on the issues that a typical technician would face, including network cabling and network protocol issues. Network+ is often accepted as an alternative to vendor-specific network technology exams within larger certification programs.

- **I-Net+**   An Internet certification designed to show baseline knowledge within the key networking and Internet service areas to ensure that the certified technician will have the basic skills necessary to implement and deploy Internet, intranet, and extranet solutions.

- **Server+**   A hardware-based, server-centric exam that is designed for technicians with 18 to 24 months of experience. (See the next section, "The CompTIA Server+ Certification," for more information.)

- **Linux+ (not yet released)**   This certification is designed to measure vendor-independent Linux knowledge. Although it's unclear how this certification will fit in the market with the existing vendor-neutral certification program of the Linux Professional Institute (LPI), it has the potential to become a driving certification in the Linux industry.

All of CompTIA's certifications are designed to meet a specific need within the industry. They are often sponsored initially by a vendor or series of vendors who feel that a need exists for baseline knowledge within an area.

The CompTIA Server+ Certification

The Server+ Certification represents an extension of the A+ Certification that has become so popular. The A+ Certification shows a baseline knowledge of PC hardware, but that knowledge doesn't necessarily translate to server hardware.

Other vendors, most notably Compaq, have managed their own server-based certification programs (Compaq ASE) that show competence with their specific server hardware. These two factors, together with the growing difference between PC hardware and server hardware, led to the need to develop a new certification.

The Server+ Certification is exciting because it combines the hardware aspects of installing a server with the planning and preparation steps that most organizations need when they deploy servers. In addition to the limitations of the A+ Certification in the hardware arena, CompTIA and the cornerstone members of the Server+ Certification initiative realized that environmental planning, disaster recovery, and documentation are key differences between working with PCs and working with servers.

The Server+ Certification continues to attract support from new vendors, and those vendors who already support the initiative continue to formalize the ways in which they will implement support for the exam. In their initial statements, Intel, Adaptec, IBM, and Hewlett-Packard indicated their desire to incorporate Server+ into their vendor-specific certification programs. These statements show the strong industry support that the Server+ exam already has.

One of the challenges that any vendor-neutral exam has is in deciding what vendor's products to cover. While by and large the committee was able to steer clear of including hardware or software that didn't belong within the exam, there is one exception. Despite the relatively low penetration of the market by IBM's OS/2 operating system, it's included in the exam blueprint as an operating system that you need to know about. It's covered there at the same level as Windows NT/2000, Novell NetWare, and Linux.

CompTIA's own Job Task Analysis survey, used to verify the exam blueprint, consistently put OS/2 at the top of the list of topics that were not necessary for the exam. After not seeing any questions regarding OS/2 on the Server+ exam, and knowing of its relatively small market share, we decided to provide only minimal coverage of OS/2 within this training kit.

Although OS/2 is mentioned sporadically throughout the training kit when its operation is similar to that of other operating systems, no effort is made to discuss its differences. We hope you find that this results in the best possible learning, in terms both of the Server+ Certification and your environment.

Server+ Benefits for Employers and Organizations

Through certification, computer professionals can maximize the return on investment in server technology. CompTIA Server+ Certification provides organizations with the following:

- Excellent return on training and certification investments by providing a standard method of determining training needs and measuring results
- Increased customer satisfaction and decreased support costs through improved service, increased productivity, and greater technical self-sufficiency
- A reliable benchmark for hiring, promoting, and career planning
- Recognition and rewards for productive employees by validating their expertise
- Assurance of quality when outsourcing computer services

Technical Training for Computer Professionals

Technical training is available in a variety of forms—via instructor-led classes, online instruction, or self-paced training—available at thousands of locations worldwide.

Self-Paced Training

For motivated learners who are ready for the challenge, self-paced instruction is the most flexible and cost-effective way to increase your knowledge and skills.

A full line of self-paced print and computer-based training materials is available direct from the source—Microsoft Press. Microsoft Official Curriculum courseware kits from Microsoft Press, designed for advanced computer system professionals, are available from Microsoft Press and the Microsoft Developer Division. Self-paced training kits from Microsoft Press feature print-based instructional materials, along with CD-ROM-based software. The Mastering Series provides in-depth, interactive training on CD-ROM for experienced developers. They're both great ways to prepare for Microsoft Certified Professional (MCP) and other exams.

Online Training

For a more flexible alternative to instructor-led classes, turn to online instruction. It's as near as the Internet, and it's ready whenever you are. Learn at your own pace and on your own schedule in a virtual classroom, often with easy access to an online instructor. Without ever leaving your desk, you can gain the expertise you need. Online instruction covers a variety of Microsoft products and technologies. It includes options ranging from Microsoft Official Curriculum to choices available nowhere else. It's training on demand, with access to learning resources 24 hours a day. Online training is available through Microsoft Certified Technical Education Centers.

Technical Support

Every effort has been made to ensure the accuracy of this book and the contents of the companion disc. If you have comments, questions, or ideas regarding this book or the companion disc, please send them to Microsoft Press using either of the following methods:

E-mail

TKINPUT@MICROSOFT.COM

Postal Mail

Microsoft Press
Attn: Server+ Certification Training Kit Editor
One Microsoft Way
Redmond, WA 98052-6399

Microsoft Press provides corrections for books through the World Wide Web at the following address:

http://mspress.microsoft.com/support/

Please note that product support is not offered through the above addresses.

P A R T   1

Planning for a Server and Its Environment

C H A P T E R   1

Laying the Groundwork

About This Chapter

This chapter lays the foundation for the concepts covered in the Server+ exam. It describes the steps involved in preparing to deploy servers as well as some of the core concepts that you should be familiar with before planning an installation. The focus in this chapter is on the fundamentals you need to be successful in planning, both for passing the Server+ exam and, ultimately, for deploying servers.

As we mentioned in the "About This Book" section, the Server+ exam is heavily focused on procedures and documentation. Questions about which documentation to refer to, which organization to contact, and the next step in the process are pervasive throughout the test. Although documentation, activity logs, and architectural basics may not be terribly exciting, these topics are the foundation of the exam. You can expect to revisit them throughout this book as we work through the issues involved in disaster recovery, backups, and troubleshooting.

Before You Begin

To complete this chapter, you should have

- An A+ Certification. Although not required, it's recommended for a Server+ Certification.
- A basic working knowledge of PCs and their component parts.
- A notebook to take notes in.
- A computer with Internet access.

Lesson 1: Why and When to Read Documentation

One of the last things most people like to do is read the documentation for a product. Most of us would rather play around with the product, and only if we get stuck will we go back and read the documentation. Although some of us have managed to get our VCR clocks to stop flashing "12:00" without consulting the manual, we cannot expect to implement a server in the same way. It requires preparation, which includes reading the documentation.

After this lesson, you will be able to

- Identify important documentation and read it
- Use alternatives to documentation

Estimated lesson time: 20 minutes

Identifying Important Documentation

People have many reasons for not reading documentation. Almost all of us have seen manuals translated from Chinese to English that make about as much sense as betting on the Jamaican bobsled team. We've come to expect that documentation won't provide us with the information we need.

Unfortunately, documentation exists for a reason. It allows the manufacturer of the product to communicate how to use or implement the product, but also, perhaps more important, it gives the manufacturer an opportunity to highlight potential problems with the use or installation of the product. It may, for example, outline a special setting that is required for the product to work, or it may identify a quick troubleshooting procedure.

The documentation supplied by a vendor can make your experience with the product less painful by helping you avoid some of the most common problems. It can also provide you with clear procedures for common tasks you'll need to perform. Documentation is helpful when it ultimately improves the installation of the product or reduces your frustration with an installation.

Some people decide that they would rather wing it, reading the documentation only when they encounter a problem. It's best to resist this temptation, however, because so many problems are easily avoided but difficult or time-consuming to resolve once they occur. If, for instance, you neglect to get the BIOS (basic input/output system) and RAID (redundant array of inexpensive disks) settings correct before formatting a hard disk or a RAID array, you may find yourself with the unpleasant task of reformatting that disk and redoing any work saved on it between the time you formatted it and the time you noticed the problem.

Those people who wing it often find themselves confronting these kinds of problems, and as a result they must often reschedule the same installation or upgrade over a period of days or weeks. This erodes the confidence of the user base and causes problems in larger environments where interrelated upgrades are necessary to accomplish corporate goals.

It's important to understand that, realistically, you won't read all of the documentation before implementing every new product. The sheer volume of the documentation involved would far exceed your available time.

One way to control the amount of documentation you read in a year is to limit your reading to specific types of documentation. Most products today come with a quick start guide, an installation or administrative guide, and a user's guide. For the purposes of installing a product, your best bet is to read the quick start guide before beginning.

Another good source of information is the errata sheets and other pages that are inserted into the box at the last minute. These pages generally indicate problems that other users have had with the product. (You can decide whether the vendor includes them to enhance your installation experience or just to save on technical support costs.) If one of these pages has been printed on hot pink, red, or some other conspicuously colored paper, you should definitely read it, as it probably contains urgent and important information about the product.

Once you've started the installation process, you can review the installation or administrative guide to learn any details you may need to know about the product. If you read the installation or administrative guide before starting the installation (as is recommended), the quick start guide will normally let you know.

Another way to control the amount of documentation you have to read is to use techniques that allow you to get the information you need without reading every word. These techniques are particularly helpful when a quick start guide isn't provided or doesn't cover the kind of installation you need.

The basic techniques for increasing the speed at which you can process documentation are

- Skimming
- Scanning
- Leafing

The following sections describe these techniques in more detail.

Skimming

Skimming involves reading every third to fifth word, trying to quickly pick up a general idea of what is being said by stringing the context clues together with the words you're reading.

This technique is effective when you need to get a rough understanding of what the documentation is saying without fully understanding the material. It is particularly useful during the planning phase because it allows you to gain a quick understanding of what a product can and can't do without researching every detail.

Scanning

Unlike skimming, *scanning* is more of a visual technique than a reading technique. Instead of reading every third to fifth word, you look for nonparagraph text and text set off with icons, and you read these elements completely.

The idea of scanning is that writers tend to identify the most important detailed information by including it in a bulleted list or by adding some kind of a tip or warning icon to it. When scanning, you're looking for details rather than an overview of the information being discussed.

This technique works well when you have experience with similar products because differences are almost always set off in blocks of text that you can locate with ease.

Leafing

Most of us are familiar with leafing as it applies to magazines. We generally do no more than leaf through the tons of magazines and leaflets crossing our desks each year. That is, we look through the titles and pictures on each page and stop to read only information that interests us.

In terms of documentation, *leafing* generally involves flipping through manuals looking for topics that apply to our use or implementation. It often means looking over the table of contents, selecting chapters that will be of interest, and then reading or skimming them.

Practice: Scan a Printer Manual for Warnings and Cautions

Most printers installed today have at least a quick start guide and a user's guide. If you're like most people, you haven't read the user's guide. You may not even have removed it from the protective cellophane. Use the scanning technique just described to extract important details from your printer manual.

▶ **To scan a printer manual**

1. Gather the printer documentation.

2. Identify the important documentation.

3. Identify warnings and cautions pertaining to how you use the printer.

When you identified the important information from the printer manual, did you find that you've been doing anything that is not recommended or even dangerous?

Note This practice wasn't chosen completely at random. Most people never read their printer manuals and therefore do things that the manufacturer doesn't recommend. Those things tend to add up, eventually causing problems.

Using Alternatives to Documentation

In the old days, maybe 10 years ago, when you wanted to get information about a product that wasn't in the documentation, or you wanted an explanation for something you didn't understand, you had three choices. You could

- Call the reseller who sold you the product (and be charged for support).
- Call the vendor's technical support line (and wait on hold forever).
- Dial into the vendor's bulletin board system (and hope they answered your message).

All of these options were relatively painful, so people generally used them as a last resort, after they had exhausted the provided documentation. Or they would read the documentation while on hold for tech support. Those days are long gone. In today's world of high-speed connections to the Internet, vendors with extensive online knowledge bases have found a new and better way to give you the information you need.

Recall that the goal of reading documentation is to improve the installation experience. The tools available on the Internet to make the installation go more smoothly are sometimes much more powerful than the documentation.

Internet Newsgroups

Perhaps one of the greatest benefits of the Internet is that it allows groups of people who normally wouldn't have been able to find one another to communicate about their common interests. While lots of community-based Web sites are being created today, the original mechanism for communicating with large groups of people on the Internet was Usenet, or what we now call *Internet newsgroups*.

Since there's a newsgroup for practically everything related to computers (and even more on noncomputer topics), chances are good that you can find a newsgroup dealing with the particular product you're working with, and perhaps even with the particular problem you're having.

When you start investigating a product for purchase, one of the best things you can do is go to a newsgroup search engine and search for the name of the product. This search should return a list of messages regarding the product. The search mechanisms aren't perfect, but they allow you to rapidly get information from users of a product.

The information you obtain in a newsgroup search can be invaluable for learning of the kinds of problems being reported for the product and the magnitude of the problems, so that you can anticipate and plan for your installation.

If you're looking for information on a popular product, it may help to narrow your search by including key words such as "setup" and "installation" so that you end up with a smaller list of messages to read through.

Note Internet newsgroups are also an excellent way to get an answer to a particularly odd or thorny problem. Consider adding Internet newsgroups to your "bag of tricks" when solving a problem, provided you have the time to wait for the answer.

Vendor Web Sites

In addition to the user feedback and solutions that you can get from Internet newsgroups, most vendors have provided Web sites with technical documentation and parts of their own base of knowledge on the product. The information contained on the Web site is generally more up-to-date and includes more workarounds and installation tips than the printed documentation does.

In the early days of the Internet, the three-letter acronym FAQ, short for frequently asked questions, came to be synonymous with useful information. FAQs were designed to avoid having the same questions asked over and over in the newsgroups. Most vendors have adopted the FAQ as a mechanism for eliminating some of the calls they get to their tech support department. The FAQ generally includes the top 10 to 50 questions that technical support is asked and includes the complete answers to those questions. The FAQ is an excellent first stop in any search for information.

Another means of getting information is to search a vendor's knowledge base for the product name and either "setup" or "installation." This search generally results in a list of installation problems that aren't covered in the release notes or any of the printed documentation.

By reading the FAQ and searching the knowledge base, you'll have prepared yourself for the most common problems during installation, the ones that might make the difference between a successful implementation and a monumental disaster.

Tip You can also use Internet search sites such as http://www.northernlight.com to search for information on a product or an error message. These global searches sometimes find things that the newsgroup searches don't find.

Practice: Search Newsgroups for Product Information

In this practice, you will search for information about a product and review comments from other users to determine whether there are any critical problems you should be aware of. Figure 1.1 shows the results of one such search.

Note The figure you see here, and perhaps even the process of searching the newsgroups, may change; such is the dynamic World Wide Web.

▶ **To search for product information using groups.google.com**

1. Open a Web browser.
2. Type the address http://groups.google.com in the address window.
3. On the main page, select the option to search discussions.
4. Enter the name of the product about which you want to find comments.
5. Click the search button.
6. Peruse the results to see what, if any, conversations are potentially interesting.

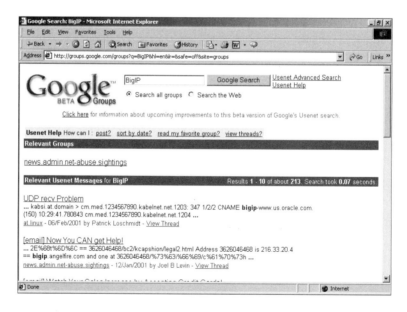

Figure 1.1   Results of a search for information about F5 Networks' BigIP product, using the keyword "BigIP"

Practice: Search a Knowledge Base for Potential Installation Issues

In this practice, you will search a vendor's knowledge base for information on a product that you're planning to install. Figure 1.2 shows the results of a knowledge base search.

▶ **To search for installation information on a vendor Web site**

1. Open a Web browser.

2. Search for the vendor's Web site, or type the vendor's Web site address in the address window.

3. Select the support section.

4. Select the option to search the knowledge base.

5. Select the product, and type **installation** in the search field.

6. Review the results to see whether there are any issues that apply to your environment or that you should be concerned about.

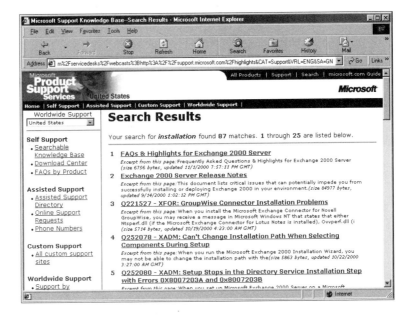

Figure 1.2   Results of a search of Microsoft Knowledge Base for Exchange 2000 installation

Lesson Summary

Documentation is an often overlooked but important mechanism for ensuring that installations go well. The more research you do into common problems, the less chance you have of being surprised by a problem, and the more successful your installations will be. Remember to do the following:

- Identify and read the important information received with a product.

- Use the skimming, scanning, and leafing techniques to extract the information you need from the documentation.

- Refer to Internet newsgroups and vendor Web sites for additional information.

Lesson 2: Logging Information

The previous lesson focused on the importance of reading at least some of the documentation and of preparing for an installation by determining what the potential problems are. This lesson recognizes that we are feeble creatures who are unable to memorize everything that we read or come into contact with, and so it discusses techniques for writing information down and organizing it so you can find it quickly.

After this lesson, you will be able to

- Take effective troubleshooting notes
- Maintain an activity log to help in troubleshooting

Estimated lesson time: 20 minutes

Taking Effective Troubleshooting Notes

Almost every successful network engineer I've met takes notes. Some engineers write themselves e-mails; some use spiral notebooks; and still others, like me, put together three-ring binders with printouts and notes mixed together. What's important is not how they log information or where; it's that they do log information, and that they log the right information.

One of the biggest struggles I have with the people I've been responsible for has been getting them to understand the importance and necessity of keeping a log of what they've done and what they've found interesting. Everyone wants to believe that they have a picture-perfect memory and will remember minute details years later. The reality is that we're all busy and involved with too many things to remember something we did a few weeks or months ago, let alone a few years ago.

One of the techniques I use to emphasize this point is to start asking somewhat detailed questions when people come to ask me for help with a problem. If the answers aren't forthcoming, I say that I'm sorry but I won't be able to help.

I don't do this to be cruel. I am invested in their success, so their failure to solve a problem hurts me too. However, they have to understand that they must be able to explain what they did, in what order, and when. Without that information, attempting to troubleshoot a problem is a thousand times more complex.

About 20 percent of the problems I help others solve involve simple steps that they generally tell me they have already done. Either they don't remember whether they've performed the step or they think they did perform the step but that it didn't work.

When we finally get to the point of approaching the problem from the beginning again, we often find that one step was left out or wasn't executed well. The end result is that a problem they may have been working on for weeks is solved in a matter of hours, simply by taking things one step at a time and documenting what has been done.

Creating a log of what you've done and the effects that your actions had will accomplish two things for you. First, it will clarify in your mind what you've done and make it easier for you to determine the nature of the problem. Second, it will allow you to communicate more effectively when you ask for help. This improved communication will benefit everyone because you'll spend less time getting help, both internally and externally. The people you are asking for help will also be happier to work with you because they'll feel that their assistance is more likely to be successful. I cannot stress enough the importance of taking notes while working on computer projects. It always pays off in the end.

The High Cost of Not Taking Notes

One of the most extreme examples I've seen of the cost of poor note taking involved a support person who was responsible for supporting and updating a product that only a few customers used. This person had a problem with the debug environment at our company. No matter what he did, he ended up with the same results. The build of the product would always end with an access violation error shortly after starting.

About a month after he started having this problem, I was asked to help him resolve it and subsequently repair the customers' perception of him and the company. We had one very upset client, and our entire organization was aware of the problem.

In my conversations with him, he would insist that nothing had changed in the environment. We even went so far as to get the machines that the software had originally been built on to try to determine the cause of the problem. It wasn't looking good.

Throughout the process, I continued to ask pointed questions about what tests he had performed and what the results were. I practically begged him to start logging his efforts so we could evaluate where the problem was.

He became incredibly discouraged. He spent days repeating the same or similar steps, trying to figure out what he was doing wrong, believing that some simple misconfiguration during installation was causing his problems. He must have rebuilt his development environment at least a dozen times.

Finally, I had to insist that he start logging all of the things he did and what the results were. Once he did so, it didn't take long to find the two problems leading to the errors that had plagued us for so many months.

You see, when the support person rebuilt the machines he was using to compile the code, he loaded the latest version of the development environment, a more recent version than the one in which the product was originally developed and compiled. As it turns out, Microsoft had added a new feature that placed static strings in read-only pages of memory. A string could be almost any non-numeric information, such as the name of someone who sent an e-mail or the name of the program itself. As a part of the error-handling routine, we converted some of those strings to uppercase for comparison purposes. These altered strings caused an error in the new environment because we no longer had write access to the memory the strings were in. A simple compiler switch solved that problem.

The other problem was that we weren't using the exact Oracle driver we had developed the application with. There happened to be a problem with the debug libraries provided with the particular Oracle driver the support person was using. A quick change to the current Oracle driver resolved the problem.

He could have found each of these errors quickly if he had been paying attention to his build and taking detailed notes so the original developer could see the changes. As a result of this consultant's lack of desire to take notes, a simple problem took months to resolve, and we almost lost an important client.

Don't wait until you get into a situation in which you're stuck performing the same steps over and over again. Take detailed notes of your actions so you'll be able to communicate to others what you've done.

Maintaining an Activity Log

Up to this point in the lesson, we've been talking about the need to keep notes for yourself, to help you remember what you've done and the results you have received. Unfortunately, with complex networks and servers, a single person is rarely responsible for everything. Most people share responsibilities with other parts of the organization or with other people within their department.

If you keep your own notebook describing what you've done and tested, and the other people do the same, the only way to determine what happened to the network and when it happened is to get everyone in the same room to review their notes together. There's also little or no group awareness of what is happening to the network, the server, or any other shared responsibility.

That's why it's so important to establish a mechanism for recording changes and activities on the network. This mechanism can be as simple as a shared folder to which people submit change sheets or problem reports, or it can be as complex as a multinational help desk repository containing all of the problems and actions for a network. The mechanism isn't important, just that there is one.

Practice: Create an Activity Log

In this practice, you'll create an Exchange-based activity log that everyone can use. This log is a simple way to track activities and problems in environments that are too small to justify a help desk system.

▶ **To create a public folder to hold an activity log**

1. Open Microsoft Outlook 2000.
2. If the folder list isn't displayed, select Folder List from the View menu.
3. Expand the Public Folders folder by clicking the plus sign to the left of it.
4. Right-click All Public Folders, and select New Folder from the shortcut menu.
5. Give the folder a name, such as Activity Log, and click OK.
6. If Outlook asks you to create a shortcut on your Outlook bar, click No.
7. Close Outlook, and open the Exchange System Manager.
8. Expand the Administrative Groups folder.
9. Expand the site folder that your account is in. This will generally be the name of the company, and it will be the only folder showing for small organizations.
10. Expand the Folders folder.
11. Expand the Public Folders folder.
12. Right-click your folder, and select Properties from the shortcut menu.
13. Click the Exchange Advanced tab.
14. Clear the Hide From Exchange Address Lists check box.
15. Click OK to save your changes.
16. Close the Exchange System Manager.

You now have a folder that you can send e-mail to whenever you have a problem or whenever you make a change. If your colleagues do this as well, you will all have a central repository for changes and problems on the network that you'll be able to refer to when you have a problem.

Lesson Summary

Creating logs for yourself and for the network you work within is an important part of being successful. In this lesson, you learned why activity logs are important and what each type is used for.

Lesson 3: Determining Need

Understanding why you're doing something is key to being successful. For instance, if you know only that you need to build a car, you might build a Ford Escort. If you know, on the other hand, that you need to be able to race the car on the stock car circuit, you might build a different car, and you'd build a still different car if you know that it needs to operate on the African plains.

This lesson looks first at how your organization approaches risk and then at the kinds of services a server might provide and the relative load that each of these services places on memory, processor, and disk access speed.

After this lesson, you will be able to

- Identify your organization's risk tolerance
- Identify the services to be run on the server
- Develop a guideline for the amount of resources you'll need in each area for good performance

Estimated lesson time: 25 minutes

Identifying Organizational Risk Tolerance

One of the core components in determining need is assessing the capability of the organization to accept risks. Some organizations avoid risk like the plague, and others are comfortable making calculated risks.

Risk is something that surrounds us each day. For instance, there is a risk of injuries in the office, in the home, and certainly in the cars that most of us use to get to and from work. Some larger organizations have developed whole departments that manage risk. In smaller organizations, upper management or the owner typically handles risk management.

Every organization has some tolerance for risk. In other words, it will accept a certain amount of risk in order to forgo the expense of avoiding it. In information systems terms, a *risk* is generally something that could happen that would cause a service outage. Risk management has been particularly important in information systems, and many organizations have gone to great lengths to develop ways to avoid almost every risk that could occur. For disk failures, they have mirroring and RAID-5 drive arrays. For complete system failures, they have clusters. For an act of nature, they have regional data centers, or *hot sites*. No matter what the risk is, someone can engineer a solution around it. However, these solutions cost money. Spending this money may or may not make sense for a particular organization.

Risk tolerance generally breaks down into two categories: lost opportunity and perception. Each of these is very important, and either one can be the overriding factor in terms of your solution. Let's look at lost opportunity first.

Lost Opportunity

When you hear a company say that an outage cost it $5 million, it's generally not talking about the amount of money that it had to pay out. In other words, the company probably didn't write a check for $5 million because of the outage. What it's referring to is the lost opportunity to make money.

Before we discuss the things to look for when you're trying to understand the opportunity loss involved in a risk, let's look at two radically different scenarios to clarify this concept.

Let's say you're running a dot-com company that sells widgets. You have two competitors that also sell widgets on the Internet. Your prices are competitive, and you generally retain 95 percent of your customers. In other words, given no other factors, your customers will go to your competitors to buy widgets only 5 percent of the time.

If a customer buys all of its widgets from you, that customer's average yearly value is $500. You expect that you'll have the average customer for 15 years. That makes the lifetime value of a customer $7,500. Now let's say that you get 1000 orders per hour and that those orders are worth $50,000.

For every hour your site is down, you're losing $50,000 in direct revenue, and you're also losing customers. The loss of 10 percent of those customers might be estimated at $375,000 per hour. This is half of their lifetime value multiplied by the number of customers. Half of their lifetime value is used because on average the customer you lose will be halfway through its lifetime with your company. A one-hour shutdown might cost more than $400,000.

It's those kinds of numbers that really get people's attention. A simple Web site taking orders might generate huge opportunity losses if it's down. Although we've greatly simplified the math involved in performing an opportunity loss analysis, it's clear that the numbers add up.

An organization in this situation probably has a very low tolerance for risk because such a high cost is attached to it. The risk could justify all kinds of additional systems and hardware just to avoid a failure.

Now let's look at another scenario. Suppose you have a five-person office. Each person works primarily at his or her own PC, but occasionally refers to previous work stored on a file server. If the server is down for an hour, there is no real impact on the business. You could say that the staff wouldn't be able to do their work without the server, but that's probably a stretch. If you estimate $20 per hour per person for the cost of the staff, you're looking at a cost of about $100 per hour for every hour the server is down. In this scenario, it's probably not worth spending much money to avoid downtime.

The two scenarios just described don't have much in common, and neither will their servers. The first company will invest very heavily in redundancy and mechanisms to prevent failures, whereas the second one will probably take only minimal steps to ensure that the system is available.

Here are some factors to consider when determining the opportunity loss of a risk:

- What are the risks? The starting point is knowing what kinds of failures can happen. Common failures include disk failures, central processing unit (CPU) failures, failures caused by acts of nature, and so on.

- How does each risk affect the ability to make money? Systems pertaining to an organization's ability to make money are always a priority. Don't forget, however, that some businesses can use a manual system, such as taking orders on paper, until the system is returned to service.

- Will the staff that normally use the system be totally idle if it is down? The answer to this question will determine whether you should include the cost of the staff in your calculation for the loss. If some members of your staff are only order takers, there's little possibility that they can do something else when the order system is offline. However, if you're working with staff that have more varied duties, it might not make sense to include staff wages.

- What impact will a failure have on your customers? If a system outage will have a negative impact on customers' perception of your organization, your calculations have to account for the cost of lost customers.

The bottom line is that every risk has some negative impact; you're just trying to quantify it.

Note This may seem like an involved process to go through just to be able to determine whether you should have dual power supplies in a server or whether you should establish a fault-tolerant environment, but this step, more than any other, will help you justify your proposal to management.

Perception

So far we've been talking about numbers and figures. However, the way your organization perceives the various risks is also an important factor. We each have our own perception of reality and our own view as to whether a given issue is important or not.

In the end, any risk tolerance analysis needs to look at how a risk feels, more than the potential costs. People have an internal governor that controls how much risk they are willing to take. Organizations get their risk tolerance from their people. You'll want to take a look at how the owners and senior management feel about risk.

The following are some factors that can help you determine the management's or owner's risk tolerance:

- How much insurance do they carry on the company? The larger the amount, the less risk they are willing to tolerate.

- What are the deductibles on the insurance they do carry? Higher deductibles mean a higher risk tolerance.

- Do they carry loss-of-business insurance? This type of insurance is very expensive; if it's being carried, and it's not a bank requirement, it usually indicates a low tolerance for risk.

- Is the company publicly traded? Publicly traded companies generally have a lower risk tolerance.

- How much working capital is on hand? Carrying a lot of working capital in bank accounts generally indicates a low tolerance for risk.

Although some of this information may not be made available to you, find out what you can, and use it as a starting point for your observation of the owner's risk tolerance.

Avoiding Risk

You should now have a good sense of how risk-tolerant your organization is. This section covers three techniques for addressing risk concerns:

- Scalability

- Availability

- Clustering

These solutions avoid risks and should be considered when your organization's risk tolerance is low.

Scalability

A solution that is *scalable* is simply capable of scaling to meet the future needs of your organization. In the past, having a scalable system meant working with larger hardware platforms. Scalability was often used to tout UNIX solutions because of their ability to run on larger machines and thus serve more users.

Today Intel machines running Microsoft Windows can be configured with multiple CPUs, and the resulting processing capacity rivals even the largest UNIX-based systems. That capability, coupled with the use of clustering solutions (described later), has led to scalability being less of an issue than before. In today's environment, a server's scalability generally refers to the number of processors that can be installed or the number of drive slots that the server case has.

The number of processors that a server can accommodate can be an important issue if the server is providing a service that is CPU intensive, such as one for a client/server application, or if the server is being used to provide terminal services.

Most servers can accommodate only between four and eight processors. Beyond that, rather specialized hardware is required.

The greatest challenge with processor scalability in Intel-based systems is that you have to ensure that the stepping level of the processor is the same for all of the processors installed in the machine. The *stepping level* refers to the specific manufacturing process used to manufacture the chip. CPU manufacturers such as Intel sometimes make small changes to a processor to fix identified problems or to improve the success rate of their manufacturing process. The problem is that these relatively minor changes sometimes cause timing inconsistencies that can bring about a multiprocessor system failure.

Technically, the recommendation is to keep the stepping level within one revision; however, it is always better for stepping levels be exactly the same if possible.

Note Because of the requirement to match stepping levels of the processor, I recommend that you fully populate all of the processor slots in a server. That way you'll know that all of the processors are the same stepping level. The trade-off is a few thousand dollars more up front in return for fewer hassles later.

Another measure of a server's scalability is the number of hard disks the case can support. A standard computer might have room for two or three hard disks at most, whereas server machines typically have room for five or more. This type of scalability is beneficial in smaller environments in which keeping a separate case for the hard disks is not desirable.

The more disks a server can hold, the more storage space it can have and also the faster it can return results. In terms of scalability, the more drive slots that are available, the more times the hard disk space can be upgraded without getting an external drive cabinet.

An external drive cabinet isn't generally a big issue, although it does require more space, a separate power connection, and often a separate SCSI bus. (SCSI stands for Small Computer System Interface.) All of these are easily addressed as long as the server has space to add another SCSI bus.

Availability

Scalability refers to a system's ability to grow to meet future needs, which is always a bit of a prediction. *Availability* refers to a system's ability to avoid and quickly recover from failures, and it is very much a concern of the present.

Availability is one of those 80/20 rules in life. Making a system mostly available—say 80 percent of the time—is easy. You can just put a standard PC in the role of a server, and you'll get at least 80 percent uptime. As an organization's needs for availability grow, however, it becomes more and more difficult to squeeze those last few percentage points of availability out of the system.

You can improve availability in a variety of ways. For instance, power (or the lack of it) can be responsible for a significant amount of downtime in a system. It can be addressed by uninterruptible power supplies, generators, surge suppressors, and dual power supplies. These solutions minimize the effect of power problems on a server and increase availability. We'll be discussing these options in Chapter 2, Lesson 2, "Addressing Power Needs."

Hard disk failure is one of the most common failures in a server. (There are only two types of mechanical devices in a computer that are always running: hard disks and fans.) That's why this book, and the press in general, spend so much time on RAID-5 and RAID-1 (mirroring). We'll discuss RAID and its impact on availability in Chapter 3, Lesson 3, "Disk Storage."

The less-frequent reasons for system failure include network adapter failure and complete system failure. Network adapter failures are covered in Chapter 3, Lesson 4, "Network Connectivity." You can avoid a complete system failure by using a technology called clustering, which we'll discuss next.

Clustering

Clustering occurs when several computers work together as one large computer so they can respond to clients more quickly and take up the slack if one of the clustered servers fails. Clustering has become popular because it allows a large number of smaller computers to mimic a large computer for a fraction of the cost.

With clustering, simple Intel-based servers can provide a level of performance that was previously available only with large UNIX servers or IBM mainframes. It has changed the way we think about scalability because we're no longer limited to tasks that can be performed with a single machine. Rather than focusing on the number of CPUs that can be put into a single machine, we now look at the number of machines that can be tied together.

Clustering is a great concept, and when implemented correctly it can be a great benefit. Its downside is that it's difficult to set up and maintain, since upgrades have to be carefully coordinated among the servers within the cluster. Additionally, all of the software running on the cluster has to be aware of the cluster. As a result, clustering is generally used only in very specific applications in which high performance is required.

Note One excellent example of an application requiring high performance is a database server. As you might expect, databases are the most commonly implemented software in a clustered environment. If you're interested to see the impact clustering can have, visit the Transaction Processing Performance Council's (TPC) Web page at http://www.tpc.org. The TPC keeps statistics on the performance of different databases, using its standardized test. As of this writing, the four top-performing database engines were running in clustered environments.

Practice: Identify Your Processor's Stepping Level

In this practice, you will use Windows 2000's diagnostic tools to identify the stepping level of the processor you're running. If you have an open processor slot, this practice will let you know which processor stepping level to request when ordering a new processor.

▶ **To determine the processor stepping level**

1. Log on to your Windows 2000 computer with an administrative account.

2. Click Start, and then select Settings, Control Panel, Administrative Tools, and Computer Management.

3. Expand the System Information folder by clicking the plus sign to its left.

4. Click on the System Summary folder.

5. Read the processor line(s) from the right-hand pane. The stepping level is clearly indicated. Figure 1.3 shows an example of a System Summary.

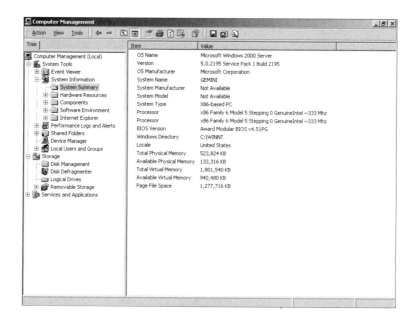

Figure 1.3   System Summary for a system containing two Pentium II processors, both with a stepping level of 0

Note Windows 2000 is better than most operating systems at coping with processors at different stepping levels. However, both Intel and Microsoft recommend using processors with the same stepping level whenever possible.

Deciding What Services the Server Will Perform

Determining what a server is going to do is the first step in planning for the server. In large environments, each server might have a very specific, focused role, providing only one service to the network. In smaller environments, a single server might be asked to provide a variety of services.

The number of services a server can or should provide depends largely on the number of users you're supporting. As you might expect, as the number of users for a particular service increases, so does the load that service puts on the hardware.

Table 1.1 indicates the relative load that a particular service puts on a server. It is meant to give you a feel for the kind of a load an application will create and may not precisely reflect your environment. The amount of hardware you'll have to provide to accommodate a given load depends on the number of users who will be using the service.

Table 1.1   Relative Load of Various Services

Type of Service	Number of Users	Processor Load	Memory Load	Disk Load
Domain controller	2000	Moderate	Moderate	Moderate
Gateway	1000	High	Moderate	Low
Router	250	High	Low	Low
Bridge	250	High	Low	Low
Firewall	250	High	Moderate	Low
Proxy	250	High	High to moderate	Moderate
Database	50	High	High	High
Client/server*	50	Extremely high	Extremely high	Low to moderate
Mail	5000	Low to moderate	Low to moderate	Low to moderate
FTP	2000	Low	Low	Moderate
SNA	1000	High	Moderate	Low
RAS	50	High	Low	Low
File and print	250	Low	Moderate	Moderate to high
Fax	250	High	High	Moderate
DNS	10,000	Moderate	Moderate	Low
WINS	2000	Low	Low	Low
DHCP	10,000	Low	Low	Low
Web*	1000	High	High	Low

* The load created by these services can vary wildly depending on the type of use they receive.

Client/server applications have their own unique needs, with loads that can vary a great deal. You should consult the software manufacturer for their sizing requirements. Web servers are another special case. Some Web servers just display static content, and others interact with databases and provide customized content. The latter are the ones that most companies today are looking to install, and so the table reflects that kind of server.

The tricky part of sizing a server is taking the general perceptions discussed here and converting them to a server configuration that meets the needs of your organization. Generally speaking, you can place three or four services that involve a moderate load on the same server. Likewise, you might be able to combine as many as a dozen services with low resource requirements on a single machine. Services that create a heavy load on a server should be combined with a few low-priority services or with nothing at all.

Once you've determined the kind of load your current environment will place on a server, spend a moment determining how much growth the organization is planning. In general, you want to make sure that the server you install will be sufficient for at least two years, if not three. This means that you should project how many users each service will have in three years and build that capacity into your server now.

Lesson Summary

Determining the needs of an organization is a complex task that involves assessing both the organization's risk tolerance and the number of users the organization has and is projected to have. Organizations with low risk tolerance or a large number of users will need to investigate availability and scalability options. In this lesson, you have learned to identify risk tolerance and project the load that users will put on a server.

Lesson 4: Selecting an Operating System

Although most people select an operating system even before they know what their organization needs, it is generally best to try to hold off on this decision until you have assessed your organization's needs. In this lesson, you'll learn the key features and benefits of several popular operating systems so that you can make an intelligent decision.

After this lesson, you will be able to

- Identify the strengths and weaknesses of various operating systems

Estimated lesson time: 10 minutes

Methods for Selecting an Operating System

If the only tool you have is a hammer, you tend to see every problem as a nail.
—Abraham Maslow

I selected this quote because it mirrors how most people choose an operating system. If they're familiar with NetWare, they propose a NetWare solution. If they're familiar with Windows 2000, that's what they recommend.

This approach has some advantages: if you already know the operating system, installation and support are easier. Eventually, however, sticking with what you know rather than exploring all of the options can leave you with inferior or outdated solutions.

Another technique that people use to choose an operating system is to look at what is currently popular in the market. Their reasoning is that device drivers and upgrades are sure to be available because of the operating system's popularity. This too is a relatively good way to evaluate which operating system to use, but it tends to cause people to switch operating systems more frequently than necessary as the popular operating system changes.

Finally, people sometimes use a variation of the previous technique and choose an operating system based on what they think will be popular. This is perhaps the most risky way to choose an operating system because industry projections tend to be so inaccurate. No one really knows what will be popular a year or two from now.

Features and Benefits of Popular Operating Systems

Table 1.2 shows the three most popular operating systems for servers in today's market, along with an assessment of their strengths and weaknesses based on my experience and on industry reports. Conspicuously missing from the table is IBM's OS/2 Warp operating system. It is omitted simply because it has only one benefit, and that is its seamless integration into IBM midrange and mainframe environments. Other than that, almost all other areas are weak.

Table 1.2   Strengths and Weaknesses of Popular Operating Systems

Feature/Benefit	Novell NetWare	Microsoft Windows 2000	Linux
Directory services	+		–
Stability	+	+	+
Developer support	–	+	+
Scalability	–	+	
Cost			+
Support			–
Ease of use			–
Internet compatibility		+	+
Security	+	+	–
Popularity		+	+

By reviewing the table and determining which criteria are important to your organization, you should be able to quickly and easily decide which operating system is appropriate for your environment.

Lesson Summary

In this lesson, you learned about the methods that people use to choose an operating system, and you decided which operating system is right for your environment by looking at the benefits and drawbacks of each. The three methods people use to choose an operating system are

- What they know
- What's popular
- What they think will be popular

Lesson 5: Architecture Basics

Before determining what server you're going to deploy to meet the needs of your organization, you must understand some of the basic architectural issues that can affect your decision. This lesson addresses these issues.

After this lesson, you will be able to

- Discuss the performance implications of different buses
- Determine the PCI features necessary in your server

Estimated lesson time: 25 minutes

PC Buses

Before delving into the details of PC buses, it's important to understand what a bus is. A *bus* is, simply, a connection between devices that can be used to communicate information. PC buses are electrically connected circuits that allow communication between the CPU and the other components of the system. The *throughput* of a bus, or its speed, is determined by the frequency at which it transfers data (generally expressed in MHz) and the width of the data transferred (generally 1 byte to 8 bytes). The total throughput of the bus is found by multiplying the frequency by the width of the data.

The original IBM PC ran at a mere 4.77 MHz. With CPU speeds now in excess of 1 GHz, it's amazing that the basic architecture of the PC has held up. Processor speed has increased by a factor of more than 200. And although the rest of the components in the architecture have improved as well, they haven't increased as much as the processor speed.

The original PC bus, Industry Standard Architecture (ISA), ran at the same 4.77 Mhz as the 8088 processor. The ISA bus fell out of favor after the 80386 was released because it just couldn't keep up with the higher and higher processor speeds.

It was at this time that some industry leaders got together and designed the Extended Industry Standard Architecture (EISA) bus. This bus was designed to be used either alongside the ISA bus or instead of it. EISA was specifically designed so that an ISA card could work in an EISA slot. This was accomplished by doubling the number of contacts in the slot. When an ISA card was inserted into an EISA slot, the card would hit two connectors. The slot detected this and operated as if it were an ISA slot.

EISA was faster than ISA, which was operating at 8 MHz by that time, because it allowed up to 4 bytes to be transferred at once instead of the 2 bytes that ISA supported. In addition, while ISA required two clock cycles to complete a transfer, an EISA card could complete the transfer in one clock cycle. (The 4-byte transfer limit just happened to be the limit of the 80386 processors.) In theory, an EISA card in an EISA slot would be four times as fast as an ISA card. This extra performance came at a cost, however. Both the EISA cards and EISA-based motherboards were expensive to purchase, and as a result they were installed almost exclusively in servers in which performance was paramount.

Note IBM had a failed attempt prior to EISA to convert the market to its Microchannel bus. The failure was attributed primarily to IBM's refusal to let the industry have the technology. IBM insisted on charging royalties on all Microchannel devices, which essentially killed the technology.

Shortly after EISA was released, there was a push to come up with another, faster, bus that could be used to communicate with video cards. By that time, graphical user interfaces had become well established, requiring large amounts of information to be communicated to the video card. The resulting bus, the Video Electronic Standards Association (VESA) local bus, was designed specifically to communicate with an 80486 processor, although Intel warned that this architecture would be short-lived. The VESA local bus, popularly referred to as the Video Local Bus (VLB), was much faster than ISA or even EISA, and it wasn't as expensive as EISA to develop for.

Intel's warning was based on the different design that its Pentium processors would be using. As a result of the different processor design and an understanding that the bus design must be abstracted from the processor design, Intel designed a new bus, Peripheral Component Interconnect (PCI), to replace ISA, EISA, and the Video Local Bus. PCI was designed for growth and was relatively independent of the internal timing considerations that the Video Local Bus had to contend with.

Because of PCI's relative abstraction from the CPU and its ability to accommodate growth, PCI systems were more expensive than their Video Local Bus cousins. This led to PCI being used primarily in high-end systems, with the Video Local Bus maintaining a firm hold on the low to midrange systems.

Once the Pentium processor was released, the Video Local Bus became hard to support because additional electronics were needed to convert the native output of the Pentium processor to something that Video Local Bus cards could handle. Still, Intel's new PCI bus wasn't universally accepted until well after the Pentium processor became the mainstay of corporate computing.

Although the PCI bus is still the most common bus used in computers, there is another bus or, more accurately, port, that you'll be expected to know about for the Server+ exam: the Accelerated Graphics Port (AGP). The AGP was created specifically to address the continuing pressure from video card manufacturers and consumers for a faster way to display data. It is substantially faster than the PCI bus. Current configurations include only one AGP slot, and so it's generally reserved for video cards.

Note In practical terms, AGP is not a consideration for a server. Whether the server has an AGP slot built in or a video card on the motherboard should not be a consideration. Servers are designed to work with little or no console-based activity, and therefore the graphics on the console should be of little concern.

Table 1.3 shows some of the progress that has been made in the performance of PC buses. The sharp rise in bus speeds hasn't kept pace with CPU speeds, however. Despite that, the advances in bus technology have been substantial.

Table 1.3   Relative Performance of PC Buses

Bus Type	Clock Rate	Width (Bytes)	Transfers/Cycle	Throughput
ISA (8 bit)	4.77 MHz	1	½	2.3 MBps
ISA (8-bit)	8.00 MHz	1	½	4 MBps
ISA (16-bit)	6.00 MHz	2	½	6 MBps
ISA (16-bit)	8.00 MHz	2	½	8 MBps
EISA	8.33 MHz	4	1	33 MBps
VESA VLB	33.00 MHz	4	1	132 MBps
PCI (32-bit)	33.00 MHz	4	1	132 MBps
PCI (64-bit)	33.00 MHz	8	1	264 MBps
AGPx1	66.00 MHz	4	1	264 MBps
AGPx2	66.00 MHz	4	2	528 MBps
AGPx4	66.00 MHz	4	4	1056 MBps

Features of the PCI Bus

Since PCI is the main bus in use today, it makes sense to explore some of its features and how they relate to performance and reliability within a system. The following features of the PCI bus are of greatest interest in a server context:

- Bus mastering
- Interrupts
- Hierarchical PCI
- Peer PCI buses
- Hot swapping

Let's explore each of these features in turn.

Bus Mastering

While bus mastering is an important feature, it's not unique to the PCI bus. Other buses, such as EISA, supported bus mastering. *Bus mastering* allows a card in one of the slots to control the PCI bus so that it can perform an entire operation without the intervention of the CPU. This frees the CPU to perform other tasks and can substantially increase overall system performance.

Although bus mastering is great, it isn't implemented in every PCI slot. In general, only the first three slots on a motherboard are PCI bus mastering slots. This means that the highest-performing cards in a server generally need to be in the three slots closest to the CPU. While most cards will function, albeit at a reduced speed, if they're not in a PCI bus mastering slot, some require this type of slot.

In addition to bus mastering, PCI now offers a technique known as concurrent PCI that separates the traffic on the ISA, PCI, and CPU, or system, buses, allowing simultaneous operations on all three buses and thus further increasing throughput.

Interrupts

Interrupts are signals to the CPU that one of the computer's components needs attention. Traditionally, serial and parallel ports, as well as almost every type of device, use interrupts to communicate with the processor. When the IBM PC was released, it had a single interrupt controller capable of 8 interrupt request (IRQ) lines. When the IBM AT was released, it added a second interrupt controller that was chained into the first controller, yielding a total of 16 interrupts, of which 1 is generally not usable because of the chaining arrangement.

One of the challenges in a modern computer is managing the interrupts because so many devices want them. Table 1.4 shows the IRQ lines in a PC and their traditional uses.

Table 1.4   Standard and Extended Uses of IRQ Lines

IRQ	Standard Use	Extended Use
0	System timer	
1	Keyboard controller	
2	Cascade to second interrupt controller	
3	COM2	
4	COM1	
5		LPT2
6	Floppy diskette controller	
7	LPT1	
8	Real-time clock	
9		
10		
11		
12	PS/2 port	
13	Math coprocessor	
14	Primary IDE controller	
15	Secondary IDE controller	

As you can see from the table, only four IRQs are available for all of the other devices in the system, including the sound card, network card, Universal Serial Bus (USB), video card, and so on. This can make getting an available IRQ quite difficult.

One of the solutions to this problem was to allow multiple PCI interrupts to be mapped to a single IRQ line. This mapping conserves the number of interrupts that are available for other devices and allows the system to determine where the interrupt came from by examining the PCI hardware.

Technically speaking, there are four possible PCI interrupts that a PCI card could be mapped to. Rarely, however, are that many standard interrupts available for the PCI devices to use. As a result, one or two interrupts are mapped to the PCI bus and all of the PCI cards use those interrupts to signal to the CPU that they need attention. The CPU receives the interrupt, notes that it came from a PCI bus shared interrupt, checks the PCI hardware to determine exactly which card signaled the interrupt, and calls the appropriate driver to communicate with the card.

Hierarchical PCI and Peer PCI Buses

PCI buses are generally required to have four or fewer devices per bus, due to signaling and timing issues. As a result, systems that need to accommodate more than four PCI devices generally have either multiple PCI buses that interface directly with the processor, or a PCI-to-PCI bridge that allows multiple buses to share a single interface. In the first case, where multiple PCI buses interface with the processor, the PCI buses are considered peer buses. In the case of PCI-to-PCI bridges, the buses are considered to be hierarchical because all of the traffic from all of the PCI buses runs through a single PCI-to-host chip. Hierarchical buses are cheaper to implement, but their performance will not match the performance of an implementation using peer PCI buses.

Hot Swapping

Throughout the history of PCs and the increasing bus speeds, there has been one fundamental truth: once you plug a card in and turn the power on, it's in the PC until you turn the power off. For most people and in most implementations, this isn't a big issue. If, say, a network card fails, you just turn the machine off, replace the card, and turn it back on—no big deal. However, the more heavily a server is relied upon, the less downtime is acceptable.

Compaq therefore developed a PCI specification that allows for cards to be inserted and removed while the power is on. *Hot swapping* is the ability to insert and remove cards while the power is on and the server is running. Intel has recently adopted this specification and is supporting it in its new processors.

Hot-swappable PCI slots allow you to replace cards, such as a failed network card, without powering down the computer. The system will detect the new network card and will install it automatically.

Meeting the specification for hot-swappable PCI slots results in additional cost for the hardware manufacturer. Your system documentation will indicate whether it supports PCI hot swapping and will give you instructions and precautions for using this feature.

Intelligent Input-Output (I2O)

Manufacturers of add-in hardware have two major categories of problems. The first involves how their hardware interacts with the other hardware in a PC. The second concerns the need to create stable drivers so their hardware will work with various operating systems.

Server manufacturers must contend with the fact that CPUs in servers must spend increasing amounts of time translating messages from one device to another. For instance, they must translate a file that a user is saving from the format used by the network card to the format that the disk controllers need.

For these reasons, a new standard, aimed at simplifying hardware development, is emerging. Known as Intelligent Input-Output (I2O), this standard proposes a single unified messaging format that could be used in any operating system. The operating system itself would support the I2O protocol, or the system would have an additional card installed to process I2O messages.

It's not clear as yet whether the I2O initiative will be successful. It has support from various hardware vendors, but the operating system establishment and consumers have not embraced it yet.

Lesson Summary

This lesson covered some of the architectural basics you'll need to know to pass the Server+ exam and to plan for the appropriate server for your environment. You learned about the evolution of PC buses and their relative speeds. You also learned how the advanced features of PCI allow for greater performance through the use of peer buses, as well as for reduced downtime through the use of PCI hot swapping.

Review

Here are some questions to help you determine whether you have learned enough to move on to the next chapter. If you have difficulty answering these questions, please go back and review the material in this chapter before beginning the next chapter. The answers to these questions are located in the appendix, "Questions and Answers."

1. You've just received a new product that you ordered. Your boss walks by with someone from another division who's considering the same product. He wants to know whether the product has a particular feature. How would you go about finding out for sure?

2. You're evaluating three different products with similar features and similar costs. You're concerned about making the right decision. How should you determine which is the best product?

3. You've been on vacation for a week, and you get in early your first day back to read your e-mail and get settled. As you're walking in, however, a user stops you and says that she can't log on. After a quick check at her computer, you determine that you can't log on either. What should you do to figure out what is going on?

4. You've done the necessary analysis for a new server. You've taken into consideration the needs of the organization and have quantified the issues around the need. However, management doesn't seem pleased with the solution. What might have you forgotten?

5. Your company is planning a phase of rapid growth. You're trying to determine the best course of action for purchasing servers. What options should you consider?

6. You're getting ready to add a new server. What method might you use to choose the operating system to run on that new server?

7. Which will perform better, hierarchical PCI buses or peer PCI buses?

8. When is hot-swappable PCI important?

CHAPTER   2

Planning a Server's Environment

About This Chapter

The previous chapter covered some of the core concepts that server support personnel need to know. This chapter begins the more practical exploration of environmental planning issues. These issues are key to a successful implementation, and they also help ensure the long-term reliability and availability of the servers that you install.

Chapter 1 discussed server availability and the outside factors, such as temperature, humidity, and power, that can negatively affect it. This chapter addresses those environmental factors in more detail. In addition, it begins to address disaster recovery, describing how to plan basic tape-backup management and monitoring functions and how to create a disaster recovery plan. Not only is this information important to your long-term success, it is a meaningful part of the Server+ exam.

Before You Begin

To complete this chapter, you should have

- An Internet connection

Lesson 1: Space Planning

When planning for a server, it's easy to get so wrapped up in the technical details—the amount of hard disk storage, the number of processors, and the amount of memory—that you forget to establish a place to put the server once you have it. That's the subject of this lesson.

After this lesson, you will be able to

- Identify physical security issues
- Assess the impact of the climate on a server

Estimated lesson time: 20 minutes

Providing Physical Security

Most discussions of security for a server involve users, groups, access permissions, and audit trails—in other words, software security. These issues involve how one controls access to the server's resources via software. However, when installing servers, their physical security is also important.

Physical security refers to the ability to control physical access to the server hardware. The first level of physical security for any implementation is to have a lock on the room in which the server is kept. A card access system, shown in Figure 2.1, is a good solution. Such systems log all comings and goings to the room, generating an audit trail. This will presumably limit the number of people who have access to the server and reduce the chances of unauthorized access.

Figure 2.1   A card access system

Although a locking device sounds like a simple precaution, it's one that is rarely taken in smaller environments. This failure to provide a locked space for the server is very dangerous because once someone has physical access to a server, he or she can steal it or hack into it with relative ease.

By default, physical access to a server gives one access to every file on the hard disk. In every server operating system, the administrator can get access to any and every file on the system. Admittedly, some operating systems make access by the administrator more difficult than others, but they all allow it to be accomplished unless file-level encryption is in use.

An intruder who gains physical access to a server can remove it to another site and reinstall the operating system, setting a new administrative password in the process. The intruder can then use that password to gain access to all of the files on the system.

Some operating systems are also vulnerable to having their security database downloaded onto a floppy or other medium and taken to another computer, where a password-cracking program can be run to retrieve the password for every user. Having these passwords might allow someone to access other systems for which the users have the same passwords.

Although it is true that by default any operating system can be easily hacked into once someone has physical access to the server, Windows 2000 does have the ability to further deter this kind of an attack.

Windows 2000 allows for files on NTFS file systems to be encrypted. When a file is encrypted, only the security administrator and authorized users of the files can open them. Because of the mechanisms involved, if Windows 2000 is reinstalled on the same machine, the new security administrator will not be able to decrypt the files.

In other words, the operating system will not allow access to encrypted files after a simple reinstallation. That doesn't prevent the intruder from running hacking and decrypting programs against the files to try to restore their contents; it just makes the process significantly harder and more time-consuming.

Encrypting files is a nice option for machines such as notebooks, for which physical security is impossible to provide. However, although encryption is available at the server level, it's not recommended as an alternative to physical security. The additional overhead of encryption isn't warranted when a lock will suffice.

Providing Climate Control

Climate control means maintaining both temperature and humidity within the optimum range for the server hardware. Temperature and humidity are generally controlled by an air conditioning unit placed in the computer room.

Although today's servers can operate under a much wider range of temperatures than their mainframe forebears, there are still optimum temperatures that should be maintained to maximize a server's life span. Above a certain temperature, the circuitry and disk-drive media begin to deteriorate. Although this temperature is much higher than the ambient room temperatures most of us are used to, it's the temperature of the component or hard disk that is important. The internal environment of most servers is several degrees higher than the ambient room temperature.

Although server cases are designed with high-speed fans to minimize the impact of this temperature differential, the temperature in the server case can sometimes be a full 25°F higher or more than the ambient room temperature. This means that a server in a room with an ambient temperature of 85°F could have a temperature of 110°F or higher at the hard disk. It's at these temperatures and above that circuitry and hard drives begin to deteriorate.

Generally speaking, it's desirable to keep the ambient room temperature between 65°F and 70°F. This range provides a relatively wide safety margin for temperatures inside the server. Although 65°F to 70°F is preferable, it's acceptable to allow the ambient room temperature to reach as high as 75°F. Air conditioning units, shown in Figure 2.2, help regulate ambient room temperature.

Figure 2.2   Server air conditioning units

In addition to controlling the temperature, you must closely control the humidity so as not to short-circuit the server or cause the components to become brittle. Humidity is simply the amount of water vapor in the air. When we talk about humidity, we mean relative humidity, which indicates how much water vapor is in the air compared to how much water vapor the air can hold. That is why relative humidity is given as a percentage. The higher the air temperature, the more water vapor the air can hold.

Although most servers can operate safely at between 10 percent and 90 percent relative humidity, a more conservative range of 45 percent to 65 percent is often recommended. As with the recommended temperature range, this provides a wide safety margin.

This humidity range is used because servers contain a number of printed circuit (PC) boards that are manufactured using a process where humidity is present. This humidity becomes a part of the board material itself. When the humidity is vastly different, the PC board either loses the water vapor it originally contained or takes on additional water vapor. This causes expansion or contraction of the PC board material that can cause the fragile solder traces used to connect the components to break and fail.

One of the other common stipulations for humidity in a server's operating guidelines is that the humidity be noncondensing. That is, no water should condense on the metal surfaces. Condensation generally occurs when air that is high in humidity at a given temperature comes into contact with an object at a lower temperature. Because the temperature of the object is lower, the object lowers the temperature of the surrounding air through convection. The air can then hold less water, and its relative humidity increases. If the relative humidity exceeds 100 percent, water condenses onto the object.

All of us have seen condensation in action. When you go to a restaurant and you're given a glass of ice water, the glass initially has a dry exterior (unless you have a sloppy waiter). After several minutes, however, the outside of the glass generally becomes covered with small water droplets. These water droplets don't come from inside the glass; they come from the air surrounding the glass, which cools to the point that it can no longer suspend all of the water vapor it holds and so releases some of the water vapor onto the glass in the form of condensation.

By the way, glass is a reasonably good insulator, preventing the transmission of heat energy. Metal is a good conductor of energy, including heat energy, and so is much more susceptible to this condensation effect. Because so much metal is used in the construction of computers, condensation buildup on the case is a real concern due to the damage it can cause.

Since computers use electricity to perform their work, condensed water vapor is a shorting hazard, and it can also cause oxidation that corrodes contacts, eventually leading to intermittent electrical problems because a contact between components is no longer being maintained.

Planning for Floods

The preceding section discussed the hazards and damage that condensed water can cause. These risks are even more of a concern in environments where water may pool on the floor or an area may become flooded.

In this discussion, a flood is not just an act of nature, where a river overflows its banks. Flooding can also occur when a condensation drain from an air conditioner is not functioning properly, when a floor drain backs up, or in other situations involving standing water on the floor.

Flooding problems can be serious if not identified and corrected quickly. Since most power runs across or under the flooring, there is a real danger of electrocution and other hazards as the water comes into contact with the electrical wiring. As a result, it is recommended that you install a water sensor in any space where you'll have a server. This sensor can generally be attached to the card access system or to an alarm system and can provide an immediate indication that there is a problem.

One situation where a water sensor would have come in handy occurred several years ago when I was given some space in my company's building for a new computer room. Unfortunately, I wasn't allowed to choose the space myself. A certain location in the center of the building was allocated for this purpose.

We addressed all of the environmental issues discussed in this chapter and put together a quality computer room to support our AS/400 and network servers. It had two different uninterruptible power supply (UPS) units, a two-compressor air conditioner (in case one compressor failed), raised flooring, a floor drain, and a water sensor.

One evening in the dead of winter, I was called into the computer room because water was streaming down the back wall of the computer room. That wall just happened to house the electrical distribution panel for one of the two UPS units. Although no sparks were flying, it was quite disconcerting to see water flowing down the wall. We quickly shut down the systems and initiated an emergency power outage in the computer room itself. (The UPSs were getting splashed with water, so no one really wanted to go over and shut them down manually.)

When we investigated where the water was coming from, we discovered that the computer room was on the edge of one of the outer walls of the original building, which had been added on to, and that roof drains were positioned directly above it. The drainage pipe had frozen at its exterior outlet, causing the water from the melting snow and ice to fill up the drainage pipe and eventually pool above the drains. As a result, the drains had collapsed in such a way as to allow the water to flow down through the roof into the areas below.

The result this day was a flood of water coming down the wall. The solution was relatively simple: a thermostat-controlled heater at the outlet of the drain to prevent it from freezing shut. With that fix we never had the same problem again, but it just goes to show that no matter how well you try to plan your environment, there will always be factors you didn't consider.

Lesson Summary

In this lesson you learned about physical security and why it is important. You need to be confident that your system is secure. You also learned about climate control, including the need to keep temperatures low so that you have a wide margin of safety for the temperatures inside the cases. Humidity also plays an important role in climate control. In particular, you don't want water condensing on the servers. Finally, you learned about flooding and the sometimes unexpected ways in which it can occur.

Lesson 2: Addressing Power Needs

After hard disk failures, one of the most common causes of server problems is power irregularities. The power coming into most facilities is very "dirty" in that it has a series of spikes, surges, and other problems that are potentially dangerous to the components inside the server. In this lesson you will learn what electrical power is, what kinds of problems it presents, and what you can do to protect servers from power problems.

After this lesson, you will be able to

- Explain the basic principles of alternating current and direct current
- Identify power problems and resolutions

Estimated lesson time: 30 minutes

Understanding Direct and Alternating Current

Most consumers in the United States don't really understand the electricity that comes out of their walls or how it works. While a complete discussion of the physics of electricity is well beyond this book, it is helpful to understand what electrical power is on at least a basic level before talking about the kinds of problems that can occur.

The electricity that most of us are used to is the kind that comes from the outlets in the walls of our houses and offices. That kind of electricity, *alternating current* (AC) electricity, is produced by power plants miles and miles away and transported to our homes via electric wires for our use. Alternating current gets its name because the flow of the electricity reverses, or alternates, many times per second. In North America, AC electricity alternates at a frequency of 60 Hz, while in much of the rest of the world the frequency is 50 Hz.

This kind of electricity is used because it is easier to transport (or conduct), without significant loss, over long distances. It can be moved efficiently from where it is produced to where it will ultimately be consumed. It can also be transferred at extremely high power levels without generating a great deal of heat.

Alternating current forms a sine wave. That is, it forms a sine wave when displayed on a device such as an oscilloscope that shows the relative amount of electricity flowing. Because you may or may not remember from your trigonometry class what a sine wave looks like, Figure 2.3 shows an example.

Note Most people attribute the harnessing of electrical power to Thomas Edison, and although Edison was a great inventor and contributed significantly to our use of electricity, it was another man, Nikola Tesla, who pioneered the use of alternating current. If you would like to find out more about Nikola Tesla, log on to http://www.hightension.org or search for Nikola Tesla on your favorite search engine.

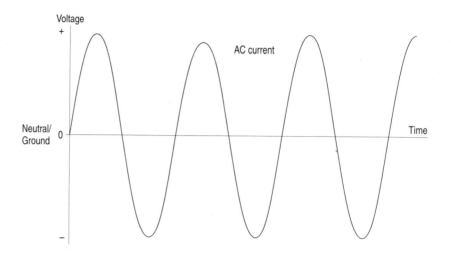

Figure 2.3   Alternating current as it appears on an oscilloscope

Another kind of electricity that we're all familiar with is *direct current* (DC).
Unlike alternating current, which changes its direction of flow, direct current
always flows in a single direction. This is the kind of electricity found in batteries. Direct current is easy to store but tends to give off more heat than alternating
current when conducted over long distances, so it is generally used for electronics and devices in which the storage of power is more important than its transmission. Direct current is also generally used at much lower power levels than
alternating current. On an oscilloscope, direct current forms a straight line rather
than a sine wave, as shown in Figure 2.4.

Figure 2.4   Direct current as it appears on an oscilloscope

Your server is an electronic device that requires direct current to function. Direct current provides power for all of the components in the computer. Therefore, the first thing that happens to the alternating current electricity when it enters the computer is that it's converted into direct current.

Converting Alternating Current to Direct Current

The job of converting alternating current to the direct current needed by the components of the server is handled by the power supply or power supplies in the server. There are several different methods of performing this conversion, but by and large, most of the power supplies found in today's servers use a "switching" technology and are thus called *switching power supplies*.

Switching power supplies are relatively hardy devices that can sustain many power problems before failing, and they can generally work with a wide range of input voltage levels without changing their output voltage. This comes in handy when you're dealing with the power grids of most industrialized nations, because heavy power drains can decrease the voltage being supplied to each office.

Understanding Circuit Breakers and Capacity

Electricity in either AC or DC form is potentially dangerous. Either type can cause serious damage to internal organs and skin tissue at high enough voltages. Another nasty habit of electricity is that if you attempt to pass too much of it through a circuit, the conductors will heat up and eventually melt or catch fire.

Because of the risks involved with electricity, when it first came into use fuses were employed to limit the amount of current that could pass through any given circuit (consisting of a set of wires and attached devices). When a fuse begins to conduct too much current, the filament inside the fuse begins to melt, and eventually it will open up to disconnect the circuit.

While a fuse is a cheap and effective method of preventing potential problems, it is also a destructive process: once a fuse fails you need another one to get the circuit working again. Given this problem, most homes and offices have switched to circuit breakers. Circuit breakers also interrupt the circuit when too much current is flowing; however, they can be reset once tripped.

Note Fuses are still used today, particularly in environments where a large amount of power may be drawn for a very short period of time. Because fuses are slower to react than equivalent circuit breakers, large electrical motors sometimes use fuses rather than circuit breakers to prevent the accidental disconnection of the circuit.

A key point here is that a circuit breaker will allow only a certain amount of current to flow through a circuit before it shuts down. In practical terms, most circuits are set up for 15 amps of current. Any more than this will trip the breaker and shut down power to all connected devices. This fact is important when planning an environment for your server because servers in particular and computer rooms in general tend to draw a large amount of power.

In planning a computer room, you'll want to gather the approximate amperage that all of the devices will draw. You can then determine the number of circuits you need by dividing this total amperage number by about 7 amps, so that you can keep each of the circuits about 50 percent loaded. This reduces the risk that a single new device will accidentally cause a circuit breaker to trip. Alternatively, you can use 10 amps if you request 20-amp circuits.

The location of the outlets for circuits may also be an issue, since you need to get the power from the correct circuit to the devices that need it. If you're lucky enough to have a raised floor, you can generally have circuits tied to a "floating" outlet or double outlet under the floor that can be dragged to the desired location. If not, you'll have to plan on routing the power from the wall outlet to the devices. When doing this, pay particular attention to the amperage ratings of all of the connecting power cords and power strips. Failure to use a sufficiently sized connecting cord can result in melting of the cord, creating a fire hazard.

Tip Don't coil power cords. Electrical power flowing through a wire generates a magnetic field. When a power cord is coiled, the magnetic field creates additional resistance, and that additional resistance causes the cord to heat much more rapidly than if it were laid out normally. Although a single loop or even a few loops shouldn't be a significant issue, do try not to coil cords when you can snake them in an ordered way.

Identifying Power Problems

Power problems come in two varieties: too much power and too little power. Although this distinction may seem simple, it is made because the two types of problems cause different kinds of results.

The most frequent types of power problems involve the receipt of too much power. These types of problems are dangerous primarily because they decrease the lifetime of the power supply and, if severe enough, can reduce the life of the components in the computer itself. The two kinds of power problems in this category are spikes and surges.

Spikes are momentary, dramatic increases in voltage. They generally consist of a thousand or more volts that last for up to a few power cycles. Spikes can have a variety of causes, ranging from an electrical motor, such as a compressor, starting to a lightning strike within the area. Spikes are one of the most common power problems.

Surges are longer, less dramatic increases in voltage. A surge might last for several power cycles but increase the voltage only by 100 volts or so. They are much less troublesome than spikes because they are less dramatic, often falling within the operating tolerances of the power supplies converting the energy. They too can be caused by compressors or other electrical motors starting or stopping. Figure 2.5 shows what a spike and surge might look like.

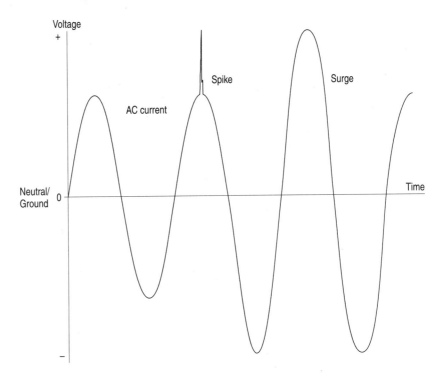

Figure 2-5   Effect of spikes and surges on the normal alternating current sine wave

The other category of power problems involves insufficient power. These kinds of problems are not damaging to the equipment, but if they last long enough they could cause the server to shut down unexpectedly because there's not enough power to sustain it. They can also cause intermittent problems when the server components don't receive enough power. The types of problems in this category are sags, brownouts, and blackouts.

A *sag* is a momentary reduction or loss in power that typically lasts a few power cycles. Sags are generally relatively harmless but may cause a reduction in power to the server, which is sometimes enough to cause problems. They are generally caused by motors starting or a momentary short circuit somewhere close on the power grid.

A *brownout* is a much longer reduction in power. It may last several minutes and can represent a severe decrease in the input voltage to the power supply. Most people recognize brownouts because they see their lights get dimmer. In a severe brownout, or a *blackout*, the lights go out entirely. Because brownouts are so easy to spot, most people assume that they are the best indicator of bad power. Unfortunately, other types of power problems are more difficult to see. It's always best to assume that every type of power problem exists in your area and to plan for all of them. Figure 2.6 shows the effect of sags and blackouts on alternating current.

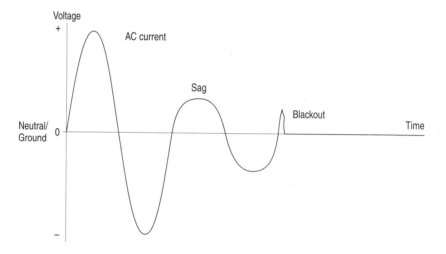

Figure 2.6   Effect of sags and blackouts on the alternating current sine wave

Solving Power Problems

There are two basic ways to resolve power problems. You can either condition the incoming power or provide your own power. All of the devices designed to solve power problems will use one or both of these mechanisms. The following three basic devices can be used to address power problems:

- Surge suppressors
- Uninterruptible power supplies (UPSs)
- Generators

The following sections discuss how to select and use each of these devices.

Surge Suppressors

The most common and most cost-effective way of dealing with spikes and surges is to use a *surge suppressor*. Surge suppressors work by clamping the voltage at a certain tolerance level and not allowing it to rise above this level (shown in Figure 2.7). They offer a relatively cheap and effective way to protect a server's power supply and components and are recommended for every computer.

Surge suppressors are designed to absorb the excess energy received during a voltage spike or surge and convert it into heat. Most modern surge suppressors use metal-oxide varistors (MOVs) that allow voltage to rise to a certain level but not beyond that point. Unfortunately, every time an MOV is forced to divert power to generate heat, it becomes slightly damaged. Eventually, after diverting enough power, the MOV will no longer be functional. Most high-quality surge suppressors have an indicator light that indicates when the MOVs can no longer absorb any more energy.

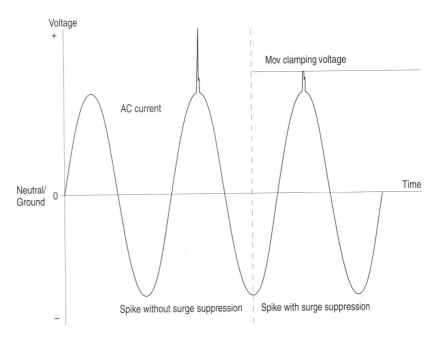

Figure 2.7   Effect of surge suppressors on spikes and surges

There are three key points to evaluating surge suppressors (the specifications for a particular surge protector are usually available on the packaging and on the manufacturer's Web sites). The key points are

- The number of joules of energy they can divert
- How low their clamping voltage is
- Which lines are protected against spikes and surges

A *joule* is a measure of power. The more joules a surge suppressor can divert, the more spikes it will take before it becomes ineffective. The clamping voltage indicates when the MOVs become effective. The lower the clamping voltage, the less harmful electricity can make it through to the server. The number of electrical lines protected is important because spikes and surges can occur on all three lines in a U.S. grounded outlet. The best surge suppressors protect all of the lines from surges or spikes.

Tip One of the secrets in the power management industry is that surge suppressors are *parallel devices*, not serial devices. This means that they protect the entire branch circuit that they are plugged into. You could, for instance, plug a surge suppressor into one socket of an outlet and your computer into the other socket of an outlet, and the surge suppressor would still protect the computer.

Due to some fairly complicated electrical interactions, the farther a surge suppressor is connected from the devices you want to protect, the less effective it is. This is one of the reasons that it's recommended that you plug your computer directly into a surge suppressor rather than just plugging the surge suppressor in down the hall.

However, if you have an office full of computers, each with its own surge suppressor, and you have one new computer that doesn't yet have a surge suppressor, the new computer is not at great risk because the other surge suppressors on the same circuit will protect it.

UPSs

Surge suppressors are great for handling spikes and surges, but they don't help for sags or brownouts. That's what UPSs are for. A *UPS* is exactly what its full name implies: an uninterruptible power supply. It works by keeping a battery from which it can draw whenever the electrical power from the utility falls below an acceptable range.

Historically, UPSs were distinguished from a similar device known as a standby power supply (SPS). However, marketing has managed to eliminate the meaning of an SPS in today's market. Most devices sold as UPSs actually would be better described as SPSs. Technically speaking, a UPS never allows an interruption of power to the servers connected to it. It does this by converting the incoming power either to direct current for storage in a battery or into motion. The direct current or the motion is converted into alternating current by separate circuitry. This is the cleanest type of power because it is generated at the UPS and thus isn't affected by problems in the power grid feeding the building. However, this purity comes at a price; UPSs waste some of their energy in the conversion processes.

SPSs, in comparison, simply maintain their batteries and watch the power going by until they are needed. When an SPS detects that the power from the utility company is outside the acceptable parameters, it switches on its inverter to convert the direct current stored in its batteries to the alternating current that the server expects and disconnects the utility power from the system. This continues until the SPS is told to shut down, the SPS runs out of battery power, or normal power is restored from the utility company.

The switching time in SPSs used to be a problem, but with the switching power supplies in most servers and the improved switching times, they are now relatively indistinguishable from UPSs and the term SPS has declined in use.

Two measures for UPSs are important in planning: the maximum load they can sustain and the length of time they can sustain it. The maximum load is almost universally the only number that is prominently displayed on literature and packaging. UPSs are often marketed as having a maximum load of, for example, 1400 volt-amps (VA) or 6 kilovolt-amps (KVA), without indicating how long they can sustain this load. In larger UPSs, this omission occurs because the amount of time that the load can be sustained is determined by the number of batteries connected to the UPS. The more batteries connected, the longer the UPS can sustain the load.

To determine how powerful a UPS you need, you first need to determine what servers and peripherals you want to connect to the UPS. You then need to account for the amount of power that these devices draw. Don't forget to include any nonserver devices that you may want to protect from power failures. This includes routers, telephone systems, and any other devices that may need an orderly shutdown in the event of a power failure or that will be necessary for communication.

Note When determining the amount of UPS protection you need, do not include any laser printers. Although larger UPSs are able to handle a laser printer, in general it's advised that you not plug a laser printer into a UPS.

To determine the draw of a device, you need to convert its power usage to the measure that is used for UPSs, the volt-amp (VA). This is done by multiplying the voltage—in our case 120 V—by the number of amps that the device requires. For instance, if you have a monitor that takes 1 amp of current, the monitor has a VA of 120.

If the device you're looking at has two numbers for the input amperage, always use the higher number to be safe. Although most devices use peak current (peak amperage) only when they start up, it's safer to assume the maximum amperage in your calculations. Using this maximum gives you an additional degree of safety because manufacturers tend to set the maximum slightly higher than the device will ever draw.

Once you've got all of the numbers from all of the devices, add them up to get the total number of volt-amps you need in your UPS. Generally, UPS manufacturers recommend that you add 25 percent to this number to handle growth, but you have already built in more than this margin of safety by using the higher power utilization numbers.

Once you have a volt-amp rating, you can start looking for UPSs that exceed that number. If you need more than about 1500 volt-amps, you'll be looking for UPSs rated in KVA, which is simply 1000 VA. If this is the case, divide your total by 1000 to determine the KVA of the UPS you need. For example, 1850 VA would be equivalent to 1.85 KVA.

If your power needs are large, it may make sense, or even be necessary, to split the load across two or more UPSs. Although it's generally a bad idea to have separate UPSs providing power for different computers because of the maintenance issues involved, there are times when it is appropriate. For instance, you may be required to fit the UPS into a rack mount configuration. There's a limit to the size of a UPS that will fit in a rack mount environment.

The second part of selecting a UPS is knowing how long the UPS can provide power when necessary—something the industry calls *run time*. Run times vary from manufacturer to manufacturer for the same size UPS, and they depend to a great extent upon the true load that the UPS has to maintain. Most UPSs are best at supporting loads of about 50 percent of their rated capacity. However, you should refer to the run-time performance charts available from the UPS manufacturer to determine the peak operating efficiency and overall run time.

In general, smaller UPS units are equipped with batteries that are not replaceable. Medium-sized UPSs (650 to 3000 VA) have replaceable batteries. Larger UPSs, like the one shown in Figure 2.8, usually allow for external battery cabinets to be attached, extending the run time. These can be particularly useful when your support personnel are off-site or if you want to be able to maintain normal operations for a longer period of time than that required to power down the systems.

Tip If you're already tired of planning for your environmental needs, and your server is going to be used for Internet hosting, you may want to consider a co-location facility. These facilities take care of all of the environmental issues and rent locked rack space and bandwidth to you for your purposes. They provide the environmental and power protection that you would otherwise have to supply yourself.

Figure 2.8   A large UPS with huge racks of batteries for power

Generators

When adding batteries to a UPS, there is a point beyond which adding additional batteries becomes prohibitively expensive. It's at that point that you should consider a generator. A *generator* (shown in Figure 2.9) is a miniature power plant for any device you want or need to keep running. Generators are generally diesel fueled and are designed to start automatically during a power outage (blackout). During the delay while the generator is starting, a UPS provides power to the connected equipment. After the generator is operational and producing suitably clean power, the UPS transfers the load to the generator and begins recharging its batteries.

Figure 2.9   A generator at a co-location facility

Generators are used primarily in operations that can accept zero downtime. Examples are network operations centers, telephone operator centers, hospitals, and other locations where continuous operation is essential. Although they are relatively expensive to set up and maintain, they can generally run continuously for days if necessary during periods of natural disaster. The main concern when using a generator is running out of fuel. Most generators are set up with 48 to 96 hours or more of fuel—plenty of time to call for more.

Practice: Size a UPS System for a Small Environment

In this practice you will select the appropriate size UPS system for a small environment. You can choose from the four hypothetical UPSs shown in Table 2.1.

Table 2.1   Hypothetical UPSs

UPS Size	Run Time at 25 Percent Load	Run Time at 50 Percent Load	Run Time at 100 Percent Load
1000 VA	80 minutes	44 minutes	15 minutes
2200 VA	80 minutes	44 minutes	15 minutes
3 KVA	80 minutes	44 minutes	15 minutes
6 KVA	80 minutes	44 minutes	15 minutes

This environment has the following equipment:

- One server rated at 6 amps
- Two servers rated at 3 amps
- One 15-inch monitor rated at 1 amp
- Two network hubs rated at 0.5 amp

Using this information and Table 2.1, answer the following questions.

1. What is the total number of volt-amps that are necessary?

2. If you require 30 minutes of run time, which UPS is necessary?

3. If you require 60 minutes of run time, which UPS is necessary?

Practice: Size a UPS System for a Larger Environment

In this practice you'll use the hypothetical UPSs from Table 2.1 to choose a UPS for a larger environment.

In this environment, you have the following equipment:

- Three servers rated at 6 amps
- Five servers rated at 2 amps
- Network equipment totaling 4 amps
- One 15-inch monitor rated at 1 amp

Using this information and Table 2.1, answer the following questions.

1. What is the total number of volt-amps that are necessary?

2. If you require 30 minutes of run time, which UPS is necessary?

3. If you require 60 minutes of run time, which UPS is necessary?

Monitoring Power Problems

The final consideration in power planning is knowing when a power problem or event has occurred. In the case of spikes and surges, this isn't much of a problem, because no action is generally necessary. However, in the case of extended brownouts or blackouts where the UPSs or generators are being used, it's important to know so that you can take corrective action or so you can monitor the situation.

Even if you have automated systems to manage the shutdown of the servers connected to the UPSs, you will still want to know that a problem has occurred, either to manage other systems not protected by the UPS or just to make sure that everything goes smoothly. The ability to monitor power problems is an essential part of power planning.

When planning for notification (described in Chapter 6, "Installing Hardware and Peripheral Drivers"), make sure that all of the systems you'll need to accomplish the notification will be kept operational by the power protection. For instance, it makes no sense to have the server send e-mail to your pager if your Internet connection isn't protected by UPSs. Nor does it make sense for a system to try to page you directly if a UPS isn't protecting the phone system.

Lesson Summary

In this lesson you learned that servers use DC electricity for their circuitry and drives. It's the job of the power supply to convert the alternating current (AC) from the electrical outlet to the DC electricity that the computer needs.

AC electricity coming from the utility company can have a wide variety of problems. These problems can be addressed by the use of surge suppressors, UPSs, and generators. A UPS keeps systems running for a limited time even after the utility power has been lost, in addition to addressing other power problems. UPSs are measured by the amount of load that they can carry and by how long they can carry that load.

If it may become necessary to support the load for a long or potentially indefinite period of time, you should consider using generators in conjunction with UPSs to provide a more permanent source of power. Whether or not you use generators, it's a good idea to monitor your system for power problems and to arrange to be notified when they occur. This notification will allow you to monitor the automated shutdown procedures and to intervene immediately when appropriate.

Lesson 3: Planning the Physical Installation

The first lesson in this chapter discussed the overall environmental issues involved in an installation and how they affect planning decisions. The previous lesson dealt with the role power plays in planning for an installation. This lesson turns to issues closer to the server itself. We'll be discussing how the server is installed, how cables are connected, and issues concerning physical access to the server.

After this lesson, you will be able to

- Identify important characteristics for racks
- Plan the installation of servers and peripherals within a rack
- Install keyboard-video-mouse (KVM) switches
- Manage the cable layout to minimize problems

Estimated lesson time: 20 minutes

Understanding the Importance of Racks

Server installations involving more than a few machines are often arranged in specially designed racks. Racks and rack-mount equipment are expensive, sometimes quite expensive, and yet most medium to large installations use racks. That is because this equipment provides a number of important benefits.

When considering rack-mount equipment, it's important to realize that it's not an all or nothing thing. It's a continuum of options that allow you to become more and more efficient. Basic rack-mount environment consists of a freestanding rack that is anchored to the floor as well as at the top. From there you can add shelves that can hold standard servers in standard cases. The ultimate in rack-mount environments is a locking cabinet that houses rack-mounted servers and devices.

The primary benefit of rack equipment is density. Because racks use floor space efficiently, they allow more servers to be placed in the same amount of space. Even if you don't work in Manhattan, where office space is at a premium, computer room space is expensive because of the special requirements for climate control. Racks are frequently used when space is at a premium.

In addition to using less space, racks allow for a secondary level of physical security. In larger environments where several divisions of an organization share a common computer room, a locking rack cabinet can limit the number of people with physical access to the server. This is particularly important for Internet servers located in co-location facilities. That's why most co-location facilities use locking rack cabinets.

Finally, racks allow for better airflow because they are generally equipped with fans on the top to help the fans in the servers pull air through. This keeps the internal temperature of the servers lower and prolongs their life spans.

Planning Installations in a Rack

Although racks provide great advantages, their use raises three additional concerns that are not normally associated with computers. These are vertical space, loading, and placement.

Vertical space refers to the height of the equipment. Height is measured in a unit called a *U*, which is 1.75 inches. Thus, a rack-mounted device that is 2U is 3.5 inches in height. By reviewing the heights of each of the units to be installed in a rack, you can determine whether there will be enough space. Expressing heights in U allows you to perform a simple subtraction of the number of U you need for equipment from the number of U available in the rack to determine whether there's enough space. It also eliminates the potential problem of the holes not being lined up correctly. Because the manufacturers build the racks and rack-mount equipment to a certain height, they know where to place the mounting screw holes.

How equipment is installed inside a rack is an important safety concern. In general, it's advisable to place the heaviest items near the bottom. This gives the rack more stability and a lower center of gravity. In addition to the general rule of loading the heaviest items at the bottom, it's important to adhere to any recommendations from the rack manufacturer. There may be additional requirements based on the design of the rack's fans or other auxiliary equipment. Individual components also sometimes have spacing requirements, but these are generally listed as a part of the space requirement for the component. This additional space is necessary to provide airflow through the device.

Finally, when placing enclosed racks in the computer room, you'll want to ensure that the doors of the racks can swing open freely. Generally, you should allow at least 3 feet of clearance at the back of a rack and at least 6 feet of clearance at the front. This allows the doors in the back to open fully and also gives you room at the front to slide equipment out on rack slides and still have room to work on it.

Installing Keyboard-Video-Mouse Switches

As I indicated previously, one of the greatest advantages of rack systems is that they allow a greater density of servers in the same space. However, most of the space in a server installation is taken up by the keyboard, mouse, and monitor. These peripheral items often take several times more space than the server itself.

Since servers only infrequently need to be accessed via these devices, keyboard-video-mouse (KVM) switches were developed. These switches are designed to allow more than one server to be connected to the same keyboard, monitor, and mouse.

KVM switches are significantly more complex than just a manual switch of electrical wires. They have to communicate with the servers simultaneously, letting each believe that it has its own keyboard, mouse, and monitor. Some of these switches can generate an on-screen menu of the servers that are attached and allow you to select the server from that menu.

The number of servers that can be controlled from a single keyboard and monitor depends upon the switch, but typical quantities range from 4 to 32 or 64. The larger switches often allow for two or more keyboards, monitors, and mice. This helps eliminate contention in environments with large numbers of servers. KVM switches are attached to each server by means of three cables. These cables, which are sometimes bundled together, are plugged into the monitor, keyboard, and mouse ports of the server. The KVM switch is then connected to the shared monitor, keyboard, and mouse via the standard cables.

Tip Because KVM switches must communicate with the servers individually, they must support the personality of the mouse you have attached to them. Most KVM switches aren't aware of the newer "wheel" mice. If you intend to use this type of mouse with your KVM switch, make sure that it's supported.

Although KVM switches can greatly reduce the amount of space needed for servers, they often cause cabling problems because of the sheer number of cables that must be connected to them.

Routing and Managing Cables

Imagine for a moment a computer rack that has 10 computers in it. Each computer has 5 cables coming from it (a power cord, a network connection, a keyboard connection, a mouse connection, and a video connection). That rack therefore has at least 50 cables routing power and communications from one machine to another.

Fifty cables may not seem like a lot, but once they've all been woven around each other, it can be difficult if not impossible to remove a single server without accidentally disconnecting another one. Because of the potential for problems with cable routing and management, it's important to consider the methods for managing them. Figure 2.10 shows one well-groomed trellis leading wires from one rack to another.

Figure 2.10   A trellis for routing cables at a co-location facility

One of the most fundamental issues in cable management is labeling. With 10 cables of the same type in each rack, you'll find it difficult to know which port the video cable is connected to. Labeling can be done with specialty labeling products or with something as simple as a permanent marker. Whatever you use, you'll want to make sure that you label each end. If possible, label the cable every few feet or so as well. This will ease the cable identification process.

Once the cables have been labeled, it's a good idea to bundle together all of the cables that will always go to the same location, so that they work like a single cable. For instance, most KVM switches require three separate cables. If you bind all of these cables with wire ties or electrical tape every 18 inches, those three cables become one cable. Bundling can significantly reduce the number of cables you have to manage.

Tip When bundling cables, try to have the ones with connectors that screw in or lock on be slightly shorter than the other cables. This ensures that the locked-on cable is the one that is pulled on should the cables get tugged, and it will reduce the number of times that cables are accidentally unplugged. This practice is particularly useful when working with KVM cables because the keyboard and mouse connectors do not lock on and thus are often disconnected accidentally.

The final consideration in cable management is how to route the cables so that they don't get tangled. Routing is generally done through cable management channels built into the rack, but it can also be accomplished with cable ties. In any event, you'll route cables on the right or left of the cabinet and then horizontally over to the server once they are at the right height.

Lesson Summary

In this lesson you learned about the importance of racks and how to use them effectively in your environment. Racks are an efficient way to use space as well as to enhance the life of the servers by maintaining a lower internal temperature.

In addition, you learned that KVM switches can further reduce the amount of space consumed by servers in a rack. Finally, you learned how to route and manage cables within a rack to make management easier.

Lesson 4: Preparing for Backups and Monitoring

No installation plan is complete without considering the issues surrounding backups and monitoring. These are both essential maintenance functions that should be considered before the installation. Although we'll cover monitoring and tape backups in more detail in Chapters 13 and 14, we need to go over the planning concepts here so that you can complete the planning phase of your installation.

After this lesson, you will be able to

- Select the correct tape backup device
- Plan for tape rotations
- Plan for meaningful monitoring of your backups, as well as of your server as a whole

Estimated lesson time: 20 minutes

Selecting the Correct Tape Backup Device

When planning a server installation, you may not have to worry about how the server gets backed up, because a network backup system might already be in place with the capacity to back up the new server. In most environments, however, backup will be a serious consideration for the new server. This is because backup systems are one of the more expensive components of a server. When selecting a tape backup system, you need to consider the following three issues:

- Previous backup tape format
- Tape backup window
- Media life span

Previous Backup Tape Format

One of the biggest factors influencing the kind of tape backup system you select is the type and capacity of the media you're using on other servers, especially the type of tape backup system used on the old server, if the machine you're planning for will replace an existing system. This is true not only because you're already familiar with the media and drives but also because you've already got an investment in tape media and because you need to have a way to restore the old backups.

Obviously, to restore backups from an older system it's necessary to have the tape format that was previously used. For instance, if you have a new Digital Linear Tape (DLT) drive system and the old system was a 4-mm system, you'll be unable to restore those 4-mm tapes unless you keep the 4-mm drive that the tapes were backed up on and install it in the new server as well. This isn't a bad idea for two reasons. First, you know that the tape drive will read the tapes it wrote. Second, it gives you a fallback for backups on the main system should the new tape backup fail.

The most common change when adding a new server is to upgrade to the newest tape drive within that family. For instance, if you were using 4-mm tapes for backups, you're likely to purchase a Digital Data Storage (DDS) IV 4-mm tape drive because that format has the ability to read the previous media, and it allows for greater capacities. However, capacity isn't the only issue.

Tape Backup Window

A *tape backup window* is the amount of downtime that the organization can accept while performing backups. An organization that is primarily office-based and doesn't use the computers for more than 12 hours a day on average has a 12-hour backup window available. This means that the users can reasonably be expected not to be on the system for 12 hours each day. An organization that operates 24 hours a day must perform all of the backups while someone is on the systems.

Even in organizations having 24-hour operations, there are times when the systems are being lightly used and when backups might more easily fit within the system load. Backups generally involve an incredibly intense load because they try to move massive amounts of data through the system and off to the tape backup device. The intensive nature of the backup process can cause some real contention and performance issues for users on the system.

It's important to try to fit backups within the window available. The amount of time a backup requires is dictated partially by the rotation scheme you use and partially by the amount of data to be backed up and the type and model of tape drive you select. The amount of data to be backed up should be fairly easy to calculate: Just use the total disk capacity of the new server. Although you won't always be backing up everything, your backup scheme must be able to handle at least that amount of data within the backup window.

Each tape drive has a different *throughput*. The throughput is how much data the drive can write to tape under ideal conditions. This value is a good starting point for determining how quickly backups will be performed.

Table 2.2 shows a variety of information about the popular tape backup formats, including their throughput, storage capacity, and expected media life span. You've seen all of these formats in the preceding text except for 8-mm systems and the new Advanced Intelligent Tape (AIT). When estimating capacity, you should base your calculations on the uncompressed throughput figure for each drive, because compressed figures are roughly double these numbers. This will help allow for growth as well as for the fact that the drive will never be able to maintain the best backup rate because the server will have some gaps in its ability to push data to the tape drive.

Table 2.2   Tape Drive Models, Capacities, and Throughput

Drive Type	Model	Capacity	Media Type	Media Life Span	Throughput (Uncompressed) MB/Sec
DLT	DLT-8000	40 GB	DLT IV	30 years	6.0
	DLT-7000	35 GB	DLT IV	30 years	5.0
	DLT-4000	20 GB	DLT IV	30 years	1.5
4 mm	DDS-4	40 GB	DDS-4	>10 years	3.0
	DDS-3	24 GB	DDS-3	>10 years	1.0
	DDS-2	8 GB	DDS-2	>10 years	0.5
8 mm	Mammoth-2	150 GB	225m AME	>30 years	12.0
	Mammoth (EXB-8900)	20 GB	170m AME	$\geq$30 years	3.0
	Mammoth LT	14 GB	125m AME	>30 years	2.0
	Eliant 820	7 GB	160mXL	>30 years	1.0
AIT	AIT-2	50 GB	AIT-2	>30 years	6.0
	AIT-1	35 GB	AIT-1	>30 years	3.0

Another consideration is whether the tape drive will be backing up across the network. If the network is slow, or if its throughput is slower than the drive, you'll have to account for the slower network speeds when calculating the amount of time each type of device will take to back up your environment.

Note To achieve the maximum sustained throughput for a backup device, the server needs to be able to provide data at that rate. If the server you're planning to install won't be able to sustain the rate of speed that the backup needs, you will have a problem. You should also consider that some backup software may not be able to maintain the kinds of data rates necessary to keep the backup drive active. Check with the backup software manufacturer before you make your final decision on either a drive or a software vendor.

In some environments, a single tape drive may not be able to back up all of the data within the time frame available. You may need to team two or more drives that work simultaneously in order to get the backup done within the window provided. Although multiple drives are sometimes necessary, it's best to avoid them when possible because software that supports *striping* (a storage scheme that spreads a backup's data across several tape devices) is still relatively rare, and without striping it becomes necessary to manually assign the storage areas that each drive backs up.

Once you've selected the drive type and know that it will back up your system in the given backup window, you can begin to investigate options to improve the capacity, such as autoloaders and libraries. In other words, if you can accomplish your backup goals within a given time window, but the drive doesn't have enough capacity on one tape, you need to look for solutions that can change those tapes for you—or look for a higher-capacity medium. An *autoloader* automatically changes the tape in the tape drive when one is filled. It is generally just a carrier holding more than one tape that is inserted into the front of the tape device.

Libraries, on the other hand, tend to have more than one carrier and a locking front door. The carriers are inserted into the unit but are not connected directly to a single tape drive. Libraries also tend to have the capability to install more than one drive. Libraries are recommended when more than one drive is necessary to address throughput issues and when the capacity of the two (or more) drives still doesn't provide sufficient capacity to back up the entire system.

An important point should be made here: Autoloaders and libraries can dramatically increase the capacity of a backup solution, but they don't reduce the amount of time it takes to back that data up, as compared to the same number of drives. As a result, autoloaders are a good solution when large backup windows are available. Libraries are a good solution only when multiple drives are needed to achieve backup speed and multiple tapes are necessary.

Note It is not a good idea to use autoloaders or libraries to hold all of your tapes, or even a week's worth of tapes. Should a disaster occur, the latest backups won't be protected. Although convenient, this is a risky method for handling backups.

Media Life Span

In environments where long-term records must be maintained, the amount of time that backup media will hold on to the information stored on them can be important. Some industries, such as aerospace, are required by law to maintain records for many years after production or after a repair. In these industries, and in other situations where maintaining information for long periods is important, the life span of the medium factors into the purchase decision. Although most server-class tape backup systems have media life spans of 30 years and beyond, it's important to realize that not all media have the ability to retain data for this long.

Although the media life spans shown in Table 2.2 might seem long enough, it is strongly recommended that any data being kept for archival purposes, where it may be needed for more than 10 years, be written to an optical medium. Tape drives are excellent at backing up large amounts of data very quickly, but their retrieval properties are really best suited to complete restorations. Archived data should probably be handled via a more stable, optical medium. A variety of write once, read many (WORM) drives are available that provide life spans that can't yet be measured because they are so long.

Choosing a Tape Rotation Scheme

Purchasing a tape drive is a big expense, but it may represent less than half of the total cost of the backup solution. The media used to store the backups are often a significant part of the total solution cost. Often this is because even an efficient tape rotation mechanism requires several tapes.

Types of Backups

Before exploring the tape backup rotations, it's important to understand the three basic types of backup that can be performed. They are

- **Full.**   All files are backed up.
- **Incremental.**   Files that have changed since the last full or incremental backup are backed up.
- **Differential.**   Files that have changed since the last full backup are backed up.

Although these are the terms used for file-based backups, the same principles apply to database and mail system backups as well. A *full backup* is easy to understand, as it backs up all of the files. *Incremental backups* are also easy to understand in that they incrementally back up files that have changed since the last full or incremental backup. *Differential backups* are similar to incremental backups, except that they back up all of the files that have changed since the last full backup, not just since the last differential backup.

Incremental and differential backups are used to balance the amount of time spent backing up the systems on a daily basis with the need to perform a restoration in a reasonable time. Differential backups back up more data than incremental backups because each one includes everything that has changed since the last full backup, whereas incremental backups back up only the files that changed that day. As a result, differential backups take longer to run. However, they have the advantage of allowing for much quicker restores.

If you were doing daily incremental backups and you had to restore the system, you would first have to restore the last full backup, and then you'd need to restore each successive day's incremental backup. Just managing the tapes during this process can be time-consuming. Consider also that the files that change on the first day tend to keep changing on successive days. For instance, if you kept your timesheet in an Excel file on the server, you would have changed the file when you entered your time on Monday, so it would get backed up. On Tuesday you'd edit the same file and it would get backed up again, and so on until the failure. The same spreadsheet would now be on the full backup as well as on each incremental backup. The result is that the same file would be restored over and over again.

If you were doing differential backups, you'd restore the last full backup and then only the most recent differential backup. Not only does this reduce the number of tape swaps, but it also significantly reduces the amount of time required because each file is being restored at most two times (once from the full backup and once from the differential backup.)

Tape Rotation Schemes

Now that you understand the types of backups that are available, it's time to consider rotation schemes. There are two tape rotation schemes that most people consider because they are easy enough to be managed by humans. Although more-complex tape rotation schemes exist that are more tape efficient, they are generally used only when extremely large backup sets are being created, and then only when the software being used for backup supports the rotation method within the software.

The two most popular tape rotation schemes are as follows:

- Sets
- Grandfather-father-son (GFS)

The sections that follow describe these schemes.

The Sets Rotation Scheme

Although generally used only in small environments, a valid backup rotation is to use a series of backup sets, each of which has all of the tapes needed to back up a complete week. In this rotation there are generally five or six tapes per week—for Monday, Tuesday, Wednesday, Thursday, Friday, and sometimes for Saturday. Each tape is put into the drive on its day of the week. The complete set of tapes is swapped out each week for a new set. As a rule, for simplicity all backups are full backups.

Generally, this scheme uses only between two and four sets of tapes; having to use more than that tends to require so many tapes that the GFS rotation scheme described next becomes much more effective. The sets method of rotating tapes does have some nice advantages, the first of which is that it is very simple. The second advantage is that it wears the tapes evenly so that tape wear generally isn't a concern before the server is replaced. Finally, only one tape is necessary for a restore.

However, this tape rotation scheme requires a lot of tapes, and it doesn't provide much of a history, so all of the errors or missing data must be noticed fairly quickly. Missing or erroneous data that isn't located quickly can't be recovered.

The Grandfather-Father-Son Rotation Scheme

The most widely used tape rotation scheme by far is the grandfather-father-son (GFS) scheme. This scheme is used because it's easy to understand and minimizes tape use. While the sets tape-rotation mechanism requires one set of tapes for each day of the week, the GFS mechanism allows a single set of tapes to be reused through most days (generally Monday through Thursday), then weekly tapes, and finally monthly tapes.

The idea behind this rotation scheme is that you rarely need a specific version of a file from more than a week ago. In other words, files tend to fall into two groups: those that change daily, in which the daily changes are important, and those that change infrequently and therefore have no daily changes that need to be restored. This scheme allows the same tapes to be reused each week, without concern for files that may not be able to be restored.

In the GFS tape rotation scheme, the daily tapes are rotated each day throughout the week. The weekly tapes are rotated each week throughout the weeks of the month, and the monthly tapes are rotated each month throughout the months of the year. In cases that may require restoration from further back than a year, yearly tapes are sometimes made as well. (This would technically be a great-grandfather-grandfather-father-son (GGGFS) scheme, although some backup software documentation lumps it under GFS.)

Planning for Monitoring

No matter how great a rotation scheme you set up or how great a tape backup device you select, they will be meaningless if a problem occurs that you don't notice because you aren't monitoring the backup. The greatest challenge in any installation is maintaining the system and knowing when problems occur. Some problems are impossible to miss; if the server goes down, you're likely to hear from several hundred users asking what happened. However, problems with the backup system aren't quite so easy to detect.

This section discusses the importance of monitoring the tape backup process, using the monitoring systems built into your tape backup software, as well as some more general mechanisms for monitoring the server.

Monitoring Backups

For the most part, people don't pay attention to the backups because they run fine most of the time. Even the best-intentioned support personnel will eventually get used to the backup running successfully and will quit looking at the printed backup reports.

As human beings, we're subject to something called conditioned response. We get lazy because we expect the same result every time. That's why we stop looking at the printed backup reports and why we begin to ignore warning messages when we see them all the time. For instance, when was the last time you read the flammability warning on a pillow or upholstery tag before you clipped it off? (Or maybe you're so used to these tags that you just ignore them altogether?)

The problem with reporting only errors is that we don't know whether the operation succeeded. Thus, we don't know whether the backup completed successfully or failed to complete. For tape backups, it's generally advisable to establish notification on both success and failure, so you can ensure that the backup operation completed successfully. Most backup software on the market today allows for printed and e-mail notification of success and failure.

Note In most backup software packages, the final entry in the log file for the backup indicates the overall success or failure of the backup. If you want to have printed copies of the logs, you should train the person responsible for managing them to look at the last page. If a failure is indicated, he or she should notify the appropriate person or resolve the problem.

Sometimes people are aware of the cause of a failure but don't feel that resolving it is important, and so each successive report indicates the same failure. The result is that the report is ignored and other problems crop up within the backup process that aren't noticed. For this reason, you should address every failure message.

Monitoring the System

Two other monitoring mechanisms that support more than just a single backup application should also be a part of your planning process. One of these mechanisms monitors hardware events, and one monitors services and network operations. They are

- Desktop Management Interface (DMI)
- Simple Network Management Protocol (SNMP)

Both protocols are similar in that they allow you to query a device for information and to manage the device; however, DMI is PC-centric, whereas SNMP is network based, allowing for the management of both network equipment and servers. Although there has been a great deal of discussion of how to bring the DMI and SNMP standards together so that a single management interface can be used between management applications and hardware, to date those efforts have been ineffective.

Both mechanisms support notifications when a predefined threshold is exceeded. In SNMP, these notifications are called traps, and in DMI they are called alerts, but the goal is the same. The process alerts a management application or console to a problem. The management application may attempt to resolve the problem itself using predefined scripts, or it may notify support personnel, or both.

Practice: Select a Tape Drive and Rotation Scheme for a Small Office

In this practice, you'll decide on the best tape drive and rotation scheme for a small office. Refer back to Table 2.2 for the basic characteristics of the tape drives.

Suppose that you need to choose the right backup solution for a small office that maintains a large number of faxes and therefore has a large amount of online storage. The office currently has approximately 40 GB of data, and its server currently has a capacity of 60 GB. The growth rate of the data is slow, and a very small percentage of it changes each day.

The office's backup window is approximately 14 hours each evening and 60 hours over the weekend. What solutions would be good for this environment?

Although the total storage capacity is high, there's no urgency in completing the backup, so an autoloader is a good solution here. Getting all of the data backed up will take more than one cartridge unless compression is used on the largest-capacity tape drives available.

In this environment, the best rotation is probably a simple set rotation with a full backup every night. To accomplish that, a tape drive with a throughput of 1.2 megabytes per second (MBps) is necessary. The formula for determining this is (60 GB * 1000 MB/GB) / (14 hours * 60 minutes/hour * 60 seconds/minute). This calculation indicates that an autoloader with a DLT-4000, DDS-4, Mammoth LT, AIT-1, or better will be sufficient for the environment's needs.

Practice: Select a Tape Drive and Rotation Scheme for a Manufacturing Company

In this practice, you'll choose the best solution for backing up a manufacturing firm's data. Again, refer back to Table 2.2 for the characteristics of the tape drives.

In this environment, you have a manufacturing firm that makes widgets in three shifts. A large number of production and administrative staff are on the system during the first and second shifts. The third shift has roughly half the people of the second shift, so activity is relatively light.

The firm has a 10-GB production database as well as 60 GB of other data that needs to be backed up. For the 30 minutes that the third shift is on its lunch break, it's acceptable to have a slowdown associated with a backup. The production database tracks the movement of widgets on the job floor and is very active, as is the 60 GB of additional data being backed up. It's estimated that 20 percent of the data on the system changes each week.

The plant shuts down for 48 hours each weekend, so backups during that time are not a problem. What are good solutions for this environment?

In this environment, the solution is more complicated because you must first determine how much data will be backed up each week. Given the 70 GB of data and a 20 percent change rate, you can calculate that approximately 14 GB of data will have to be backed up throughout the week. Although incremental backups throughout the week would reduce the total backup to approximately 2.8 GB, the environment wouldn't be able to tolerate much downtime because the system routes the widgets through production. As a result, differential backups should be performed throughout the week to minimize the impact of an outage.

Because of the need to perform differential backups rather than full backups during the week, a GFS rotation would make sense.

On weekdays 30 minutes are available to back up 14 GB. This requires a sustained backup rate of at least 7.8 MBps. On weekends 70 GB of data must be backed up in 48 hours, requiring a backup rate of 0.4 GBps.

Only one of the drives in Table 2.2 can achieve the 7.8 MBps backup rate needed to complete the weekday backup in time: the Mammoth-2. Otherwise, at least two drives will be necessary, since the highest uncompressed backup rate for any other device is 6 MBps. The need for high speed drives up the capacities of the tapes, and so the best solution for this environment is probably either two DLT-8000s, two AIT-2 drives, or a single Mammoth-2 drive. Autoloaders aren't a good option because two drives are necessary. Although a library is an option, it is not a necessity, because the entire system can be stored on the one tape in each drive.

Lesson Summary

In this lesson, you learned the considerations for selecting a tape backup unit and for developing a tape rotation scheme. You learned that the previous tape format used is important because of the need to be able to restore previous backups and archives. You learned that your tape rotation scheme can significantly affect the number of tapes needed. You also learned to be cognizant of the organization's backup window and how your backup solution can fit into that window.

Finally, you learned the basic monitoring terms and solutions that you should be aware of when planning so that you can establish proper monitoring of the system.

Lesson 5: Creating a Disaster Recovery Plan

The previous lesson discussed how to plan for tape backups and monitoring. This lesson discusses the events that make these practices important. It focuses on the mechanics of a disaster recovery plan so that you can modify the organization's existing plan or develop a new one.

After this lesson, you will be able to

- Develop a disaster recovery plan
- Plan for and select catastrophic recovery options

Estimated lesson time: 20 minutes

Developing a Disaster Recovery Plan

None of us like planning for unpleasant events. We avoid it simply because even planning for them is, well, unpleasant. Unfortunately, unpleasant things can happen, and plan for them we must. A *disaster* in a server context is an unscheduled service outage, whether that outage is caused by an act of nature or by equipment failure inside or outside of the organization.

You've already learned about some of the mechanisms for disaster recovery. Lesson 2 discussed UPSs and generators. All of these mechanisms are designed to minimize the possibility and impact of a power-related disaster. Chapter 1, Lesson 2, addressed mechanisms for minimizing the impact of component failures. You haven't, however, seen how to develop a comprehensive plan that addresses the technical aspects of a disaster as well as how to proceed once a disaster has occurred.

Disaster planning, often called contingency planning, is a developing profession of its own. The Disaster Recovery Institute (DRI) International is currently developing certifications and a body of knowledge to support the profession. Its Web address is http://www.drii.org. The information covered here is consistent with its current body of knowledge.

Obviously, if your organization has a department for risk management or contingency planning, your first action in planning for disaster recovery should be to contact that department to coordinate your activities. If your organization doesn't have a department that is responsible for disaster recovery planning, you may want to visit the Disaster Recovery Institute's site, as it has contact information for government, educational, and private organizations that have an interest in contingency planning and materials that you can use to begin your planning process.

When developing a disaster recovery plan, there are several key steps to take. They are

- Evaluate the risks
- Measure the business impact

- Develop strategies
- Plan emergency operations
- Train staff to use and maintain the disaster recovery plan

Each of these steps is discussed in the sections that follow.

Evaluating the Risks

The first step in developing a disaster recovery plan is to determine what the risks to your business operation are. In the context of deploying servers, this generally means evaluating the potential causes of server failure. For this step, simply list each of the possible risks.

Some common risks are as follows:

- Power failure
- Server component failure
- Hard disk failure
- Network equipment failure
- Data communications failure
- Acts of nature (such as tornadoes, hurricanes, and earthquakes)

Measuring the Business Impact

For each of the risks you've listed, you now need to determine the impact it would have on your business. The business impact of a given risk is measured in two dimensions. The first dimension is frequency. In other words, what is the likelihood that the event will occur? For instance, you might reasonably estimate that a hard disk failure will occur once per year in a large server. A power supply failure might occur once every five years.

The second dimension is the severity of the risk. How severe an impact does the failure have on the internal and external customers of the organization? Is the failure simply a nuisance, or is it a business-stopping event? Business-stopping events and those that affect external customers are oftentimes the first ones to be addressed.

Developing Strategies

Once you have identified and quantified the risks, it's time to evaluate potential solutions to the problem. You'll put those potential solutions and their costs together with the risks to determine which solution, if any, is warranted for the risk. Although ideally you would develop an algorithm to determine how much solution cost the risk could bear, most of the time the assessments are too imprecise for a precision formula.

Once you have identified the risks and selected the solutions, you should implement the solutions in the plan for the new server or as soon after installation as is practical. This will ensure that the solutions you've identified are implemented before the risks actually occur. Because of the shortage of qualified IT people, more organizations are being forced to become reactive rather than proactive.

Planning Emergency Operations

When planning for a disaster, most people have no difficulty determining what the risks are or developing potential strategies for preventing the risks from occurring. Frequently, however, the planning falls short when it comes to the steps to take if a particular risk occurs. Whether the risk is covered by a strategy or not, the recovery often requires human involvement, either to supervise the operation or to perform certain manual steps.

When more than one person or department is involved in the response to a disaster, you need a plan for how their activities will be coordinated. This coordination is necessary to reduce confusion and eliminate overlap. A major portion of an effective disaster recovery plan will focus on how the risks will be addressed when they become disasters.

Training Staff to Use and Maintain the Plan

The final step in a good disaster recovery plan is training. You need to train your personnel in what the plan is, how it is executed, and how it needs to be maintained. Training is perhaps the most critical yet most neglected task. It helps ensure that new risks and solutions are put into the plan and that everyone knows what is expected when a disaster occurs.

Planning for a Catastrophic Disaster

While most of our disasters will be little more than nuisances that disrupt the operations of a single department or a few departments for a few hours or days, there are some circumstances that could totally destroy the data center and thus render the entire company inoperative. These kinds of disasters are extremely rare, but they do occur, and most large organizations need to address them in disaster recovery planning.

From the perspective of a server implementation, you need to consider two primary options when thinking about a catastrophic disaster. They are

- Hot backup sites
- Cold backup sites

The following sections address each type of site.

Hot Backup Sites

Hot backup sites are duplicate operating environments maintained in different geographic regions. These sites are expensive to maintain because they require you to maintain a duplicate of the existing environment, including every driver, patch, and service-pack update.

A hot backup site is, however, the ultimate in contingency planning. It allows an organization to resume business very rapidly after a catastrophic failure because most of the setup is already done. All that you would need to do, ideally, would be to restore the backups onto the systems at the hot site.

Cold Backup Sites

While hot backup sites provide a complete duplicate of the systems in operation, *cold backup sites* provide only space and in some cases duplicate equipment. This type of site allows systems to be recovered fairly quickly because the facility is already ready and most of the equipment should already be available. However, because the systems are not operational, recovery time is longer than at a hot site. In most cases, the substantial difference in cost leads organizations to choose cold sites.

Lesson Summary

In this lesson you learned the basic steps for preparing a disaster recovery plan. They are to evaluate the risks, measure business impact, develop strategies, plan emergency operations, and train staff to use and maintain the plan.

You also learned where to find additional information about disaster recovery planning and how hot backup sites and cold backup sites are used as a part of a disaster recovery plan to address the risk of a catastrophic disaster.

Review

Here are some questions to help you determine whether you have learned enough to move on to the next chapter. If you have difficulty answering these questions, please go back and review the material in this chapter before beginning the next chapter. The answers for these questions are located in the appendix, "Questions and Answers."

1. Why is climate control important? What impact does it have on performance or availability?

2. Your organization's business offices are located on the Florida Keys, where hurricanes are a real concern. The organization wants to make sure that if a natural disaster strikes it will be able to get back up and running right away. What is the best disaster recovery solution?

3. Your organization is an application service provider (ASP), hosting applications for companies across the United States. One of the biggest concerns that customers express to the sales people is the potential for your systems to be down, preventing them from getting their work done. What power precautions should you take to minimize the risk that a power failure could keep your systems from operating?

4. Your organization has a computer room with a raised floor. Some people in the organization say you shouldn't be worried about flooding because the computer room is 12 inches above the floors in the rest of the building. Why isn't this true?

5. You're installing a new server and you don't have any new circuits available to you, so you have to use an existing circuit. What should you do before plugging in the new server?

6. Your organization has just hired a new director of information technology, and as a part of his initiation to the organization he wants to know what everyone does and has asked to see any materials that you have to show the processes you go through. You're responsible for monitoring backups. When you show him the five failed backup reports over the last six months, he seems concerned. What might be concerning the new director of information technology?

7. You're installing a new server in a new rack, complete with a very heavy rack-mount UPS. Your boss likes the fact that the UPS has LEDs on it indicating load and battery availability and wants the UPS mounted at the top of the rack where everyone will be able to see these LEDs. Why is this a bad idea?

8. Your organization is in the pharmaceutical industry and must maintain records of clinical studies for several years. Although most clinical study information is archived on optical media, you're concerned about the ability to restore the study data from the regular tape backup and archive mechanisms. What consideration should you give to tape backup systems?

C H A P T E R   3

Planning the System

About This Chapter

The previous two chapters focused on issues that you should decide prior to planning for the server itself. We've now covered every aspect of planning for implementation and maintenance, including the environmental issues surrounding implementation. This chapter focuses on the core issues of planning and selecting the actual server. It reviews all of the major components of a server and discusses the considerations for selecting those components. Combine this information with the information you gathered in Chapter 1 to determine how the server should be configured.

Before You Begin

To complete this chapter, you should have

- Internet access

Lesson 1: Processing Capacity

Processing capacity—the speed of the CPU or CPUs—is the most widely used metric for measuring how fast a server is. After all, the CPU is the brains of the server, controlling everything that happens. Therefore it is often thought that the speed of the processor is the primary indicator of the speed of the system. While that's certainly the case, this lesson also looks at other processor characteristics and how they can enhance server performance. Although the CPU and its associated chipset ultimately determine the kind of memory that can be used, we'll delay our discussion of memory until Lesson 2.

After this lesson, you will be able to

- Identify CPU characteristics
- Select the appropriate processor cache size
- Explain the benefits and drawbacks of symmetric multiprocessing

Estimated lesson time: 20 minutes

Identifying CPU Characteristics

While most of us could easily identify clock speed as an important CPU characteristic, other CPU characteristics also affect performance. The main factors in CPU performance are

- **Clock speed.** The frequency of internal CPU cycles. Clock speed indicates the internal timing of the CPU. For the same CPU architecture, clock speed indicates relative speed.

- **Cache size.** The CPU must wait for information to be fetched from memory. An onboard memory cache allows the processor to speed up that process because cache can be accessed much faster than system memory. The cache controller tries to guess what the processor will need next and to load as much of it as possible into the cache to speed up operations. The larger the processor cache, the greater the chance that the needed information will be in it.

- **Memory bus.** The incredibly high speeds of a processor indicate only the internal frequency that the processor runs at. When the processor is communicating with other devices, it operates at a much slower rate. A variety of memory speeds and architectures, described in Lesson 2, affect the overall performance of the server and are dictated by the CPU and CPU support chips.

- **Architecture.**   The clock speed of a processor, measured in megahertz or gigahertz, indicates how many cycles a processor can complete in a second. However, a single clock cycle in one processor may accomplish more or less work than a single clock cycle in another processor. The architecture of the chip determines how many clock cycles a given instruction will take to execute and the optimization techniques that can be applied. Thus, a chip's architecture and the optimization techniques it incorporates can significantly affect the chip's overall performance. Some examples of architectures are the AMD K6-3, AMD Athlon, Pentium, Pentium Pro, Pentium II, Pentium III, and Pentium 4.

The best way to determine overall processor performance is to use the standardized benchmarks available from several PC publications. These benchmarks are designed to simulate the way that the CPU is used in the real world. Benchmarks such as those maintained by the Standard Performance Evaluation Corporation (SPEC) and Ziff-Davis can help you determine the overall speed of the processor.

Selecting a Cache

For most professionals, selecting the CPU consists of selecting the architecture and the speed. They generally spend very little time selecting a cache size that makes sense for the application of the server. However, the cache size can affect a processor's overall performance by 10 percent or more.

The performance improvement gained by a larger cache has a cost, however. The processor with the largest cache can cost more than twice as much as the one with the smallest cache. Although there is no hard-and-fast rule for choosing a cache size, there are two guidelines you can use:

- **Installed memory.**   As more main memory is installed, the ratio between main memory size and cache size increases. This larger ratio decreases the effectiveness of the CPU. To maintain the processor's effectiveness in using the cache, it is a good idea to increase the cache as memory increases. You may want to consider upgrading the cache size of the processor if you are planning on installing more than 256 MB of RAM.

- **Processor utilization.**   If you expect that the application for the server will be processor intensive, the 10 percent or more improvement in CPU performance provided by a larger cache may be worth the extra cost. Server applications such as terminal servers, applications servers, and database servers may benefit substantially from additional cache.

In general, the more cache that is available, the better the performance. The additional investment in cache memory is usually worth it for servers that will be heavily used.

Considering Symmetric Multiprocessing

Chapter 1, Lesson 3 discussed scalability as it relates to both multiprocessing and clustering. Multiprocessing, you may remember, is the use of multiple processors in the same machine, with an operating system that can take advantage of the additional processors.

The primary reason to use multiprocessing is that it allows systems to be scaled in a more effective and simpler way than by using clustered solutions. The additional processors can share the same memory and can communicate with the other processors almost instantaneously. This provides a level of efficiency that cannot be found in a clustered environment.

This efficiency is important. Although there is a point beyond which adding processors to a system is not effective, adding a small number of processors usually produces an almost linear improvement over a single processor. Put another way, multiprocessor-enabled applications that use the processor extensively almost double their performance when another processor is added. In fact, according to research done when Microsoft Windows 2000 was being released, scalability for processors—even for those simply providing file and print services, which are not traditionally processor intensive—improved by a factor of 3.5 when four processors were used.

Although multiprocessor systems are quite useful in most environments, in some cases adding more processors to the system does not improve performance. For example, additional processors are not effective when the system either is performing a single task or when it already has surplus processing capacity. In these cases, the operating system simply can't take advantage of the additional processing power that is available.

Most servers provide a variety of services and run multiple execution threads to get work done for the clients quickly and efficiently. There are, however, applications that use a single execution thread for all or most of their processing needs. A *thread* represents an indivisible series of coded instructions. A given thread can be executed only by a single processor.

The arrangement of services on a server can be likened to the environment of a supermarket. In any given supermarket, dozens of shoppers may be wandering through the store selecting their groceries. However, they must all pass through a cashier to leave the store. If only one cashier is on duty and more than one shopper needs to check out, the additional shoppers will have to wait. Adding more cashiers will allow the supermarket to serve more and more shoppers at one time and will get them out of store quicker—that is, if there are shoppers waiting to be served. In this analogy, the cashiers are CPUs in a server. When they become a bottleneck, adding more of them will improve performance. The shoppers are the threads, going about their business until they need a cashier (processor).

An important point here is that adding cashiers can reduce the total time the shoppers spend in the store only by the amount of time the shopper would stand in line. They still require the same amount of time to do their shopping. Similarly, if the bottleneck is not the processor, adding more processors won't solve the problem.

Since a single-threaded application can be executed on only one processor at a time, adding processors will have a marginal impact on this type of application. Basically, the second processor will end up taking care of I/O and system issues while the first processor spends all of its time executing the application. In most environments, servers run multiple applications or one multithreaded application, so not being able to take advantage of additional processors isn't an issue. Microsoft SQL Server is an example of an application designed with multiple execution threads so that it can take advantage of additional processors. Adding multiple processors to a SQL server will therefore generally improve performance.

The other situation in which additional processors aren't helpful is when the primary limiting factor, or bottleneck, for the system isn't the processor. When another component of the system is the primary limiting factor, increasing the number of processors won't appreciably improve the performance of the system because the operating system can't use the additional processing power. For more information about bottlenecks, how to identify them, and what to do about them, see Chapter 8, Lesson 3.

Once you've determined that a multiprocessor system is required or desirable, consider purchasing all of the processors that you intend to put into the unit at one time. As we mentioned in Chapter 1, Lesson 3, multiprocessor systems rely on the processors being identical or nearly so. By ordering all of the processors at the same time, you can be reasonably assured that they are all at the same stepping level.

Lesson Summary

This lesson identified the basic CPU characteristics and discussed how they affect performance. It also explored symmetric multiprocessing as an alternative to a single-processor configuration and discussed how to determine whether symmetric multiprocessing is appropriate for your environment.

Lesson 2: Memory Requirements

In Lesson 1, you learned about the importance of the CPU, which controls all that happens in the system. This lesson describes the different types of memory that can be installed in a server and discusses how they differ in terms of both cost and performance. As was mentioned in Lesson 1, the memory type that a server uses is primarily driven by the CPU and support chips. However, different memory choices are sometimes available.

After this lesson, you will be able to

- Identify the different types of memory
- Describe the importance of ECC memory

Estimated lesson time: 20 minutes

Memory Types

Because processor speeds have increased so dramatically since the first PCs, memory speeds have also been forced to increase. These increases in speed have necessitated changes in the design of the memory itself. Today, servers contain either a variation of synchronous dynamic RAM (SDRAM) or Rambus dynamic RAM (RDRAM) for their main memory. The sections that follow describe the various types currently in use.

Note PC memory has gone through a series of iterations to get to this point. To keep this discussion brief, I've refrained from providing a history of memory types, other than when required for clarity. I've also avoided discussing other forms of memory that still appear in older workstations. If you're interested in more historical references or information pertaining to workstation computers, please refer to the *A+ Certification and Training Kit,* also available from Microsoft Press.

SDRAM

SDRAM is the most common form of RAM in use today, both in servers and in workstations. It is cheap to manufacture and has a high memory density. It is currently defined in three speeds: 66 MHz, 100 MHz, and 133 MHz. The basic functioning of SDRAM is synchronized to the memory bus of the processor or, more technically, to the Northbridge processor support chip. For today's 64-bit-wide processor buses, this means that SDRAM can transfer memory to the CPU at a maximum rate of slightly more than 1 GB per second. Although this may seem like a substantial speed, with processors today exceeding 1 GHz, the memory technology is already the limiting factor in the processor's ability to get work done.

SDRAM comes in two varieties: *unbuffered*, which does not attempt to regenerate control signals; and *buffered*, or *registered*, which has circuitry to regenerate the control signals. The term "registered" refers to the registers on the module that hold and regenerate the control signals for use. The use of registered memory is important when more than four memory slots are present or when large amounts of RAM are present because the added modules of memory create a larger drain on the memory bus. Although the design of the motherboard determines whether registered memory is required or not, most servers require registered memory.

DDR SDRAM

Double data rate SDRAM (DDR SDRAM) is exactly what the name implies: an SDRAM module with double the data rate. This means that the total throughput of a DDR SDRAM chip is slightly more than 2 GB per second. This substantial improvement is useful for processors that operate at or above 1 GHz. The design changes to get the double data rate out of an SDRAM chip are relatively trivial, meaning little additional manufacturing cost. DDR SDRAM chips are likely to be the largest player in the server RAM market in the coming years.

RDRAM

RDRAM is very different from SDRAM. While SDRAM transfers at most 8 bytes of information at a time, each RDRAM module always transfers 2 bytes of memory at a time. Although each transfer involves fewer bytes, RDRAM typically runs at 800 MHz, allowing for a transfer rate of 1.6 GB per second. In addition, RDRAM modules have the ability to be accessed two or four chips at a time. This can lead to performances of 3.2 GB per second and 6.4 GB per second, respectively. SDRAM chips do not have this capability, so RDRAM chips can be substantially faster, at least on paper.

Note The field testing of RDRAM machines against SDRAM machines has seemed to indicate that RDRAM actually performs slightly slower in most applications, but these tests were not done with the latest processors, and they probably don't reflect the way the story will play out in the end.

RDRAM speed has a price, however. RDRAM modules are substantially more expensive than SDRAM chips because of the additional circuitry required to maintain the 800-MHz rate and to support the special access methods required by RDRAM.

Intel's Pentium 4 chip is shipping with CPU support chips that support only RDRAM. In fact, they access two RDRAM modules at a time, allowing for a total memory bus throughput of 3.2 GB per second. The trade-off is that the Pentium 4 requires that either two or four RDRAM chips be used. It cannot operate with an odd number of RDRAM chips.

Note Buying the absolute highest in performance follows a universal rule: 80 percent of the cost is in getting that last 20 percent of performance. As this is written, Intel's Pentium 4 is the performance king, but the AMD Athlon processor follows it closely. Because of the Pentium 4's requirements for expensive memory and Intel's pricing, Pentium 4 systems are substantially more expensive than the associated AMD Athlon–based systems, which perform almost as well.

When making your decision about how much processing power you need, ask yourself whether that last 20 percent of performance is worth the substantial cost. It may be more effective to pursue alternatives to the highest performance in a single processor. For servers, a multiprocessor system using AMD processors may perform better and be cheaper because of the lower cost of the CPUs and the associated memory.

Parity

Memory chips of any type have many more transistors etched into them than their processor cousins. A transistor and a capacitor represent every bit of information within a DRAM chip. In a 256-megabit (Mb) RAM chip, that means more than 256 million transistors. By comparison, the AMD Athlon CPU has 22 million transistors. All of those pathways need to function perfectly for the system to work. Sometimes, however, a momentary dip in power will cause a failure, and sometimes a marginal component will fail for no apparent reason.

Since it's difficult to prevent a failure, the next best thing is to be able to identify that an error has occurred. That is what *parity* does. For each byte, an additional bit, called a *parity bit,* helps determine whether there was a failure in one of the transistors representing a memory bit. The parity bit is set to either 1 or 0 to make sure that the total number of bits set to 1 in the byte is an odd number. So if the byte has an even number of bits that are set to 1, the parity bit is set to 1. If the byte has an odd number of bits that are set to 1, the parity bit is set to 0.

If the memory controller reads the byte of memory and the parity bit and finds an even number of bits set to 1, it generates an error known as a nonmaskable interrupt. Depending on the operating system, this may cause the system to halt unexpectedly, or it may simply display an error message. In either case, the only solution is to replace the affected memory because the parity scheme cannot identify the bad bit, only indicate that there is an error.

Error Checking and Correcting

Although knowing that there is a problem is a good start, it would be best for the memory to keep going if a single bit fails. Although detecting and fixing memory errors was initially not practical for most applications because of the additional storage space required, most memory today is error checking and correction (ECC) memory.

It takes 5 bits of information and a special algorithm to be able to detect and fix a single bit error in a byte. The algorithm is able to correctly identify the failed bit and reset it when returning data to the CPU. The cost of ECC memory when memory was accessed 1 byte, or 8 bits, at a time was prohibitively expensive. However, now memory is accessed 64 bits at a time. Because of that a strange thing happens. Take a look at Table 3.1, and notice that the number of bits required for parity and ECC are the same at 64-bit word lengths.

Table 3.1   Bits Required for Parity and ECC

Word Length	Bits, Parity	Bits, ECC
8	1	5
16	2	6
32	4	7
64	8	8
128	16	9

If you were to use the parity mechanism to determine whether there was a fault on the 64 bits, you would require 8 bits of information simply to detect the error. However, using those same 8 bits, the ECC algorithm can both detect and correct single-bit errors across 64 bits. When memory modules came out in 64-bit widths, most of them had ECC built in. Dual-inline memory modules (DIMMs) were the first memory modules to come in 64-bit widths, and they were thus the first to have ECC as a standard option.

Although DIMMs can be had without ECC on them, we strongly advise that ECC be used for all applications, and ECC's use in server environments should be considered an absolute requirement.

Tip Always use ECC memory. The large amounts of RAM typical of servers dramatically increase the potential for problems. In the 1980s and 1990s, the second leading cause of server crashes was memory failure. (The first was hard disk failure.) Using ECC memory will eliminate most memory-caused crashes.

Lesson Summary

In this lesson, you learned about the two major types of RAM used in servers today: SDRAM and RDRAM. You also learned about common mechanisms for detecting and correcting single-bit memory errors and that ECC memory should be considered a requirement for servers.

Lesson 3: Disk Storage

In choosing a CPU or memory, your array of options is rather limited, as you saw in the previous two lessons. With disk storage, however, you have a wealth of options that involve different technologies, speeds, and implementations. This lesson reviews all of the major technologies for drive connectivity and logical drive representation.

After this lesson, you will be able to

- Explain the difference between physical and logical storage
- Identify RAID levels and RAID options
- Identify drive connectivity buses, their performance characteristics, and their requirements

Estimated lesson time: 40 minutes

Physical vs. Logical Storage

The first step in understanding server disk storage is to grasp the difference between physical and logical storage. This distinction is important because in today's operating systems and hardware environments a physical disk does not necessarily mean the same amount of logical storage. The ability to partition a single physical disk into multiple partitions, and the corresponding ability to join space from two or more physical disks into a single logical volume, means that there is little relationship between the size of the physical disks and the size of the various logical volumes made available for storage. Figure 3.1 shows some simple ways in which disks can be divided into partitions and the partitions can be arranged into volumes.

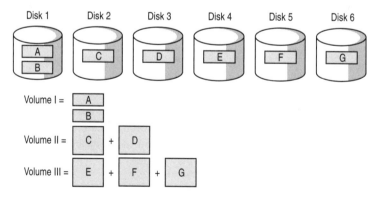

Figure 3.1   Examples of ways in which disks can be broken into partitions and partitions assembled into volumes

Redundant Arrays of Inexpensive Disks

In 1987 the University of California at Berkley released a paper titled "A Case for Redundant Arrays of Inexpensive Disks," which changed the way people looked at disk storage. Prior to that paper, most fault-tolerant hard disks were large monsters that were incredibly expensive. The five methods that the paper described, RAID-1 through RAID-5, consisted of various mechanisms that could be used on smaller drives to create a larger logical space and fault-tolerant solutions. In more recent history, a sixth RAID option, RAID-0, has been added to extend the definition to include a solution that does not have any fault tolerance.

Of the total of six RAID levels that are defined, only three are in popular use. They are

- **RAID-0.**   Also known as *striping*, RAID-0 uses two or more equal-sized segments of space from different drives that are interleaved, increasing access speeds. The total logical volume space is equal to the number of disk space segments multiplied by the size of a segment. RAID-0 does not provide fault tolerance but does offer enhanced speed.

- **RAID-1.**   Also known as *mirroring,* RAID-1 uses an even number of equal-sized segments from an equal number of disks. The total logical volume space is equal to the sum of all of the disk space divided by 2. This technique provides enhanced read performance with a slight impact on write performance, but it is fault tolerant.

- **RAID-5.**   Also known as *striping with parity,* RAID-5 requires three or more equal-sized segments from different drives. Information stored is striped across the disks, and parity is also written in a rotating manner. The total logical volume space is equal to the sum of the disk space segments minus the one segment of disk space used to store parity information. The best general-purpose RAID level, RAID-5 is a good mix for read and write performance and is fault tolerant. Its one drawback is reduced overall performance when a drive has failed.

The other RAID levels defined by the Berkeley document either required specific hardware or were found to have poorer performance characteristics than the RAID-1 and RAID-5 schemes in popular use today.

Figure 3.2 illustrates these three RAID levels.

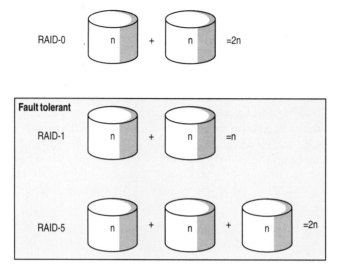

Figure 3.2   Storage options of different RAID levels

RAID Options

The introduction of RAID significantly reduced unscheduled downtime and re-duced costs for minicomputers and PC-based servers. However, the growing need to minimize scheduled downtime as well as unscheduled downtime led to the development of several additional technologies and options. The most important of these technologies are as follows:

- **Hot swap/hot plug.**   This drive bus technology allows you to remove a drive from an array and replace it with a new drive while the system is on line. With the software that detects the new drive, you can replace a failed drive without shutting down the server.

- **Failover/hot spare.**   In this configuration, an extra drive is kept powered up in the array. When a drive fails, or when a certain threshold of errors for the drive has been exceeded, the extra drive is loaded with the information from the failed or failing drive and inserted into the array. The bad drive is then taken off line to be addressed later. This reduces the impact of the perfor-mance penalty on RAID-5 arrays when a drive has failed by putting a new drive into service automatically.

By using these two new technologies, you can reduce, if not eliminate, even scheduled downtimes. This helps meet the organization's availability goals and makes technicians happier because they don't always have to come in at 2 A.M. to fix a problem.

Another development that improves the performance of RAID is dedicated hardware controllers that support the calculations that must be performed to generate the parity information in a RAID-5 environment. Although some operating systems, such as Windows 2000, allow the CPU to perform the parity calculations, performance is usually better with a hardware card, and the load on the system CPU is greatly reduced.

Operating systems that support RAID in software often can't use all of those RAID options for the boot partition. For instance, Windows 2000 cannot use a RAID-5 partition as a boot partition. And although a RAID-1 (mirrored) partition is an option, it requires a boot floppy to work correctly should the primary hard disk fail. Having a boot floppy is inconvenient; it's also hard to ensure that the disk stays with the server.

Hardware-based RAID-5 configurations can also now have a dedicated cache on the RAID-5 controller card to service read and write requests. You learned in Lesson 1 that the amount of cache on a processor helps to speed up the processor by reducing the number of slower accesses to regular memory. The amount of time spent waiting for regular memory to return a result is measured in nanoseconds, or billionths of a second. The amount of time spent waiting for disks is measured in milliseconds, or thousandths of a second.

The cache on the RAID card works in the same way that the cache for a processor works. It reduces the number of times that the server must go to the disk to retrieve information by maintaining copies of previously requested information and reading the next several sectors from the disk. This caching improves the overall perceived speed of the drives and of the RAID array.

In addition, cache is sometimes used to allow writes to the disk to be confirmed before they actually happen. This is useful because it allows the server to release the resources associated with writing the sector to the disk. The RAID controller then writes the information to the disks when it has time. This mechanism is called *write-back cache*. If the RAID controller doesn't implement this mechanism for writing data, it is said to be a *write-through* controller because write operations go through the controller cache directly to the disk.

The SCSI Drive Bus

The SCSI drive bus was the first universal drive bus designed to eliminate the proprietary buses. At the time that SCSI was first developed, there were several competing standards for drive buses. Each had its own benefits and weaknesses, but all were proprietary. Although SCSI was originally designed by a single company, it was quickly turned over to a committee so that it could become a standard.

SCSI brought a series of features that were revolutionary for their time. Perhaps the most profound of these was that the drive media, motors, and electronics were packaged together into a single unit. Most systems, such as the modified frequency modulation (MFM) and run-length limited (RLL) controllers used in PCs, had the drive media and motors in one package and a separate controller that accessed the media at an incredibly low level, controlling everything about how the media were used. That's why a 20-MB MFM drive could be reformatted with an RLL controller to a 30-MB capacity.

SCSI changed this by packaging a controller on the drive. The controller was responsible for all low-level functions of the drive and accepted higher-level commands from the system. This configuration allowed the manufacturer to precisely tune the controller's operation to the media, heads, and motors used in the construction of the drive, which in turn resulted in performance improvements and higher drive densities.

SCSI also allowed nondisk devices to be connected to the same bus. This provided a standard bus for scanners, tape drives, and other peripherals that were, at the time, using proprietary buses as well. This versatility would be one of SCSI's defining features for the first 12 years of its existence.

Since the original SCSI specification was approved in 1986, many changes have been made to increase the overall speed, the number of devices per bus, and the length of the bus. What was originally a single standards document covering the entire standard has been replaced with a series of documents defining different parts of the standard. This separation has allowed for the more rapid development of the standard. There are three current SCSI standards: SCSI-1, SCSI-2, and SCSI-3.

Starting with SCSI-2, features were added to the standard to allow devices to receive more than one command from the host controller and to respond to those commands when they were able. The new features also allowed the devices to reorder the commands so that they could be completed more efficiently. This ability was particularly useful for servers that would be receiving multiple requests. The drives could now reorder the commands to minimize the amount of time wasted repositioning the read-write heads.

Because of SCSI's features and its high rate of transfer, SCSI drives are the preferred storage for most servers. Although some low-end servers use the Integrated Drive Electronics (IDE) drive technology, and high-end systems use Fibre Channel–attached drives, most servers don't need the performance of Fibre Channel drives, and they need more flexibility than IDE provides.

SCSI Bus Types

When the original SCSI standard came out, it specified two bus types. The first was the single-ended (SE) specification that was widely adopted by the market. This specification allowed for the manipulation of voltage on one wire within a pair. The receiving circuitry measured the voltage and determined the binary digit being represented. The SE specification used low-level voltages (3.3 V) for signals.

The other form of SCSI, high-voltage differential (HVD), was used in some less popular implementations such as minicomputers but was never adopted by the market at large. HVD SCSI buses allowed for much greater cable distances because the differential mechanism employed by HVD was more reliable, but the higher voltage (5 V) that was required meant that the circuitry on SE devices could and often would be burnt out if they were accidentally installed on the same bus as an HVD device. This type of accidental installation was a distinct possibility because the cables and connectors for HVD devices were the same as the cables and connectors used for SE devices. In addition to the risk of burning out circuitry, HVD devices were more expensive to manufacture.

Ultimately, differential signaling was reintroduced to SCSI in the SCSI-3 standards documents, but using low voltage. At the same time, HVD was eliminated from the specification. The new low-voltage differential (LVD) bus can be longer than the associated SE bus, but no damage occurs if LVD devices and SE devices are plugged into the same bus. In fact, some LVD devices are designed to be capable of operating in an SE mode. These so-called multimode devices operate in LVD mode when they can, but fall back to SE mode when connected to an SE bus.

SCSI Terminators and Timing

Whenever an electrical signal is conducted, a problem can occur in which the signal reflects off the end of the cable and returns back down it, causing garbled signals. To prevent this, terminators are used on both ends of the bus to absorb the electricity before it can be reflected. Any high-speed bus has some mechanism to terminate these reflected signals.

The SCSI standards contain two different types of terminators:

- **Passive.**   A 132-ohm terminator, for use with SCSI-1.
- **Active.**   A 110-ohm terminator with voltage regulation, for use with SCSI-2 or higher.

Active terminators are substantially better at eliminating the signal bounce that occurs when a signal reaches the end of the wire, and they are therefore recommended for all SCSI implementations above SCSI-1.

The reason for this superiority is that the bus clock rate, or speed, increased with each revision of SCSI. At SCSI-2's 10-MHz rate, the passive terminators are not always effective at preventing the signal from being reflected. Today's SCSI bus clock rates of 40 MHz are totally incompatible with the passive terminators designed for SCSI-1.

Those companies marketing SCSI devices decided that each bus speed within SCSI should be referred to by a more appealing name than the names defined in the standards. As a result, the terms "fast" and "ultra" have gained specific meaning with regard to SCSI. SCSI-2, when it came out, defined a 10-MHz bus. This bus speed became known as Fast SCSI. Ultra SCSI-3 increased the speed of that bus to 20 MHz. With SCSI-3, the bus speed was increased again to 40 MHz, and it became known as Ultra2. Although Ultra3 technically exists, and it transfers data twice per bus cycle, marketing forces took over again, and Ultra3 became Ultra160 because it could transfer 160 MB per second.

This transfer rate is possible because of the addition of a wide bus that was developed during SCSI-2. A wide SCSI bus transfers data 16 bits (2 bytes) at a time rather than 8 bits a time, as in the original standard. Once the wide bus had been added, the original SCSI bus became known as the narrow SCSI bus. Using a wide bus doubles the throughput. Thus, a bus running at 40 MHz can transfer 2 bytes at a time, twice per cycle, and can therefore achieve 160 MB per second, as in Ultra160 (2 transfers per cycle * 2 bytes per transfer * 40-Mhz transfer rate = 160 MB). Table 3.2 compares the different versions of SCSI, showing the number of devices per bus, maximum speed, and maximum cable length.

Table 3.2   Comparison of SCSI Versions

Version	Devices per Bus (Excluding Host Adapter)	Maximum Speed (MB/ Second)	Maximum Length in Meters (SE)	Maximum Length in Meters (LVD)
SCSI-1	7	5	6	N/A
SCSI-2 (Fast)	7	10	3	N/A
SCSI-2 (Wide)	15	10	6	N/A
SCSI-2 (Fast/Wide)	15	20	3	N/A
SCSI-3 (Ultra)	7	20	3	N/A
SCSI-3 (Ultra/Wide)	15	40	3	N/A
SCSI-3 (Ultra2)	7	40	N/A	12
SCSI-3 (Ultra2/Wide)	15	80	N/A	12
SCSI-3 (Ultra160)	15	160	N/A	12
SCSI-4 (Ultra320)	15	320	N/A	12

The IDE Drive Bus

IDE is a drive bus that was designed specifically for the needs and architecture of PCs, unlike its SCSI cousin. In fact, IDE's official name is AT Attachment (ATA) because it was designed to attach directly to the AT bus in the IBM AT. From this point on, we'll refer to IDE drives as IDE/ATA drives, or as ATA drives only. This name is more technically correct, and it allows for the distinction between the different standards.

Like SCSI devices, ATA drives have their low-level controller connected directly to the drive. However, instead of talking to another controller plugged into the motherboard, the drive controller on an ATA drive talks directly to the ISA or PCI bus on the motherboard. This makes adding an ATA controller on the motherboard a rather trivial process of putting on the connectors and connecting them to the bus.

ATA's advantages are also its disadvantages. ATA is simple to manufacture and to install. There are also fewer translations and less overhead in ATA than in SCSI, so throughput is higher. The disadvantage to ATA is that because of it's simple design it doesn't implement SCSI's additional features, particularly command queuing.

In single-user systems and small servers, this omission isn't a major issue; the systems can perform adequately. As more and more users access a server, however, the access to the hard disk becomes more random. At that point, SCSI's command ordering and queuing features begin to play an important role in the server's overall performance. SCSI drives perform better under more diverse loads. IDE is generally a poor choice for anything but small servers.

IDE/ATA Modes of Operation

Just as SCSI has adapted and grown over the years, so has the ATA standard. The original standard defined three modes for programmed I/O (PIO) and three modes for direct memory access (DMA). Today that's been expanded to five PIO modes and seven DMA modes. The reason for the more expansive list of DMA modes is that DMA modes are the preferred method of operation, since they have a performance advantage over PIO.

The PIO modes operate by notifying the CPU that a transfer needs to be accomplished. The CPU then intervenes and retrieves the data from the drive. In the DMA modes, the drive itself, or a separate memory controller on the motherboard, transfers the data from the drive to memory. This separation allows the CPU to continue working on other tasks. Because of the additional CPU overhead in managing PIO, most of today's drives use the DMA modes.

Table 3.3 shows the various modes and their maximum throughput, as well as the standard that defines each mode.

Table 3.3   Maximum Transfer Rate of IDE/ATA Modes

Mode	Maximum Transfer Rate (MB/Second)	Standard
PIO Mode 0	3.3	ATA
PIO Mode 1	5.2	ATA
PIO Mode 2	8.3	ATA
PIO Mode 3	11.1	ATA-2
PIO Mode 4	16.6	ATA-2
DMA Single Word 0	2.1	ATA
DMA Single Word 1	4.2	ATA
DMA Single Word 2	8.3	ATA
DMA Multiword 0	4.2	ATA
DMA Multiword 1	13.3	ATA-2
DMA Multiword 2	16.6	ATA-2
DMA Multiword 3	33.3	ATA-4
DMA Ultra ATA/66	66.6	ATA-5
DMA Ultra ATA/100	100.0	N/A

As you can see, IDE/ATA drives have a much slower bus speed than SCSI drives. However, an IDE/ATA drive bus supports at most 2 devices, far fewer than the 15 drives supported on a SCSI bus. For both buses, the current speeds exceed the maximum sustained transfer rates of the disks. (The *sustained transfer rate* is the greatest amount of information that can be retrieved from or stored on the hard disk if sequential sectors are accessed.)

IDE/ATA Cables

The ATA standard has had to adapt to the changes brought about by greater bus speed, just as the SCSI standard has. Although the ATA standard has managed to keep the same connector configuration, the cable itself has changed to improve the reliability of the data transmission.

When ATA drives were first designed, a 40-pin cable was needed to convey the data and control signals to the drive. To minimize the number of pins, the data and ground signals shared two ground wires. Two ground wires could be used because in theory all signals are referenced from a single ground state. Thus, only one ground line is absolutely necessary to be able to understand the signals. Using one or a few ground wires was a common practice in earlier computer development to keep the pin and wire count low. Unfortunately, this technique makes the design more susceptible to noise, particularly as speeds increase.

The solution to this problem was quite elegant. A hybrid cable-connector combination that has a 40-pin connector and an 80-wire cable was chosen. Both grounds are connected together and then tied to the 40 additional wires in the cable. This dramatically improves reliability because the additional wires more accurately conduct the ground between the drive and the host adapter.

All drives that operate at Ultra ATA/66 mode or higher require this special hybrid cable. Most drives and adapters detect the presence or absence of this cable and will refuse to operate at Ultra ATA/66 mode or higher without the hybrid cable. This is good, since the result of trying to use a 40-wire cable at such high speeds would likely not be effective at all.

Fibre Channel

Both IDE and SCSI are legacy interfaces that have been around for more than 10 years and have been going through evolutionary changes. Fibre Channel (note the French spelling) is a revolutionary new interface. Although now able to be implemented on either fiber or copper, Fibre Channel was originally designed to take advantage of the new properties of fiber optics.

In our discussions of both SCSI and IDE, you saw how the designers had to overcome the limitations of the interfaces as they pushed them to higher and higher speeds. These issues are primarily related to the characteristics of an electrical signal. There are two basic factors that affect an electrical signal: imperfect conductors and magnetism.

No matter how purely we distill copper, aluminum, or other conductors, they still have characteristics that get in our way when we try to conduct signals down a wire. In particular, two properties are difficult to address. The first is *resistance*, the measure of how much the conductor resists the electricity flowing through it. The higher the resistance, the less power makes it to the other end. The other is *capacitance*, the tendency for the conductor itself to hold on to some of the electricity. Capacitance is particularly bad for digital signals that transition rapidly between high and low voltage states. The conductor absorbs some of the electricity when driven to a high voltage, making it potentially indistinguishable from the low voltage state. And during the next low voltage state, some of the electricity held in the conductor is released, making it difficult to determine that it is the low voltage state.

The end result is that only a very small amount of voltage might distinguish a high voltage state from a low voltage state. The low voltages that we use for signaling make maintaining a reasonable differential between the high and low states very difficult, which makes deciphering the message on the other end of the wire more challenging. Although today's conductors are defined so as to limit the amount of resistance and capacitance they have, there's no way to completely eliminate these properties of wire.

Magnetism is the other issue affecting conductors, and it sets the ultimate limit on the transfer of electrically-based signals. Most of us studied magnetism and how it works in school. We watched iron filings move on a piece of paper or made a crude electromagnet out of a battery, some wire, and a nail.

In our science class, when we ran the power through a wire wrapped around a nail, we were trying to create an electromagnet. Unfortunately, in computers magnetism is more often an unwanted side effect than a desired result. As we pass electrical signals through the conductors in a system, a small magnetic field is created. The magnetism isn't so much of an issue in and of itself. However, there's an inverse property that causes problems.

When a magnetic field and a conductor move in relation to each other, an electrical charge is inducted in the conductor. This charge is inversely proportional to the space between the conductor and the source of the field. As a result, problems occur when two wires are run in parallel close together. The power, or signal, on one wire creates a fluctuating magnetic field that induces unwanted currents in the wire next it, bleeding away power and creating interference. There are methods for reducing the impact of inductance, but it can't be eliminated.

Fiber optic cables experience neither of these problems because the signal is conducted with light rather than electricity. Thus, resistance and capacitance are not concerns, nor is magnetic induction. Fiber optic cables thus have the potential for much higher speeds than standard cables. In fact, no one is really sure what their maximum speed is. They are currently running at 2 GHz in production systems, and 4-GHz standards are in development. Our biggest challenge is converting the optical signals in the fiber optic cables into meaningful electrical signals.

For Fibre Channel to run on copper, some fundamental shifts in thinking had to occur. Both SCSI and IDE interfaces are parallel in that they communicate multiple signals at one time. Fibre Channel running on fiber optic cable transmits only one signal at a time, but it does so very quickly. The same serial communications technique was used with copper. By transmitting only one signal but transmitting it very fast and to only one device, the kind of performance available with fiber cabling became available on copper, over short distances. Of course, very highly distilled copper is required to minimize the electrical considerations of resistance, capacitance, and magnetism.

In addition to their faster speeds, fiber optic cables can connect devices across much greater distances. Fibre Channel supports 30 meters between devices when using copper connectivity and 10 kilometers when connected optically. And that's the distance between each pair of devices, not the total bus length. With fiber optic cables, Fibre Channel should support even the largest campus environments.

Note As you'll see when we discuss networking in Lesson 4, Ethernet has trounced Token Ring for many years. The ease of setup for Ethernet and the cheap adapters have made Token Ring obsolete. Token Ring was an excellent technology. The dual paths and the automatic disconnection of missing adapters through the Multistation Access Units (MAUs) made Token Ring incredibly stable and gave it predictable performance.

Although the market has abandoned the Token Ring protocol, many of the same technologies have made their way into Fibre Channel, where they provide additional stability.

Another advantage to Fibre Channel is that it supports as many as 126 devices directly and many, many more with a switch fabric installed. (A *switch fabric* is a network, or fabric, of switches interconnecting the Fibre Channel devices.) Contrast this with the maximum 15 devices supported by Wide SCSI. The ability to support a large number of devices can be helpful in large environments where disk capacity is an issue. Admittedly, disk densities have made the number of drives connected to a single server much less of an issue; however, there are still applications that need higher performance or higher total disk capacity.

With all of Fibre Channel's great features, you might ask why we're not all using it. The simplest answer is cost. Fibre Channel products have been getting cheaper as inexpensive electronics have been developed to transfer data at these incredibly high speeds. However, such products still have a premium price associated with them.

The other serious deterrent to using fiber optics in Fibre Channel, which is the preferred method, is the fact that most people are not used to working with fiber optic cables. Fiber has a tendency to break when asked to make tight bends, and installing ends on a fiber cable is much more difficult than putting an end on a copper cable, although progress has been made in recent years.

Hard Disk Performance

Before leaving our discussion of hard disks, it's important to talk about the disks themselves and the factors affecting performance. Hard disks are not much different from the floppy disks we're all familiar with; they're essentially a small piece of disk medium spinning around underneath read/write heads inside the drive. The medium stores information by having its magnetic material rearranged by magnets in the read/write heads.

Unlike the information on CDs and LPs, which use a single groove that spirals its way across the disk, the information on magnetic media is read and written in a series of concentric rings called *tracks*. These tracks are broken up into small sections called *sectors*, each of which can hold 512 bytes of information. The number of sectors in a track is determined by how far out on the disk the track is. Because the tracks farther out on the disk have more area, these tracks have more sectors.

Today, besides the bus to which the drive is attached, two other factors affect the performance of hard disks. They are the speed at which the drive can move the read/write heads from one track to another (access time) and how fast the medium spins beneath the read/write heads. Access time used to be the primary indicator of drive performance because all hard disks spun at the same speed. The few milliseconds that it took to move the heads from one track to another was important because it was the only factor that changed from one drive to another.

Many years ago, however, hard disk manufacturers began to realize that spinning the disk at the same 3600 RPM that it had always spun at was inefficient. The faster they could spin the disk, the less time it would take for the sector being requested to be back under the read/write head so that it could be read. Initially, disk rotation speeds were increased to 5400 RPM. This was followed by 7200 RPM and finally 10,000 RPM and 15,000 RPM in some of today's fastest hard disks.

Increasing the disk's speed to 15,000 RPM reduces the latency—the time it takes for a sector to come under the read/write heads—to a mere 2 milliseconds. A drive spinning at 3600 RPM would need to wait approximately 8 milliseconds for the same information to become available. These performance improvements can make a big difference, particularly in a busy server environment where the drives are constantly kept busy.

Practice: Select a Hard Disk Configuration for a DHCP Server

Selecting the right hard disk configuration for a server is an important part of the overall server configuration.

Using Table 1.1 in Chapter 1, Lesson 3 and the information in this lesson, choose the best configuration of hard disk drives for a server that provides only Dynamic Host Configuration Protocol (DHCP) services to an organization of 500 users.

The first step is to determine the amount of disk activity the disk will receive as a result of providing DHCP services. Table 1.1 shows that the amount of disk activity for a DHCP server will be very low.

A pair of IDE disks that have been mirrored (RAID-1) will suffice for this application because of the extremely low use. Of course, SCSI disks on a RAID controller are valid too. A Fibre Channel solution for disks is probably not warranted for this server due to the organization size and the low disk storage requirements.

Practice: Select a Hard Disk Configuration for a Database Server

Database servers rely heavily on their disk subsystem for performance because of the large amount of data being stored.

As you did in the previous practice, refer to Table 1.1 in Chapter 1, Lesson 3 and the information in this lesson to decide what size and type of hard drives to use for a large database server.

The database server will house a 60-GB online database that is used to handle orders and shipments for an organization with thousands of users. The organization works 24 hours a day, six days a week to get orders out in a timely fashion.

Six or more SCSI disk drives on a pair of SCSI buses is probably warranted here, if not a Fibre Channel implementation. The hard disk requirements of a database server are large. Additionally, the short backup window on the weekend indicates a need for good performance just for backups. The disks should be partitioned so that a RAID-5 volume is created to house the database. This will establish fault tolerance and will maintain performance. The reason for using six or more hard disks is to give the server more disk arms to use to service requests. Fibre Channel would also be a good option, particularly if there's a need to centralize storage, since the total requirements of the database may indicate that the organization has a lot of data to store and back up.

Lesson Summary

In this lesson, you learned that perhaps the most difficult decision in putting together a server is selecting the hard disks. The variety of ways for connecting the hard disks, and the variety of hard disks themselves, makes for a difficult decision.

You learned that there's a difference between the logical storage that servers use and the physical disks that make up that logical storage. You also learned that RAID technologies allow you to use multiple drives in order to create volumes that are larger than your physical disks, and that RAID-1 and RAID-5 are fault tolerant.

You learned that there are three basic options for drive connectivity: IDE/ATA, SCSI, and Fibre Channel. IDE is simple, cheap, and best for small servers. SCSI is more complex and slightly more costly; it is most appropriate for mid-level servers. Fibre Channel has some nice distance and speed advantages, which makes it a good choice for large environments.

Finally, you learned that the performance of the hard disks themselves can significantly affect performance. The rotational speed of a hard disk can reduce the latency substantially.

Lesson 4: Network Connectivity

Until now, this chapter has covered the same components that you find in a stand-alone computer, although some of them have special performance considerations when used in a server environment. This lesson is different; it discusses network connectivity and how to connect a server to the network.

After this lesson, you will be able to
- Identify various network topologies and their advantages
- Explain fault-tolerant options for adapter failure

Estimated lesson time: 20 minutes

Network Topologies

Connecting computers together in a local area network (LAN) requires a closely coordinated set of wires, network cards, and physical signaling protocols. The combination of electrical and logical guidelines that make up basic connectivity between two or more computers is known as a *topology*. With today's LANs, there are two basic topologies to be aware of:

- Ethernet
- Token Ring

Ethernet

Ethernet is currently the most popular network topology. It uses a communication method very similar to a CB radio. When you use a CB radio, you first listen to find out if anyone is talking, and you transmit if you don't hear anyone. Ethernet works in the same way. If a network card needs to transmit a packet, it first listens to the medium; if it doesn't hear any other network card transmitting, it transmits.

However, this technique leads to the same problem that CB radios have: if two people are listening for a break in the communications, and they both hear one, they might transmit at the same moment, garbling both signals. In Ethernet, if two network cards do transmit at the same time, they detect this condition and then wait a pseudo-random amount of time before attempting to transmit again. This pseudo-random amount of time helps ensure that the two cards don't transmit over one another again.

This method of communication is called Carrier Sense Multiple Access/Collision Detection (CSMA/CD). In networks that use this method, all of the computers are connected together on a single bus, to which each can transmit at any time.

CSMA/CD is an effective way to communicate until the utilization gets high—beyond about 50 percent of the theoretical capacity. When that occurs, many computers have to wait for an opening. When they see one, the computers begin transmitting at the same time and their signals collide, and then another set of computers sees the opening after the collision and collide in their transmissions too.

In extreme cases, the entire network can become saturated with rebroadcast attempts until the logical connections fail and the computer quits attempting to communicate. These so-called "broadcast storms" eventually settle down on their own, but they can disconnect a lot of logical connections before they do.

Because it's so important to keep Ethernet from being highly utilized and because networking needs have increased, several improvements have been made to Ethernet since its introduction. Not the least of these was the implementation of Fast Ethernet. Ethernet originally ran at speeds of 10 megabits per second (Mbps). Fast Ethernet runs at 10 times that speed, 100 Mbps. In addition to Fast Ethernet, there's also growing support for Gigabit Ethernet that runs at 1000 Mbps, or 1 gigabit per second.

These changes, as well as a need for cabling to become easier, have led Ethernet to convert from coaxial cables to twisted-pair cables. Originally Ethernet was available via a thick cable, called 10Base-5 because it could support 500-meter lengths. Later, Ethernet was supported on a thinner coaxial cable, called 10Base-2 because it could be used in 200-meter lengths. Because of the relative difficulty of installation and longer supported lengths, 10Base-5 cables were traditionally used only for backbones, and 10Base-2 cables were used to connect PCs to the backbone.

Because both types of coaxial cables required a terminator at each end of the cable, if a cable connection was broken for some reason (because a cable end became unplugged, the cable was cut, or someone disconnected a cable), the entire segment of the Ethernet would go down. In many smaller environments, this meant that the entire network would be inoperable. In larger environments, each segment of Ethernet was attached to a repeater that essentially copied the information from one medium to the others. Repeaters were useful for isolating failures in an Ethernet environment, but coaxial cable was still prone to errors.

Eventually, Ethernet added support for twisted-pair wiring. This wiring was given the designation 10Base-T. The addition of twisted pair as a cable type was a major advance because it meant that each computer got its own connection to the Ethernet network from a hub, and so the network wasn't susceptible to the line breakage problems that 10Base-2 had. Twisted pair also eventually allowed for speeds to be increased.

Note The fact that the wire is twisted is very significant. In coaxial cable, the construction limits the amount of electromagnetic noise and interference that the cable receives. Regular pair-based wiring doesn't have this automatic rejection of interference. Since electromagnetic noise tends to shift the voltage of a circuit, and because the DC circuits used in electronics measure the difference between the two sides of the circuit, it's possible to encourage the interference to affect both wires of a pair to nearly the same degree. The net effect is that the differential between the two wires doesn't change and the signal can still be read on the other end.

The final cabling adaptation for Ethernet was the inclusion of fiber optic cabling as an option. Although twisted pair was easier to install and maintain, it couldn't go as far as the old 10Base-5 cabling, and even 10Base-5 cables weren't long enough for some systems. When Ethernet began supporting fiber optics, these distance limitations were overcome. Fiber optic cables can be run for several kilometers without problem.

By the time Fast Ethernet appeared, both the 10Base-5 and 10Base-2 coaxial cables had fallen into disfavor, and so Fast Ethernet was supported only on twisted-pair or fiber optic cable. Fast Ethernet requires new category 5 cabling, which supports the 100-MHz frequencies necessary to transmit data at 100 Mbps. The requirements for fiber optic cable didn't change.

More recently, Gigabit Ethernet has become available. Although initially available only on fiber optic cable, some copper-based Gigabit Ethernet options are now becoming available. Gigabit Ethernet is used primarily between servers and the network and between network switches on a backbone.

One of the other ways that Ethernet improved performance was through the use of switches. A switch allows different speeds of Ethernet to be mixed and minimizes overall traffic by routing all directed Ethernet traffic straight to the computer that it's destined for. It does this by looking at the hardware address of the Ethernet packet to determine which port that address is connected to. In environments with multiple servers and multiple clients, this switching can dramatically improve performance.

The primary limitation of switches is that they can't restrict the transmission of broadcasted information, or information without a specific destination address. As a result, on networks using protocols that do a lot of broadcasts, such as NetBEUI (NetBIOS Enhanced User Interface), the performance improvement may not be noticeable. Although all protocols need to broadcast from time to time, those that can limit their broadcasting will be best able to take advantage of a network switch.

Ethernet or one of its variations is more than likely already installed in your organization. The real choice when selecting a network topology for a server is determining whether Fast Ethernet is sufficient or whether it will need a Gigabit Ethernet connection. For most small to medium-sized organizations, Fast Ethernet is probably sufficient for today's needs. This is particularly true if the server you're planning for won't be the organization's primary server. However, consider using Gigabit Ethernet for primary servers or in larger organizations where the throughput of the server may need the additional bandwidth.

Token Ring

The competing standard to Ethernet is Token Ring. Although it is a great technology and a good choice for a networking topology, Token Ring has fallen out of favor because it is more expensive than Ethernet. Token Ring runs at two speeds, either 4 Mbps or 16 Mbps. However, due to the method of access, a 4-Mbps Token Ring network appears to run at almost the same speed as a 10-Mbps Ethernet network.

Token Ring uses a token-passing mechanism in which a system passes a token to its neighbor, which passes the token to its neighbor, and so on until the token makes it all the way back around the ring. The token grants a computer the ability to transmit data on the ring. The computer appends the data to the token and then sends it to the next computer in the ring. When the originating computer gets the token back, it removes the data and passes the empty token to its neighbor.

The Token Ring system is excellent because it has a very predictable time when a computer will be able to transmit. Unlike Ethernet, which must listen for an opening and hope that it doesn't collide when transmitting, a Token Ring–attached computer receives a token after a fixed period of time. This is very useful for situations when you need to be able to guarantee delivery within a certain fixed amount of time. The 16-Mbps version of Token Ring allows for multiple tokens to be going around the ring at one time, effectively improving performance and decreasing the response time for any single computer. It also allows for other techniques, such as early token release, that further enhance performance.

In the early 1990s, I worked for a telecommunications company and was writing a program to read the telephone switches in real time and record the data on the LAN, where it would be picked up and entered into the billing system.

The design of the system was such that if the LAN went down the system was supposed to start recording data to the local hard disk. In this way, no data would be lost even if the LAN went down. (Ultimately the program was implemented on two different PCs, each recording to a different server on the LAN.)

At the time, we didn't want to invest in UNIX or VAX systems to perform this task because of their relative expense. With some reluctance, we started working on the project in DOS with an intelligent serial I/O card. We found that the program would work fine while everything was OK, but when we disconnected the LAN while the system was on Ethernet it would sometimes lose a few bytes of data. When we used Token Ring instead of Ethernet, there was no data loss when the network went down. Needless to say, we left the solution on Token Ring.

This isn't to say that Fast Ethernet wouldn't have cured the problem, nor does it mean that DOS is the right platform for a fault-tolerant application. It just goes to show that sometimes the predictable response from Token Ring can be quite useful in solving problems.

One of Token Ring's other advantages was that the Multistation Access Units (MAUs) were connected together with redundant cabling. Should one of the cables between two MAUs be cut, they would continue to operate. This redundancy was particularly useful for adding new MAUs. You could break the ring between two MAUs to add the new MAU without disrupting the network. The MAUs in the network would detect the break and use the redundant cabling to keep the network functioning. Once the new MAU was connected and the loop reestablished, operations would continue normally.

Despite the advantages of Token Ring, it's no longer in widespread use, although you'll see the same token-passing method in use in technologies such as Fibre Channel. Token Ring as a networking topology is, for all intents and purposes, dead today.

Network Card Performance

In a server, the network interface and its capacity for transmitting and receiving data can easily become a bottleneck. Since a server's real purpose is to serve its clients, it only makes sense that the communication with those clients needs to be as fast as is practical. Although you've already seen the different topologies that can be used to connect servers to clients, we haven't yet talked about the performance impact of the network card itself.

Network interface cards (NICs), like all other add-on cards, use resources from the system to accomplish their tasks. These resources can take the form of bus time, interrupts generated, or processor time. The goal of a good component is to minimize the resources used while maintaining performance. Although desktop-class NICs sometimes minimize CPU and bus usage through on-board processing, specialized server-class NICs should guarantee that the card minimizes the utilization of the CPU and PCI bus.

Most modern NICs are fairly good citizens and will behave well in a server. Sometimes, however, the needed bandwidth exceeds what one card can produce. In those cases, it makes sense to install multiple NICs so that a network switch can be used to help increase the total throughput. The technique of using more than one adapter to access the same medium with the same logical address is called *load balancing* or *teaming*. In these scenarios, the network drivers manage the multiple adapters as if they were one larger adapter.

Adapter load balancing works well because each card has its own physical address, and when the client attempts to resolve the hardware address of the network adapter, the driver decides which adapter's hardware address to respond with. This allows the server to manage the amount of traffic bound for each network adapter, greatly increasing the throughput.

Although load balancing is an option, the additional CPU load of determining which hardware address to respond with and the complexity of the drivers managing this configuration are generally not warranted. More often, it's better to select a higher-speed connectivity option, such as a Gigabit Ethernet card, rather than two Fast Ethernet cards. Doing so allows for greater total throughput with less CPU overhead.

Fault Tolerance

Although using two NICs for performance reasons isn't always the best solution, there are cases when multiple NICs do make sense. For example, you may want them for redundancy in a fault-tolerant environment where there's a concern that a NIC may fail. While NIC failures are fairly unlikely, they do occur, and they do cause outages. Adding a second network adapter to the system and using the fault-tolerance features built into the operating system or driver allows the server to adapt to a NIC failure and reroute traffic before the users even notice.

Lesson Summary

In this lesson, you learned the types of network topologies that are in common use today, as well as how to select network adapters for performance in a server application. You learned when adapter teaming, or load balancing, makes sense for a server application, and what adapter fault tolerance means.

Review

Here are some questions to help you determine whether you have learned enough to move on to the next chapter. If you have difficulty answering these questions, please go back and review the material in this chapter before beginning the next chapter. The answers for these questions are located in the appendix, "Questions and Answers."

1. You're working for a medium-sized organization that needs a new terminal server. What kind of server should you select?

2. You're putting together a file and print server for an organization with a few hundred users. You're trying to determine how much cache to order for the processor. What guidelines should you use?

3. A soft memory error has been recorded on a server. What should be done?

4. You're putting together a server to be a firewall. What kind of hard disk is appropriate?

5. Your organization has grown and has just built a huge new data center. It wants to standardize on a set of high-performance drives in one cabinet. What kind of bus is appropriate?

6. Your organization recently upgraded the backbone to support additional growth and has given you the task of selecting a new file and print server. You've settled on CPUs, memory, and hard disks. What kind of network connectivity should be provided?

P A R T   2

Installing and Configuring a Server

CHAPTER 4

Gathering and Configuring Firmware and Drivers

About This Chapter

In Chapter 3 you learned about the various components of a server. In this chapter you will start performing the preinstallation and installation activities by gathering and updating firmware and drivers. *Firmware* is the software that is burned onto a card to allow it to function. Most devices have firmware that controls their operation. A *driver* is the software that connects the hardware (and its associated firmware) to the operating system.

Updating firmware and drivers is important for all hardware platforms, but particularly for new hardware. This is true because drivers often have bugs and performance issues when they are first released. These problems are normally dealt with quickly, and new drivers are posted to the vendor's Web site. Although these drivers are put into production as soon as they are tested and released, the process of duplicating CDs and integrating the new CD into the production process for the server might take several weeks or even months. As a result, the drivers that you receive with the server can be outdated and might have bugs and performance problems that will affect your environment.

In addition to drivers and firmware, this chapter addresses the BIOS and RAID settings you will need to configure before installing the server operating system on the hardware. Reviewing these settings will ensure that you know what they were when the operating system was installed as well as that all of the settings are optimal for the system.

Before You Begin

To complete this chapter, you should have

- An Internet connection

Lesson 1: Downloading Firmware and Drivers

While neither fun nor glamorous, the process of ferreting out the current and correct firmware and drivers for all of the devices in a new server is an important part of the installation. It helps to minimize problems in the future by addressing all of the problems other organizations have had that led to the firmware and driver updates—before the problems happen in your organization.

After this lesson, you will be able to

- Locate firmware and drivers on a vendor's Web site
- Select the appropriate drivers and firmware for installation

Estimated lesson time: 10 minutes

Locating Firmware and Drivers

Because locating firmware and drivers on a vendor's Web site is so dependent upon the specific site, this lesson first reviews the general process of retrieving drivers, as well as some common pitfalls in navigating Web sites to download the drivers. It then asks you to practice downloading two drivers from two different Web sites.

Most hardware vendors use their Web sites to help control support costs, in addition to marketing their products. For that reason, locating support information online is usually a relatively trivial task. Although the name may be technical support, customer support, or customer care, a link to these resources is usually on the home page and only one click away.

The difficult part generally starts when you try to locate the drivers for your particular device. Oftentimes a vendor will refer to a device in two or more ways. For instance, Hewlett Packard may refer to an HP LaserJet 5Si printer as an HP LJ5Si printer or by the model number, C3167A. Trying to tell the Web site which product you have is often quite frustrating. To make things easier, many vendors, including Hewlett Packard, are now providing multiple ways of gaining access to their drivers.

After you have selected the device, you're sometimes redirected to a product that is the same as the one you have, only packaged differently. For instance, motherboard manufacturers used Adaptec's 78xx chipset, and Adaptec also used this chipset in its widely popular AHA-2940 card. If you search for the drivers for the AHA-2940 card, you're suddenly dropped into a section dealing with drivers for the 78xx chipset. This can be somewhat disconcerting if you're not expecting it. Most Web pages indicate at the top what the drivers on the page are good for. If this information is not clearly stated, the best plan of attack is to download and extract the drivers, and check the README file to verify that they will work with your device.

Once you've navigated your way through the maze to your product's support page, you may or may not need to go to the download page to select the drivers to be downloaded. The drivers themselves are most often tailored to a specific operating system, although sometimes the drivers for every supported operating system are placed in a single large bundle. The download for the 3Com Gigabit Ethernet card in the practice bundles all of the available drivers into a single file.

Firmware updates are generally on the same page as the driver downloads, and they usually come in two parts. The first part is the binary image of the firmware that is to be loaded. The other file is the utility used to load the firmware. To find this utility, you often have to follow a link from the downloads page to a separate page. This is because the firmware loading utility is generally common to most, if not all, of the devices that the manufacturer makes. Some manufacturers use the approach of bundling both the loading utility and the image in the same file.

Practice: Download Novell NetWare 5 Drivers and Firmware for a 3Com 3C985-SX Gigabit EtherLink Server

Use the following steps to retrieve Novell NetWare 5 drivers and firmware for a 3Com 3C985-SX card. These steps take you through the navigation process and describe how we selected each option.

▶ **To download drivers and firmware for a 3Com EtherLink Server**

1. Start a Web browser.

2. Go to http://www.3com.com.

   Click the Service & Support link from the menu bar.

3. Select the product category, Network Interface Cards (NIC), from the list of product categories.

   Select the technology, Gigabit Ethernet, in the combo box that initially comes up as "Choose Technology."

   Alternatively, you can enter the family or the part number.

4. Select the 3C985 link from the page that appears.

5. Scroll down to the "Shipping Drivers" section and select either the FTP or HTTP link for each of the three EtherDisks, and save them into a directory.

6. Close the Web browser.

Extracting Firmware and Drivers

Once you've downloaded the drivers and firmware, you need to extract them to verify that they are the correct ones. Although each vendor packages its drivers and firmware differently, the general process for extracting and reviewing them is the same:

1. Move the downloaded driver or firmware file into an empty directory.

2. Double-click the driver or firmware file.

3. The effect of double-clicking the driver or firmware depends upon how the driver was packaged by the vendor. It should be one of the following:

    - A DOS window opens and extracts the files. You don't need to do anything more.

    - A DOS window opens and prompts you to agree to a license. After that the files are extracted. You don't need to do anything more.

    - A window opens asking where you want to place the extracted files. Select a directory, and click the Extract or OK button.

    - You're prompted for a floppy disk. Provide a disk at the prompt. Although this is rare in today's market, some vendors extract their files directly to a floppy disk.

    - A ZIP file extraction utility starts and then extracts the files to the directory.

Once you've extracted the files, you'll want to review them to see if any README files exist. These files usually have a .TXT, .WRI, or .DOC extension. Double-clicking the README file should bring up information about the drivers or firmware included in the downloaded package.

Reviewing the Extracted Files

Review the files you've extracted to make sure they are the ones you need. Here's a checklist of things to look for:

- **The correct operating system.**   Are the drivers for the correct operating system?

- **The correct hardware.**   Does the README file indicate that the driver supports the hardware you have? In other words, did you get the driver for the right device?

- **Cautions.**   Are there any cautions in the README file that would indicate areas of concern or that the driver should not be used in your environment?

- **Procedure.**   The installation procedure varies from driver to driver and from operating system to operating system. Failing to follow the recommended procedure can lead to installation problems.

Lesson Summary

This lesson reviewed the basic process for finding and extracting drivers and firmware from various manufacturers. It also covered the kinds of things to look for in the README files accompanying the drivers to reduce the possibility of problems.

Lesson 2: Implementing Firmware Updates

Having the firmware is one thing; implementing it is quite another. This lesson describes a process for implementing firmware updates while minimizing the potential impact of loading an incorrect version.

After this lesson, you will be able to

- Save the current version of the firmware
- Load the new version of the firmware

Estimated lesson time: 10 minutes

Preparing for Firmware Upgrades

Implementing new firmware is sort of a risky proposition. Most cards and motherboards that you load new firmware on can get so confused in the process that you can't recover them without sending the card in to the manufacturer.

Although this type of problem is very much the exception and not the rule, you should take a few precautions when working with firmware. They are

- **Ensure that power isn't lost.**   Your server should have a UPS that it will be connected to. Make sure that the server is connected to the UPS while performing the firmware upgrades. Power loss during a firmware load can render the card inoperable. You'll also want to test the UPS to make sure it's working.

- **Make each reboot a cold reboot.**   Every time you reboot while upgrading firmware, do so by powering off the system and powering it back on, unless otherwise instructed by the firmware load program. This ensures that the entire system is given a chance to reinitialize from scratch each time.

- **Back up, back up, back up.**   If you happen to be upgrading firmware on an existing system, make sure that system is backed up. Should the firmware upgrade change something unexpected, or should it fail, you may need to restore the system.

- **Be sure that it's necessary.**   After the system is installed, firmware updates should be done only to correct problems. The additional instability caused by changing firmware is generally not worth it, unless there is a specific problem or problems. Before upgrading the firmware of a production system, make sure you've got a good reason.

Tip I myself have had to recover from a firmware upgrade gone wrong. When upgrading the firmware and driver for a NetWare server many years ago, I didn't realize that the SCSI card manufacturer had changed the drive geometry translation. As a result, I needed to perform a complete rebuild of the server. The rebuild was necessary because the updated firmware was necessary, but the point remains—be judicious in your firmware upgrades.

Booting for Firmware Operations

When booting the system to perform a firmware upgrade, you should boot in as minimal a configuration as possible. Minimizing the software that is running reduces the potential that software will interfere with the firmware writing process and cause the process to fail. As a result, a clean bootup—that is, one without extraneous drivers and software—is preferred.

If the firmware utility runs from DOS, a DOS boot floppy is all you need to ensure that nothing is loaded that will cause problems. This assumes, of course, that you don't load anything special on the boot floppy.

If the firmware load utility must be run from Windows, the task of performing a clean bootup gets a little more difficult, because Windows stores much of its configuration information in a database called the registry. The registry contains most of the configuration information for the server, and as a result you should be extremely careful when making registry changes. However, you'll want to rename the entire HKEY_LOCAL_MACHINE\SOFTWARE\Microsoft\Windows \CurrentVersion\Run key to something else, and hold down the Shift key while rebooting. Finally, you'll want to stop all services that you can. This will eliminate all unnecessary software from running on the system.

The HKEY_LOCAL_MACHINE\SOFTWARE\Microsoft\Windows\Current-Version\Run key contains programs that run when you log on. Renaming that key prevents the programs from running. Holding down the Shift key during logon prevents the items in the Startup menu from running. Finally, stopping all of the services turns off any of that software that might be running. Once the firmware updates have been completed, you should remember to change the HKEY_LOCAL _MACHINE\SOFTWARE\Microsoft\Windows\CurrentVersion\Run key back to the original name to allow the items that are supposed to run for each logon to run once again.

Saving the Previous Version of the Firmware

Whenever you upgrade to new firmware, it's important to save the previous firmware. The simple reason for doing so is that you know the existing firmware functions at least to some degree with the card you have. If the new firmware doesn't work correctly, you may be able to reload the old firmware and continue as before. If you don't save the previous version of the firmware, however, you'll have nothing to fall back on.

If the firmware you received was bundled with the firmware writing utility, a batch file (ending in a .BAT extension) might be included with the image and writing utility to allow you to upgrade the firmware directly. You'll want to skip this batch file unless it's clear that the utility will prompt you to save the previous firmware. Review the batch file to see the parameters it uses in conjunction with the firmware writing utility. These parameters can help you determine whether the batch file will save the existing firmware and see if there are specific options that you should use when writing the firmware to the card.

Run the utility manually and use the option to save the existing firmware, unless the utility does not have such an option. Although they are by far the minority, a small number of firmware upgrade utilities do not have an option to save the current firmware. Thus it is possible that you won't be able to save your current firmware in case you need to revert back to it.

If you're running on a DOS boot floppy, make sure that the floppy has room to save the firmware from the card or motherboard. It's also a good idea to copy this file to a hard drive on another system before proceeding with the upgrade. Floppies are notoriously unreliable, and this will ensure that you still have the file should the floppy disk become corrupted.

Upgrading the Firmware

Once you've performed all of the steps just described, the actual process of installing the new firmware is trivial. All you have to do is to run the firmware update utility with the option to load an image file and tell it where to find the file. The utility itself will then load the new firmware onto the card. The process generally takes only a few minutes, and when complete the utility usually gives instructions to reboot or to take other actions necessary to allow the new firmware to take effect.

Although we mentioned this point earlier, it bears repeating: during this process it's extremely critical that the computer not be rebooted and that the power not be lost. Incomplete updates to firmware can leave the card in a state in which it will no longer respond and may require return to the manufacturer.

Lesson Summary

In this lesson, you learned the important preparation steps for implementing new firmware, including saving the previous version of the firmware and performing a backup of any existing configuration.

Lesson 3: Optimizing BIOS Settings

Working with BIOS settings is analogous to taking your car in for a tuneup. Incorrect settings can rob a server of performance or in some cases make it unstable. Optimizing the BIOS settings for your environment will allow your organization to get the most out of the new server.

After this lesson, you will be able to

- Identify settings that shouldn't be changed
- Establish optimized settings for your server

Estimated lesson time: 10 minutes

Getting into the BIOS

Before you can do anything with a server's BIOS, you have to get in. The BIOS setup screens are generally fairly easy to enter and require only a simple keypress. Often there's a message on the startup screen indicating which key to press—sometimes Delete, other times F1. Sometimes, however, you'll have the problem that the message indicating which key to press has been turned off, and the documentation that might indicate which key to use has been lost.

The quickest method of getting into the BIOS—albeit a brute force one—is to turn the computer off, press down and hold one key on the keyboard, and turn the computer back on. By holding down a key on the keyboard through the boot process, you'll force the BIOS to indicate a keyboard error. The screen that indicates the keyboard error almost always specifies a key to press to get into the BIOS setup. If you have to do this, snoop around in the BIOS options to find the message to display the key to enter setup, and reenable it.

Recording Settings

Although the thought of recording each of the BIOS options and how they are set isn't anyone's idea of fun, it's an important documentation step that can help you should a disaster occur and you need to install on a new piece of identical hardware. By noting all of the settings, you can minimize the differences between the original installation and the new system and, in doing so, reduce the risk of problems.

Unfortunately, BIOS screens can't be easily captured directly. As a result, you must either write down all of the options and the settings or make a photocopy of the BIOS screens in the documentation and write the settings next to them. Generally, copying the screens out of the system installation guide makes the process slightly less painful.

As we review the settings on each of the following pages, you should sit in front of the server and copy the BIOS settings into your logbook, or locate a copy of the BIOS screens in the documentation and write the current settings next to the options.

Tip Another way to document the BIOS settings is to take a digital camera and take a picture of the BIOS screen while it's up. You can then print this picture and put it in the server's log. You'll have to be careful to watch out for flash glare, but the resulting picture should be reasonably legible.

Configuring Basic Settings

Every BIOS has settings that are considered to be standard. They include the date/time, the floppy drives, the hard disk configuration, the video card type, and other miscellaneous items. These settings appear on a basic settings screen that is used to set up the system so that it will, presumably, boot. This is the screen that was available many years ago before additional features were added to the BIOS. Figure 4.1 shows a basic BIOS screen.

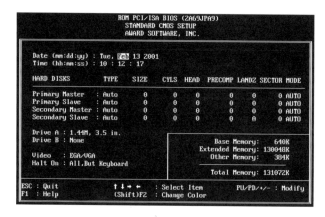

Figure 4.1   A standard BIOS configuration screen

The following list discusses some of the options commonly found on the basic settings screen in the BIOS and gives suggestions for setting them.

- **Date/time.**   Setting the date and time in the BIOS may seem unnecessary in today's environment because all operating systems allow you to set the time from within the operating system and have it propagate back to the BIOS. However, it's never a bad idea to get the date and time set up correctly.

- **Floppy drives.**   It may seem obvious, but the system needs to be configured for your floppy disk drives. Most machines today have a single 1.44-MB, 3.5-inch floppy disk.

- **Hard disks.**   Although it's possible to set up IDE hard drives manually in the BIOS, there's generally an auto-detect option on the BIOS's main menu

that you should select. Some BIOSs require that CD-ROMs be set up using
this option as well.

- **Video type.**   This option should almost always be VGA in today's computer
  environment. Historically, it was possible to use older adapters in servers, in
  part to reduce cost; however, there are currently no practical alternatives to
  VGA-based video cards and monitors.

- **Halt on errors.**   By default, when the power-on self test (POST) detects an
  error, the computer stops and displays a message about the error and prompts
  for input to continue. The halt on errors settings allow you to change how the
  system behaves at startup. These settings generally allow you to specify
  whether or not the BIOS should stop when it encounters an error. Some
  BIOSs allow for halting on anything except a keyboard error. This is handy
  when you don't want the fact that a keyboard was accidentally unplugged to
  stop the server from booting.

In addition to the settings listed here, the basic settings screen usually indicates
total installed memory, in case you missed it on the bootup screen. You should
review this number and make sure that it matches the amount of memory that
was supposed to be installed.

Note Historically, memory had to be reset in the BIOS after a change in the installed memory. Although some BIOSs still require that you enter setup and save
changes, most don't bother to stop the booting process for a memory size change.

Configuring Advanced Settings

Many years ago a series of new options for BIOSs started emerging. They were
designed to make the setup more user-friendly and allow more flexibility. There's
quite a bit of variation in what these items are called, but the options are generally the same. Figure 4.2 shows a BIOS configuration screen with some of
these options.

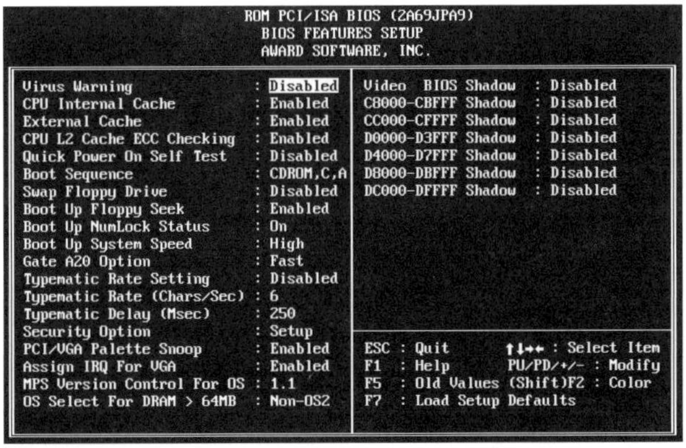

```
                       ROM PCI/ISA BIOS (2A69JPA9)
                          BIOS FEATURES SETUP
                          AWARD SOFTWARE, INC.

 Virus Warning             : Disabled    Video  BIOS Shadow  : Disabled
 CPU Internal Cache        : Enabled     C8000-CBFFF Shadow  : Disabled
 External Cache            : Enabled     CC000-CFFFF Shadow  : Disabled
 CPU L2 Cache ECC Checking : Enabled     D0000-D3FFF Shadow  : Disabled
 Quick Power On Self Test  : Disabled    D4000-D7FFF Shadow  : Disabled
 Boot Sequence             : CDROM,C,A   D8000-DBFFF Shadow  : Disabled
 Swap Floppy Drive         : Disabled    DC000-DFFFF Shadow  : Disabled
 Boot Up Floppy Seek       : Enabled
 Boot Up NumLock Status    : On
 Boot Up System Speed      : High
 Gate A20 Option           : Fast
 Typematic Rate Setting    : Disabled
 Typematic Rate (Chars/Sec) : 6
 Typematic Delay (Msec)    : 250
 Security Option           : Setup
 PCI/VGA Palette Snoop     : Enabled     ESC : Quit        ↑↓←→ : Select Item
 Assign IRQ For VGA        : Enabled     F1  : Help        PU/PD/+/- : Modify
 MPS Version Control For OS : 1.1        F5  : Old Values (Shift)F2 : Color
 OS Select For DRAM > 64MB : Non-OS2     F7  : Load Setup Defaults
```

Figure 4.2   An advanced BIOS settings screen

- **Virus Warning.** Determines whether the boot sector of the hard disk has changed between boots. When enabled, an error message appears whenever the boot sector changes. This option is probably not necessary for most servers, since viruses that infect the boot sector are not prevalent in today's environment and the use of floppy disks on a server is rare. It's better to run a virus scanner on a regular basis. Leaving this feature enabled will often lead to a false virus warning immediately after the operating system installation.

- **CPU Internal Cache.** CPUs have internal caches to speed up memory access, as we discussed in Chapter 3. This option allows you to turn off the CPU's internal cache. This cache should be enabled.

- **External Cache.** Allows you to enable or disable the L2 cache. Like the internal cache, the L2 cache is located on the CPU module in most cases, but it's separate from the internal cache. This cache should be enabled.

- **CPU L2 Cache ECC Checking.** Enables or disables ECC checking on the L2 cache. This option should be left enabled.

- **Quick Power On Self Test.** Allows the POST to skip certain tests in order to speed up the booting process. Often these tests include the memory test. Because of the need for servers to be reliable, the extra few minutes the full test takes while rebooting are probably warranted. Thus, you should disable this option. However, you might want to enable it while installing the operating system to speed up the installation process. Just remember to disable the feature when the installation is done.

- **Boot Sequence.** Controls the order in which devices are tried for booting. This option is important because if you leave the order as CD-ROM, A, DISK, as the option is set when a system is shipped, a bootable CD-ROM left in the drive will boot before the hard disk. Most server operating system CDs are *bootable*, meaning that the setup routine may start again if the operating system CD is left in the drive. On the other hand, if you change the option to DISK, A, CD-ROM or something similar, and at some point the operating system boots but will not start up, inserting the setup CD-ROM for recovery won't work because the CD won't get a chance to boot. The shipping option is often the best setting.

Note Windows 2000 will return to disk booting if a key is not pressed shortly after booting from the CD-ROM. This is a nice feature when the boot order is set to CD-ROM, A, DISK. It allows you to leave the CD-ROM in the drive without disturbing the ability of the server to boot from the hard disk. Although other operating systems haven't taken advantage of this kind of setup yet, it's probably not too far off.

- **Boot Up System Speed.**   Older systems used to have a switch on the front to set the speed of the processor. This option is long gone, but sometimes there's still an option to slow down the processor. We are at a loss as to why anyone would want to slow down a server. It should always be set to high.

- **Security Option.**   Controls how the BIOS password protection is configured. If this option is set to Setup, a password is required to enter the setup screen (assuming a password has previously been set). If it's set to Boot, a password is required to boot the system. This option should be set to Setup.

Note The password security option for booting isn't a good idea, because the battery on the motherboard maintains it. If the battery is removed or a special jumper on the motherboard is changed, the password will be removed. However, the Setup password setting is useful to prevent unauthorized people from easily changing the BIOS.

- **Assign IRQ For VGA.**   Some video cards need a designated IRQ to be able to support advanced features, such as onboard graphics processors. However, because graphics display is a very small part of a server's role, this option should be disabled. This is true even for terminal servers because although graphics activity is going on, only the graphics displayed on the console are routed through the video card.

- **PCI/VGA Palette Snoop.**   Helps specialized video add-on cards work in conjunction with the primary video display while in 256-color mode. This option should be disabled in a server.

- **MPS Version Control for OS.**   Controls the version of the Multi-Processor Specification (MPS) standard that the multiprocessor system is set up for. Set this option to the highest available setting unless the operating system documentation requires that it be set differently.

- **OS Select For DRAM > 64MB.**   OS/2 accesses memory greater than 64 MB in a way that is different from other operating systems. If you're installing OS/2, set this option to OS/2. Otherwise, set it to non-OS/2.

- **Video and system BIOS shadowing.**   BIOS shadowing allows the motherboard to copy the ROM from the system and from video cards to RAM. RAM is quicker than ROM, and thus this option can improve performance for some operating systems. Although you can turn these options on, they will have little effect on most operating systems, which don't use the system or video BIOS anyway.

Configuring Chipset Settings

Chipset settings control the timing and access features of the chipset. Figure 4.3 shows a chipset settings BIOS page and all of the complicated options. These settings are generally best left alone. However, there are some settings that you may want to be aware of:

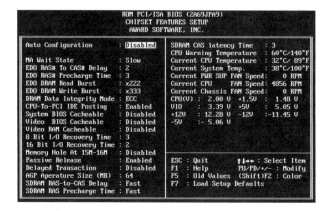

Figure 4.3   A chipset settings screen

- **Memory auto-configuration.**   If enabled, allows the system to determine the speed of the memory and configure the CPU support chipset appropriately to access the memory. This option should be left at its default setting.

- **DRAM Data Integrity Mode.**   Allows you to turn off ECC for the main memory. For servers, this option should always be set to enable ECC.

- **AGP Aperture Size (MB).**   Sets the amount of memory from the AGP video card that can be mapped into main memory. In a server, this setting should be set to the smallest available value because video card performance is not important. The smallest aperture is generally 16 KB.

- **CPU Warning Temperature.**   Sometimes servers provide a thermometer on the motherboard for the purpose of warning the administrator when the temperature of the CPU exceeds a threshold. This setting is best left to the default. If that setting causes a warning to go off, contact the manufacturer to determine whether a new higher setting is acceptable. Sometimes a temperature warning will cause an alert in the system log, and other times it will sound an audible warning.

- **Auto-detect DIMM/PCI clock.**   Allows the motherboard to detect the presence or absence of memory or PCI cards in DIMM and PCI slots. If no cards are detected, the system clock signal is not sent to the empty slots. This reduces electromagnetic interference and signal problems related to lack of termination.

- **Chipset special features.** Controls the behavior of the chipset. This option may disable certain advanced features and behaviors. Its exact functioning will depend on the chipset. Leave it enabled unless advised by technical support to change it.

In addition to the options listed here, there is generally a long series of memory-specific settings that control wait states and other timing-related issues. These settings absolutely should not be changed without assistance from technical support. Changing the timing for how memory is accessed can cause instability problems that are difficult to diagnose.

In addition to these memory settings, you will often also see information related to the CPU's current temperature as well as to the power currently being received by the motherboard and fan speeds. This information can help you determine if there is a power supply problem or a fan failure.

A power supply is supposed to output power at several different voltages. A tolerance of 10 percent is generally allowed for each voltage. Next to each current voltage is the reference voltage that the power should be at. If the current voltage differs from the reference voltage by more than 10 percent (positive or negative), you should consider replacing the power supply.

Setting Up Plug and Play, PCI, and Integrated Peripherals

Plug and Play (PnP) and PCI are associated because all PCI cards are PnP compliant by definition. The options on this setup screen are most often used to configure interrupts and other PnP settings. Some of the settings for integrated peripherals, such as serial, USB, and parallel ports, are also sometimes found on the PnP/PCI BIOS setup screen. Figure 4.4 shows an example of this type of screen. Here are some of the important settings that can be found there:

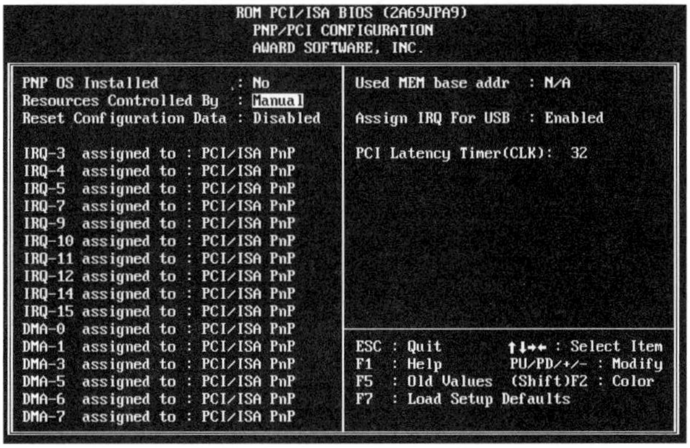

Figure 4.4 A PnP/PCI BIOS screen

- **PNP OS Installed.**   Tells the BIOS whether a PnP-compliant operating system is installed and should be allowed to initialize devices, rather than having the BIOS initialize the devices. This option should be set to Yes if your operating system is Plug and Play compatible. Windows 2000 is Plug and Play compatible, but many other operating systems, including Novell NetWare, are not.

- **Resources Controlled By.**   Determines whether the IRQs and other devices are set automatically or controlled manually in the BIOS. This option should be set to Automatic when a PnP-compliant operating system is installed and set to Manual otherwise. It allows you to specify the IRQs being used by non-PnP cards and devices. This helps PnP configuration utilities when they are trying to determine what IRQs are available.

- **Reset Configuration Data.**   Each Plug and Play card stores a small amount of configuration data on itself. A bad driver or extended power loss sometimes corrupts this information and can prevent the proper configuration of the card. Allowing the configuration data to be reset can fix this problem. This option is set once and will clear itself automatically. Use it as a last resort when a PnP operating system is not installed, because it may require the manual setup of every PnP card. When a PnP operating system is installed, setting this option is generally not a big issue because the operating system will reconfigure the PnP cards from its database.

- **On-board IDE controller (primary/secondary).**   Controls whether the on-board IDE controllers are turned on or off. If your server has an ATAPI (IDE) CD-ROM drive, at least one of the on-board IDE controllers must be enabled.

- **On-board parallel port.**   Controls whether the on-board parallel port is enabled or disabled. If you're not using the server's parallel port (and you shouldn't be), disable this option to make IRQ 7 available for other peripherals.

- **Parallel port mode.**   Selects the operating mode for the parallel port. The options are generally bidirectional, ECP, or EPP. ECP, or Enhanced Capabilities Port, is the preferred mode of operating a parallel port.

- **EPP version.**   Controls the version of EPP that the onboard parallel port emulates.

- **Onboard serial ports.**   Controls whether the onboard serial ports are enabled or disabled. Enable the onboard serial ports only if you will need them. Generally, one port is used for UPS connectivity, and the other is not used. In such cases, you should disable the second serial port so the interrupt is available for other peripherals.

Lesson Summary

This lesson reviewed the common BIOS options and indicated what their settings should be in most cases. Setting these options to the correct values will ensure that the server achieves optimum performance and operates without error.

Lesson 4: Configuring RAID Settings

In this lesson, you'll learn about the basic RAID settings and configuration that you should perform to establish RAID arrays and prepare them for operating system installation. Although the settings are relatively simple, they are important because proper setup of the RAID arrays can make the difference between a fully fault-tolerant, high-performance drive array and a slow, problematic one.

After this lesson, you will be able to

- Establish RAID drive arrays and hot spares
- Identify failing drives and their location

Estimated lesson time: 20 minutes

Verifying Controller and Drive Status

The first step in setting up the RAID controller is to verify that it recognizes the connected drives. A quick check of the drives and their status is recommended before starting the process of building the array.

To perform this check, enter the RAID controller's BIOS. This is generally done by pressing Ctrl+A during the bootup sequence, but some RAID controllers require a different key sequence.

In most systems the BIOS will perform a quick bus scan and then show a tree view of controllers, buses, and drives. The RAID controller generally displays its BIOS information as well as any pertinent information, such as host bus and cache memory, on this screen. Configuration options may also appear on this screen, but they are generally located on another screen. This is a good time to verify the onboard cache memory and battery backup status, if the card supports battery backup of the cache.

You should see a series of drives listed under each bus. Verify that all of the drives you have installed on the system are listed under the appropriate buses. If there are more drives than can be listed on one screen, scroll down to review the installed drives. If drives that you believe should be installed don't show up, verify the bus settings to ensure that termination and transfer rates are set correctly, as discussed next.

By scrolling down to the first SCSI bus, you'll see the type of the bus and will have the opportunity to change the configuration options. In particular, you can change the termination settings, the termination power, and in some cases the device-specific transfer rates. If all of the devices are new, the transfer rates generally shouldn't be an issue. The controller should provide termination power on the bus and should be terminated unless the bus connects both internal and external devices.

Scrolling down to the first hard disk will display its configuration information. Often the firmware revision as well as the size, block size, and capabilities will be listed. If it displays an error or lists incomplete information about the size of the drive or the block size, there may be problems with the device. You should reattempt the installation of the drive. Some RAID cards also give you a specific indication of the overall status of the drive.

Once you've reviewed each drive and bus to confirm that the drives are installed and functioning properly, you can move on to create a RAID array.

Creating a RAID Array

The process of creating a RAID array is incredibly simple. Essentially, you select the type of RAID array and the devices you want to include and tell it to go. Most controllers can create three kinds of arrays. They are the same RAID-0, RAID-1, and RAID-5 we discussed in Chapter 3.

Let's walk through the array-creation process step by step. You can repeat this process to create multiple arrays.

1. Once in the RAID BIOS select the array creation command. This menu option allows you to specify the type of drive array you want to create.

2. Select the kind of array to be created. If the array is either RAID-0 or RAID-5, you'll be given the option of setting the stripe size of the array. It's generally recommended that you accept the default setting for the cache size.

3. Select the drives that you want to insert into the array. The available drives should be listed. Do not select the drives you want to use as hot spares. If you're creating a RAID-1 array, you'll be limited to two drives.

4. When the settings are complete, select OK. If you're creating a RAID-1 array, you'll be prompted to indicate which drive has the information on it that you want to keep.

Create all of the arrays that you need for your system and then commit the changes. As soon as the changes are committed, the controller will start building the arrays.

Note Some RAID controllers allow you to create RAID-0 arrays on top of RAID-1 and RAID-5 arrays. This technique permits you to maintain the individual array sizes at a reasonable level while still allowing for higher capacity.

Marking Drives as Hot Spare

In the preceding section, you specifically did not include any drives that you wanted to have as hot spares in the initial build of the array. This is because hot spares are not generally members of any array; they are simply drives connected to the controller that you've indicated can be used when a drive fails. Therefore, the hot spare will replace the first drive that fails within the array, assuming that it is large enough to do so.

The process of creating a hot spare drive is as simple as selecting the drive and then selecting the menu option to make it a hot spare. No other configuration steps are necessary. The hot spare drive will automatically take over for a failing drive.

Identifying Failing Drives

A RAID controller doesn't prevent hard drives from failing; it just prevents a drive failure from stopping the system. Although the RAID array may prevent the system from shutting down when a failure occurs, the failure should still be addressed.

There are a few basic ways to identify a drive failure. Perhaps the most obvious way is to notice that its drive light is off. The RAID software driver installed in your server operating system will also issue some sort of alert when a drive fails. You might see this alert when you review the server log, or you might receive it via the monitoring and notification systems. The alert will let you know that a drive has failed as well as the bus and ID of the drive.

Lesson Summary

In this lesson, you learned how to configure RAID settings so that RAID arrays would be available for operating system installation. You also learned how to verify that the drives were functioning properly and how to establish hot spares to accommodate drive failures.

Review

Here are some questions to help you determine whether you have learned enough to move on to the next chapter. If you have difficulty answering these questions, please go back and review the material in this chapter before beginning the next chapter. The answers for these questions are located in the appendix, "Questions and Answers."

1. What is the greatest risk when installing new firmware?

2. What precautions should you take when installing new firmware?

3. When should firmware updates be performed?

4. What kind of a reboot should be performed after a firmware installation?

5. What BIOS settings should never be changed?

6. Several options deal with video settings. How should the video settings be set up for a server?

7. You are installing Novell NetWare as your server operating system. How should the PnP/PCI settings be set?

8. You've added a new hard disk to a RAID controller and want it to be used as a hot spare. What must you do to accomplish this?

CHAPTER 5

Installing and Configuring the Network Operating System

About This Chapter

In Chapter 4, you finished the last of the preinstallation activities by downloading the latest drivers and implementing the latest firmware. In this chapter, you will install and configure the operating system on the server hardware.

This chapter is different from most of the other chapters in this book in that a large portion of its content is operating system–specific. Although you will be using only one of the operating systems discussed here, it's recommended that you read the entire chapter, including the sections on operating systems that your environment doesn't use. Doing so not only will prepare you for the Server+ exam but also will give you an understanding of how other operating systems are installed. You will find this understanding helpful when installing any operating system.

Note This chapter is not intended to replace the installation instructions provided with the operating system. Rather, it's meant to give you a quick overview of the process so you'll know what to expect.

Before You Begin

To complete this chapter, you should have

- Your server hardware
- Your network operating system medium and documentation

Lesson 1: Choosing an Installation Method and Type

Back in Chapter 1, Lesson 4, you learned how to select an operating system. By this point you should have made your decision. Now you must decide how you are going to install the operating system you've chosen. In this lesson, you'll learn about the various ways an operating system can be installed.

After this lesson, you will be able to

- Select the appropriate installation method for your server
- Identify the advantages and disadvantages of each installation type

Estimated lesson time: 15 minutes

Installation Methods

There are two basic methods of installing server operating systems today: CD-ROM/DVD installation and network installation. The following two sections review each of these installation methods and discuss their advantages and disadvantages.

CD-ROM/DVD Installation

The most common way to install a network operating system is via a CD-ROM or DVD. This installation is the easiest type to set up, and it is supported by all operating systems. The advantages of installing from CD-ROM/DVD are as follows:

- **Simplicity.**   Perhaps the best reason to select a CD-ROM/DVD installation is its simplicity. You don't need to perform any special network setup.
- **Least chance of problems.**   Since you're not depending upon anything other than the CD-ROM/DVD and the CD-ROM/DVD drive, there are fewer potential interruptions and problems when installing from a CD-ROM/DVD.
- **Speed.**   Generally speaking, CD-ROM/DVD installations are quicker than other kinds of installations.

CD-ROM/DVD installations do have some disadvantages, however. The most serious of these is the possibility that a media error will occur on the CD-ROM or DVD. Should a media error occur during installation, the installation will obviously not complete successfully, unless you can locate a replacement CD-ROM or DVD. For organizations that have multiple servers, this is certainly a possibility. However, locating different media in the middle of the installation is often awkward and difficult.

The other disadvantage of installing from CD-ROM or DVD is that any time you want to install a new option you'll be prompted for the installation medium. You can copy the installation files to the hard disk and change the location each time you're prompted for them, but this is a little less elegant than just having the setup take place without prompting. If you install from the network, the location will always be the network installation location. As long as you maintain the installation server, you won't have to worry about finding the installation medium or redirecting the location to the installation files. In most cases you won't even be prompted for the files; the setup program will detect their presence in the default location and continue automatically.

Lesson 2 assumes that you are installing via CD-ROM or DVD, because this is the most popular method and because it is universally supported by server operating systems.

Network Installation

Although not as easy as CD-ROM/DVD installations, network installations are particularly useful when the server will be one of many servers at a site. It allows the installation files to be copied onto one server and for that server to be used as the source for all of the installations at the site.

The primary advantage of a network installation is that all of the installation files are kept in one place, so you can add components to the operating system without having to locate the installation CD-ROM or DVD. Generally, when administrators go to the trouble of setting up a network server from which installations can be performed, the server also contains some of the latest patches and fixes needed to rebuild a server completely should a problem arise.

The disadvantage of network installations is that they are harder to set up because they involve creating an installation floppy disk or, even more difficult, a network bootable image, which the network card on the new server will automatically download. Although both processes are doable, most people choose to create the installation floppy disk.

Each network operating system has different rules for how the network installation floppy disk should be created, and some don't support network installations at all. The preparation involved in a network installation is generally warranted only when many servers are going to be installed at the same site.

Installation Types

Just as there are two basic methods of installing an operating system, there are also two different types of installation: new installations and in-place upgrades. This section discusses each of these types in turn.

New Installations

Until this point in the book, we've assumed that you will be installing a new server into a new environment, and so we've covered all of the planning issues associated with installing a new server. This emphasis is in no small way related to the fact that installing a new server requires much more planning than upgrading an existing server.

Installing an operating system on new server hardware is generally a very low-risk process that goes smoothly. All the devices in the system have drivers for the operating system, and few incompatibilities are to be found.

In-Place Upgrades

An in-place upgrade involves installing a server operating system over the top of an existing operating system. This type of upgrade is often dramatically different from a new installation in that it involves answering far fewer questions than when installing the operating system for the first time, because the existing operating system already has the information and the setup program can extract it.

Another difference is that the server already contains data that you want to preserve. This changes how the installation will proceed. Most installations, as you'll see in Lesson 2, begin by preparing the drive for installation. Generally, this means installing a partition table and formatting one or more partitions, a process that wipes out existing data.

During an in-place upgrade, on the other hand, the setup program tests the existing drives and partitions to ensure that there are no errors. Setup programs vary as to whether they will fix the errors themselves or require you to run fix utilities from the existing operating system. In either case, the setup program starts by ensuring that the drives have no errors and there is sufficient space to install the new operating system.

Although in-place upgrades are often used to upgrade existing servers, it's better when possible to perform a new installation on a new server and then migrate the users and data to the new system. This minimizes the impact of the small glitches that sometimes occur during an upgrade.

The biggest challenges when upgrading an existing server are to make sure that you have valid backups and to allow yourself enough time for the upgrade. Allow enough time not just to complete and verify backups but also to handle any problems that arise. Technicians commonly underestimate the time they will need to upgrade a server. In particular, they often don't allow time for coping with unexpected issues.

Installation Timing

An installation, whether it's a new one or an upgrade, can involve a great deal of time. The time can be spent configuring the system or waiting for the installation program to complete its operations. Every operating system has a slightly different installation procedure and thus has different points when you may be able to let the system perform its own activities unattended.

There are certain points during an installation when the installation program needs time to process. Although these points vary as to when they occur and how long they last, depending on the hardware and the operating system being installed, some components are common to most installations. Most of the steps that follow don't allow access to the system at all while they are under way. In some cases, although access is allowed, it is ill advised because of the severe performance penalty. Some of the major steps that may require a wait on your part are as follows:

- **Building the RAID array.** Although you can continue to work on a system while the RAID array is building, it's better to start this process, leave the server alone, and then come back once the array has been built to partition, format, and load the operating system. Doing so will make those procedures go much faster. Start building the RAID array just before you go home for the evening or before you go into a long meeting. Depending upon the size of the array, the building process may take several hours.

- **Formatting the drives.** Formatting the drives may take quite a long time, particularly when you haven't let the RAID array build before starting the process. Formatting can take hours if the drive space is quite large. In general, it's recommended that you format the system/boot partition as a relatively small area of the disk (4 GB or less) that can be formatted in less than an hour. Once the system is up and running, you can format the additional partitions in the background. While the system is formatting the system/boot partition, you can go to lunch or go into a short meeting.

- **Installing the operating system.** Installing the operating system files generally takes about 20 minutes, during which time there's no need to interact with the setup process. It's probably too short for a meeting or a lunch (unless you bring it back to your desk), but it's long enough to tend to other tasks, such as reading e-mail.

- **Detecting the hardware.** If the operating system enters a hardware detection phase at the end of file copying, the first part of this phase generally detects devices that have support shipped with the operating system. These devices don't usually require intervention on the installer's part. Later in the hardware detection phase, however, nonstandard devices and devices whose drivers are not packaged in the operating system arc detected, and as a result your intervention will be required to provide the additional drivers. The hardware detection phase generally lasts for about 10 minutes before needing intervention—just enough time to go get a drink.

Lesson Summary

This lesson reviewed the primary methods for installing new operating systems and for upgrading existing servers. You should now have a basis for deciding what kind of installation to perform. The lesson also reviewed the major steps involved in installing an operating system, indicating when there would be breaks in the action so that you could plan your day efficiently.

Lesson 2: Installing the Operating System

Installing the operating system is the moment that most people remember when asked about the installation of the server. They don't remember placing the server in the rack or preparing the computer room. They remember turning on the power and inserting the operating system CD. This lesson gives you an important overview of the process of installing an operating system, covering the installation process for Microsoft Windows 2000, Novell NetWare, and Linux.

Note You'll notice that OS/2 isn't included here. We elected to refrain from walking through the installation of OS/2 for several reasons: it has not had a recent release, there are no questions on the Server+ exam directly relating to it, and the market generally lacks support for it. If you need to install OS/2, review the following sections to get a general idea of the process, and then refer to OS/2-specific literature for details.

After this lesson, you will be able to

- Plan an operating system installation
- Perform an operating system installation

Estimated lesson time: 120 minutes

Understanding the Basic Installation Procedure

Although the methods for installing the various operating systems are all different, the outcome is the same. The outcome should be a bootable hard disk or hard disks that contain the configured operating system. To achieve that outcome, the following basic steps have to occur:

- **Performing a preliminary hardware scan.**   This scan is done just to make sure that the hardware can install the operating system. It may involve checking for a VGA adapter, hard disks of sufficient capacity, or installed memory. This scan generally happens at the very start of the installation process.

- **Partitioning the hard disk.**   This step breaks the available hard disk space into reasonable chunks. Linux requires swap and root partitions. Practically speaking, Linux requires a boot partition as well. Because of BIOS and master boot record limitations, there are special considerations for using disk space above 2 GB. To ensure that the system will be able to continue to boot, a separate boot partition is strongly recommended. Novell NetWare needs a SYS volume. For Windows 2000, a boot and system partition are needed. (They can be the same partition.)

- **Formatting the partitions.**   Reserving space with the partitioning process is only the first step in preparing the hard disks; the next step is to format the partitions. The formatting process writes the root data structures that the operating system uses to locate all of the other data stored on the hard disks. It's required for every kind of partition.

- **Loading the operating system.**   Once the hard disks are prepared, you can load onto the system the files necessary for the operating system to run. In the case of Linux, the files are loaded to the root partition and the boot partition, if present. Novell loads them to the SYS volume, and Windows 2000 loads them to the boot and system partitions.

- **Configuring the system.**   During the installation, the setup program accepts configuration information from you specifying how you want the system to be set up and then writes those settings to the hard disk to be used the next time the operating system boots up. This configuration process may also include a more detailed hardware scan to determine what other devices are present in the system.

When you install any operating system, you can expect to encounter each of these phases. Although some of them may not take long, and they may not occur in the same order, the basic process is the same for each operating system.

Installing Windows 2000

Windows 2000 is one of the easiest operating systems to install. Its mechanisms for detecting hardware and the wizard-based installation of drivers make the installation process simple. The Windows 2000 recovery console even makes recovering from problems during an installation easy. Although installing Windows 2000 involves a lot of configuration, the process is straightforward and simple.

The first thing that happens when you boot from the Windows 2000 CD, if there is an active partition on the hard disk, is that you're prompted to press a key to boot from the CD. As we mentioned in Chapter 4, this is a great option because it allows you to set the system to boot from the CD-ROM drive first without worrying that a CD left in the drive will prevent a normal bootup.

Immediately after booting from the Windows 2000 CD, the setup program performs a quick hardware check to ensure that Windows 2000 will be able to install on the system. After that, a text screen is displayed that prompts you to press F6 if you need to install a third-party SCSI driver. When you press this key, the setup program will then further identify hardware, trying to load all of the drivers for any SCSI cards that may be present in the system. Once this process is complete, the installation will prompt you for any third-party SCSI drivers you have. When you have provided the drivers and chosen to continue, or if you let the installation run rather than pressing F6, you see a menu prompting you to indicate what action you want to perform. You can either install Windows 2000, repair an existing installation, or exit the installer. Figure 5.1 shows the initial setup screen for Windows 2000 after drivers have been loaded.

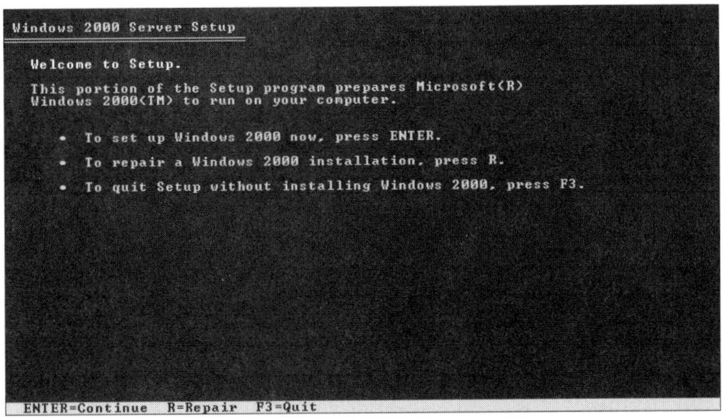

Figure 5.1   Initial Windows 2000 Server Setup screen

Note The repair option is present even if no other installations of Windows 2000 are present on the computer.

Press Enter to begin the setup process. The first step of this process involves accepting the license agreement. You do this by pressing the F8 key. Windows 2000 then searches for previous installations. If any are present, you're given the option of installing over them. If there are no previous installations, you're asked how you want to partition the hard disk or disks on the system. Figure 5.2 shows the partitioning screen on a new system.

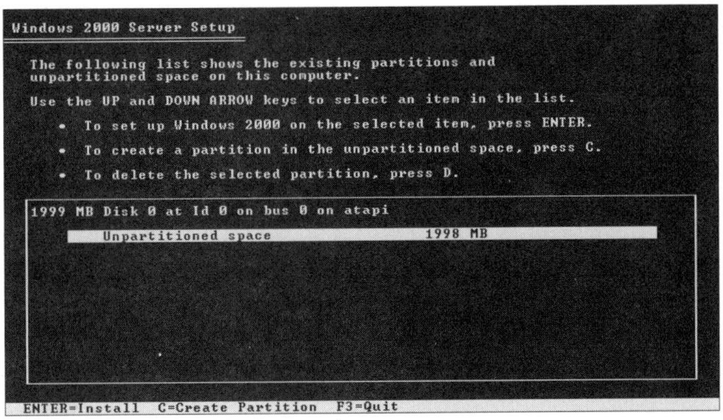

Figure 5.2   Partitioning screen, showing all drives and partitions for a system with a single 2-GB hard disk

In general, you should create only the system and boot partitions at this time. (These are usually the same partition.) Because some SCSI controllers limit the size of this partition to 4 GB, it's recommended that you create a 4-GB partition and format it with NTFS. Sometimes problems occur if the system partition is too large.

Once the partition is formatted, the installation program begins copying the installation files to the system. It then reboots the system to begin the graphical part of the installation. Do nothing when you see the prompt about booting from the CD; after a few seconds, the system will automatically boot from the hard drive. After another hardware detection phase, you're presented with an opportunity to change the current locale and keyboard. The locale is Windows 2000's way of determining the language you want to use as well as the kind of separators you use for thousands and decimals. It combines all of the little details that users from different locations around the world will want to change. Figure 5.3 shows the localization screen.

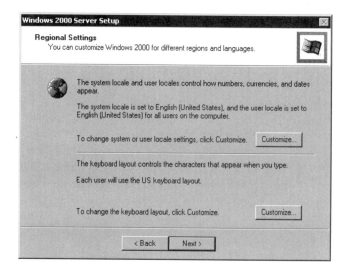

Figure 5.3 Regional Settings screen—the first graphical screen in Windows 2000 Server Setup

The next screen allows you to enter your user name and organization. Although you could provide your own user name here, it generally makes more sense to enter the name of the computer. Figure 5.4 shows the personalization screen. The next steps are to enter your product key and to select the licensing mode for the server. Since Windows 2000 is a proprietary operating system, access licenses are sold individually, and it needs to know how many you have—and whether you're licensing by server or by seat. Figure 5.5 shows the licensing screen with the default answer of five concurrent licenses.

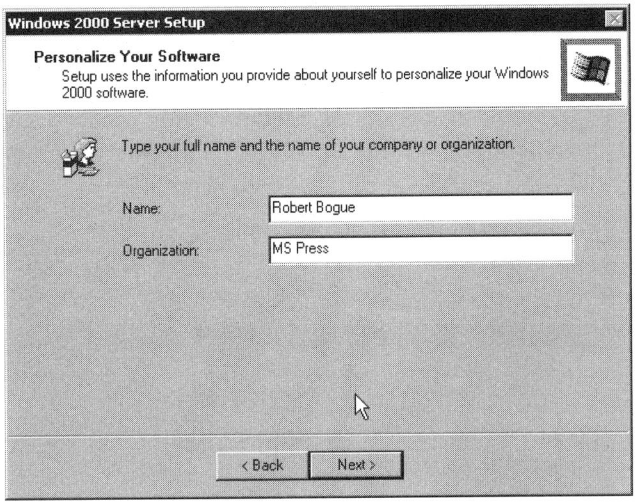

Figure 5.4   Personalize Your Software screen

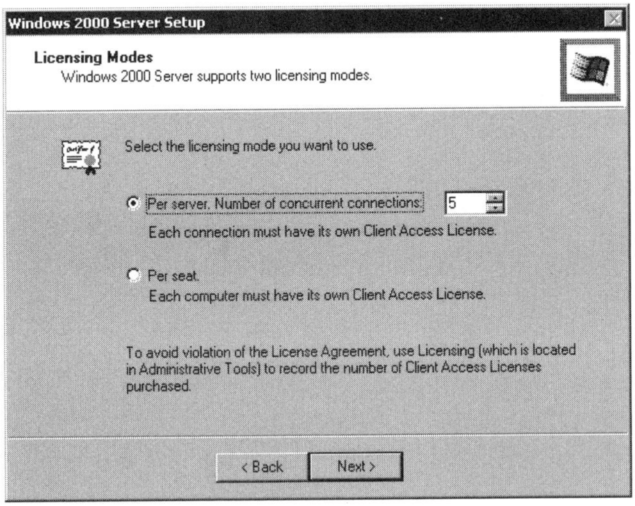

Figure 5.5   Licensing Modes screen

Note Deciding which licensing method is best, or which one to use in your environment, is beyond the scope of this book. You can find information about Microsoft's licensing programs at https://eopen.microsoft.com.

Once you've selected the licensing mode, the next screen allows you to assign a computer name and select the password for the administrator account. By default, Windows 2000 selects a unique name for the server, which is less than intuitive. You can rename the server to anything you want, but you should avoid names that might already exist on the network. Choosing a name that's already on the network can cause problems with the setup of this server and with the other computer that has the same name. Figure 5.6 shows this screen for a Windows 2000 computer that's been named TESTCOMPUTER.

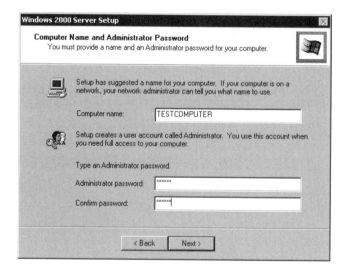

Figure 5.6   Specifying a computer name and administrator password

The next screen shows the options to be installed with the operating system. Several items are selected by default when installing a server, but many more are not selected. You can choose to continue with the default options or install more or fewer of the optional components. You can always add or remove components of Windows 2000 later through Add/Remove Programs in Control Panel, should your decisions now not anticipate all the future needs of the server.

The next screen sets the time, date, and time zone for the server. Although setting the time zone may appear to have little impact on the server's initial operation, it should be set correctly. An incorrect time zone setting can lead to some interesting and subtle time-related errors that are difficult to find. This is particularly true when some of the servers in an organization are set to the correct time zone and others are not. Figure 5.7 shows the Date And Time Settings screen.

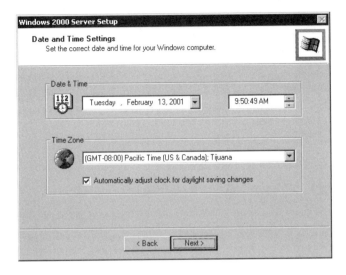

Figure 5.7   Setting the date and time, as well as the time zone

Note Active Directory needs correct time and time zone information to function properly. Failure to set the time zone correctly or to synchronize the server clocks may lead to inconsistent update posting.

If a modem is present, the installer will now request regional dialing information. This is followed by the installation of network components. This step proceeds automatically until you're asked whether you want to accept typical network settings or to specify settings manually. In the interest of expediency, assuming that you still have drives to partition and format, which can't be done during the setup, it's recommended that you accept the typical settings.

Note You can always reconfigure the network by clicking Start, pointing to Settings, and selecting Network And Dialup Connections. This section allows you to configure all of the adapter and protocol settings related to networking. You can add or remove services using Add/Remove Programs in Control Panel.

The next screen asks whether the newly installed server will be part of a domain. If the answer is Yes, a computer account must already exist for the new server in the domain or, more commonly, you must provide a user name and password with sufficient rights to add computers to the network to include the server in the domain. Figure 5.8 shows this screen.

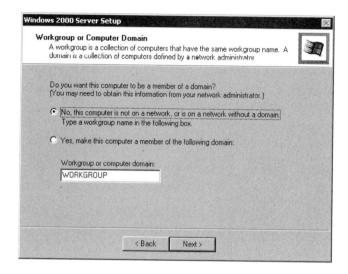

Figure 5.8 Workgroup Or Computer Domain screen

Once the network adapter is successfully identified and membership in the domain has been established or forgone, the setup program will proceed without intervention for some time and complete the configuration of Windows 2000. After this process, the system will ask you to complete the installation by clicking Finished. The system will then reboot, and the Windows 2000 logon will appear.

At this point, the operating system is installed on the hardware. However, many additional steps are still needed to make the server ready for users, as you'll see in Lesson 3. These steps involve configuring the system for your environment and clients.

Installing Novell NetWare 5

Whereas Windows 2000 is the easiest operating system to install, Novell NetWare is perhaps the hardest. It's difficult primarily because it requires a series of steps before you can even launch the installation program. In fact, another operating system, DOS, must first be installed on the server. This requirement, which is a result of NetWare's history, is a disadvantage in today's environment, when almost no one runs DOS any longer. Despite Novell's good installation program, the steps required to prepare for installing NetWare make the process more difficult than that for the other operating systems addressed here.

Note I was once a system administrator of a large NetWare 3.*x*/4.*x* environment, and I'm still quite fond of some of NetWare's features. My evaluation of the operating system here is based on its ease of installation (or lack thereof), not on how good the system is once it is installed. NetWare is a very respectable network operating system that is very stable.

Preparing the DOS Boot Partition

In order for NetWare to boot, the server must be prepared with a DOS partition of not less than 50 MB. I'd recommend that the partition be at least twice this size to accommodate future releases of the operating system. You can create this partition by using the NetWare license disk.

The NetWare license disk is a bootable disk containing the portions of DOS 7 necessary for creating the DOS partition. You create this partition by using the FDISK command, creating the partition, and then formatting the drive with the FORMAT command. (Don't forget the /S switch to transfer the system, or boot, files to the new partition.)

After you've created the partition, you need to modify CONFIG.SYS to include the lines FILES=40 and BUFFERS=30. Additionally, you must load a DOS CD-ROM driver for the CD-ROM drive. This is sometimes an issue, since most new hardware doesn't ship with DOS drivers at all. However, a generic IDE CD-ROM driver generally works with the CD-ROM drives in today's servers.

Tip If you're looking for a DOS CD-ROM driver, search the Internet for the keywords "ATAPI," "DOS," and "CD-ROM," using your favorite search engine. This will list several sites with IDE/ATAPI CD-ROM drivers that may work.

Running the Install Program

Once you've created the DOS partition, located and installed a DOS CD-ROM driver, modified the CONFIG.SYS file, and rebooted, you're ready to start the installation program. This is done by running the INSTALL command from the root of the CD-ROM.

The first screen is a license agreement that you must accept. The second screen prompts you for the installation location for the NetWare server files. Figure 5.9 shows this screen. The default installation directory is C:\NWSERVER. Unless you have some compelling reason to use a different directory, accept the default by selecting Continue.

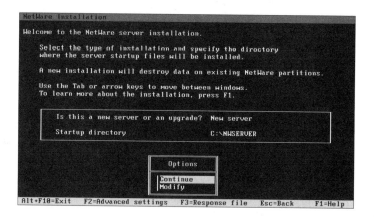

Figure 5.9 Specifying the DOS directory where the NetWare server files will be installed

The next few screens prompt you for information about the server's internal IPX network ID, or server ID, and ask whether the NetWare server should be started at bootup. The answer to this question is yes.

The next screen prompts you for the current country, code page, and keyboard. Although these are standard identifiers established by the American National Standards Institute (ANSI), most United States citizens aren't aware that they are in country 001 or that they use code page 437. Again, unless you've got a compelling reason to change these values, such as having a different keyboard layout or speaking another language natively, you should leave these settings at their defaults. Figure 5.10 shows the regional settings screen with the default settings.

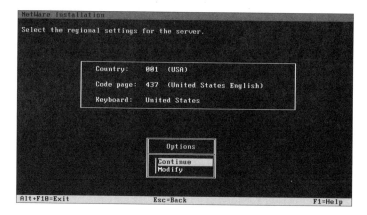

Figure 5.10 Specifying regional settings for NetWare

The next screen asks you to verify the mouse and video card being used. Unlike Windows 2000, which detects the specific make and model of the video card, NetWare, not being based on a graphical user interface (GUI), cares only whether the video card is VGA or Super VGA compatible. Most video cards today are what NetWare would consider to be Super VGA cards. Figure 5.11 shows this screen.

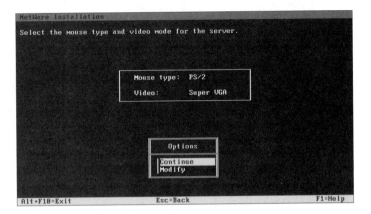

Figure 5.11   Specifying the mouse type and video mode for NetWare

In the next step, the installation program attempts to detect any Platform Support Modules (PSMs) that may be appropriate for the server. PSMs might be used if the server has multiple processors or if it supports Hot Plug PCI. Note that this is not the same as Plug and Play; NetWare 5 is not a Plug and Play–compliant operating system.

Next the installation program identifies the disk controllers and drives. Historically this has been done through the use of .DSK modules, but in NetWare 5 Novell decided to use only the NetWare Peripheral Architecture (NWPA). This replaces the single .DSK module with a Host Adapter Module (HAM) and a Custom Device Module (CDM). By default, NetWare will detect standard disk controllers and install these modules for you, for disk controllers whose drivers ship with NetWare. However, you may need to provide a disk with nonstandard host adapter drivers. Figure 5.12 shows the screen prompting for platform and storage adapter information.

```
┌─NetWare Installation────────────────────────────────────────────────┐
│                                                                      │
│ The following device drivers were detected for this server.  Add, change, or
│ delete device drivers as needed.                                     │
│                                                                      │
│   ┌─ Device types ──────────── Driver names ──────────────────────┐  │
│   │                                                               │  │
│   │  Platform Support Module:    (optional)                       │  │
│   │                                                               │  │
│   │  HotPlug Support Module:     (optional)                       │  │
│   │                                                               │  │
│   │  Storage adapters:           IDEATA,IDEATA                     │  │
│   │                                                               │  │
│   └───────────────────────────────────────────────────────────────┘  │
│                            ┌─ Options ──────────┐                    │
│                            │ Continue           │                    │
│                            │ Modify             │                    │
│                            └────────────────────┘                    │
│                                                                      │
│ Alt+F10=Exit  Esc=Back                                     F1=Help   │
└──────────────────────────────────────────────────────────────────────┘
```

Figure 5.12   Specifying driver names for the disk drive controllers

The next step is to identify the network card. This process is similar to the one used to identify hard disk controllers and disks. If the installation program doesn't detect the network card automatically, you can provide a floppy disk with the .LAN drivers for the network card. Figure 5.13 shows the screen used to confirm the types of storage devices and network boards that NetWare detected.

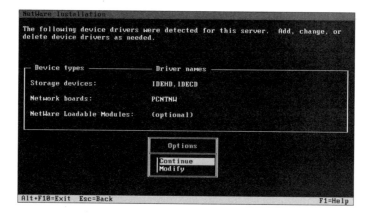

Figure 5.13   NetWare installation screen reporting detection of an IDE hard disk, an IDE CD-ROM, and an AMD Ethernet card

After the drivers for the disk controllers and network card have been loaded, you're taken to a screen at which you can set up the SYS volume for your NetWare server. By default, NetWare will attempt to create a SYS volume as large as the remaining space on the first hard disk. Although this volume can be as small as 350 MB at the absolute minimum, it's recommended that you allocate 1 GB or more so that additional space is available for server-based application installations. Figure 5.14 shows this screen.

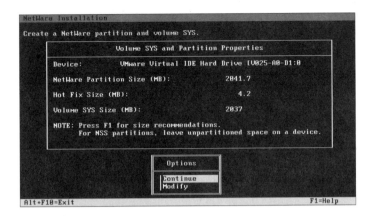

```
NetWare Installation
Create a NetWare partition and volume SYS.
            Volume SYS and Partition Properties
    Device:        VMware Virtual IDE Hard Drive [V025-A0-D1:0
    NetWare Partition Size (MB):        2041.7
    Hot Fix Size (MB):                     4.2
    Volume SYS Size (MB):               2037
    NOTE: Press F1 for size recommendations.
          For NSS partitions, leave unpartitioned space on a device.

                        Options
                        Continue
                        Modify
Alt+F10=Exit                                        F1=Help
```

Figure 5.14   Setting up the SYS volume for a NetWare server

At this point the installation program will copy all of the files necessary to start
the pseudo-graphical version (with menus and pop-up windows) of the installation program. The first step in the graphical installation is to name the server. The
server name can be between 2 and 47 characters in length and should be unique
on the network.

Next you're given an opportunity to create additional volumes in either the traditional Netware volume format or Novell Storage Services (NSS) format. The new
NSS format offers increased flexibility and is advisable for new installations.
After you've created all of the volumes you need, you are asked whether you
want to mount the volumes immediately or at the end of the installation when the
server reboots. Depending upon the size of the additional volumes, mounting
them can take quite a while, so you may want to delay this until the next reboot.

The next step is to select the networking protocols for the installation. Historically, NetWare has used its own Internetwork Packet Exchange (IPX) protocol,
although in recent years it has begun to support the more widely used Internet
Protocol (IP). IP can now be the exclusive protocol installed on your NetWare
server. When installing IP, you must provide an IP address, a subnet mask, and a
default gateway.

Next you must set the time zone for the server. As with Windows 2000, setting
the time zone is important, particularly when multiple servers are present. Problems can occur when the time zone is set correctly on some servers but not on
others. The time zone is also particularly important when using NetWare Directory Services (NDS), because NDS needs to have an understanding of relative
time so it can post changes in the correct order.

The next steps are related to establishing an NDS tree or joining this server to an
existing tree. Essentially, to add the server to an existing tree, you select the tree,
select a location within the tree for the server, and provide a user name and password with the authority to add servers.

Now you need to supply your licensing information. This information is provided on the license floppy disk, and it is necessary to allow more than two connections to be made to the server. The license floppy disk contains the number of users that the server is licensed for, and it should have been included in the same box as the CDs you used to install NetWare 5.

The final step in the installation is an opportunity to install additional included products on the server. This step involves little more than specifying the options to be installed and then selecting the Next option. The system then copies the files from the CD onto the system.

Once you've completed this step, all that's left is a reboot to make the server available and the configuration that must take place on a Novell server to make it suit the needs of the environment.

Installing Linux

Linux was once probably the hardest operating system to install. Although great progress has been made over the last few years in terms of reducing the complexity of a Linux installation, it's still more complex than a Windows 2000 installation.

There are several Linux distributions, each with its own installation procedures, quirks, and requirements. For this discussion, we'll focus on Red Hat Linux 7 because it's one of the most widely accepted Linux distributions, particularly for servers.

One of the concerns with Linux, more so than with other operating systems, is selecting the correct driver for the devices you have. Linux doesn't detect all devices automatically, and often you must specifically select the appropriate device driver from hundreds and even thousands of possible drivers for each type of device. The server log (discussed in Chapter 1) that you've started for the server should include the specific device information for every device and the version of the installed firmware. It's even a good idea to get the information on the motherboard chipsets and BIOS before starting the installation.

Starting the Installation

Starting the Red Hat Linux 7 installation is generally as simple as inserting the CD-ROM and rebooting the server. Most servers today will boot from their CD-ROM drives, and since the Red Hat Linux 7 CD-ROM is bootable, you should be brought directly to the installation program. If you downloaded Red Hat Linux (other than as an ISO image for burning your own CD-ROM), you'll need to create a boot disk. You can do this by extracting the files, navigating to the DOSUTILS directory (which contains utilities designed to be used in a DOS/ Windows environment), and running the rawrite program. When prompted, you'll want to provide the images\boot.img file that was also extracted. This will create a bootable floppy disk that you can use to start the installation process.

This procedure for creating a bootable floppy is also useful when an older machine with an older BIOS refuses to boot directly from the installation CD-ROM.

Running Anaconda

Anaconda is the Red Hat installation program. It's the text-based and graphics-based program that guides you through installing Red Hat Linux. Its very first screen, shown in Figure 5.15, asks you to make a significant decision as to type of installation you want to perform: graphical, text, or expert. The text installation is not quite as flexible as the graphical version, so you should begin by selecting the graphical installation. If Red Hat Linux is unable to detect your graphics adapter and the display becomes unreadable, just reboot your system and select the text installation. You can use the text-based installation program and then adjust any settings or add any additional features after the operating system is installed. The text mode has many of the same screens as the graphical mode, but not always in the same order. Figure 5.16 shows the text-based welcome screen.

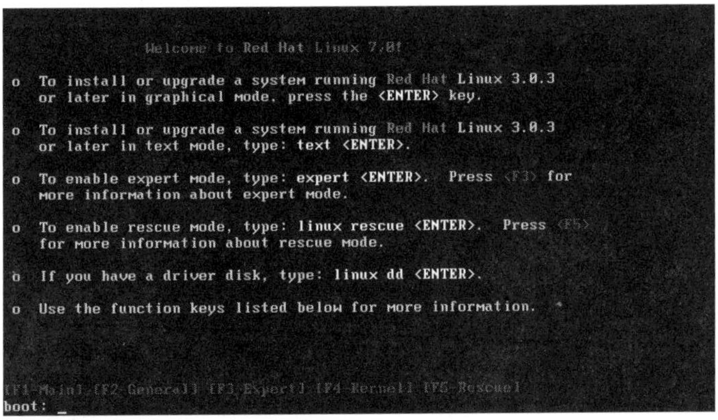

![Welcome to Red Hat Linux 7.0 installation boot screen showing options for graphical, text, expert, and rescue modes]

Figure 5.15 Choosing an installation mode for Red Hat Linux

Figure 5.16 Red Hat Linux welcome screen in text mode of installation

The next two screens allow you to configure your keyboard and mouse. These critical input devices are often easy to configure. Keyboards are relatively standardized at 101 keys, and mice are generally either serial or PS/2. Choosing them should not represent any great trouble.

Next the installation program displays a welcome screen and then asks what kind of Red Hat system you wish to install: a workstation, a server, a custom installation, or an upgrade to an existing system. Select the server option. This will install most of the components that your server will need. Although it won't install some options that can be useful, such as the X Window server that allows Linux to support graphical interfaces, this predefined setup will most closely mimic the installation you will probably want for your server. It will later allow you to install the Berkeley DNS Server, Apache Web Server, Sendmail (e-mail support), Network File System (NFS), Samba, and many other services.

The next screen to appear is the automatic partitioning screen. This screen allows you to let Linux size your partitions for you. Automatic partitioning is probably not the best option for a server. It will remove any existing partitions, including any vendor utility partitions, from the system.

If you don't intend to let Linux partition your disks automatically, you can partition them manually, using either Disk Druid or fdisk. In either case you'll want to create boot, root, and swap partitions. You can create any additional partitions you would like now, or you can wait until later.

After partitioning the hard disks, you'll need to format the partitions. This is the next step in the installation process. You're given the option to format only or to format while checking for bad blocks. Checking for bad blocks takes significantly longer, but it can be useful when you're first installing a server and you're not sure whether there are errors on the drive.

Note You can skip bad block checking if you're using a hardware RAID controller. The RAID controller will check for bad blocks, or sectors, when building the array.

Once you have completed the formatting step, if your network interface card or cards were detected, you will be prompted to enter IP information for each of them. It's not recommended that you allow servers to use DHCP-assigned addresses, although that option is listed.

After configuring the network card, you're prompted to set up the time zone that the computer is in. The graphical display of the world and the cities can be useful if you're not sure of your time zone. Unfortunately, if you're stuck configuring your server in text mode you won't see the global map. All you'll see is a list of cities, as shown in Figure 5.17.

Figure 5.17   City list in the text-based installation of Red Hat Linux

The next step is to add a local user account for yourself as well as for anyone else you would like to provide specific access to this machine. It's probably enough to add yourself at this point. You'll have that account in addition to the root account that you can use for logins.

Note If you're installing Linux/UNIX servers and clients and you're not using a unified security structure like Network Information System (NIS), you should consider investigating it. It will keep you from having to create separate accounts on each machine.

The next step in the installation involves selecting the software and documentation that you want to install on your server. Each software package and its associated documentation is collected into a package that you can select or deselect. Package groups are created from a series of packages that seem to fit together. This step shows you a list of package groups that you can select or deselect. You can either allow the default selections for the installation group you selected earlier, or you can select individual packages for installation. Selecting individual packages for installation can be a tedious job, because so many are listed; however, it's a process that you'll have to go through at some point to install options that are not included in the server installation by default.

Note Because of the open source heritage of Linux, it's more a collection of separate works than a single, unified operating system. The number of packages available for installation in Linux is evidence of this. There are several packages that do the same thing. If you're confused, you should accept the defaults now and come back later to install the packages for the additional services you need.

If, when you click Next, you receive a message stating that there are unresolved dependencies, simply select the option to install packages to satisfy dependencies and click Next. This will install any of the packages required by the packages that you have already selected.

The final step is to let the installer copy all of the selected packages to your hard disks. Depending upon the packages you selected, this might take a while. After the files are copied, your system will reboot and will then be ready for you to complete the installation by configuring devices and downloading updated drivers.

Lesson Summary

This lesson described the major steps involved in installing an operating system. It also walked you through the basic steps of installing Windows 2000, Novell NetWare 5, and Red Hat Linux.

Lesson 3: Configuring the Network Operating System

The details of configuring any one of the operating systems discussed in this chapter would fill an entire book. In fact, for each operating system there are dozens of books dedicated to the installation, configuration, and maintenance of servers. It is not my intention here to cover all of the material that may be located in each of these volumes; rather, I'll simply address the configuration activities that are common to all of the operating systems. These activities must be performed to make the operating systems useful to their users.

After this lesson, you will be able to

- Install service packs, patches, and updates
- Establish or implement a security system
- Install standard applications

Estimated lesson time: 120 minutes

Installing Service Packs, Patches, and Updates

After you've installed the operating system and all of the necessary options, your best bet is to gather and implement patches, updates, and service packs. It is important that you first install all of the additional components you need before applying any updates. This is because some service packs install updates only for components that are installed, and occasionally installing an option will accidentally overwrite updated files from the service packs.

Note Most of the discussion that follows applies to operating systems supported by a single vendor, but it doesn't really apply to Linux. Because Linux has no single person who tests the operating system, patches, and updates, the updates aren't gathered into neat little packages called service packs. Instead, there's just the process of monitoring the continuing stream of updates.

The process of finding updates varies by operating system vendor, but in general, updates are distributed in two ways. At first updates are distributed individually, one at a time, as they become available. After a certain number of updates have been completed, they are bundled and run through additional testing. Those bundled sets of updates are the service packs we've all become so familiar with.

Each service pack normally includes all of the patches included in the previous service pack, in addition to the new patches. As a result, you need to install only the latest service pack on a server for all of the updates to be applied.

Once you've applied the latest service pack, it's time to review all of the available "hot fixes," or unbundled patches. The vendor's Web site generally lists all of these patches. The decision to install a patch that wasn't bundled into a service pack is quite a murky one. Each patch is tested to some degree when it's released, but an additional round of testing takes place when the service pack is created. This means that an individual patch has undergone much less testing than a patch that has been bundled into a service pack. Figure 5.18 shows the Microsoft Windows Update site and the patches and service packs that it lists for a Windows 2000 server.

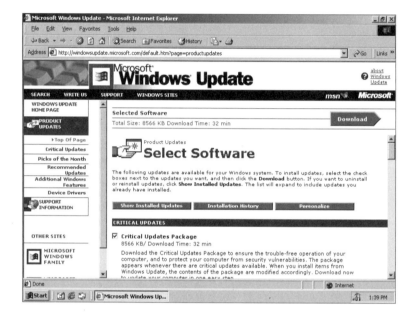

Figure 5.18   Windows Update site, listing critical updates first

This issue of testing is important because many people, myself included, exercise caution even when new service packs come out. Often I install service packs into a development environment or on personal test systems. This allows me to perform additional testing in my environment.

Understanding the caution with which many approach installing service packs will help you understand the extreme caution that most professionals exercise when installing unbundled patches. Individual patches haven't been tested as extensively, nor are they installed in as many environments, so unexpected side effects may occur. However, if there is a patch for a problem that's likely to affect your environment, you should consider testing and implementing it.

Note One of the features Microsoft included with Windows 2000 was a Windows Update feature. This feature allows for the interactive selection of updates that you want to apply to a server. There's even an add-on utility called Critical Update Notification that allows Windows 2000 to notify you when a critical update becomes available. By running Windows 2000 and the Critical Update Notification utility on your workstation, you can be notified when important updates are available that should be applied to your workstation as well as to the server.

Critical updates are updates that fix security or severe stability problems. They are often created in response to a security hole that is discovered. It should be noted that some of the critical updates that address security are focused more on preventing users from accidentally infecting a server than on actual holes in the operating system.

Implementing Security

The need to implement security to protect an organization's computing resources is ingrained into our professional culture today. Recall that Chapter 2 talked about the physical aspects of server security. This section looks at the basic software security system used by different operating systems and gives suggestions for implementing security that will protect your resources without hindering your users' legitimate needs for access.

As you know, most network operating systems establish security by means of a user name and password. Technically, however, the user name and password simply establish an identity. Security involves controlling access to resources based on that identity. Although there are different mechanisms by which operating systems establish and determine security, the basics are fundamentally the same.

How Security Works

A user is issued a user name and password that establishes that person's identity. The user is associated with one or more groups. Groups are logical groupings of users with similar characteristics. For instance, the members of the accounting group might all have access to the accounting directory or to the accounting application.

Access to resources is assigned to the resource. Resources include files, directories, printers, and so on. The access is associated with a user or a group. If the access is associated with a group, it applies to every member of that group. In NetWare, Windows 2000, and OS/2, the preference is to assign all access through groups when possible; doing so makes the administration of the system easier.

In Linux, assigning access is a bit trickier because the default file system under-stands only a single group per file. While NetWare, Windows 2000, and OS/2 inherently understand the idea of a many-to-many relationship among users, groups, and files, Linux does not. A *many-to-many relationship* between users and groups means that a user can belong to multiple groups and a group can con-tain multiple users. Although Linux allows a many-to-many relationship between users and groups, the default file system supports a single group owner and single user owner of a file. To be able to support the access control lists neces-sary to completely implement many-to-many relationships, Linux requires a ker-nel patch. This patch allows a single resource, such as a file, to have multiple accesses assigned to it.

Linux supports only three different modes of access that can be combined. They are read, write, and execute. Read access gives the user the ability to read the file. Write access allows the user to write to the file. Execute access, as you may have guessed, allows the user to execute the file.

Note The default is for Linux to support three localizations of security: User, Group, and World. These accesses are set via the chmod utility using a single numeric digit for each localization. Read access is 4, write access is 2, and exe-cute access is 1. These are added together when the localization has more than one of them.

NetWare, Windows 2000, and OS/2 understand a slightly more expansive secu-rity system based on CRUD, short for create, read, update, and delete. This mechanism allows tighter control over what can be done within the resource, particularly if it's not a file. In addition, because the file systems for NetWare, Windows 2000, and OS/2 support a many-to-many relationship among users, groups, and access control lists for a file, security can be assigned completely from groups.

Note One of the concepts that we don't cover here is *auditing*. Auditing involves keeping track of what has been done, usually via an audit trail, and it can, in some operating systems, be selected by user and by resource. If you suspect that you're having a problem with security, auditing the system will provide addi-tional information that can help you identify which users are accessing given information.

Suggestions for Implementing Security

Security is one of those features within an operating system that, when estab-lished correctly, will serve you well. It will be flexible enough to support chang-ing organizational structures and will be robust enough to prevent users from accessing files that they are not supposed to access.

However, if the plan for establishing security is not well thought out, it can be the biggest headache you'll face in supporting a network. You'll spend a great deal of time establishing security, only to find that users can't get to places that they should have access to and can get to places that they shouldn't have access to.

The following are some loose guidelines and suggestions for dealing with security. They are by no means exhaustive, but they are a good framework to start from.

- **Less is more.**   Simply put, establish as little security as is appropriate for your environment. The less complex the security is, the less time you'll have to spend setting it up, and the less chance there is for errors.

- **(Almost) always use groups.**   Establishing security by groups is an important way to simplify the process of adding security. Once you've established the appropriate groups, you can grant them access to the resources. Then, as new users are added, you need only add them to the appropriate groups. This process is substantially quicker than duplicating access for each new user, which requires duplicating every access that a user has to every resource.

- **Understand inherited rights.**   In each of the operating systems (except Linux), there are inherited rights that flow down through to the resources below. For instance, if you have write access to a directory, and the inherited rights mask hasn't been changed, you'll have write access to all of the files in the directory.

- **Set access at the highest level.**   Access should be set at the highest level possible, not on each individual file or directory. The idea is to do as little administration as practical. By establishing access at the highest possible level, you can allow the access to flow down to the lower levels. For instance, instead of setting file access on the directories \MYDIR\DIR1 and \MYDIR\DIR2, you could set it on \MYDIR and let the access flow down to \MYDIR\DIR1 and \MYDIR\DIR2. This assumes, of course, that there is no reason why the user shouldn't have access to all of \MYDIR.

- **Create password policies.**   A user name and password are supposed to uniquely identify a person, but if the password is given to another user for temporary use, is observed, or is too easy to guess, it isn't an effective identification method. Setting appropriate password policies with regard to their length, their ability to be guessed, and the length of time that they are valid helps ensure that a password does identify a user.

Installing Client Software

The first real test of a server is setting up a client to talk to it. The goal, of course, is to allow clients to get services from the server. If you can't get a client to talk to the server, there's little point in having it. Setting up a client to talk to the server has become significantly easier as Windows 95/98 and Windows 2000 clients are now assumed, having replaced MS-DOS and Windows 3.x.

Windows 95/98 and Windows 2000 support networking clients natively. That is, they allow for the installation of operating system client software that makes Windows aware of the services a server has to offer. Microsoft includes clients for both Novell and Microsoft with Windows, and Novell offers a separate NetWare client for Windows.

Linux isn't completely left out—your Linux server can pretend to be a Windows server by using the Samba software. Samba allows the Linux server to communicate using the same server message block (SMB) structure that Windows servers use. Additionally, several third-party clients allow Windows machines to use NFS shares. NFS shares are the "native" file-sharing method of Linux and its UNIX cousins.

The biggest challenge for most people is not installing the client software, because that process has become so simple. The biggest issues are generally related to cabling and hubs. Chapter 13, Lesson 3, discusses cable scanners and issues related to cabling. If you can't get a client that you've set up to talk to the server, you may want to jump ahead and read that discussion to see whether it can resolve your problem.

Installing Standard Applications

Your organization may or may not have created requirements for the kinds of software that must be installed on the servers. If you don't have these types of guidelines in place, you should give some consideration to standard pieces of software that will simplify the process of maintaining the server. The list that follows describes applications that can improve your ability to maintain the server:

- **Remote control software.**   Remote control software allows you to make changes to the server that can be done only from afar. Novell bundles a remote console application with NetWare, and Windows 2000 allows you to run Terminal Services in remote administration mode so that you can run applications on the server remotely. OS/2 doesn't include any remote control software, but you can purchase and install add-on products that allow you to take control of an OS/2 server. Linux natively supports telnet sessions and X Servers, so remote control software isn't necessary.

- **Antivirus software.**   Protecting against malicious computer viruses is a fact of life in today's environment. Antivirus software installed on the server protects the server and also keeps the clients from infecting one another through the server. If your organization doesn't have standard antivirus software, you'll want to look for an antivirus program that automatically updates its virus definition files.

- **Mini-firewall software.**   Even though most servers are hidden behind corporate firewalls, mini-firewall software that prevents access to the TCP/IP ports except for those that you specifically allow is often a good idea. This prevents internal users from taking advantage of known security issues with the operating system to access sensitive information. Mini-firewalls are most often used in conjunction with Linux, but they can also be used to help other operating systems.

- **Application metering software.**   Monitoring what software is being used from the server is not only a requirement for licensing, it's also useful in helping you determine what training might be necessary. The more an application is used, the more likely it is that training would be helpful. On the flip side, if certain applications on the server are never being used, perhaps they could be removed, or more training might be necessary to encourage people to use them.

- **Event monitoring software.**   Event monitoring software monitors and reports events or errors on the server. Various types of monitoring software exist, some of which may not need to be installed on the server itself. But establishing monitoring prior to placing the server in production is a good idea.

- **Time synchronization software.**   As directory services become more and more prevalent in corporate computing, the synchronization of the server's time with a universal clock is increasingly important. If the operating system doesn't support time synchronization internally, you should install additional software to maintain clock synchronization.

Other pieces of software may certainly be useful too, but the previous list accounts for the most commonly encountered server needs.

Lesson Summary

In this lesson, you learned the initial configuration steps that should be taken with a newly installed operating system. First you learned to apply any service packs or updates to the operating system to address vulnerabilities and to improve operation.

Next you learned how to implement the security system within the operating system—how users, groups, and access rights are used together to control whether a user has or does not have access to a resource or a file.

You also learned to test your installation from the network by installing the network client on one of the computers connected to the server, and finally you learned some of the standardized applications that you'll want to install on every server.

Review

Here are some questions to help you determine whether you have learned enough to move on to the next chapter. If you have difficulty answering these questions, please go back and review the material in this chapter before beginning the next chapter. The answers for these questions are located in the appendix, "Questions and Answers."

1. What are some of the benefits of installing an operating system across the network?

2. Why do in-place upgrades take so long?

3. You're a busy professional who needs to maximize the effectiveness of your time. You're planning on loading a new server over the course of two days. What steps should be completed the first day?

4. What is the first step in installing most operating systems?

5. What partitions are required for a Windows 2000 installation?

6. Why is the correct setting of the date, time, and time zone so important?

7. What unique partition is used to boot a Novell server?

8. What NetWare volume is required for a NetWare server?

9. Will a .DSK module work with NetWare 5?

10. What kinds of partitions are required for a Linux installation?

11. What is a service pack?

12. When should a patch be applied?

13. A user name and password are used to determine what?

14. What is CRUD?

C H A P T E R   6

Installing Hardware and Peripheral Drivers

About This Chapter

In Chapter 5, you installed the operating system on the server hardware. In this chapter, you'll finish that installation by ensuring that all of the external peripherals are properly connected and drivers are updated.

In the next chapter, you'll start documenting routine tasks related to the server. To do that, you need to have fully completed the installation of the server and the peripherals, so let's get started.

Before You Begin

To complete this chapter, you should have

- Your server hardware and peripherals
- The network operating system installed on the server

Lesson 1: Configuring External Peripherals

Now that you've installed the operating system on the server, you need to make sure that all of the external devices are attached completely and correctly. For most servers this means connecting the uninterruptible power supply (UPS), installing the UPS monitoring software, and installing the drive cabinets.

After this lesson, you will be able to

- Connect a UPS to the server
- Connect external drive cabinets

Estimated lesson time: 15 minutes

Understanding UPS Connectivity

UPSs are designed to be a solution to power problems that are transient in nature. They cannot provide an endless supply of electricity to a server. Because they are designed only for transient outages, it's important for the server to know when its UPS has been activated. If the UPS stays active for too long, the server should shut itself down gracefully before the UPS runs out of power.

Today most UPS manufacturers make software that is installed on the server to receive messages from the UPS about its operating status. Despite the many differences in this software, there are some common themes:

- **Connectivity.**   Most UPS monitoring software communicates with the server through a serial cable or a Transport Control/Internet Protocol (TCP/IP)–based network connection.

- **Event log.**   This log contains a history of all of the events that the UPS has gone through. It is sometimes contained on the device itself, rather than on the server. The event log is helpful when determining the cause of a UPS failure and in reviewing utility power reliability.

- **Event notification.**   This consists of a method of notifying the operator of problems, operational information via SNMP traps, and broadcast notifications over the network.

- **Status review.**   This interface permits you to review the operating status of the UPS unit. Often this includes the battery status and input and output voltages, as well as the temperature of the unit.

- **Scheduled testing.** Some UPSs allow themselves to be tested at regular intervals to ensure that the batteries and inverter (which converts DC to AC power) are functioning properly. The method for performing this test varies from unit to unit but sometimes involves transferring the output to the batteries, possibly resulting in power loss. It's best to schedule these tests during a time when the system is least likely to experience corruption due to open files or activity if the power to the server is lost.

In addition to these common characteristics, UPSs generally share a common set of messages that they send to the server to indicate their status. The following list is not exhaustive, but it shows some of the more important messages a UPS would send:

- **On battery.** This message from the UPS indicates that it is operating on battery. It can occur any time the UPS determines that the input power is unacceptable, such as during brownouts and blackouts. It can also be caused by power that is out of frequency range or is too high.

- **Low battery.** The UPS sends this message when the batteries are almost depleted. Sometimes the user can configure the threshold at which this message occurs. This is the message that is generally used to trigger automated server shutdowns.

- **UPS shutdown.** This message can be sent to the UPS to tell it to turn itself off. It is often used when the servers have completed (or nearly completed) shutdown and can safely have power removed. The shutdown message generally has a user-configurable delay to allow the server to complete its shutdown event.

- **UPS overloaded.** This message is sent by the UPS to indicate that, based on the existing load on the UPS, should the power fail the UPS will be unable to transfer to battery because the built-in power inverter can't supply sufficient amperage. This condition should be addressed immediately, as it effectively prevents the UPS from operating. If you follow suggestions to load a UPS at 80 percent of capacity at most, this should never be an issue.

- **Bypass on.** Larger UPSs give you the option of bypassing the unit. This is generally done so the unit can be serviced, during which time the UPS is unavailable. If a line conditioner exists within the UPS, the line conditioner may remain active and will work to maintain usable power. This message is a warning to indicate that service is being performed on the UPS.

- **Check surge suppressor.** Units with built-in surge suppression may report that the surge suppressor has become ineffective and should be replaced.

- **Emergency power-off.**   This message is generally logged to the event log of the UPS itself rather than being sent to the UPS software on the server. It indicates that the UPS received an emergency power-off event due to user entry at the keypad or a remote power-off button. This event causes immediate and complete UPS shutdown. Emergency power-off buttons are a safety feature designed to protect people from electrocution.

In addition to these messages, which may also have associated messages indicating that the condition has ended, there are other messages specific to the UPS manufacturer and model. Review the manufacturer's documentation for additional messages that the UPS can generate so you understand what they mean and what corrective action, if any, you should take.

Connecting the UPS to the Server

As was mentioned in the previous section, most UPSs can communicate with the server via either a serial cable or a TCP/IP network. The decision as to which to use is based on several factors:

- **Number of servers protected.**   If a UPS supports more than one server, it's recommended that you install the UPSs on the network and have the servers listen for UPS events. In this way the failure of a single server won't impede normal shutdown.

- **Cost.**   In many cases, the network monitoring module involves an additional cost, whereas the serial interface is built into the UPS.

- **Availability of network monitoring utilities.**   Most network monitoring utilities use SNMP, which is directly supported by the on-board network controller of most UPSs. If you've already established an SNMP-based network monitoring infrastructure, network-based connectivity is preferable.

There is one very specific caution that you should heed if the UPS is connected to communicate via the serial port. Most operating systems today automatically attempt to detect a serial mouse on the first serial port and sometimes on additional serial ports. The detection routine for a mouse has been known to cause a UPS to enter a battery-power-only mode. The only way to reset the UPS is to power it down and then power it back on. If you're running a serial connection to your UPS, review your network operating system documentation and verify that the mouse detection is turned off for the port to which the UPS is connected.

If you're connecting via a TCP/IP-based network, make sure that all routers, switches, and network equipment necessary to reach the servers to be shut down are also supplied by the UPS so that they won't lose power immediately and not convey the message to the servers. If your notification process for power failure includes e-mail or paging notification, make sure that all of the devices necessary to accomplish those tasks are connected to a UPS as well, or the message may never make it to you.

Reviewing UPS Statistics

Once the UPS is connected to the server, via either a serial cable or a network connection, and the software has been properly installed, most software allows you to review the event log as well as the operating status of the UPS.

Reviewing the event log is relatively trivial and will generally show a long list of transitions to battery power as the system detects problems with the incoming power and momentarily supports the load with the batteries. Depending upon the unit, you may be able to review historical operating variables as well.

Most units allow you at least to review the operating statistics of the system and the operating status of the UPS. The following are some common operational statistics:

- **Current status.** Provides a quick overview of what the UPS is doing. It could be on battery, charging, idle, or have some other status. Charging indicates that the batteries are being charged from the most recent on-battery event. Idle indicates that the unit is operating by providing utility power to the output and is not charging the batteries.

- **Input voltage.** Gives the actual voltage being provided by the utility company. Voltages will vary slightly from region to region and from day to day.

- **Input amperage.** Shows the total current drain that the UPS is placing on the incoming utility line. It includes both the powered load and any UPS-induced load, such as the load caused by charging the batteries.

- **Input frequency.** Lists the frequency at which the AC input-power is transitioning. Remember from our discussion of power in Chapter 2, Lesson 2 that alternating current changes direction several dozen times per second. This frequency should be 60 Hz in the United States and 50 Hz in most other parts of the world.

- **Battery temperature.** Indicates the temperature of the UPS at or near the battery. Batteries don't do well at excessive temperatures and tend to generate heat when both discharging and charging. This digital thermometer allows the UPS to monitor battery condition and adjust charging activities to maintain maximum battery life.

- **Battery voltage.** Gives the existing output voltage of the batteries. This voltage is the primary indicator of the battery's charge state and may be expressed in terms of a run time derived by applying a mathematical formula to the battery voltage, amperage, and existing load to determine how much longer this load can be maintained.

- **Output voltage.** Shows the existing output voltage. This voltage should match the input voltage unless the UPS is *line-conditioning* the power (adjusting it to the appropriate voltage) or generating the power itself through the use of the inverter and batteries.

- **Output amperage.**   Gives the existing load of the output. This statistic indicates how many amps are being drawn by the attached devices. If the load exceeds the maximum amperage rating of the unit, an overload warning message may be generated. The output amperage will generally be less than the input amperage during normal operations.

- **Output frequency.**   Shows the existing frequency of the output power. This frequency should match the input frequency unless the UPS is generating its own power.

The UPS's user manual should describe the exact operational statistics that you can review and their meaning to the operation of your particular UPS model.

Controlling the UPS

In addition to allowing you to monitor the UPS, the software bundled with the UPS should allow you to perform other functions. Although it normally doesn't make sense to use the software to control the UPS, doing so can be helpful when, for example, a component of the UPS has malfunctioned or you're trying to diagnose a problem.

Generally, you can shut down or reboot the UPS from the user interface, but it's usually better to do this from the UPS panel itself so that you can visually verify that the attached equipment has been shut down successfully.

Sometimes it's possible to use the software to lock the UPS in line-conditioner-only mode if the batteries are defective and need to be replaced. In this mode the UPS tries to clean the power supporting the systems as much as possible without the assistance of the batteries or inverter. This is a short-term measure that you should use only until you can install new batteries.

Finally, the software generally allows you to initiate each of the tests that the system can perform. These tests can include an audible indicator test, a battery and inverter test, or a complete system test. Remember that initiating testing may cause the unit to fail immediately and thus should be done when the failure of the UPS will have the least impact on operations.

Installing a Drive Cabinet

After a UPS, the peripheral most commonly installed with a server is an external drive cabinet. These cabinets hold the additional hard disks that won't fit in the server's case. Installing some drive cabinets involves little more than connecting a SCSI cable and power cable, while others are more complicated.

Note There's a trend in the industry to reduce the size of the server itself in favor of attaching external drive cabinets. This push is in part the result of the desire to squeeze as much server into as little space as possible.

The installation of a basic drive cabinet starts with connecting the SCSI (or Fibre Channel) bus. With SCSI implementations, the length of the cable is important, and therefore cables between the server and all of the drive cabinets associated with the server should be as short as possible. And don't forget to terminate the end of the SCSI chain.

The next step is to connect the power. The same basic rules for plugging in servers apply to the drive cabinet. It should be plugged into a UPS. If the cabinet has two power supplies, it's a good idea to plug each supply into a different UPS to help ensure that there are no power interruptions.

The final connection is the monitoring connection. In some cabinets, this is a network connection that can be monitored via SNMP. In other cabinets the connection is a serial cable that connects directly to the server. In either case, the vendor-supplied software will be able to monitor the drive cabinet and report on failures, such as power supply or drive failures.

Connecting and setting up this monitoring connection is an important way to ensure reliability. It allows problems to be detected quickly. In many cases, the information provided by the drive cabinet's monitoring software is not otherwise available to the server until a failure occurs. This early warning is important if you have established a RAID array for fault tolerance, because the array is still susceptible to a drive enclosure failure if more than one of the drives in the array is located in the enclosure.

Lesson Summary

In this lesson, you learned about the basic connectivity of UPSs and how you can use the software included with a UPS to check its status in addition to performing automated shutdowns of the systems.

You also learned about drive cabinets and the importance of establishing a monitoring connection with the server in addition to providing drive connectivity and power. This connection is important for fault tolerance and problem notification.

Lesson 2: Updating Manufacturer-Specific Drivers

In Chapter 4, Lesson 1, you downloaded all of the drivers from the manufacturers' Web sites in preparation for installation. In this lesson you install those drivers, using either the methods suggested in the driver documentation or the driver update functions built into the operating system.

After this lesson, you will be able to

- Identify the drivers that need to be updated
- Replace the drivers

Estimated lesson time: 20 minutes

Identifying Hardware Requiring a Driver Update

In the old days, it was simple. If you didn't manually install the device drivers, they weren't installed. In today's PCI-based Plug and Play world, it's still very easy to identify which devices weren't automatically installed by the operating system. In Windows 2000, those devices appear in the Device Manager with a yellow question mark next to them.

Even when you're working with a non–Plug and Play operating system, the process involves little more than unloading the driver that's currently loaded (if any) and manually installing the new driver, following the instructions supplied with it. Since most of the drivers for non–Plug and Play operating systems are loaded manually, you may not even need to unload the previous version of the driver.

Note Just as you should not update firmware unless there's a clear reason for doing so, you should consider not updating a driver once the system has been installed, unless there's a clear need. Although the effect of driver updates is not as dramatic as firmware updates, driver bugs can still cause a server to crash.

Working with drivers is probably one of Linux's biggest faults. Even hard-core Linux fans have admitted that device support is confusing, and it's often difficult to get devices working right. There are two reasons for this weakness.

The first reason is that drivers can be installed in several different ways. They can be compiled directly into the kernel, or they can be compiled into modules that can be dynamically linked to the kernel. Compiling the kernel is a rather involved process that will almost certainly cause support issues if you ever call the distribution's software support line. In addition, modules compiled into the kernel can't be updated or turned off, so upgrading a driver can force you to recompile the kernel. The end result is that there is no clear way to tell which modules have been compiled into the kernel and may be conflicting with the modules you're trying to add.

The second reason is that version numbers are difficult to determine, for both modules compiled into the kernel and precompiled loadable modules, unless the module sends a version string to the console. Although most drivers do output their version information in this way, some do not. If you have the C source code for a device driver module, you can look at it. The version generally appears close to the top of the file.

One way to see whether a module outputs a console message is to use rmmod to unload the module and insmod to reload the module. Reloading the module causes it to send any console messages to the console. This makes the messages appear at the bottom, or end, of the console where they are easier to find.

In NetWare, the story is much different. You determine the version number of a driver by issuing a MODULES command and reviewing the listed modules until you see the one that you are checking. If it needs to be updated, you do so by using the UNLOAD command to unload the module you need to replace, putting the new version in the correct spot on the hard disk (either the SYS:SYSTEM directory or the boot partition), and using LOAD to load the new module.

In OS/2, the procedure for determining the driver version depends upon the type of driver it is. You can review the drivers for network adapters, for instance, through the network control panel applet. The version is listed on the adapter's properties page. Network adapters are also updated through the network control panel applet, and other drivers are updated through their associated applets. The driver manufacturer will inform you which control panel applet to use.

In Windows 2000, the easiest way to identify hardware that hasn't been installed is by checking the Device Manager for items flagged with a question mark in a yellow circle. This icon indicates that Windows 2000 detected a device but couldn't find a suitable driver for it. This normally happens when you cancel the driver installation process during the hardware detection phase. If you delete the device and reboot, you'll be prompted again to find a suitable driver.

You can look at the driver version for installed devices by right-clicking the device in Device Manager, selecting Properties, clicking the Driver tab, and reviewing the driver version listed. A button on this tab also allows you to search for an updated driver.

Practice: Check Hardware Drivers in Windows 2000

In this practice, you'll check the driver version for a Windows 2000 device. This allows you to determine whether the device driver is up-to-date.

▶ **To check the version of a device driver in Windows 2000**

1. Right-click My Computer and select Properties to display the System Properties dialog box. (See Figure 6.1.) The General tab of this dialog box displays the Windows version, indicates who the operating system is registered to, and gives basic information on the processor.

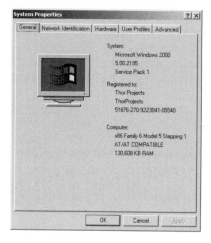

Figure 6.1   System Properties dialog box

2. Display the Hardware tab by clicking it. (See Figure 6.2.) This tab allows you to manage hardware and hardware profiles.

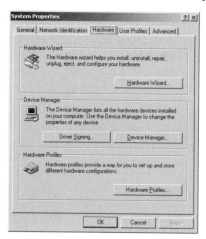

Figure 6.2   Hardware tab of the System Properties dialog box

3. Start Device Manager by clicking the Device Manager button. The Device Manager window lists all of the devices installed in your system, sorted by category. (See Figure 6.3.)

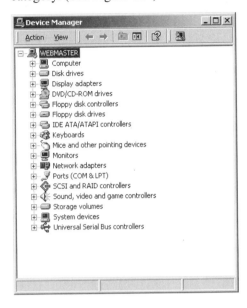

Figure 6.3   Device Manager window

4. Expand the appropriate category for your device by clicking the plus sign to the left of the category. Figure 6.4 shows the Network Adapters category expanded.

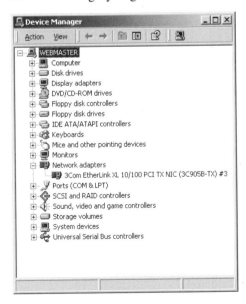

Figure 6.4   Expanding a device category

5. Right-click the device whose driver you want to review, and select Properties from the shortcut menu. The General tab of the device's Properties dialog box shows the type, manufacturer, and location of the device, as well as a summary of the device's operational status. (See Figure 6.5.)

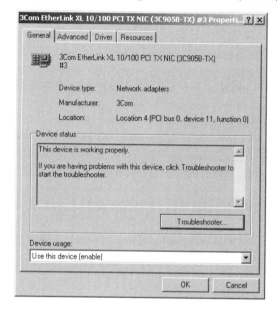

Figure 6.5   Properties dialog box for a network adapter

6. Select the Driver tab by clicking it. (See Figure 6.6.) This tab shows the version and provider of the driver and gives you the option of seeing file-level details, uninstalling the driver, or updating it.

7. Check the driver date and version shown on this tab.

By reviewing the date and version, you can determine whether the driver you downloaded from the vendor's Web site is more up-to-date than the one already installed.

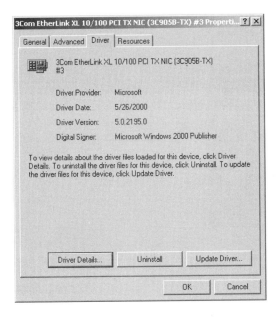

Figure 6.6   Driver tab of the device's Properties dialog box

Practice: Update a Hardware Driver in Windows 2000

In this practice, you'll run the Windows 2000 Upgrade Device Driver wizard to update the driver associated with a device.

▶ **To update a driver in Windows 2000**

1. Display the Driver tab of the Properties dialog box for the device, following the procedure in the previous practice.

2. Click the Update Driver button.

3. When the Upgrade Device Driver wizard appears (shown in Figure 6.7), click Next.

Figure 6.7   First page of the Upgrade Device Driver wizard

4. The next page displays options that allow you to search for a device driver or display a list of drivers. (See Figure 6.8.) Select the default option, Search For A Suitable Driver For My Device, and click Next.

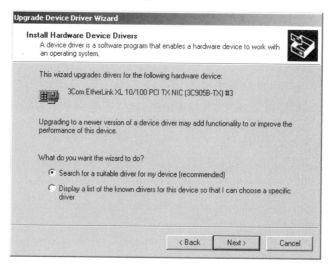

Figure 6.8   Telling the wizard to search for a driver

5. Select from among the locations to search, as shown in Figure 6.9, including floppy disk drives, CD-ROM drives, a location you supply, and the online Microsoft Windows Update service. If you downloaded a driver, select the Specify A Location option so you can give the location of the extracted drivers and select the Microsoft Windows Update option to make sure you have the latest drivers. When you've made your selections, click Next.

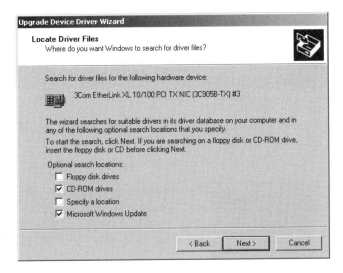

Figure 6.9   Specifying where to look for the driver

6. The wizard attempts to locate an updated driver. The following results are possible:

- **An updated driver is available.**   In this case you'll be given a choice of accepting the updated driver or keeping the existing driver.

- **Alternative drivers are available.**   Although a newer driver is not available, alternative drivers exist that are believed to work with the device, either from another provider or for a similar device. (See Figure 6.10.) To see the alternative drivers, click the Install One Of The Other Drivers option.

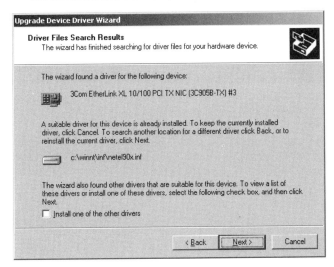

Figure 6.10   Wizard results indicating that alternative drivers are available

- **No updates are available.**   No updated or alternative drivers are available. A screen will appear indicating that there are no updates.

  If the driver you downloaded is more up-to-date than the one currently installed, you'll be given the opportunity to install it. Simply clicking Next will install the driver.

Note Even if you didn't download and extract the drivers, Microsoft Windows Update may be able to find an updated driver for your device.

7. Click Finish to close the wizard. (See Figure 6.11.)

Figure 6.11   Final page of the Upgrade Device Driver wizard

Lesson Summary

In this lesson, you learned how to identify which drivers within the various operating systems need to be updated, so that you can install them by using the features built into the operating system or by using the instructions provided with the driver.

Review

Here are some questions to help you determine whether you have learned enough to move on to the next chapter. If you have difficulty answering these questions, please go back and review the material in this chapter before beginning the next chapter. The answers to these questions are located in the appendix, "Questions and Answers."

1. Which message is generally used to initiate automated shutdown of a server?

2. How can a UPS be connected to a server for notification of events?

3. What might cause the input amperage to be higher than the output amperage in a UPS?

4. What does an "emergency power-off" message in the event log mean?

5. Why is battery temperature important?

6. Drive cabinets generally have three connections to them. What are they?

7. In Linux, how can you determine the version of a driver?

CHAPTER 7

Performing Routine Tasks

About This Chapter

In Chapter 6, you installed the last of the external devices on the server, completing the installation process. In this chapter, you'll learn about some of the routine tasks you need to perform. First you'll check the event and console logs to make sure that everything is functioning properly. You'll also learn how to perform orderly shutdowns of the server, both manually and through an automated procedure.

Before You Begin

To complete this chapter, you should have

- Your server hardware and peripherals
- The network operating system installed on the server

Lesson 1: Reviewing Event and Console Logs

Event and console logs can provide a wealth of information about the operation of the system. They frequently contain both success and failure information, allowing you to determine which components of the operating system initialized successfully and which didn't.

After this lesson, you will be able to

- Review error and console logs
- Identify critical errors that must be addressed

Estimated lesson time: 10 minutes

Reviewing the Error and Console Logs

Every server operating system keeps some kind of log or logs containing important messages about the server's status. These messages may warn of an error that occurred or may just acknowledge the successful startup of a service. In either case, a periodic review of the server's logs is an essential part of maintaining the server.

You can install server monitoring software that reads the event log directly and alerts you when an error is recorded. Although this software is a useful way to ensure that excessive errors aren't being logged, it's not a substitute for reviewing the log yourself from time to time.

There are three basic reasons to review the error logs periodically:

- **Identify critical issues.**   You can locate messages indicating issues that are causing the server to reboot.
- **Identify a progressive failure.**   You can see indications that a given error is getting progressively worse.
- **Manage the log size.**   You can limit the logs to a relatively small size, so that they will be efficient to search.

We will discuss each of these issues in turn.

Identifying Critical Issues

Each operating system records critical issues in a different way. In Novell NetWare, they're called abends and they're recorded in SYS:SYSTEM\ ABEND.LOG. Linux creates core dumps, files containing a snapshot of the system ("core") memory at the time of the failure. Microsoft Windows 2000 shows the "blue screen of death" and creates a MEMORY.DMP file in the Windows directory.

No matter what the operating system is or what the critical error is called, the results are the same: the shutdown of affected services and often a server reboot. Although most professionals believe that they don't need to review a log to know when the server reboots, there are times when a server reboot will go unnoticed. For instance, the server may reboot at a time when no one is using it.

Every operating system logs critical errors in the main server log in addition to the special log and dump files created when the error occurs. Although it may take a more knowledgeable resource, such as one of the operating system programmers, to interpret the contents of a dump file, its mere presence warns the system administrator that something is wrong. You should be on the lookout for critical problems by checking the associated log entries or dump files periodically.

Resolving a problem that is causing critical errors is a bit harder than identifying it. For instance, an IRQ_NOT_LESS_EQ message in Windows 2000 indicates a bad driver. In NetWare, the abend message may or may not indicate the root cause of the error.

The best approach when dealing with a critical issue is to check the vendor's Web site for suggestions as to how to resolve the issue. For good measure, search the newsgroups and the Web for additional input. If neither search leads to a clear answer, try calling the vendor.

Because critical issues can cause the server to reboot, they can remove it from service and eventually cause corruption of the files and/or databases on the server. Unlike the issues that we'll discuss next, these issues require immediate and focused attention to prevent further reboots.

Note Many professionals are hesitant to call for vendor assistance, either because of the cost of the call or because they want to feel as though they have solved the problem on their own. I urge you to spend the money, swallow your pride, and call the vendor immediately. The opportunity loss of downtime generally far outweighs the cost of the call to the vendor. As for your pride, try to remember that the quicker you solve the problem, with or without help, the more competent you will look to others in your organization.

Identifying Progressive Failures

Not all problems are as clearly defined as abrupt service failures or server rebooting. Some problems that start out as minor or intermittent issues progressively get worse, either causing performance issues or indicating an imminent failure. The next chapter discusses performance problems in detail and describes how to create a performance baseline. Here we'll simply look at factors you can use to determine whether a problem is becoming critical. When dealing with critical issues, you need to take the most comprehensive, drastic measures possible. With progressive failures, you should use a more cautious continuum of options.

The following is a list of key indicators of a progressive problem that you should address promptly:

- **Increasing frequency.**   Errors that occur infrequently at first and become more and more frequent indicate a potential for a complete failure. Investigate the service or module that is generating the errors, and research the error.

- **Increasing severity.**   Errors that are increasing in severity should be considered a potential failure. For Windows 2000, this might mean a transition from informational to warning messages or from warning messages to error messages.

- **The presence of any warning or error.**   Any warning or error indicates that something unexpected or undesirable has happened. If possible, investigate these messages and eliminate the cause. In addition to helping ward off potential problems, reducing all kinds of errors minimizes the sheer volume of warning and error messages in the log, helping make it clear what services and modules are not performing correctly.

Managing Log Size

In all operating systems, log files continue to grow larger and larger as new messages are added to them. These logs need to be pruned or archived periodically so that they don't become unmanageable.

In some operating systems, the method for archiving logs is simply to copy the log file and then delete the original file. In both Linux and NetWare, this is the best method for archiving the log files. Windows 2000 has an Event Viewer interface that allows you to save or clear the log. This method has the advantage of allowing transaction-based programs to write to the log. These programs, which process each operation or series of operations atomically, can maintain an open handle to the event log without having to worry about preventing the log from being renamed or moved.

If you're keeping an e-mail log of network activities, as suggested in Chapter 1, you'll probably want to e-mail the archived log files to the distribution list (or to the shared folder) so that they can be retrieved if there's a problem with the server. This will allow everyone to review the previous log entries.

In Windows 2000, each log file has a fixed maximum size. This size is generally too small for most servers. By using Event Viewer, you can expand the maximum size of the log to allow more entries. If you get a message that a log file is full, you should either check and clear the log more frequently or double the size of the log. Transactions that are written to a full log file are discarded, so obviously you'll want to ensure that the log does not become full.

Practice: Review an Error Log in Windows 2000

As mentioned earlier, Windows 2000 has a special utility that allows you to view the error logs. In this practice, you'll use this utility to view your error log and identify critical issues. For the purposes of illustration, I've developed a couple of errors on a machine named WEBMASTER.

▶ **To use Event Viewer to view the error log**

1. Log on to Windows 2000 with an account that has administrative privileges.

2. On the Start menu, select Settings and then Control Panel.

3. Double-click Administrative Tools.

4. Double-click Event Viewer. Figure 7.1 shows the Event Viewer window for the server WEBMASTER.

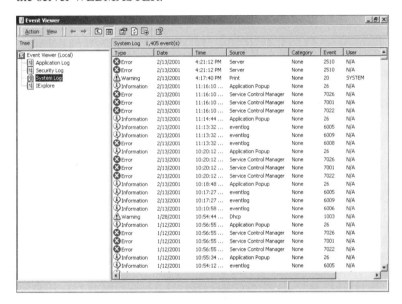

Figure 7.1   Event Viewer for WEBMASTER with the system log selected

5. Select the log you want to view in the pane on the left. (In the figure, the system log is selected.)

6. Double-click one of the errors or warnings in the log. (Figures 7.2 and 7.3 show the first warning and error from the top of the log.)

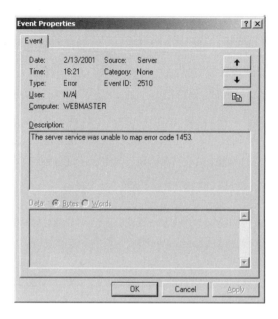

Figure 7.2   A server error message from the system log

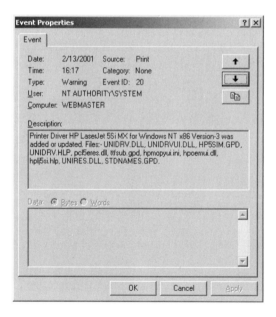

Figure 7.3   A print system warning from the system log

7. Review the message, and determine whether action is necessary.

Note The error shown in Figure 7.2 was caused by an incomplete installation of Windows 2000 Service Pack 1. This was determined by searching the Internet and finding a newsgroup mention of a behavior change between the released Windows 2000 and Windows 2000 Service Pack 1. The print system warning simply indicates that the system downloaded a new driver for the printer. This message lets you know that DLLs were changed, in case there is a conflict.

Viewing the error log is simple and easy. Event Viewer allows you to sort the log by severity and by source, making it a powerful analysis tool.

Practice: Change the Log Settings for Windows 2000

The default log settings in Windows 2000 might work for some environments, but in most it's necessary to adjust them to more reasonable numbers so that events are never discarded because the log is full. In this practice, you'll adjust the settings for your logs.

▶ **To change the log settings for Windows 2000**

1. Log on to Windows 2000 with an account that has administrative privileges.

2. On the Start menu, select Settings and then Control Panel.

3. Double-click Administrative Tools.

4. Double-click Event Viewer. Figure 7.4 shows the Event Viewer window for the server WEBMASTER.

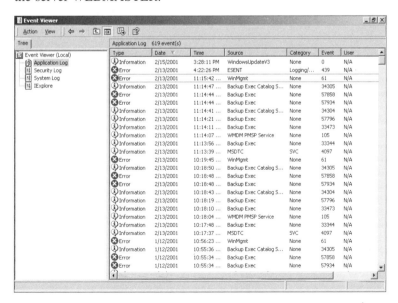

Figure 7.4 Event Viewer for WEBMASTER with the application log selected

5. In the left pane, right-click the log whose settings you want to modify and select Properties. The Properties dialog box for the log appears. Figure 7.5 shows the Properties dialog box for the application log.

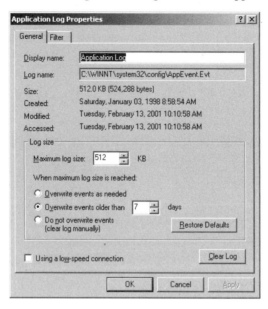

Figure 7.5   Properties dialog box for the application log

6. Set the maximum log size that you want. Logs as large or larger than 8 MB are common.

7. Change the behavior when the log becomes full. For servers, you'll want to set the log to Do Not Overwrite Events.

8. Click OK to accept the changes.

Change the settings for each log. This is particularly important for the application and system logs, as they log the most errors.

Lesson Summary

In this lesson, you learned about the location and makeup of critical error logs. You also learned the criteria to use when reviewing the server logs to identify potential problems. Finally you learned procedures for maintaining the logs and managing their size.

Lesson 2: Performing Manual and Unattended Shutdowns

Starting a server is as simple as pressing the power button and waiting for it to boot. Shutting a server down often isn't that easy because the services on the server need to be shut down first. This lesson reviews the normal shutdown procedures for each operating system and discusses problems that can occur during shutdown. Finally it looks at the issues involved in unattended shutdowns.

After this lesson, you will be able to

- Perform a normal shutdown of a server
- Determine how to handle abnormal shutdowns
- Prepare for unattended shutdowns

Estimated lesson time: 10 minutes

Performing a Manual Shutdown

Shutting down the system should be as simple as pressing a button. For Windows 2000 running on machines that support the Advanced Configuration and Power Interface (ACPI), it can literally be that easy, but in most cases it's not. The reason for this is that the services that are started when the server boots may need to be shut down in a specific sequence or may need to be shut down before you shut down the operating system. In addition, most server operating systems don't understand ACPI and the messages received by the operating system when the power button is pressed.

Note In most operating systems, the order in which services and modules start up is controlled by the modules themselves, or via the service control manager. In any case, the operating system controls the startup of services but rarely specifies or controls the shutdown order.

No matter which operating system you're using, you should always allow the operating system to shut down completely before removing the power, if you can. Powering off before the shutdown is complete can leave the file system and databases in an inconsistent state and generally requires a file system check upon restart. In rare cases, data corruption can occur.

Note Our discussion here relates specifically to shutting down a single server. When multiple servers are involved, dependency issues can make it necessary to bring up or shut down one server before another. Be aware that these kinds of issues exist, and consider them when establishing your startup and shutdown plans.

Shutdown Considerations for NetWare

Shutting down a NetWare server is relatively simple. You simply issue a DOWN command at the console. The command takes effect immediately, unloading all modules and returning to a console prompt. After that, you can power down the system, issue an EXIT command to return to DOS, or reboot the server. EXIT reboots the server if DOS has been removed from memory, and it returns to DOS if DOS is still loaded into memory.

Problems with NetWare shutdowns are relatively rare and generally result in the server not responding after the DOWN command. However, it's not a bad idea to shut down modules before issuing the DOWN command. You can do this by exiting any modules that have screens and unloading any modules that you know consume a large amount of resources.

Shutdown Considerations for Linux

In Linux, startup and shutdown is controlled by the init command. As with most tasks in Linux, rebooting the system can be done in several ways. Each requires root access and is much the same as the others. The first way to shut down the Linux system is to use the shutdown command. This command allows you to specify a delay by using the –t parameter, or you can just pass the now parameter to shut the system down immediately. If you want to reboot, you can pass the –r parameter as well. Alternatively, you can just issue a reboot command that reboots the system for you.

Finally, as the root user you can issue an init command directly, indicating the next state you want the system to be in. An init state of 0 means that the system should be shut down.

Shutting down Linux is generally as straightforward as shutting down NetWare. In very rare cases, programs running on Linux don't want to shut down when Linux asks them to. If the program refuses to respond to a shutdown request, Linux terminates it by removing the program from the run queue and forcibly releasing its resources. It's a rather brutal way to shut down the program, but it generally keeps any problems that the program was having from preventing the shutdown from completing.

Shutdown Considerations for Windows 2000

Windows 2000 is a GUI-based operating system, and thus its shutdown command is issued from within the graphical interface. Generally, you must log on to the server before you can shut it down. However, you can modify the registry on the server to allow it to be shut down from the logon prompt. Directions for doing this are in the Microsoft Knowledge Base at http://support.microsoft.com.

Windows 2000 can sometimes be delayed in its shutdown by rogue programs that resist termination. These programs, including Microsoft's own Exchange Server, can delay the shutdown process by repeatedly responding to the service control manager that they need more time to shut down. Sometimes Windows 2000 will shut down more quickly if all of the services on the server are stopped first, or at least the services that have been known to delay the shutdown. You may want to create a batch file that contains the commands necessary to shut down trouble-some services.

Performing Unattended Shutdowns

Shutting down the system while you're on-site is one thing. Setting it up to shut down on its own is a different matter altogether. Unattended shutdowns are generally accomplished via software, usually UPS software. As we discussed in Chapter 6, Lesson 1, the UPS software can be configured to shut down the server before the UPS runs out of battery power.

An unattended shutdown performed by UPS monitoring and shutdown software is susceptible to the same kinds of problems as a normal shutdown. In addition, there is one other consideration: the server should restart when power is restored. If you don't configure it to do so, the server will shut itself down and won't turn back on when the power is restored.

The process for making sure that the server restarts when power is restored involves two steps. First you must configure the server to turn on automatically when power is restored. This is generally accomplished through a BIOS option. The second step is to configure the UPS to shut down when the server completes shutdown and to restart when power is restored. Shutting down the UPS is generally accomplished through the server software. You should test this process to make sure that the UPS doesn't shut itself down before the server is completely shut down. Ideally, the shutdown process will look something like the one depicted in Figure 7.6.

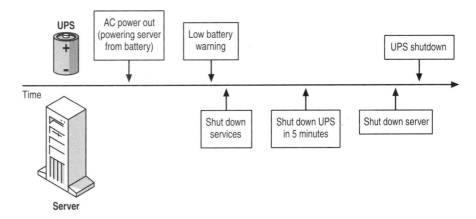

Figure 7.6   The shutdown process during a power outage

The real danger is that the power might be restored for a short period and then go off again before the server can be started and then shut down normally. To avoid this, you should set the UPS to delay restarting after power is restored. The ability to restart the UPS when power is restored is normally available only on larger UPSs. This setting sometimes has a delay option. If there's an option for a power-on delay, it should be set to no less than two minutes, as most repeat outages occur within two minutes.

If the UPS is connected to the server and all of the settings are correct, the server should detect the loss of power and issue any appropriate notifications. The server will then detect the low battery signal and begin the shutdown procedure. Once the server has shut down, the UPS will shut down.

When power is restored, the UPS will wait the specified amount of time and then restart. After the UPS restarts, the server will restart. The UPS will then recharge the battery until the next power outage. Figure 7.7 depicts what should happen if everything is set up correctly.

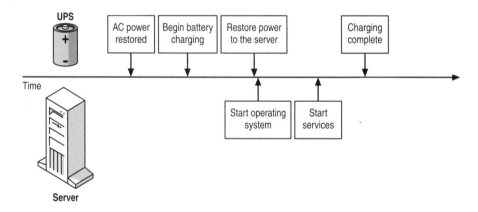

Figure 7.7   The startup process after power is restored

Lesson Summary

This lesson reviewed the shutdown procedures for Novell NetWare, Linux, and Windows 2000. It also discussed the uses for automated shutdown procedures and the settings necessary to make them successful.

Review

Here are some questions to help you determine whether you have learned enough to move on to the next chapter. If you have difficulty answering these questions, please go back and review the material in this chapter before beginning the next chapter. The answers for these questions are located in the appendix, "Questions and Answers."

1. What is the name and location of the Novell NetWare log file that records critical errors?

2. What is the file that Linux records when an abnormal process termination occurs?

3. How does the procedure for resolving progressive errors differ from that for resolving critical errors?

4. What are the two different signs of a progressive error?

5. Why is it important to review the log files of a server?

6. What is the shutdown procedure for a Novell NetWare server?

7. How can Linux be shut down?

8. What two settings should be established for unattended shutdowns to be completely effective?

C H A P T E R   8

Monitoring a Server's Performance

About This Chapter

Chapter 7 began our transition from installation issues to maintenance issues and issues affecting server operation. This chapter focuses on performance information. This information is used to identify servers that are not performing as they should, as well as to identify components of a server that should be upgraded to improve overall system performance.

Before You Begin

To complete this chapter, you should have

- A server on which to collect performance data

Lesson 1: Understanding Performance Data

Before you can use performance data to analyze a system, you have to understand what performance data is as well as what it isn't. In this lesson you'll learn what performance data is, how to gather meaningful performance data, and what performance data can't tell you.

The purpose of performance monitoring is to identify real and potential performance problems. In other words, the goal of performance monitoring is to identify and eliminate real and potential bottlenecks in the server that may affect its performance.

After this lesson, you will be able to

- Identify the steps necessary to collect performance information
- Select the appropriate data to collect

Estimated lesson time: 20 minutes

Establishing Baseline and Trend Data

Most of the data we deal with in computers we analyze comparatively, although we rarely think of it that way. We base our analysis of whether we have enough disk space not only on the amount of free space reported but also on how much space we have used and believe we will use in the near future. We analyze the speed of our CPUs based in part on the speed of CPUs that are currently available. We analyze our need for memory based on how much memory we can have.

Think back five years, when memory was expensive and CPUs barely reached 100 MHz. Even the best server then, the top of the line, would be considered inadequate in today's environment. When purchasing that server, our comparison would have been based on the other systems available, which ran at speeds below 100 MHz. Today, however, when compared with processors exceeding 1 GHz, a 100-Mhz system seems slow.

Most professionals don't realize the extent to which their analysis of data involves more than just the data itself. Part of their analysis is based on their experiences with similar data in other environments. Understanding that most analysis is comparative in nature is essential to understanding how to view performance data. Many decisions regarding performance data are relatively subjective, based on the previous experience of the professional evaluating the performance data.

Since analysis of performance is always relative, performance data by itself says little. To be meaningful, it must always be compared with a reference point. That reference point is called a *baseline*. The baseline consists of performance data collected when the system is operating normally. It establishes what normal performance for the system is so that future runs of performance monitoring can identify what has changed.

Note There is sometimes limited value in reviewing performance data for a system for which no baseline performance data is available. In such cases, you're using experience as your reference point, rather than hard numbers. Avoid doing this when possible. Every system and every environment is different, and assumptions made based on other performance data in other environments may lead to incorrect assumptions about what is and isn't functioning correctly.

Comparing current performance data against a baseline is an effective way to review performance data, but perhaps a more meaningful analysis is done with a series of data leading from the baseline to the current performance data. This type of analysis helps identify trends and the rate at which the trends are progressing. In other words, performance monitoring should be done periodically, not just once a problem occurs. Collecting data periodically also helps you detect slowly moving trends, such as disk space usage, that are not likely to change measurably during the period of time that the performance monitoring utility is running.

Note There is a class of utilities that continuously monitor performance and create the kind of trend reporting discussed here. These kinds of tools are generally, but not always, SNMP-based and offer automatic log management utilities that help you manage appropriate amounts of historical information.

For servers that you maintain, you should consider running the performance monitoring tool every quarter or at least twice a year. The performance data you capture by doing this will allow you to identify subtle trends involving slowly changing data, help you to plan for potential problems, and help you to be proactive.

Tip Slowly changing data can be difficult to spot until it's too late. Set up recurring entries on your calendar to review key measures that are likely to change slowly. This will help ensure that problems don't sneak up on you.

Monitoring Specific Components

Now that you understand the need for a baseline as well as for periodic performance monitoring, you need to know what components to monitor and what to watch for in the performance of each component. In Microsoft Windows 2000, a component or collection of components being monitored is known as an *object,* and a *counter* is a specific aspect of that object to be monitored. For example, Processor is an object, and % Processor Time is a counter, as is % User Time. Windows 2000 further defines an *instance* as an occurrence of a given item. For example, a system that has more than one processor would have an instance of the Processor object's % Processor Time counter for each processor and one for the total value of all the processors combined. I'll adhere to this terminology while describing the aspects of the server's performance that can be captured.

Note Technically, what I'm calling performance monitoring here is actually utilization monitoring. We are analyzing how much various components of the operating system are being utilized. Actual performance monitoring would involve monitoring the various response times to the clients. In practice, measuring response time is difficult to do and is relatively unimportant. The true indicator of whether a system is performing too slowly is when the user community feels that the system is responding too slowly.

The areas that are of the most interest to people are those that closely map to the physical components of a server. They are

- Processor
- Memory
- Disk
- Network

Notice that this terminology is not specific to any particular operating system. These are generic categories that are available in all performance monitoring tools. We'll review each of these objects in turn, as well as the counters they contain.

Note Many of the counters listed here are not available in every operating system. I list them because you need to be aware of them, both because other operating systems include them and because they are good indicators of specific performance problems. I've used the naming convention of Windows 2000 for objects and counters because of its integrated performance monitoring tools. Other operating systems will have different names for the same counters.

Processor

Processors seem to get an undue amount of attention in performance monitoring, probably because of the emphasis manufacturers place on them when marketing servers. Despite this undue emphasis, several important indicators show how extensively the processor is being used and what is making up that activity. The following are some of the counters you should monitor:

- **% Processor Time.** The total amount of processor time consumed by the operating system and all user programs. This counter shows the total average processor utilization for the polling interval. It is generally regarded as the litmus test for whether the processor is the bottleneck. A rule of thumb is that total processor utilization should not exceed 80 percent for a sustained period of time.

- **% Privileged Time.** The total amount of processor time spent in a privileged or system mode. This is an expression of the amount of time that the operating system is using for its needs. This number will frequently include all device drivers. Tracking this indicator is generally recommended, but you should use it primarily to get a feel for what is making up the processor time rather than basing decisions on it.

- **% User Time.** The total amount of processor time spent on nonprivileged or user tasks. This number may or may not reflect services provided by the server, depending upon how the operating system implements the services. Like the % Privileged Time counter, this counter should be used primarily to get a feel for the makeup of the processor activity rather than for direct decisions.

- **% Interrupt Time.** The amount of time that the processor spent servicing interrupts. At high loads this counter shows the efficiency of the interface cards by indicating how effective they are at minimizing CPU involvement. When this number climbs above 15 to 20 percent, the installed cards are beginning to consume the processor's time, and it may make sense to replace them with cards that are more efficient.

- **Interrupts/Sec.** The average number of interrupts generated per second during the polling interval. This counter is similar to the % Interrupt Time counter but is expressed differently. If this number remains low and the % Interrupt Time number climbs, it generally indicates a problem with a driver.

Memory

While the processor gets too much attention, physical memory often gets too little attention. Memory is a mechanism for improving the performance of a server. It is nearly 100 times faster than a disk access, so the more memory you have and the fewer disk accesses you have to do, the better the system will perform overall.

Tip Since the days of Windows 3.11 and the advent of virtual memory on PCs, one of the best upgrades for a PC has been memory. Although historically memory has been expensive, the cost of memory today makes it one of the first upgrades that you should attempt.

Before we discuss the individual counters for tracking memory, there's one very important point to be made about performance monitoring where memory is concerned. Insufficient physical memory will look like a disk problem if you look only at the disk drives. This is because physical memory is used to cache the disk drives and thus reduce the number of accesses to the drives. In addition, when most operating systems need memory and no physical memory is available, they use virtual memory, or hard disk space, instead. When a server has insufficient memory, this virtual memory tends to get used very frequently, which exercises the hard disk substantially.

The following counters are useful for measuring memory performance:

- **Pages/Sec.** The number of times per second that the computer was forced to read a page of memory from the disk drive or was forced to write a page of memory to disk to make physical memory available. A *page* is the unit that the memory manager uses to move information to or from disk. It's most often a 4-KB page of memory. This paging rate should be low, but it might not stay at zero. The internal processing of some services may cause a small amount of paging. Although this counter is frequently used to identify memory issues, it's better to refer to the Available Physical Memory counter (available through Windows Task Manager in Windows 2000) to determine whether enough physical memory is available.

Note Even when a large amount of physical memory is available, the operating system may continue to show that there are page faults (via the Pages/Sec counter). For instance, I have a server running with 512 MB of RAM in my lab. With all services loaded, it still has 120 MB of physical RAM available. The machine continues to show page faults even after a long period of inactivity. For that server, a small amount of paging is normal. No amount of memory will prevent it from paging.

- **Available Physical Memory.** The current amount of physical memory (RAM) that is available for use. Although most server operating systems use both physical and virtual memory, it's the available physical memory that is generally the most important. If the number is excessively low (less than 5 to 10 percent of memory), the system will be swapping out virtual memory for physical memory, creating page faults that will show in the Pages/Sec counter.

Note NetWare has historically required significantly more available memory than other operating systems. Novell's official requirement was 55 to 65 percent of total memory for cache buffers. Cache buffers are essentially available memory on a NetWare server. This requirement has recently changed somewhat. For the current available memory recommendation, please refer to Novell's Web site.

- **Committed Bytes.** An indication of all the memory, both physical and virtual, that has been allocated to the operating system or running applications. This counter is useful to ensure that memory isn't being "leaked" by an application or the operating system. *Leaked memory* is memory allocated to an application or to the operating system that the application or operating system no longer tracks as being allocated, so it allocates new memory. This indicator should climb until the system has been under normal load and should then level off and quit climbing. If the counter continues to climb, it generally indicates a memory leak that should be investigated further.

- **Available Bytes.**   The overall number of bytes of memory that can be allocated by an application or the operating system. This counter reflects both physical memory and virtual memory on the hard disk. If this number is small, the virtual memory size currently defined for the operating system may be insufficient. Although some operating systems allow the virtual memory size to grow on the fly, it's a good idea to define a maximum amount of virtual memory so that it doesn't grow. This reduces fragmentation and improves performance.

- **Cache Bytes.**   The number of bytes currently being used to cache disk accesses. The larger this number, the greater the chance that a disk read can be served from memory rather than from disk. Therefore, the larger this number the better the performance will be. This number is useful primarily in trend analysis to show how memory is being used by the server.

Note Sometimes the operating system reports only cache bytes and not available memory. If the operating system doesn't report available memory separately, you can think of cache bytes as the total available memory.

Disk

Unlike processors and memory, disks require you to track two kinds of information. In addition to looking at the standard performance information that shows how busy the disks are, you must also track how full the disks are. This is necessary because disks are the persistent storage in the server. The counters discussed here address both needs.

Another difference between disks and the other components we've discussed is that disks can be viewed in two different ways. The first way of viewing them is as physical disk drives. This perspective allows you to monitor the utilization of the disk drive arm and other information about the physical disk. This is generally the best way of viewing the performance of drives because you're looking at them as physical components.

Another way of viewing disks is as logical volumes. A logical volume, you may remember, can be made up of more than one physical disk. By reviewing performance counters for logical volumes, you can see the total utilization of disk space and can view most of the other counters that are available for physical disks.

Tip Windows 2000 turns off logical disk (volume) performance counters by default. This saves the small amount of overhead involved in keeping these statistics. If you run performance monitoring software and find that all of your disk counters are 0, you'll want to run DISKPERF /? at the command prompt and follow the instructions to turn on the logical disk performance counters.

The following counters are important for monitoring disk performance:

- **% Disk Time.**   The percentage of time that the disk is busy. This is measured by calculating the time that at least one command is pending for the drive vs. the total time available. If this counter begins to be consistently high, about 80 percent or so, additional disk drives or faster disk drives may be called for.

- **Current Disk Queue Length.**   The number of pending requests to the disk. When this number consistently exceeds two times the number of disks being viewed, you may need additional or faster hard disks. Note that when viewing the current disk queue length for a physical disk in a RAID-5 array, the number of disks for calculation should be one less than the number of drives in the array.

- **% Free Space.**   The percentage of the disk that is available for files. This number should be greater than 10 percent of the disk space because fragmentation becomes prevalent when less than 10 percent of the disk space is free. This counter reports on free space and may indicate the need for additional storage, not faster drives.

Note If disk utilization is consistently high, you should consider defragmenting the drive, particularly if the free disk space is low or has historically been low. Defragmentation of the hard disk will help improve performance and may allow you to delay slightly the need for additional hard disks.

Network

Although the performance monitoring tools on the server are not the best way to monitor a network, these tools should be used as part of a comprehensive monitoring of the server. By monitoring how the server thinks the network is performing, you get all of the information about the server's functional areas together.

Note Some network adapter drivers don't fully (read "properly") support the performance monitoring counters. You'll want to validate any information obtained from network performance monitoring on the server before making any significant network decisions.

If the network in general appears to be the problem, specialized software or hardware called a packet sniffer is a better choice for performing a detailed examination of the network. For more information on packet sniffers and network troubleshooting, refer to the *Microsoft Network+ Certification Training Kit* (Microsoft Press, 2001).

Most of the information that the server monitoring software can provide involves the amount of traffic the server is transmitting and receiving as well as how the adapter is performing. Some of the counters for the Network Interface object you want to pay attention to are as follows:

- **Bytes Total/Sec.**   The total number of bytes received and transmitted per second. This counter represents only the traffic that the server is involved with. Other traffic on the network that is directed between two other machines won't appear in this number. It is a good indication of how much overall traffic the server's network interface is being asked to handle. If this number is getting close to the capacity of the network segment, upgrading the network segment and server network interface to a faster medium may be appropriate. For instance, a 10-Mbps Ethernet interface can handle approximately 1 MBps of traffic.

- **Output Queue Length.**   The number of packets currently in the outbound buffer of the network card. A consistently large number indicates that the network card is unable to transmit the data the server needs to send. This may indicate that insufficient network bandwidth is available or that additional network cards are necessary.

- **Outbound Errors.**   The number of errors encountered while trying to transmit a packet. A high number of outbound errors indicates a network problem. Generally the problem is the result of the failure of a network card other than the one on the server, or in some cases it can indicate a cabling problem. Outbound errors on some adapters can be the result of normal Ethernet collisions.

- **Inbound Errors.**   Similar to the Outbound Errors counter, except that it tracks packets that the adapter received that had a problem, such as a bad cyclic redundancy check (CRC) or a length that didn't match the length reported in the header. A high number of these errors generally indicates a problem with a network card in a connected system or with the cabling or extremely high activity on the network segment.

- **Packets Received Non-Unicast/Sec.**   The number of non-unicast (multicast and broadcast) packets received by the adapter and passed on to the server. Generally speaking, a high number of these packets indicates a nonoptimal environment for the use of network switches. If your network uses switches and you're experiencing a large number of non-unicast packets, you can improve network performance by reducing the number of these packets.

Performance Monitoring vs. Benchmarking

Our discussion here is related to performance monitoring—in other words, determining how the system is performing. A very closely related, and hotly debated, topic is that of benchmarking. *Benchmarking* is the identification of how fast a system is relative to other computers by use of a measurement or set of measurements.

While benchmarking has little practical use to the professional with a single server, the benchmarks provided by vendors can be useful when you're selecting various components for the server and when you're planning for additional capacity. The primary limitation of benchmarks is their inability to accurately reflect the amount of performance improvement you'll receive by implementing the hardware on your system.

This difficulty is based on two factors. First, it's impossible to completely isolate a single piece of hardware for benchmarking purposes. For example, the Linux BogoMips Mini-Howto compares 11 systems based on a 386SX 16-MHz CPU. These systems yielded ratings varying from 1.99 to 2.49 BogoMips. Although the BogoMips measurement isn't the best measure of a CPU's performance, even a measurement such as this one that was designed specifically to determine the CPU speed of a system isn't immune to the effects of other hardware.

The second factor is that the item being replaced may not have a significant impact on your performance. A benchmark represents a relatively isolated performance assessment. That assessment may or may not reflect what you can expect to see in your system. As an analogy, suppose that you replace the tires on your car with Z-rated tires. (Z-rated tires are rated to exceed 126 miles per hour.) It's true that the new tires might be able to go faster, but unless the engine can get the car going that fast, replacing the tires will have little effect (other than draining your wallet; these tires cost $200 or more each).

Managing the Performance Recording Interval

The previous section addressed only a few of the counters that are available for performance monitoring. The total number of counters exposed by a system can be substantial—so substantial, in fact, that the performance data files can get quite large. To control the size of the performance logs, you need to regulate not only which counters are captured but also the frequency with which they are captured.

When reviewing performance data in real time, you generally want to capture and display the data quickly. You want to know precisely what the system is doing and what kind of resources are being consumed for its processing. This might mean a refresh rate as frequent as every second. Real-time performance monitoring is how most people go about making a spot diagnosis of problems. When they're notified of a problem, they open the performance monitoring tools and watch the performance of the server at that particular moment.

Conversely, when capturing performance data for baselines or later review, the goal is to identify trends and overall changes in performance. These changes can sometimes get lost in the detail of data captured every second. Typically, a performance capture will include data collected no more than once every 15 seconds. This rate provides a relatively good definition of periods of activity but takes one-fifteenth as much space as a file captured at intervals of every second.

Some systems that continuously capture long-term data on servers have intervals measured in minutes—typically between 5 and 15 minutes. This data is used more for long-term trend analysis, where even the detail of 15-second intervals becomes cumbersome.

Note Software designed for continuous long-term monitoring generally allows counters to be captured at different intervals. This is useful when you want to monitor different items at the same time but at different intervals, such as free disk space, which might change very slowly, and CPU performance, which might vary dramatically throughout the day.

When capturing a baseline, remember that each counter takes up space and that the frequency with which the performance data is captured can have a profound effect on the size of the performance file. Select an interval that creates a file that is manageable and provides the level of detail necessary to properly evaluate the problem or trends.

Lesson Summary

In this lesson, you learned that performance analysis involves both comparing performance data against a baseline and analyzing data captured over time to identify long-term trends. You also learned about the four basic areas to focus on for performance monitoring—processor, memory, disk, and network—as well as the counters that are important to monitor within those categories. Finally, you learned how the frequency of data capture affects the size of the log file.

Lesson 2: Running Performance Baselines

In Lesson 1, you learned that you need at least one reference point with which to compare performance data. This baseline information should show what is normal for your system, so that when there is a performance problem you can compare the current performance data to your baseline. This lesson discusses what a good baseline is and describes how to actually run the performance monitoring tools for Windows 2000.

After this lesson, you will be able to

- Run the performance monitoring tools necessary to capture your performance data
- Save the performance data to a file for later review

Estimated lesson time: 20 minutes

When to Take a Baseline

Lesson 1 indicated that you need a baseline to compare performance against, but it didn't spend much time talking about what an effective baseline is. There are several times when it might make sense to capture baseline data on a server: before software is installed, after software is installed, and after some users are put on the system.

In general, a baseline produced without any load, such as one taken before you've installed all the software or before you've begun to move the server into production, is of limited use. Although this type of baseline represents the characteristics of the server, it doesn't represent these characteristics while clients are accessing the server.

When possible, it's best to capture a baseline for the server immediately after deployment. In the case of a phased deployment, you'll probably want to create an initial baseline immediately after you deploy the first group of clients and then create another baseline after the installation of all clients is complete. This comparison will be useful for capacity planning. By measuring the change in server performance from a smaller set of users to a larger set, you can reasonably predict the impact of adding more users.

Tip Don't forget that performance is rarely linear. In other words, just because the system's CPU utilization increased from 10 percent to 20 percent when you added 20 clients doesn't mean that adding 20 more clients will cause only another 10 percent increase. Performance tends to remain relatively predictable up to a point, and beyond that point it tends to degrade rapidly. When doing capacity planning, remember to add a slight margin for nonlinear performance.

Generally, baselines are run for a 24-hour period, or at least from one hour before the start of business to one hour after the end of business on a typical day. If the amount of work performed can vary widely from day to day, it may make sense to capture the baseline over several days or even a week. This helps to ensure that you have an accurate picture of how the server is being used.

A good example of when you might want to run a baseline over several days is when the server is used by an accounting department that typically has different processing requirements immediately after the end of the month, when it conducts its end-of-month processing.

You should also rerun baselines any time you make significant changes to the system, such as when you add new hardware or software. In these cases the performance of the server may change radically, making the previous baseline data ineffective for identifying problems. Additional memory, more disks, or a faster processor will generally improve performance and reduce the relative load that is measured on the server.

Tip Most modern operating systems optimize themselves to the demands that they are presented with. This subtle optimization takes the form of disk caching and the swapping out of unused components from physical RAM. For this reason, you should run your baseline and subsequent performance monitoring at the same relative amount of time after a reboot. You may want to perform your baseline after a reboot, since the first thing you're likely to do when you have a performance problem is to reboot the system to see whether it improves performance.

Options for Performance Monitoring

Operating systems differ in how they facilitate performance monitoring. As you might expect, Windows 2000 has integrated performance monitoring tools as well as an SNMP agent capable of reporting the counters discussed in the previous lesson. Novell NetWare allows for performance monitoring through SNMP information and sells a product called Manage Wise that can display and monitor this information. True to form, Linux offers several different ways of monitoring performance. They range from shell scripts and small custom programs to small utility programs to the SNMP support common in both Windows 2000 and NetWare.

Chapter 2, Lesson 4, discussed monitoring options and the traps that SNMP could generate to indicate that a problem had occurred. Here we're looking at another function of SNMP: collecting performance data. SNMP also has other functions, including the ability to perform some limited configuration.

For performance monitoring, a management console polls the SNMP agent on a machine at regular intervals and collects statistics. Those statistics are displayed graphically or are captured in a log file, just as an integrated performance monitoring tool would do. The advantage of an SNMP-based performance monitoring tool is that it can collect information from many different devices simultaneously, allowing you to look at the entire network, including all of the servers and network devices that support SNMP.

The disadvantages of an SNMP setup are that it is more complex and is usually more costly to set up than an integrated performance monitoring tool, which generally requires little or no configuration and comes bundled with the operating system. Although free SNMP monitoring tools are available for Linux, very few of them allow the kind of logging necessary to perform performance monitoring.

As I mentioned earlier, Linux can run performance monitoring via a series of scripts and Perl programs. Linux is a tinkerer's' operating system where each person is free to put together a solution. Several scripts have been designed to monitor and log performance information in Linux. The challenge is that these scripts rarely collect all of the statistics you need to be able to determine which components are not performing as expected.

Practice: Run a Performance Baseline in Windows 2000

Windows 2000 provides an integrated performance monitoring utility that allows you to capture performance data. That data can then be provided in report or chart form. This tool is appropriate for collecting both baseline data and subsequent performance data. In this practice you will learn how to run the performance monitor.

▶ **To create a baseline log in Windows 2000**

1. Log on to the server with an account that has administrative access.

Note In Windows NT, you had to stay logged on to the system to keep running a performance log. This is no longer the case in Windows 2000, so you need not worry about leaving the account logged on.

---

2. Run the performance monitoring tool by selecting Start, Programs, Administrative Tools, and Performance. (See Figure 8.1.)
3. Select the Performance Logs And Alerts option from the tree on the left.
4. Double-click Counter Logs. (See Figure 8.2.) The logs you see listed are ones that have been created previously. A red icon indicates that the log is stopped; green means it is running.

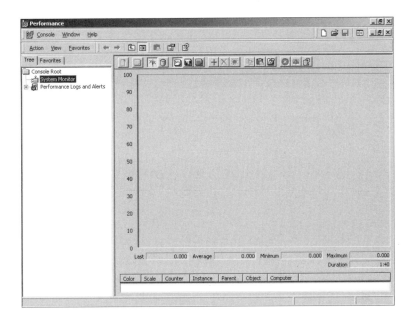

Figure 8.1   Performance monitor snap-in

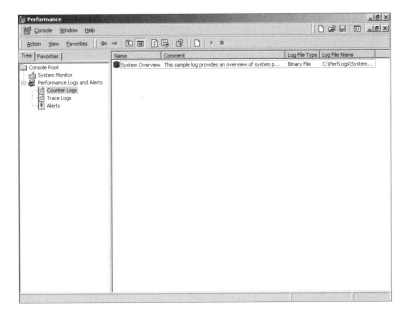

Figure 8.2   Counter Logs display

5. Right-click in the right pane, and select New Log Settings. The dialog box that appears is shown in Figure 8.3.

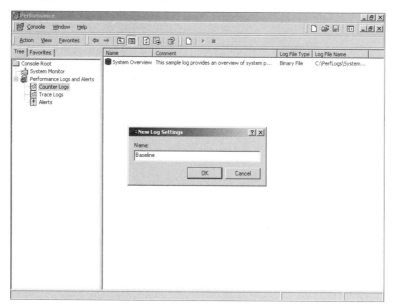

Figure 8.3 Naming the new log

6. For the purposes of this exercise, enter the name **Baseline** for your new performance log and click OK. Naming the log identifies it within the list and forms the basis of the log filename. Figure 8.4 shows the General tab of the new log's Properties dialog box.

7. Click Add in the Baseline dialog box to add counters to the log. The Select Counters dialog appears. (See Figure 8.5.)

8. In the Select Counters dialog box, select the server from which you want to capture counters. Generally this is the local server and will not need to be changed.

9. Select the object to which the counters belong.

10. To capture all counters for the object, select All Counters. To capture an individual counter, select the one you want to capture from the list.

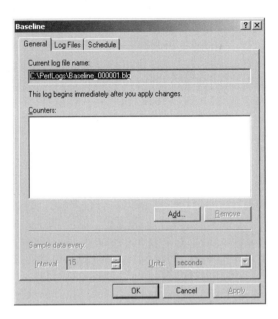

Figure 8.4 General tab of the Baseline log's Properties dialog box

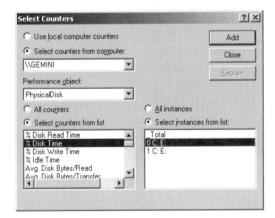

Figure 8.5 Adding counters to a log

Note When creating log files in Windows NT, you had to take every counter within an object. Windows 2000 allows you to select individual counters or all counters within an object. When monitoring certain objects, such as processes, it's advisable to use the All Counters option.

---

11. If you elected to capture an individual counter, and that counter has multiple instances, select either All Instances or a specific instance of the counter.

12. Click Add. The selected counter will now be listed in the Baseline dialog box.

13. Repeat steps 9 through 12 until you've added all of the counters to the log that you want. Click Close in the Select Counters dialog box when you are finished. This returns you to the Baseline log's Properties dialog box (shown earlier in Figure 8.4).

14. At the bottom of the Baseline dialog box, change the sample frequency to something more reasonable. An interval of 1 minute or 5 minutes should be sufficient for your baseline performance needs.

15. Click the Log Files tab to change where and how the files are logged. (See Figure 8.6.)

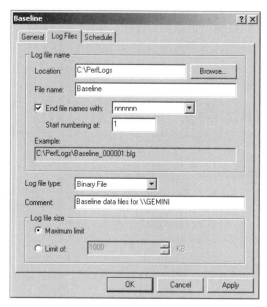

Figure 8.6   Log Files tab of the Baseline log's Properties dialog box

16. Change the location of the log files. The figure shows the default directory called C:\PerfLogs. It's important to make sure that the log file has sufficient space to grow. It's not a good idea to use your boot partition for recording log file data, since it may fill the drive. As an exercise, we will change the directory to C:\NewLocation by typing this path into the Location box. (Figure 8.11 shows the log's new location.)

17. Select a filename to identify the file. Assigning distinct names allows you to keep different kinds of performance data in the same directory.

18. Select End File Names With and specify the numbering option to ensure that each log file is given a unique name.

19. Select a file type for the log. Binary is generally acceptable; however, if you're exporting the data to another tool for analysis, you may want to choose one of the two text formats. The Binary Circular File option allows the file to reach a fixed size and then start overwriting the existing data so that the file doesn't grow further.

20. Select the Schedule tab to specify when the performance monitoring will run. (See Figure 8.7.)

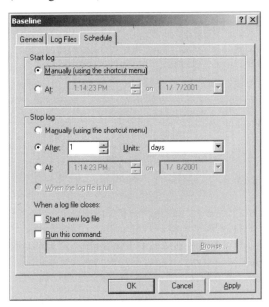

Figure 8.7   Schedule tab of the Baseline log's Properties dialog box

21. Select whether you want to start the monitoring manually or have it start at a specific time. When running a baseline, you'll probably want to set it to start an hour or two before normal working hours.

22. Select when to stop the monitoring. Allowing the log to run for a day is generally appropriate. However, if you want to conserve disk space, you can set the log to end a few hours after the end of business.

23. Specify what to do when the log closes. For a baseline, you normally would not want to start a new log file or run any specific commands. However, if you are doing continuous monitoring of a server, you might want to start a new log file and perhaps run a command to transfer the last log file to a central repository.

24. Click OK to save the performance counter log.

You can now either start the log manually or allow it to start automatically at the specified start time. When it starts, the log begins recording counters, and it continues until either the time comes to stop the log or it is stopped manually. In Lesson 3, you'll open this log file and review the data in it.

Lesson Summary

In this lesson, you learned about the various options you have within each operating system for capturing and reviewing performance data. Windows 2000 provides both integrated performance monitoring tools and SNMP support for integration with other performance tools. Both Linux and NetWare support SNMP as well, and Linux also supports scripts and third-party programs that can monitor performance.

This lesson explored the basic components of SNMP and how they are used to collect data. SNMP agents allow SNMP management consoles to query values to retrieve performance data.

Finally, you practiced collecting a performance baseline in Windows 2000. You learned that the performance monitoring tool in Windows 2000 allows you to collect as many or as few counters as you like at any interval you desire. The log files are created in a directory, and you can later review them with the performance monitoring utility or import them into another application for analysis.

Lesson 3: Comparing Performance Trends

The process of determining which component of a system needs to be upgraded and which components don't is part engineering exercise and part art form. Comparing performance and identifying the component in question requires an understanding of the overall makeup of the system.

This lesson discusses how the different counters interrelate and describes how to sort out which component is the best candidate for an upgrade.

After this lesson, you will be able to

- Identify the root cause of a performance problem
- Anticipate devices other than the root cause that may become problems

Estimated lesson time: 20 minutes

How Components Affect Each Other

One of the biggest challenges in performance monitoring and ultimately in performance tuning is that no component can be viewed in isolation from the others. Disk activity is closely related to the memory (or lack of it) on the server. The CPU speed is related to the performance of the disk controller and of the network controller. The network controller activity is influenced by almost every other component.

Because of this interrelatedness, performance monitoring will point you to the component that is being taxed the most, but that component may or may not be the root cause. Earlier I mentioned that insufficient memory often looks like a disk problem because the lack of memory forces the operating system to use the disk drive as if it were memory. I also mentioned that a high degree of processor utilization and a high number of interrupt requests mean that the add-on cards in the system may not be as efficient as they should be. You might mistakenly conclude that the processor is the bottleneck, only to find that a faster processor does not improve the system performance.

Order of Analysis

Because of the interdependence among components, it is important to conduct your analysis of performance data in a specific order. Lesson 1 identified four basic areas within a server that should be evaluated:

- Processor
- Memory
- Disk
- Network

So that you don't accidentally interpret a problem in one area as involving another area of the system, you should analyze memory data first, followed by processor, disk, and network data. The sections that follow describe what to look for in each area.

Note Although the network can ultimately affect the performance of the server, it's rare for the network to be the bottleneck in today's environment of 100-Mbps Ethernet cards and switches. It's generally the last thing that should be considered as a potential problem for server performance.

Analyzing Memory Trends

The goal in looking for memory trends is to predict when the amount of memory will be insufficient to maintain the server's performance. This prediction can be particularly difficult because the various operating systems have different ways of allocating memory, and the amount of memory they reserve for internal operations also varies.

Even different versions of the same operating system can allocate memory differently and thus have different needs when it comes to maintaining available memory. For instance, at the time of this writing the updated Linux kernel, 2.4, had recently been released, with dramatic changes in how Linux uses and manages memory. When making decisions based on the memory counters and whether sufficient memory remains, use the documentation available for the operating system. The discussion here provides general information that should be roughly applicable to any server-based operating system.

As we discussed earlier, the total memory (including both cache bytes and available physical memory) should not drop below 10 percent of total physical memory. When the available physical memory is less than 10 percent, additional RAM should improve performance.

Note Linux can sometimes be efficient even when it has no available memory and limited cache bytes. NetWare, on the other hand, generally requires more available memory.

When reviewing the memory performance data for trends, make sure that the system is not consuming significantly more memory than at the time of the last data capture, reducing the amount of memory available for caching and for running applications.

If you believe the system is memory bound, you should ignore all disk-related counters, as it is virtually impossible to determine how much disk activity is real and how much is a result of insufficient memory. The counters for the CPU should be relatively stable, although utilization may drop slightly when you add more memory.

Analyzing Processor Trends

The biggest problem with analyzing processor trends as opposed to memory trends is that processor usage tends to be less stable than memory usage. The same amount of memory is generally used over a long period of time. CPUs, on the other hand, tend to have large spikes in usage and then settle back down into troughs of inactivity. This volatility makes determining a pattern or a meaningful average very difficult.

The shorter the frequency of the sample data, the more difficult it is to determine what exactly is going on with the processor. Most performance monitoring tools won't automatically put a "best fit" line through the data, showing the trend for you. You will have to guess whether the activity is increasing or not. (You can export the performance data into an application that has a graphing tool, such as Excel. Most graphing tools allow you to put a best-fit line through a data series.)

Although small spikes of 100 percent CPU utilization can be disconcerting, they are normal and even expected. Seeing any indicator at 100 percent makes one think that it is a bottleneck. In the most precise definition of the word, the CPU probably is a bottleneck for that short period of time, but the rapid return of the utilization back to a more reasonable level indicates that replacing the CPU with a faster one won't improve the overall performance that much.

The trick when analyzing CPU performance is to identify when the CPU is a bottleneck (at 100 percent) for significant periods of time. When this occurs, an additional CPU or a faster CPU is warranted.

If, however, a high degree of CPU utilization is accompanied by a large amount of time spent servicing interrupts, you should consider a more efficient adapter or set of adapters instead of a CPU upgrade. Today's PCI-based, coprocessor-enabled add-on cards can handle a significant amount of the processing and data transfer that the CPU would normally have to do. The impact of faster add-on cards shouldn't be underestimated.

Ultimately, if the CPU does appear to be the bottleneck, and if you followed my earlier recommendation to build the server with the CPU capacity maxed out, you won't have any room to expand the CPUs. When this is the case, it's time to start looking for a larger server or, more likely, to move some of the services that the current server performs onto one or more additional servers. This will reduce the load on a single server.

Analyzing Disk Trends

Upgrading disk drives is the easiest and most frequently performed upgrade to a server. You need to monitor two types of disk trends: % Disk Time and % Disk Space In Use. Both of these counters are fairly simple, and determining trends is relatively easy.

Although % Disk Time will fluctuate just as CPU utilization does, it is generally more stable. However, very frequent data captures will make it difficult to determine the average disk utilization. As the disk utilization climbs higher, consider improving access speeds by adding another drive to the RAID array or converting a single drive to a RAID array.

The total amount of disk space used is much like memory utilization in that it's very stable, and trends are easy to determine if the data points are gathered at long enough intervals. Disk space utilization tends to grow at such a slow rate that any individual performance capture will probably not detect the change. As with the % Disk Time counter, the remedy is to add another disk drive to the RAID array.

The use of the server determines how large the disk for that server should be. File and print servers have a relatively high amount of storage capacity for their level of access activity. Conversely, database servers and transaction-based systems tend to have more access activity for the same amount of disk space.

The significance of this difference is that when you're using larger-capacity hard disks, you need fewer disks to reach the required capacity. With smaller disks, you need more for the same capacity. The more disks there are in a RAID array, the faster the array will perform. This is because having more disks allows reads and writes to be distributed across more devices for a higher total throughput. If each disk is capable of a throughput of 4 MBps and you can spread the requests over four disks, the total throughput may be 16 MBps. However, if three larger disks are used and they perform at the same 4 MBps, the total throughput of the array won't be more than 12 MBps.

Another factor influencing the choice of disks is the speed at which the disk spins. You looked at this issue when planning for a server, but it's also important when you're reviewing performance data. The faster the disk spins, the less time it will take for a requested sector of information to pass below the read-write head. This improves performance.

High-activity applications, such as databases and e-mail servers, call for small, fast disks. For file and print servers, you don't need to invest in smaller, faster disks; larger disks will work just as well for a lower total cost.

Analyzing Network Trends

Looking at network trends is perhaps the best way to determine how the server is servicing clients. The more activity there is on the network interface, the more information is being exchanged with the clients. Still, observing the network traffic from the server is a poor indication of exactly how the system is responding to the clients.

The challenge when you're trying to measure network throughput by looking at network statistics from the server is that you can't really determine when the capacity of the network segment has been reached. Complicating this is the

CSMA/CD (Carrier Sense Multiple Access/Collision Detection) method that Ethernet uses, which prevents 100 percent utilization of the theoretical bandwidth. In practice, Ethernet networks begin to become saturated at as low as 50 percent utilization. The final challenge is that the use of Ethernet switches can cause the overall performance of the network to significantly exceed the simple measure of the transmission speed.

Ethernet switches allow each port to be connected dynamically to every other port in the network. By watching the physical addresses of connected network interface cards, a switch can determine which cards need to receive each transmission. Switches then send the traffic only to the ports necessary. When switches are used with a mix of clients and servers, rather than with a single server, performance is greatly enhanced by the selective filtering of messages.

The best approach when looking at server-based network performance trends is to ignore the performance of the network itself and leave that to a separate analysis, one that can use SNMP to monitor the network devices on the network to determine how they are performing and what traffic they are seeing.

What you can tell from server-based network performance monitoring is the total throughput of the server card. This number can increase until it eventually reaches 50 percent utilization, at which point Ethernet no longer performs consistently. If this becomes the case, upgrading the server to the next higher network channel, or implementing an Ethernet switch between the server and the clients, may be appropriate.

In addition, if the network card begins to consistently show queued packets, you may need to add another adapter and team it with the current adapter to allow the server to fully utilize the bandwidth available to it. Note, however, that the queued packets may also be the result of a saturated network. Before adding a second, teamed adapter, determine whether the network is saturated. If it is, adding the teamed adapter won't help.

The other indicator to look for when reviewing network performance is the non-unicast packets received. Most (or all) of these packets are the result of broadcast traffic. This broadcast traffic reduces the effectiveness of switches by requiring that the traffic be sent to every port. Broadcast traffic can come from many different sources for many different reasons, but most of it can be eliminated.

DHCP broadcast traffic, which is used to configure IP addresses and related information, must be broadcast based and can't be eliminated. However, here are some suggestions to reduce broadcast traffic on your network:

- If you're running the IPX/SPX (Internetwork Packet Exchange/Sequenced Packet Exchange) protocol, don't bind the protocol to different Ethernet frame types. IPX/SPX and the NetWare Core Protocol periodically use the Service Advertising Protocol (SAP) to announce available services on every frame type bound to IPX/SPX. The fewer frame types, the less broadcast traffic is generated.

- If you're running NetBIOS over TCP/IP, as is generally the case with Windows-based systems, use Windows Internet Name Service (WINS) to cause the clients to communicate directly with the WINS server for name resolution, instead of broadcasting for name resolution. You'll also want to change the node type to hybrid to require that the Windows-based client resolve via WINS first and then broadcast if the name isn't found. This will ensure that clients that have not yet been configured for WINS will still be found.

- Remove unused protocols from servers and clients. The fewer protocols that are installed, the fewer ways there are for servers and clients to advertise themselves via broadcasting.

- Remove the NetBEUI protocol. NetBEUI uses only broadcasts for name resolution, and as a result it tends to be very broadcast oriented. Removing the NetBEUI protocol from every machine can significantly reduce the amount of broadcast traffic on the network.

- Identify other broadcast-based protocols and try to eliminate them from your environment. For instance, in Digital Equipment Corporation's Local Area Transport (LAT) protocol, each device announces its presence periodically via a broadcast. Reducing or eliminating the use of LAT on a network can reduce broadcast traffic.

Chain Reactions

Before leaving the topic of performance monitoring, it's important to talk about the impact of new components on monitoring. As you know from our discussion of baselines, changing a hardware or software component invalidates the baseline because doing so changes the server's basic performance characteristics. That discussion didn't go into how those performance characteristics change, however. We'll look at that topic here.

Performance monitoring is the process of identifying and isolating performance issues so that they can be solved. Solving a performance problem generally involves identifying the component that is causing the bottleneck and replacing or upgrading it. This removes the bottleneck or limit from the system and increases the throughput.

However, the inevitable result of such an upgrade is that a new bottleneck is created. If memory was the bottleneck on the server, increasing the memory might improve performance to the point that the processor becomes the bottleneck. The fact is that most of the time, when you go looking for a bottleneck you'll find one.

When planning upgrades, remember that upgrading one component may not make the performance issue go away. When asking management for funds to complete an upgrade, be careful not to promise that it will resolve all performance problems.

Practice: Review a Windows 2000 Performance Log File

In Lesson 2, you created a log file. Now you need to review the data you captured. In this practice, you'll graph the results of the log file so you can see pictorially what was happening on your server.

▶ **To review a log file in Windows 2000**

1. Log on to Windows 2000 with an administrative account.
2. Run the performance monitoring tool by selecting Start, Programs, Administrative Tools, and Performance.
3. Click the View Log File Data button on the toolbar. (See Figure 8.8.)

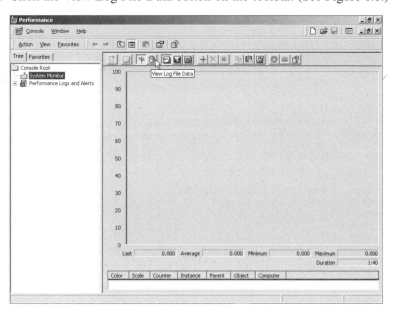

Figure 8.8   Preparing to view log file data

4. Select your performance log file and click Open.

5. Click the Add button (the plus sign) on the toolbar to add performance counters that you captured in the log file to the display. (See Figure 8.9.)

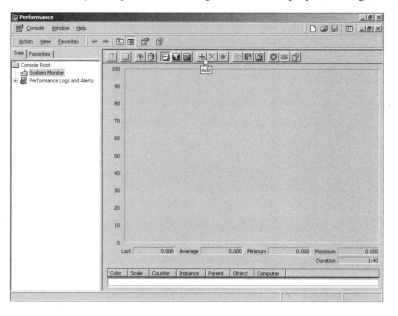

Figure 8.9   Adding performance counters to the graph

6. Select the object, counter, and instance that you would like to have graphed, and click Add.

7. Repeat step 6 until you've added all the counters you want to review. Click Close when you're done. The graphs for the counters you selected appear in the window. (See Figure 8.10.)

Tip Don't try to review all of the counters at once. Instead, review one small subset of the counters at a time so that you don't clutter the chart area until it's unintelligible.

---

8. Initially the performance data may not look useful, as it may cover too long a period of time and some counters may be very low or very high. To fix this, right-click on the graph and select Properties.

9. Select the Source tab to choose the data you want to review. (See Figure 8.11.) This tab allows you to control whether you'll be viewing current data or log data and to specify the range of data from the log that you are viewing.

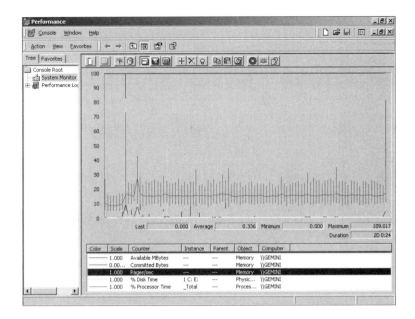

Figure 8.10   Graph of selected counters

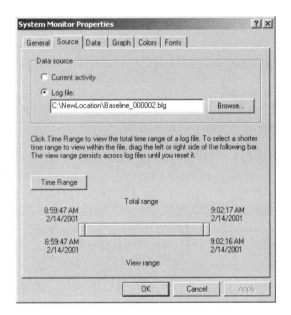

Figure 8.11   Source tab of the System Monitor Properties dialog box

10. Select the time range that you want to see displayed by dragging the box on the left end of the time range bar to set the start time for the graph. Drag the box on thc right cnd of the bar to the left to select the end time for the graph.

11. Click the Data tab to change the way that the counters you selected are displayed. (See Figure 8.12.) You may want to drag the System Monitor Properties dialog box to one edge of the screen so that you can see the graph in the background.

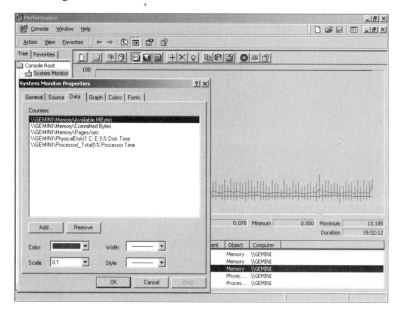

Figure 8.12   Data tab of the System Monitor Properties dialog box

12. Select the first counter in the Counters list.

13. Change the color, width, and style properties to make the counter distinguishable from every other counter. Click Apply to see the effect of your changes.

14. If the counter is either always high or always low, adjust the scale (through trial and error) by selecting a new scale and clicking Apply until the plot of the counter is displayed within the graph space.

15. Select the next counter and repeat steps 13 and 14 until you've tuned the settings for every counter in the list. Then click OK to return to the graph. (See Figure 8.13.)

16. Review the data on the graph to determine which components, if any, are the bottleneck for the system.

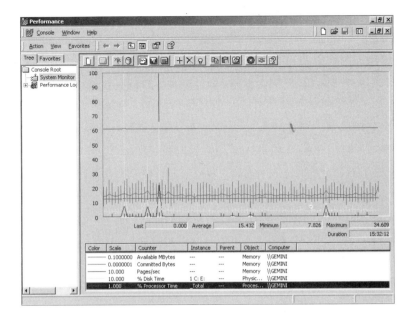

Figure 8.13   A more readable graph

Note The system whose performance you see in Figures 8.10 through 8.13 is a Dual 333-MHz Pentium II system with 512 MB of RAM. It's the system I use in my lab for some services and testing. The system has Windows 2000 installed with Microsoft Exchange 2000, Microsoft SQL Server 7.0, and Internet Information Services 5. Only one client actively uses the system.

An analysis of the data indicates that the system is more than sufficient for the load it's being asked to support. This shouldn't be a great surprise, since it doesn't support a large number of users. There are a few interesting things about the performance data, but for the most part the information is relatively mundane.

Perhaps the most interesting aspect of the data is the regular spike of the disk and CPU counters, like a heartbeat. This pattern is more than likely a result of SQL Server or Exchange Server flushing logs and performing internal checks. If the spikes were more dramatic and if this activity were important, I could capture data on the entire Processes object and then review the counters for each process until I found the one that was generating the activity. However, since so much excess capacity is available, this level of diagnosis probably isn't necessary.

Another interesting point is that even though roughly 120 MB of physical memory is available all the time, the system still generated some paging to disk. Although the paging captured in this log could hardly be considered excessive, it does demonstrate that it is not possible to stop paging on this system.

Finally, the performance data shows no appreciable increase in committed bytes. Therefore, it is unlikely that any program or service installed on the computer is leaking memory. That's a good thing.

Lesson Summary

In this lesson, you learned the order in which you should evaluate whether components are bottlenecks or not and the counters to watch to determine whether certain performance trends indicate an eventual need for additional resources. You also learned that eliminating one bottleneck will generally expose another bottleneck.

Review

Here are some questions to help you determine whether you have learned enough to move on to the next chapter. If you have difficulty answering these questions, please go back and review the material in this chapter before beginning the next chapter. The answers for these questions are located in the appendix, "Questions and Answers."

1. What is performance monitoring?

2. What are the four basic categories of counters?

3. What is SNMP?

4. Why is the amount of memory being used for a disk cache important?

5. What size disks are appropriate for database servers?

6. Why shouldn't you use the monitoring tools on the server to determine whether the network is the bottleneck?

7. What are non-unicast packets?

8. What is the most common cause of inbound network errors?

9. What mechanisms can you use to control the size of a performance log?

10. What is a baseline?

11. Why should you review performance data in a specific order when identifying bottlenecks?

C H A P T E R   9

Documenting the Installation

About This Chapter

In this chapter, you'll put the finishing touches on your server installation by collecting all of the information you've created and formally documenting the installation. This will complete the installation process. You'll then be ready to maintain the server and upgrade it as needed, as discussed in the remainder of this book.

In addition to being an important point on the Server+ exam, documenting a server's configuration is a step that separates the professionals from the rest of the class. It shows that you know how valuable preparation for problems can be. It also shows a desire to transfer responsibility for a server to someone else. Good documentation allows another person to take over the maintenance of the server, freeing you to move on to other servers and other opportunities.

Before You Begin

To complete this chapter, you should have

- A three-ring binder or folder to collect information in

Lesson 1: Creating a Hardware Inventory

When installing a server, you must sort through hundreds, if not thousands, of small hardware details that may or may not be necessary when maintaining the server. This lesson reviews some of those details and helps you develop a structure for documenting the server.

After this lesson, you will be able to

- Create a storage mechanism for server documentation
- Document server and peripheral details

Estimated lesson time: 10 minutes

Organizing Server Data

You need to keep several pieces of information that will make maintaining the server easier. Some of this documentation will be information that you create, and some will be copies of documents received from others.

Although electronic documents are normally preferred, since they allow you to make multiple copies and offer the reasonable assurance that the master copy will stay in the same place, they are probably not the best approach for server documentation. This is because if the server housing the documents goes down or is inaccessible, the documentation is inaccessible. In addition, you usually have to scan vendor information to make it available electronically, and the resulting files are large and difficult to manage electronically.

One of the best ways to handle server documentation is to get a three-ring binder that has pockets on both the front and back inside covers. You can then punch most of the documentation with a three-hole punch and add it to the binder. A binder also has the benefit of allowing you to use divider tabs to separate and index the various types of information. The front and back pockets are handy for those times when you don't have a three-hole punch available and need to include additional information, and also for those times when you've taken down information during a phone call that you haven't documented yet.

Before you start, give some consideration to how you want to gather and organize the documentation for the server. By being prepared, you can even start the documentation process before the server arrives.

Tip Any good documentation project starts with an outline. Documentation for the server is no different.

Creating a Documentation Worksheet

The best way to start documenting the server is to create a server installation worksheet like the one provided in Figure 9.1. This sample worksheet captures most of the information you're likely to need to maintain the server. It includes details on the make, manufacturer, and version for the motherboard, CPU, network card, and so on. These details are useful for inventory purposes as well as to help identify whether an upgrade to the BIOS or firmware of any device is warranted at a later date.

The goal when documenting the installation is to make the server easier to maintain. By documenting all of the manufacturers, model numbers, and firmware versions of each of the system's components, you make it easier to research the version levels of different components, and thus the causes of problems, without reviewing and rebooting the server.

The following discussion reviews the major sections of the sample installation worksheet and indicates why they are important. While it's not crucial to have a worksheet like the one shown in Figure 9.1, it is important to capture the same basic information in a way that can be reviewed by others. If you want to adopt the form in Figure 9.1 for your own use, you'll find a copy on the CD-ROM that accompanies this book.

Basic Information

Your documentation should capture the most basic information about the server. It should specify the manufacturer, model number, and serial number, as well as the server's installation location. The document should also identify exactly what server it is referring to. This is generally done by giving the server's network name.

Once you've recorded the server location and type, it's time to record the BIOS and CPU information. The manufacturer and version string of the motherboard BIOS is important because it will allow you, or someone else, to quickly determine whether an updated BIOS is available. With this information, you can download the new BIOS and review the changes file to determine what changes have been made between the latest version and the version installed in the server. You can then determine whether the BIOS changes will help and whether you should install the new firmware.

Server Installation Worksheet

Server ID/Name	
Server Mfg/Integrator	
Server Model #	
Server Serial #	
Installation Location	

Motherboard BIOS	Make			Installer		
	Version			Video Card	Mfg	
CPU	Type				Model	
	Speed				BIOS Ver.	
CPU 1 Stepping					Memory	
CPU 2 Stepping				CDROM/ DVD	Mfg	
CPU 3 Stepping					Model	
CPU 4 Stepping					Speed	

		Interface 1	Interface 2	Interface 3
Network Card	Mfg			
	Model			
	FW Ver.			

		Controller 1	Controller 2	Controller 3
Hard Disk Control	Mfg			
	Model			
	Memory			
	# of Busses	Int | Ext |	Int | Ext |	Int | Ext |
	Bus type	IDE/SCSI (LVD/SE)/FC	IDE/SCSI (LVD/SE)/FC	IDE/SCSI (LVD/SE)/FC

		Backup 1	Backup 2	Backup 3
Tape Backup	Mfg			
	Model			
	Type/Cap			

		Drive 1	Drive 2	Drive 3
Hard Disk	Mfg			
	Model			
	FW Version			
	Serial #			
	Size			
	Rot Speed			
	Interface			
	Ctrlr/Bus/ID			

		Drive 4	Drive 5	Drive 6
Hard Disk	Mfg			
	Model			
	FW Version			
	Serial #			
	Size			
	Rot Speed			
	Interface			
	Ctrlr/Bus/ID			

Figure 9.1   Sample server installation worksheet

The CPU portion of the worksheet identifies the type (Pentium III, Pentium 4, AMD Athlon, and so on) as well as the speed and stepping levels of each of the processors. The CPU type and speed probably seem obvious to you, but someone else looking at the server won't know this information. The CPU stepping levels are necessary if you ever want to add another processor. If the CPUs in a server aren't at identical stepping levels and problems arise, technical support will need to know this.

Hard Disk		Drive 7	Drive 8	Drive 9
	Mfg			
	Model			
	FW Version			
	Serial #			
	Size			
	Rot Speed			
	Interface			
	Ctrlr/Bus/ID			
		Drive 10	Drive 11	Drive 12
Hard Disk	Mfg			
	Model			
	FW Version			
	Serial #			
	Size			
	Rot Speed			
	Interface			
	Ctrlr/Bus/ID			
		Drive 13	Drive 14	Drive 15
Hard Disk	Mfg			
	Model			
	FW Version			
	Serial #			
	Size			
	Rot Speed			
	Interface			
	Ctrlr/Bus/ID			
		Drive 16	Drive 17	Drive 18
Hard Disk	Mfg			
	Model			
	FW Version			
	Serial #			
	Size			
	Rot Speed			
	Interface			
	Ctrlr/Bus/ID			
		Drive 19	Drive 20	Drive 21
Hard Disk	Mfg			
	Model			
	FW Version			
	Serial #			
	Size			
	Rot Speed			
	Interface			
	Ctrlr/Bus/ID			

Next you need to record the details of the video card. This information is necessary when updating the video card drivers and sometimes the video card BIOS itself. Video drivers are rarely updated, but you may need to do so when running remote control applications, which can be sensitive to video driver issues.

The final bit of basic information that you need to collect involves the CD-ROM or DVD drive. Although this information is pretty standard, it's useful to have if you have SCSI bus issues and a SCSI CD-ROM/DVD drive. It can also be helpful sometimes when the drive isn't recognized by the operating system.

Network Cards

The next section of the worksheet deals with network cards. The information you need here is pretty simple: manufacturer, model number, and firmware version. This is generally the only information necessary to get updated drivers and support.

Tip Pay particular attention to the network cards used in your servers. Despite the fact that Ethernet and Fast Ethernet are standards, there are still some devices that don't work consistently with other Ethernet devices of a different brand. Sometimes these incompatibility issues are related to the firmware on the network interface card. In those cases, a simple firmware upgrade may resolve the incompatibility.

Hard Disks and Hard Disk Controllers

The information you need about hard disk controllers and hard disks is a little more detailed. Because the connectivity between the hard disks and controllers is important, in addition to the makes, models, and firmware, a larger area of the worksheet is devoted to them. Considering the sheer quantity of disk drives in most modern servers, not to mention the information needed on the tape drives, it's easy to see why hard disks and controllers require so much space.

With hard disk controllers, you need the basic manufacturer and model information, and also sometimes the amount of cache memory on board the controller. This information will help you determine whether you can add additional cache memory to the controller later to improve performance. It's also important to record the type and number of buses on the controller. The worksheet also allows for the identification of internal and external buses. This is important if you're trying to find additional address space for a new device and you need to know whether the address space is available externally or internally.

Note You may want to document the termination status of each bus on a SCSI controller because termination is such an important part of connecting SCSI devices. Depending upon the complexity of your controller, bus, and drive arrangement, you may need to create separate documentation describing how the buses, drives, and cables are connected.

Tape Backup Drives

The tape backup information you need includes the standard manufacturer and model information, as well as the type and capacity of each drive. The type and capacity information is important when planning tape purchases, as well as for capacity planning.

Finally, for each hard disk, you should collect information on the manufacturer, model number, firmware version, serial number, size, rotational speed, and interface. You also need to record the controller and bus that the drive is attached to, as well as its ID.

For SCSI and Fibre Channel systems, the controller, bus, and ID combination will be apparent. For IDE-based systems, this could be primary and secondary for the controller and bus. The ID can be recorded as master or slave.

Making Additional Notes

The information captured on the worksheet provides the basic data needed for future maintenance of the server. You should also copy the notes that you made in your log during the installation of the server and include them with the server documentation. Here is some other information that you may have captured during installation that you should consider recording in the server documentation:

- The network hub ports where the network interfaces are plugged in
- The source of the server's power and the circuit breaker limits
- Quirks encountered during the server's installation
- The port number of the server's keyboard-video-mouse switch box

You may find other information helpful as well, depending on your location and environment. By capturing as much information as possible, you'll ensure that maintenance is smooth and uneventful.

Lesson Summary

In this lesson, you learned that you should document the basic information about the hardware configuration to allow for easy maintenance and capacity planning. The manufacturer, model, and version information of every component are key to easy maintenance.

Lesson 2: Gathering Vendor Contact and Warranty Information

While it's helpful to your organization to have the details of the server's configuration and location, both for capacity planning and for new support personnel working on the server, these details don't establish the authorization for support should it be necessary to contact technical support. Capturing the information that most vendors require to prove that you are entitled to service is a necessary step to ensure that future technicians will be able to get the help they need to resolve problems.

After this lesson, you will be able to

- Document the vendor contact information for technical support

Estimated lesson time: 10 minutes

Capturing Vendor Warranty Information

Depending upon the vendor, the process of getting support can be as easy as calling and asking for support or as difficult as having to fax a document showing proof of purchase, with a whole range of requirements in between. Although most vendors in today's market start support from the date of the first call, some require an invoice (or sometimes a purchase order) indicating the date of purchase.

For new servers, finding and providing a proof of purchase date is normally not an issue. For servers that are two or more years old, however, the records on the purchase may not be easily accessible by the accounting department, and thus getting the necessary documentation may be difficult.

This lesson focuses on capturing all of the information that you may need to prove that you are entitled to receive support and including it in the documentation for the server. Doing so both ensures that the information is available and simplifies the process of getting support from some vendors.

Note Even if the vendor's current policy is very relaxed with regard to providing proof of purchase or authorization for support, you should still capture as much information as possible because the vendor's policy may change at any time.

The first step in documenting the vendor contact information is to gather from the accounting department copies of all purchase orders and invoices related to the server's purchase. The next step is to review the invoice to ensure that it has enough detail that the vendor will accept it. Where possible, it should include manufacturer, model number, and serial number for all add-on peripherals as well as the server itself.

For instance, if you purchased your server from a systems integrator or value-added reseller (VAR) and you ordered the system with an additional SCSI controller or additional network cards, make sure that the invoice lists the manufacturer, model number, and serial number (if there is one) of those devices. Failing to do so may cause the vendor to refuse support simply because you can't prove that the product you're calling about was purchased on the invoice you have.

Note It's very rare for a vendor to be picky about documentation. Because technical support is there to provide support for a vendor's products and because most people base their opinion of a company largely on their experience with its technical support, most companies have loosened their technical support policies. However, an ounce of prevention is worth a pound of cure.

The next step is to gather the support telephone numbers and customer numbers (the number assigned to your organization by the vendor) so that you can easily get to them when needed. Figure 9.2 shows a portion of a worksheet where you can record this server warranty information (Figure 9.4 shows the remainder of this worksheet. The worksheets are provided on the CD-ROM that accompanies this book.)

Note Although I've separated the server hardware documentation from the warranty information, you don't have to do so. It's certainly valid to include all of the information that you need on one form.

Server Warranty Information Worksheet					
Server Name/ID			Installation Date		
Model #			Our PO#(s)		
Serial #			Vendor	Name	
Server Mfg	Name			Invoice #	
	Customer #			Customer #	
	Support #			Support #	
Video Card	Model		Hard Disk Controller	Model	
	Mfg			Mfg	
	Support #			Support #	
	Customer #			Customer #	
Network Card (Type 1)	Model		Hard Disk (Type 1)	Model	
	Mfg			Mfg	
	Support #			Support #	
	Customer #			Customer #	
Network Card (Type 2)	Model		Hard Disk (Type 2)	Model	
	Mfg			Mfg	
	Support #			Support #	
	Customer #			Customer #	
Warranty Terms:			OS Support Vendor	Name	
				Phone #	
				Customer #	
Service Contracts					
Provider	Start/End Date		Contract #	Support Phone #	

Figure 9.2 Recording information about warranties and service contracts

In addition to the manufacturer, model number, support number, and customer number for each major component of the system, this worksheet offers a place to record information about service contracts. A service contract with the original equipment manufacturer or a third party might extend the length of time that you can call in for support, or it might give you a higher priority or provide guaranteed response times.

Each service contract generally has a contract number that you need to provide when requesting support. There are places to record these numbers on the sample worksheet in Figure 9.2, but you should also always include the service contract itself in the binder with the rest of the server information.

Put the vendor contact information in the front of the binder for the server. This is the information you're most likely to need when making contact with a vendor. You may also want to come up with a log that lists when calls were made to the vendors and who made them. Figure 9.3 shows a sample service call log.

Service Call Log					
Vendor Called	Date	Task/Call ID	Initiator	Initial Contact	Notes (attach details)

Figure 9.3   Sample service call log

Lesson Summary

In this lesson, you learned how to copy and gather the documentation relating to the purchase of the server for inclusion in a binder. You also learned to record phone numbers, contract numbers, and customer numbers on a form to use as a reference when making calls to a vendor. Finally, you learned that it's a good idea to keep a central log to record all of the calls placed to different vendors regarding issues with the server.

Lesson 3: Documenting the Network Operating System

Perhaps the hardest component of a server to document is the network operating system because there are so many variables to capture. On the positive side, most operating system settings are easily checked while the server is running, so you don't need to shut down the server to check one that isn't documented. This lesson discusses the information you should capture regarding the operating system.

After this lesson, you will be able to

- Create basic operating system documentation
- Identify configuration information that is important to document in the server file

Estimated lesson time: 10 minutes

Identifying the Data to Capture

Each operating system has myriad services that a server can provide, and each service has its own settings and options. Storing the result of every conceivable option is more than difficult; it's impossible. For a Microsoft Windows 2000 server, a single registry hive used to store data about the system and its operation might have more than 10,000 unique keys, with hundreds of thousands of configuration values.

Collecting, categorizing, and documenting all of the values that represent the configuration of a server is too large a task. However, documenting some key functions and settings can be very helpful in reducing the time required to solve a problem. You should focus on the following five areas:

- Video card/monitor configuration
- Core operating system settings
- Network controller configuration
- TCP/IP configuration
- Services provided

Figure 9.4 shows the remainder of the worksheet that was excerpted in Figure 9.2. It's a place to record information about the operating system configuration and the services provided by the server, as well as the vendors and technical notes that apply to the server installation. You can use this worksheet as a template for the information you want to capture.

Services Loaded/Provided					
	DNS		Terminal Svcs		SMTP
	DHCP		Remote Control		POP3
	WINS		SNMP		IMAP4
	BOOTP		SysLog		NNTP
	DHCP		Backup S/W		HTTP
Firewall/Packet Filter			Backup Agent		HTTPS
Remote Installation Server			SMB File/Print		Database
SNA Gateway			NCP File/Print		Internet Authentication
Proxy Server			NFS File		RADIUS
Remote Access Server			NIS/NIS+		Simple TCP/IP
Virtual Private Networking			LPR Print		Mac File
Fax Server			LPD Print		Mac Print

Applicable Vendor Tech Notes, Knowledge Base Articles, and Other References (attach)		
Vendor	Article/Note ID	Summary

Additional Notes

Operating System Configuration					
Video	Resolution		Network Card 2	Speed	
	Frequency			Duplex	
	Depth			Media Type	
	Driver Version			MAC Address	
Operating System	Name			IP/Subnet	
	Version			Dft. Gateway	
	Patch Level		Network Card 3	Speed	
	Paging Size			Duplex	
	Log File Size			Media Type	
	TEMP Loc.			MAC Address	
Network Card 1	Speed			IP/Subnet	
	Duplex			Dft. Gateway	
	Media Type		TCP/IP Config.	WINS Svr 1	
	MAC Address			WINS Svr 2	
	IP/Subnet			WINS Node Type	
	Dft. Gateway			DNS Srvr 1	
				DNS Srvr 2	
				DNS Srvr 3	

Figure 9.4 Recording information about the operating system configuration, the services loaded, and relevant references

Video Card Information

The information necessary for the video card is pretty simple. It's a good idea to record the resolution, frequency, and color depth supported by the card. The first two are useful if it becomes necessary to quickly replace the server monitor or if the monitor stops working and an exact replacement isn't available. Although the color depth doesn't affect the ability to connect a monitor, it completes the set of information started by resolution and frequency. Finally, it's a good idea to record the driver version for the video card to make it easy to determine whether you have the most current video driver.

Operating System Information

Information on the operating system includes the product name, the version, and the patch or service pack level. When you call technical support for the operating system vendor, you will be asked for this information first. Knowing how much virtual memory is available, in the form of either a paging file or a swap partition, can help to identify memory-related problems. It's also sometimes important to know how big the log files can grow to, if circular logging has been enabled. This helps to determine how many events can be stored in the log. Finally, the location of temporary files is handy to know, particularly if you're trying to determine why certain disks are filling up.

Network Card Information

The network card information you need is relatively simple and consists of the speed at which the card is running, whether the card is working in half or full duplex mode, the media type, the card's hardware, or media access control (MAC) address, the assigned IP address and subnet, and the default gateway. Knowing the speed is helpful when reviewing performance issues because it will indicate the maximum theoretical throughput of the server. The media type indicates whether the interface is running copper (and which category) or fiber, which can help identify the source of network errors. The MAC address is useful when attempting to test basic connectivity and when reviewing network address conflicts, since these conflicts give the MAC address of the conflicting network interface card. Finally, recording the IP address, subnet, and default gateway can help you determine what might be causing communications problems with the server.

Information on the TCP/IP Configuration

The TCP/IP configuration information includes both the WINS and DNS name resolution mechanisms. This information will be necessary if the server is having name resolution problems.

Information on the Services Provided

Next you need to document the services provided by the server. The simplest way to do this is with a checklist like the one shown in the Services Loaded/Provided section of Figure 9.4. This list is particularly important when you need to take the server offline or perform maintenance on it because it will provide a basis for determining which users you need to notify of the outage.

Information on References Used

The worksheet also contains an area for listing knowledge base articles or technical notes that apply to the server. Use this space to record references that you used when installing the server, as well as ones you found during your research for the installation that contain cautionary notes for the installation and maintenance of the server. This additional information will alert the person maintaining the server to known problems or concerns so that he or she can focus on those issues when problems arise.

Lesson Summary

In this lesson, you learned which operating system settings to document, as well as that it's impossible to record every detail of the operating system's configuration.

Review

Here are some questions to help you determine whether you have learned enough to move on to the next chapter. If you have difficulty answering these questions, please go back and review the material in this chapter before beginning the next chapter. The answers for these questions are located in the appendix, "Questions and Answers."

1. Why do we document a server's installation?

2. Why can't we document every detail?

3. Why do we make copies of invoices and purchase orders relating to the server?

P A R T   3

Upgrading a Server and Peripherals

C H A P T E R   1 0

Upgrading Processors and Memory

About This Chapter

The preceding chapters walked you through the process of installing a new server, discussing all of the requirements for documentation, planning, and physical installation. In this chapter, the topic switches to how to upgrade a server after it's installed. As we make this transition, it's important to remember that no matter how simple or straightforward an upgrade seems, it's a good idea to have a backup. You never know what will break or what you'll have to do to recover from a bad upgrade attempt.

Caution Do a backup. Sure, it's a pain. It may even seem like a waste of time—until you have an upgrade go wrong.

This chapter deals specifically with processors and memory. Although a processor upgrade is probably the least likely upgrade to be performed once a server is up and running, it is the one with the most potential for problems. You'll see what the potential problems are, including electrostatic discharge (ESD), and how to avoid them. You'll also learn precautions and considerations for installing memory.

Before You Begin

To complete this chapter, you should have

- Your server documentation
- The parts to be installed

Lesson 1: Adding or Replacing a Processor

There is probably no more risky upgrade than replacing the processor for a server. Because the processors control everything that happens, inadvertent damage to the system's primary processor can render the server inoperative until a replacement is found.

This lesson discusses compatibility issues and precautions for installing additional processors and replacing existing processors. It also covers the operating system parameters that you should review after the installation.

After this lesson, you will be able to

- Follow the appropriate precautions for processor installation
- Physically install the CPU
- Verify operating system support of the processor
- Update operating system and application service parameters to optimize them for the new processor

Estimated lesson time: 20 minutes

Understanding Electrostatic Discharge

Before we start talking about processors, you need to know about the processor's worst enemy: electrostatic discharge. *Electrostatic discharge* is the rapid release of static electricity. Static electricity is an electrical field that is normally not flowing. The rapid release of the energy in a static electric field causes damage to processors by burning, opening, or disconnecting some of the tiny pathways within the processor.

To fully appreciate what goes on during an electrostatic discharge, you have to understand the difference between a static electric field and the types of electricity that power a server. Chapter 2, Lesson 2 discussed the two different types of electrical power and how they are used in a computer environment. We learned that electricity is the difference in potential between two conductors.

In a normal electric circuit, completing the circuit causes either alternating current (AC) or direct current (DC) power to flow. Electrons flow from the greatest number of electrons to the least number of electrons. This electron flow is what we call the current.

DC power can be stored in batteries, which generally output a specific voltage for a long period of time. The primary difference between a DC battery and a static electric field is that a static electric field is discharged nearly all at once. The other difference is that in a static electric field the electrons are holding themselves in stasis. By this I mean that the electrons are arranged into a field much like a bubble. That is why your hair stands up when you develop a strong static charge. Each hair is charged and is repelled from every other hair.

Note If you were sick the day they talked about magnets in science class, here's a refresher. Opposite poles of a magnet attract each other. Like poles of a magnet repel each other. Since electricity and magnetism behave similarly, the negatively charged electrons present in two adjacent hairs will also cause them to repel each other. If the electrical charge is strong enough, the force of repulsion between the hairs will exceed the pull of gravity.

When the tension breaks in this field, such as when you touch something made of metal, all of the electrons that make up the static electric field are rapidly discharged. This rapid discharge of energy has a very high voltage—tens of thousands of volts. However, because a static electric field does not have a huge pool of electrons, there isn't any amperage in static electricity. It's because there's no significant amperage to sustain the voltage that you aren't killed when static electricity is discharged from your body.

Note In our discussion of UPSs I mentioned that one way to measure power is in volt-amps, which is the voltage multiplied by the amperage. Even though the voltage of a static electric field is very, very high, the very small amperage means that the amount of power discharged during an electrostatic discharge is still very small.

Most people experience static electricity when they drag their feet when the humidity is very low. Then when they get close to a metal or electronic device or perhaps another person, they see a spark of electricity jump from them to the item or person. This process, called *arcing*, occurs because the extremely high voltage of the static electric field ionizes the surrounding air, allowing it to be electrically conductive.

The electrical spark that you see when arcing occurs is the result of the air being heated to an explosive temperature by the electrons passing through it. Because the number of electrons is relatively small, the explosion is very contained and generally causes only a moment of discomfort, if that. However, if this momentary explosive heating takes place inside an electrical component, it can render it inoperative.

Note Lightning is produced by the same electrostatic forces that create electrostatic discharge in humans, only on a much larger scale. Because of the higher voltages involved, the distances are much greater and the effects are much more dangerous. If you're interested in learning more about lightning and how it works, visit *http://www.howstuffworks.com/lightning.htm*.

A spark is a clear indication that there's been an electrostatic discharge. However, it takes tens of thousands of volts to arc across air, and it takes no more than 3.3 volts to power one of today's processors, and even less for other components. Thus, even static charges that are incapable of jumping across air can be very hazardous to server electronics.

Preventing Damage from Electrostatic Discharge

Because ESDs are hazardous to server components, we should keep them from reaching the components. Although there is no way to completely prevent static electricity from building up, and there is no way to prevent the charge from being conducted to the components, there is a way to control the discharges so that they don't become hazardous.

The best way to control static buildup is to maintain a constant connection to a low-resistance source of ground. The most common way of doing this is to wear a metal bracelet that is connected to a ground, known as a *grounding strap*. The bracelet maintains contact with your skin and is clipped to a ground. An alternative is setting the server on a metallic mat that has a connection to a ground. Because of your frequent contact with the mat, you drain off static charges before they can build up.

The other method of controlling static buildup is to consciously make contact with a grounded source. A good grounded source is the metal housing of the server, while it's plugged in. This is because all devices with metal housings are required to connect the housing to the ground conductor in the power cable. Making continual contact with the server's housing will neutralize any static charge before it can build up.

Caution Do not leave servers plugged in while performing upgrades unless their power supplies have a mechanical on/off switch. The server's on/off switch is a "soft" on/off switch, meaning that the server is continuously receiving power when the power supplies are plugged in and switched on. The power is minimal until the CPU asserts a signal to the power supply, but it's enough to cause damage to processors, memory, and add-on cards if they are installed or removed.

You can help to reduce the speed at which you build up static charges by purchasing antistatic fabric chairs and antistatic carpets, or by using tile rather than carpet for your floors. This is the reason that flooring used in computer rooms is typically raised tile rather than raised carpet.

A home remedy for helping to reduce static buildup is to mix a small amount of fabric softener and water in a spray bottle and use this to spray fabric and the carpet in the areas where you want to reduce static buildup. The fabric softener has antistatic ingredients that help to control the buildup.

Supporting an Additional Processor

Before adding a processor to a server, it's important to be aware of three important requirements:

- **Operating system support.** The operating system must support symmetric multiprocessing (SMP) to be able to use the second processor. Not only does the operating system have to support SMP, it must have the components and kernel for it installed. Without SMP support, the secondary CPU is just a big heating element inside of the computer.

- **Similar or the same stepping levels.** The processor you're adding should be at the same stepping level as the other processor(s). If it's not possible to get the identical stepping level, get one that is close. Failure to do so may make the server unstable.

- **An available slot.** You should have a socket or slot on the motherboard that the new processor can go into. It should also be in a location where the new processor won't interfere with any add-on cards.

If you remember these requirements, your processor installation should go smoothly.

Note In Microsoft Windows NT 4, upgrading to a multiprocessor version of the kernel from a single-processor version was not straightforward, and problems often occurred during the upgrade. If you're installing Windows NT 4 on a system that supports multiple processors, it's best to run the multiprocessor kernel even if you only have one processor installed initially.

Installing an Additional Processor

Adding a processor to a server is a relatively simple procedure, but problems can occur if it's done incorrectly. This section focuses on the steps for increasing the number of processors in a server. The next section discusses some additional concerns to be aware of when replacing a processor.

Note Sometimes installing an additional processor can make the system unstable. This may be related to the power supply, because the new processor creates an additional load. Make sure that your power supply will be able to sustain the load imposed by the additional processor. This is normally an issue only for "home-built" servers and shouldn't affect servers from mainstream providers, which typically plan power supplies for the maximum load.

The procedure for installing a new processor is basically the same for all server manufacturers as well as for all processors. The following steps walk you through this process.

▶ **To install a new processor**

1. Back up the server.

2. Read the machine-specific instructions for installing a new processor, and follow those directions if they are different from the ones presented here.

3. Shut down the server normally.

4. Remove the power from the server.

Note Before the introduction of ATX power supplies, which maintain power to the processor at all times, it made sense to keep servers plugged in while working on them. However, today the potential for problems when a system is plugged in isn't worth the additional protection from ESD that you gain.

---

5. Remove the cover and place the server on a work space.

6. Touch something that is grounded, or put on a grounding strap.

7. Remove any cables, add-on cards, or hard disks that prevent access to the processors. Be careful not to touch any installed processors, as they may be hot.

8. If your server uses a slot-based processor, such as a Pentium II or above, do the following. (Figure 10.1 shows a processor slot.)

   a. If a terminator card is installed in the next CPU slot—and one probably will be—unscrew and remove the terminator card.

┌ Processor slot

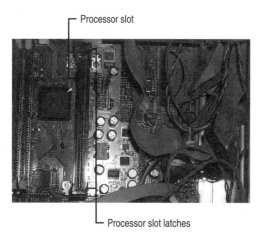

└ Processor slot latches

Figure 10.1   Processor slot, showing the black plastic riser that the processor snaps into

   b. Remove the new CPU from its packaging, and insert it into the slot from which you just removed the terminator. Do not touch the contacts on the processor card as you insert it.

   c. Screw the processor into place.

If your server uses a socket-based processor, such as Pentium, an AMD K6-3 and some Athlon processors, do the following. (Figure 10.2 shows a processor socket.)

a. Pull out and lift the bar on the side of the processor socket.

b. Remove the new CPU from its packaging.

c. Determine the correct orientation for the processor in the socket. There's often a dot on the top corner of the CPU that matches the part of the socket that is missing a pin. Visually verify the correct orientation of the processor before proceeding.

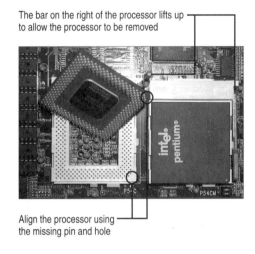

The bar on the right of the processor lifts up to allow the processor to be removed

Align the processor using the missing pin and hole

Figure 10.2 Socket-based multiprocessor board, showing a processor and zero insertion force (ZIF) socket before installation

d. Set the processor on the socket in the correct orientation, and press lightly.

e. Lower the bar on the side of the socket, and lock it in place by ensuring that it snaps behind the plastic tab.

9. Replace any fans, add-on cards, and cables you removed to gain access to the processor.

10. Close and fasten the server case.

11. Reinstall the server, and attach all cables.

12. Watch the bootup process to ensure that the additional processor is detected. If the processor is not detected, there's a problem with the hardware. For example, the processor may not be seated properly, or a jumper or a BIOS setting may need to be changed. Retrace your steps, and reread the hardware-specific instructions.

13. Next start the operating system and ensure that it detects the additional processor. Most SMP-enabled operating systems will indicate how many processors they detect. If the operating system doesn't detect the processor, refer to the operating system's instructions for adding SMP support.

Despite the number of steps involved, installing a new processor is not that difficult. By following the procedure just given, you eliminate many of the potential complications related to new processor installation.

Replacing a Processor

While the basic mechanics of replacing a processor with a new processor are fundamentally the same as the steps just given for installing an additional processor, there are some additional considerations that complicate the installation. This section assumes that you're replacing the processor with a faster processor, because replacing one processor with another of the same or slower speed doesn't make sense.

Changing the speed of the processor can have a ripple effect, ultimately changing the way the rest of the system interacts with the processor. Some of these effects are as follows:

- **Memory speed.**   Perhaps the biggest potential issue when replacing a processor with a faster one is that faster processors sometimes require faster memory. For instance, the difference between a 333-MHz Pentium II and a 350-MHz Pentium II is that the 333-MHz processor uses 66-MHz SDRAM and the 350-MHz processor uses 100-MHz SDRAM. Check to make sure that the processor you're installing can use the memory you have.

- **Core voltage.**   Sometimes, to achieve higher processor clock rates, it's advantageous or necessary to reduce the voltages supplied to the processor. Check that the core voltage in the new processor is the same as in the processor being removed to ensure that the new processor isn't burned out.

- **Clock rate and fractional clock rate.**   The speed at which the system actually runs is controlled by the clock circuitry on the motherboard. The CPU speed indicates only the maximum rate at which the processor can be run. It's important to ensure that the motherboard can support the higher processing rate of the new CPU.

In general, the motherboard should provide jumper settings to control the processor speed and core voltages. You should review these settings carefully when replacing the processor on an existing motherboard. Failure to do so can result in damage to the CPU and the motherboard, rendering both unusable.

Optimizing the Server for Additional Processors

When the operating system and server-based software is installed, it inventories the system and determines the best configuration. This configuration includes parameters that apply to multiprocessor machines, even if the system has only one processor in it when it is installed.

Although each operating system and each service configures multiprocessor support differently, there are two basic parameters that you can control to enhance performance on an SMP server. They are processor affinity and maximum threads.

Processor Affinity

Processor affinity is simply the emphasis an operating system places on running a single thread of execution on one processor. Keeping a single thread of execution on one server allows the operating system to fully realize the benefits of the processor by maximizing the effectiveness of its cache.

Before we delve into processor affinity and how it affects performance, it's important to review two points. The first is that all modern processors use a cache to help the processor perform better by predictively reading memory before its contents are necessary. This cache allows the processor to spend less time waiting for the RAM to return the requested information.

The second point is that a thread is the smallest unit of execution that can be performed. Every application must have at least one thread. However, service-providing applications, such as database servers, may have several threads of execution running at the same time.

A practical example of multithreaded execution is Microsoft Word. In the foreground is a thread that's constantly interacting with the user. It takes information from the keyboard and mouse and displays the document as it's composed. However, there are other unseen threads within Word that control its automatic pagination, as well as ones that cause the Office Assistant to pop up when you start a task that Word thinks it understands. These additional threads are doing work that doesn't have to be done by the "main" user-interaction thread.

As I mentioned at the beginning of this section, processor affinity is concerned with routing a thread back to the processor it ran on the last time, when possible, to minimize the impact that switching a task between processors has on the performance both of the overall system and of the specific service. SMP-enabled operating systems allow you to specify the amount of emphasis an operating system places on processor affinity.

Up to a point, the greater the emphasis on processor affinity within a system, the better the system will perform overall. This is true because greater processor affinity means fewer transitions of threads between processors. Such transitions cause the information already stored in the cache of one processor to be loaded into the other processor's cache. However, if you set this value so high that all processes will run only on the CPU that they first ran on, the overall performance will decrease dramatically as one CPU becomes completely loaded with activity while the others are relatively unused.

Processor affinity in Windows 2000 and in a patched version of the latest Linux kernel can be set in two ways. The first way is to express to the operating system a numeric metric that it should use to determine which processor it assigns a thread to. The higher the number, the more likely any thread is to get the same processor it had last time.

In general, the operating system default is acceptable for processor affinity, but you may want to try increasing this setting slightly to see whether overall performance improves. Depending upon the mix of services that the server is providing, increasing the processor affinity may or may not help.

The other way to set processor affinity is by having applications select a processor to run on and requiring that processor be used to execute all threads of an application. This method is rather drastic, but it can prevent one application or service from consuming all of the CPU resources in the system. The technique of forcing threads to run on a particular processor is called *binding*. It's often used for applications that don't deal well with SMP systems. Binding is also sometimes used to force all interrupt traffic to one processor, allowing the other processors to manage user threads. Review the documentation provided by the operating system vendor for these settings, and make the configuration changes that it recommends for your environment.

Note NetWare uses local thread run queues that essentially keep a thread on a processor until a threshold-based mechanism determines that a processor is either underutilized or overutilized. This mechanism is complicated to get set correctly, and it doesn't allow you to require that particular threads always run on a certain processor. The Server+ exam does not get into this level of detail regarding processor affinity. If you need specific information on how to configure NetWare, review the NetWare documentation or visit Novell's Web site.

Figure 10.3 shows binding being set for an application in Windows 2000. You can display the Processor Affinity dialog box by right-clicking the process in Task Manager and selecting Set Affinity. (The easiest way to get to Task Manager is to press Ctrl+Alt+Delete and select the Task Manager button.)

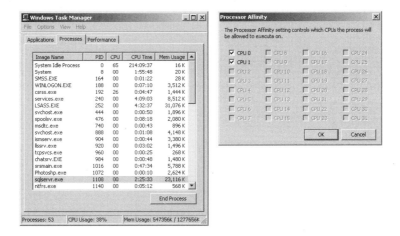

Figure 10.3   Selecting the processors an application can run on in Windows 2000

Maximum Threads

The second setting that you can use to optimize the performance of a multiprocessor machine is the maximum number of threads a service can run. This setting is only loosely related to the number of processors available. It is also related to the number of other services running and the number and speed of the disk drives on the system. This service-tuning parameter controls how many different threads a given service spawns and maintains to satisfy client requests. In general, the higher the number of threads, the more chances a thread within the service has of being scheduled for a processor.

When you install services on a server that has only one processor, the number of threads is controlled so that no one service completely dominates the performance of the server. The maximum number of threads for a service usually shouldn't be set higher than the number of processors in the system, but certain applications, in which the threads may not use all of the capacity of the server, may need a larger number of worker threads to optimize performance.

For instance, a Web server is rarely limited by the amount of processor or disk time; instead, it's generally limited by the amount of bandwidth available to the client. In such cases, the number of threads may need to be set higher than the number of processors (by a wide margin) so that the replies can get started quickly. The thread will remain active, trying to send data until it has all been transmitted. In this way, the thread will consume only a small amount of resources, but it won't be available to service another request.

On the other hand, a relational database server will use a lower number of threads because its threads generally place a large load on the system as they process data to find answers for the client. The actual transmission of the data takes a relatively short period of time.

Figure 10.4 shows how maximum threads are set in Microsoft SQL Server 7. This complex thread setup allows precise control over the resources SQL Server consumes.

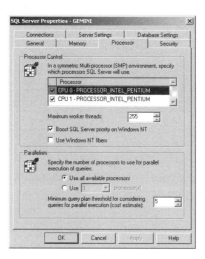

Figure 10.4   Setting the maximum threads in SQL Server 7

Each application or service should provide guidelines for maximum threads. Review these settings after installing a new processor so that you can take full advantage of it.

Lesson Summary

In this lesson, you learned that electrostatic discharge is hazardous to processors, memory, and other components due to the extremely high voltages involved. You also learned that you need to verify operating system support for the additional processor and to maintain a consistent stepping level across all processors.

The lesson also reviewed how processor affinity settings are designed to improve performance by limiting the number of transitions that a thread makes between processors. In addition, it discussed the maximum threads setting available in many service-based applications, indicating that applications that are disk or processor bound should be set for a small number of threads. Those applications that use server resources intensively should have maximum threads set equal to or slightly lower than the number of processors. Applications that don't exercise server resources can be significantly higher.

Lesson 2: Adding Memory

Memory is one of the cheapest and best ways to improve overall system performance. After disk drive upgrades, memory upgrades are the most common upgrade to be performed. This lesson covers the precautions to take when installing memory and discusses problems that can arise. It also gives procedures for installing both DIMM and SIMM memory modules.

After this lesson, you will be able to

- Follow the appropriate precautions for memory installation
- Perform the memory installation
- Verify that memory was installed correctly

Estimated lesson time: 20 minutes

Choosing Appropriate Memory

Memory chips have many, many more individual circuits than any other component in the computer. Because of this, memory is significantly more susceptible to ESD than any other system component, including the processor. Lesson 1 covered appropriate precautions to take to avoid ESD damage to components. These precautions particularly apply to memory.

Note Although memory is packaged in two different ways—DIMM and SIMM—the two types are identical internally. Don't let the different ways of packaging memory confuse you into believing that they are different from one another. They have all of the same characteristics, including susceptibility to ESD.

In addition, you should take the following considerations into account when selecting the memory itself:

- **Motherboard compatibility.**   As silly as it may seem, memory from some manufacturers doesn't get along with some motherboards. So when selecting memory, you'll want to make sure that the motherboard used in the server will support it. When in doubt, call both the server manufacturer and the memory supplier to verify support, or at least to establish that there are no known problems.

- **Same manufacturer as existing memory.**   Subtle timing differences in memory made by different manufacturers can become a stability problem for systems running multiple brands of memory. Try to stay with a single memory provider, if possible.

- **Same speed and type as existing memory.**   Additional memory should be of the same type—such as SDRAM, DDR SDRAM, or Rambus DRAM (RDRAM)—as the existing memory and should also be the same speed—66 MHz, 100 MHz, 133 MHz, and so on. Although systems will sometimes work with memory of differing speeds, most motherboards don't adjust to the different speeds. As a result, they will not take advantage of the additional speed if the new memory is faster, and they will attempt to access it at the faster rate if it's slower. This will often cause stability problems.

- **Available slot.**   Make sure the motherboard has a slot into which the memory can be installed. If it doesn't, you will have to replace the existing memory with memory that is denser (has a higher capacity). If you have to replace the memory, be sure to buy higher-density memory, and don't count the existing memory when calculating your new total because you will need to pull it to make room.

- **Interleaving.**   Make sure that the motherboard supports the number of memory boards you plan to install. To improve efficiency in memory accesses, motherboard designs sometimes use two or more memory boards at one time. If this is the case, you'll have to install the memory in the appropriate increment. This information will be in the motherboard documentation for the server. The motherboard itself will also generally indicate this by grouping one or more slots into banks.

In general, try to follow the manufacturer's recommendations and maintain as few variables as possible. By using memory with the same manufacturer, model number, speed, and so on, you can minimize the number of variables and thus minimize the number of potential problems.

Installing Memory

The process of installing memory has improved dramatically over the last 15 years. Initially, memory was sold in DRAM chips that were inserted directly into sockets on the motherboard. This meant inserting and removing each memory chip individually. In doing so, you risked breaking one of the pins off of the memory chip, leaving it unusable. It was also possible to install the memory backward in a socket. At best, memory installed in this way just wouldn't be seen by the system. At worst, it would damage the motherboard.

Today we don't have those worries. All server-based memory is packaged onto memory boards. These boards are sturdy, so it's difficult to break off the connectors, and they are notched in such a way that they can't be installed backwards.

Of course, with every advance we make, we must accept additional complexity. When memory boards (modules) were first conceived, they were laid out electrically in a way that made sense for the systems at the time. When the systems changed so did the memory board. Now we have two different types of SIMMs (with different widths) and one type of DIMM module. You need to know which type of memory your server can accept before ordering it.

Installing DIMM Memory

The following procedure applies to newer servers that require DIMMs. Follow these steps when installing DIMM-based memory:

▶ **To install memory in a server that uses DIMMs**

1. Back up the server.

2. Read the machine-specific instructions for installing new memory, and follow those directions if they are different from the ones presented here.

3. Shut down the server normally.

4. Remove the power from the server.

5. Remove the cover, and place the server on a work space.

6. Touch something that is grounded, or put on a grounding strap.

7. Remove any cables, add-on cards, or hard disks that will prevent access to the memory.

8. If the memory you're installing is more dense than the RAM currently installed in the server, you'll have to remove the existing memory, because memory must be installed from the highest capacity to the lowest capacity. To remove the memory, spread the two plastic clips on either side of the slot. This will unlock and pry up the memory module in one motion. Figure 10.5 shows this locking mechanism.

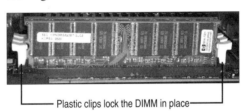

Plastic clips lock the DIMM in place

Figure 10.5   A DIMM slot, showing the locking mechanism

Note If you don't see plastic clips on either side of the installed memory, or if there is any metal involved with these clips, you probably have SIMM memory, not DIMM memory. Follow the procedure in the next section for installing SIMM-based memory.

---

9. Select the highest-capacity memory board to be installed.

10. Locate the first available (lowest-numbered) memory slot or bank. This may be labeled "slot" or "bank" on the motherboard. In general, the lower-numbered banks are closer to the power supply, and the higher numbers are farther away.

11. Orient the memory board so that the notches on the board match the raised spots in the slot. Figure 10.6 shows a DIMM, with the notches visible along the bottom.

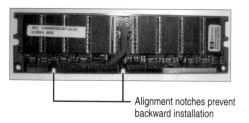

Alignment notches prevent backward installation

Figure 10.6 Notches in a DIMM, used to orient it in the slot

12. Press the memory board slowly and evenly into place, making sure you don't twist it either up or down.

13. Verify that the plastic clips on the slot have come up and grabbed the memory board firmly by locking into the notches on the side of the board.

14. Repeat steps 9 through 13 until all of the memory boards have been installed.

15. Gently press on each memory board, and wiggle it up and down slightly to ensure that it is firmly seated. Do this for memory boards that were previously installed as well.

16. Replace any cables, add-on cards, or hard disks that you had to remove to gain access to the memory slots.

17. Close and fasten the server case.

18. Reinstall the server, and attach all cables.

19. Watch the bootup process to ensure that the new memory is detected. Some BIOSs will require that you stop and enter the BIOS setup to save the change to the amount of memory. Others will bypass the BIOS setup screen and continue to boot.

20. Start the operating system, and ensure that it detects the additional memory. If the operating system didn't detect the additional memory, ensure that the BIOS setting that controls the type of OS for memory reporting is set appropriately for your operating system. Review the operating system documentation to ensure that you don't have to change any settings to have it recognize the extra memory.

Note NetWare used to require that you issue the REGISTER MEMORY command to recognize memory. Although this command is rarely needed today, it's possible that some servers will need it.

After upgrading the memory, remember to review the virtual memory sizings to ensure that they are still appropriate.

Installing SIMM Memory

The process of installing SIMM-based memory is very similar to that for installing DIMM-based memory, except for the mechanism used to latch the memory into place.

Note Although this discussion refers to 72-pin SIMM memory modules because they are the type found in a modern server, the same technique applies to the 36-pin SIMMs found in older servers and PCs.

▶ **To install SIMM-based memory into a server**

1. Back up the server.
2. Read the machine-specific instructions for installing new memory, and follow those directions if they are different from the ones presented here.
3. Shut down the server normally.
4. Remove the power from the server.
5. Remove the cover, and place the server on a work space.
6. Touch something that is grounded, or put on a grounding strap.
7. Remove any cables, add-on cards, or hard disks that will prevent access to the memory.
8. If the memory you're installing is more dense than the RAM currently installed in the server, you'll have to remove the existing memory, because memory must be installed from the highest capacity to the lowest capacity. To remove the memory, pull apart the clips on either side of the slot (as shown in Figure 10.7), tilt the memory to at a 45-degree angle, and pull it out.

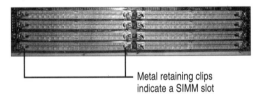
Metal retaining clips
indicate a SIMM slot

Figure 10.7 SIMM slots, showing the metal retaining clips

9. Select the highest-capacity memory board to be installed.
10. Locate the first available (lowest-numbered) memory slot or bank. This may be labeled "slot" or "bank" on the motherboard. In general, the lower-numbered banks are closer to the power supply, and the higher numbers are farther away.
11. Orient the memory board so that the notches on the board match the raised spots in the slot.
12. Insert the memory board into the slot at a 45-degree angle, making sure not to bend the pins that are in the slot (Figure 10.8).

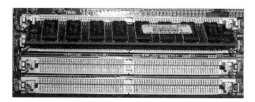

Figure 10.8   A SIMM being inserted at a 45-degree angle

13. Gently push the memory into the slot, and then rotate it back until it's perpendicular to the motherboard.

14. Secure the metal clips on the edges of the slot around the memory module, if they didn't automatically spring into place.

15. Repeat steps 9 through 14 until all of the memory boards have been installed.

16. Gently press on each memory board, and wiggle it up and down slightly to ensure that it is firmly seated. Do this for memory boards that were previously installed as well.

17. Replace any cables, add-on cards, or hard disks that you had to remove to gain access to the memory slots.

18. Close and fasten the server case.

19. Reinstall the server and attach all cables.

20. Watch the bootup process to ensure that the new memory is detected. Some BIOSs will require that you stop and enter the BIOS setup to save the change to the amount of memory. Others will bypass the BIOS setup screen and continue the boot.

21. Start the operating system, and ensure that it detects the additional memory. If the operating system didn't detect the additional memory, ensure that the BIOS setting that controls the type of OS for memory reporting is set appropriately for your operating system. Review the operating system documentation to ensure that you don't have to change any settings to have it recognize the extra memory.

Note NetWare used to require that you issue the REGISTER MEMORY command to recognize memory. Although this command is rarely needed today, it's possible that some servers will need it.

After upgrading the memory, remember to review the virtual memory sizings to ensure that they are still appropriate.

Lesson Summary

In this lesson, you learned how to identify issues that may exist when adding memory to a server, as well as the procedure to use when installing additional memory.

Review

Here are some questions to help you determine whether you have learned enough to move on to the next chapter. If you have difficulty answering these questions, please go back and review the material in this chapter before beginning the next chapter. The answers for these questions are located in the appendix, "Questions and Answers."

1. What is a thread?

2. What is processor affinity?

3. What is thread binding?

4. What are the requirements for adding an additional processor to the system?

5. What are the three concerns you need to address when upgrading an existing processor to a faster one?

6. After you've physically installed the memory and verified it in the BIOS, what is left to do?

C H A P T E R   1 1

Adding Hard Disks

About This Chapter

In Chapter 10, we started talking about upgrades, the additions necessary to ensure that the server continues to provide adequate performance to its clients. This chapter extends this conversation by discussing hard disks, specifically how to install new hard disks in a server. Although this upgrade affects performance, it affects capacity as well. As a result, hard disk upgrades are the most common upgrade performed on a server.

This chapter is largely an expansion of the coverage of hard disks that we started in Chapter 3, Lesson 3. It discusses the same bus types but focuses much more on physical installation and connectivity, rather than on planning and performance.

Before You Begin

To complete this chapter, you should have

- Your server documentation
- The parts to be installed

Lesson 1: Verifying Drive Type and Cabling

As you learned in Chapter 3, Lesson 3, there are three basic categories of hard disk: ATA/IDE, SCSI, and Fibre Channel. Within each of these disk categories are several different types of disks. This lesson discusses the various categories of disks and the connectors that each type of disk within a given category uses. It also reviews termination and jumper settings and how they relate or do not relate to where drives are connected to the cables.

After this lesson, you will be able to

- Identify the different connectors used for SCSI, ATA/IDE, and Fibre Channel
- Select appropriate cabling for the disks you're installing
- Correctly set jumpers controlling identification, termination, and other disk-related parameters

Estimated lesson time: 20 minutes

Ribbon Cable Characteristics

Before getting into the details of each disk category and the cables and connectors they use, let's go over a common cable and connector setup used with both SCSI and ATA/IDE devices, as well as by other devices inside a computer. This connector, called a *pin block connector,* consists of a series of metal pins on the device that are inserted into a block on the cable. This type of connector is very cheap and simple to manufacture and thus is often used inside PCs.

Pin block connectors are generally found on the end of ribbon cables. A ribbon cable is a cable in which parallel wires are grouped into a wide, flat plastic "ribbon." Although ribbon cables are not generally used for long distances because of the electrical interference that they are susceptible to, they are used for SCSI, ATA/IDE, floppy disk, serial, parallel, and other connections within a server.

The problem with pin block connectors is that they can easily be reversed. As a result, three mechanisms exist to ensure proper orientation of cables. They are

- Pin 1 identification
- Blocked pins
- Keyed connectors

Let's take a brief look at the strengths and weaknesses of each mechanism.

Pin 1 Identification

The pin 1 identification method of preventing accidental reversal is present on almost every ribbon cable and every device that attaches to a ribbon cable via a pin block connector, whether or not it also uses other mechanisms. Pin 1 identification is just a stripe down the side of the ribbon, showing the side to which pin 1 should connect. This stripe is generally red, but it can also be another color.

On the device itself, pin 1 is identified by a small triangle, the number 1, or sometimes the number 2. The number 2 is used when there isn't room to indicate the location of pin 1 on the board; instead, pin 2 is marked, indicating that pin 1 is located on the same end. You simply need to match the pin 1 stripe with the pin 1 identification on the device. Figure 11.1 shows an ATA/IDE hard disk with an ATA/IDE cable attached in the correct orientation. (The disk is upside down in the figure.)

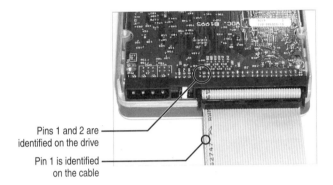

Pins 1 and 2 are identified on the drive

Pin 1 is identified on the cable

Figure 11.1   Hard disk with both pin 1 and pin 2 marked

The disadvantage to this method of identification is that it requires active thought on the part of the installer. Nothing prevents you from installing the ribbon cable incorrectly. It is up to you to locate the markings and connect the cable accordingly.

Blocked Pins

Another method that has been used to prevent incorrect cable installation involves having an unused conductor. The pin for that conductor is broken off on the pin side and blocked on the block side. The blocked pinhole prevents the cable from being installed backward. Figure 11.2 shows a cable containing a blocked pin-hole to prevent a reversed installation.

This technique is an effective way to prevent the cable from being reversed, but it comes at the expense of one of the conductors in the cable. Because the goal is to keep the number of conductors in a cable down, using a blocked pin is seen as a less than optimal solution because it wastes a connector. Thus it's no longer in common use.

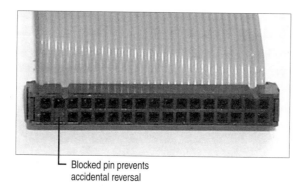

Blocked pin prevents
accidental reversal

Figure 11.2 Cable connector with a blocked pinhole

Another problem with blocked pin connectors is that if the manufacturer of the device doesn't remove the pin that is blocked, the cable won't connect, even in the correct orientation. This means that technicians have to break off pins manually or drill a pinhole in the block side of the connector. Most technicians are not comfortable doing this.

Keyed Connectors

The ultimate means of ensuring correct cable orientation involves placing a notched plastic housing around the pins on the device. The notch corresponds to a tab on the cable side of the connector, resulting in a keyed connection without the need to give up a conductor. This is the mechanism in widest use today. Figure 11.3 shows a keyed narrow SCSI cable.

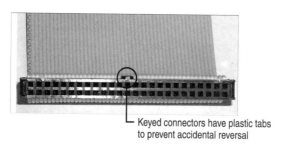

Keyed connectors have plastic tabs
to prevent accidental reversal

Figure 11.3 Narrow SCSI cable with a keyed connector

One of the reasons for the popularity of this mechanism is that it still works even if one of the components doesn't support the keyed connector. In other words, if the cable doesn't have the tab, it can still be connected to the pin side of the connector on the device. Likewise, if the device doesn't have the plastic housing, the keyed cable will still work because there's nothing to obstruct the tab. Note that if either the cable or the device lacks the keying mechanism (the tab or the housing, respectively), there is nothing to prevent the cable from being plugged in backward.

Understanding the mechanisms for ensuring correct ribbon cable orientation will help you ensure that your ribbon cables are connected correctly and are not reversed.

Caution Most systems today are not harmed when a ribbon cable is installed backward (the component simply won't work). Historically, however, improper installation has been known to result in damage components. Exercise caution when connecting ribbon cables to ensure that you use the correct orientation.

SCSI Connectors, Cabling, and Settings

Given the discussion in Chapter 3, Lesson 3, it should be no surprise that SCSI has the widest variety of connectors and cabling. SCSI's age and diversity have led to many connectors and a few different types of cabling that you need to know about when connecting a SCSI hard disk.

Internal Cables and Connectors

For the purposes of internal cabling, only two types of connector and a single type of cable are generally used. The connectors for a SCSI drive are either a 50-pin pin block connector or a D-shaped high-density 68-pin connector. These correspond to a 50-pin or 68-pin ribbon cable. The 50-pin ribbon cables are used for narrow devices, and the 68-pin cables are used to connect wide devices.

The 68-pin cable is narrower than the 50-pin cable because the wires are more densely packed. (The 68-pin cable is approximately 1.75 inches wide, while the 50-pin cable is approximately 2.5 inches wide.) Figure 11.4 shows a 68-pin SCSI cable. Refer back to Figure 11.3 to see a 50-pin SCSI connector.

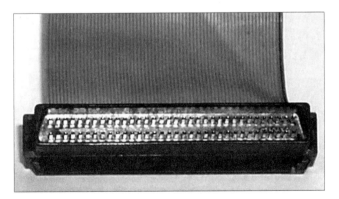

Figure 11.4   68-pin SCSI cable, showing the D-shaped connector

Unlike the 50-pin cable, the 68-pin cable uses a D-shaped connector to prevent it from being reversed accidentally. However, the pins of the 68-pin connector are much thinner than those of the 50-pin cable and are thus more susceptible to being bent. When installing 68-pin SCSI cables, be careful not to bend the connecting pins accidentally.

External Cables and Connectors

Compared to the two options available for internal cables, the options for external SCSI connectivity are considerable more complex. There are no fewer than four possible connectors and a variety of differing cable constructions. Let's review the four connectors first:

- **DB-25.**   Used primarily in the Macintosh and in early IBM SCSI controllers. The DB-25 connector is not in wide use today (except on SCSI Zip drives). The connector is secured through the use of screws.

- **Centronics-50.**   A 50-pin variant of the connector used by printers. This connector is used on many external devices because of its low cost, solid grounding, and secure connection. It is held in place by a set of wire clips on the host end that squeeze through slots on either end of the cable connector. The Centronics-50 connector was rarely used in PC SCSI cards because its large size made it difficult to fit in a slot. It is beginning to fall out of favor due to the high-density connectors that are now available.

- **High-density 50-pin.**   A D-shaped high-density 50-pin connector that has a lower profile than the 50-pin Centronics connector and thus can be used for cards in a PC. This connector is more expensive to manufacture than DB-25 and Centronics connectors, so acceptance was slow. It secures with either clips or screws. The lack of a specific standard for how to attach the connector has sometimes caused connectivity problems because the connector won't maintain a solid connection. This high-density connector was introduced with SCSI-2.

- **High-density 68-pin.**   A 68-pin variant of the high-density 50-pin connector. This connector is the only one used for external wide SCSI communications.

Figure 11.5 shows each of the external connectors. Since all of the connectors are D shaped, there's no concern that the cables will be reversed. However, the cable construction itself can be a problem.

Before leaving the topic of connectors, there's one more we should discuss: the SCA (single connection attachment) connector, a single connector that provides data, power, and configuration settings. This connector is most often used for hard disks installed in external cabinets. With the SCA connector, you can make every connection quickly and easily simply by plugging the disk into a backplane equipped with SCA connectors. Although this type of connector is still popular, disks are now being installed on swappable sleds that simplify the installation and removal of the disk within an array.

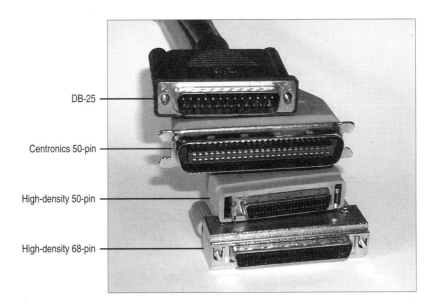

DB-25

Centronics 50-pin

High-density 50-pin

High-density 68-pin

Figure 11.5   The four types of external SCSI connectors

Chapter 3, Lesson 3 discussed the challenges involved in eliminating interference between signals in SCSI devices and the different changes that the SCSI standards have undergone to overcome this interference. Still, one of the best ways to ensure reliable SCSI operations is to use high-quality cables.

SCSI cables can be constructed in myriad ways, but the following are the three most common:

- **No shielding.**   In these cables, the conductors are all molded together, with little or no shielding from external interference. These cables are cheaper to manufacturer than shielded cables but lead to shorter usable cable lengths and to errors on the SCSI bus.

- **Outer shielding.**   In these cables, the conductors are molded together, just as in cables without shielding, but then an outer shield of foil or sometimes braid is wrapped around the conductors before the molding is added to the outside. Connecting the shield to the ground at each end reduces interference from external sources.

- **Outer and inner shielding.**   In these cables, the bundled conductors are shielded on the outside, as with outer shielding. In addition, however, the conductors are twisted into pairs internally, and each pair is surrounded by a thin aluminum foil shield. These shields are connected to the ground on each end. This type of cable is expensive to manufacture and thus expensive to purchase, but it offers the best protection from interference. These cables are recommended for SCSI implementations on a server.

Termination and Settings

SCSI uses IDs to differentiate among devices. The controller's ID is set by the controller BIOS. For hard disks and other devices, the ID is set by a series of jumpers. For narrow SCSI devices, the series will have three jumper sets (6 pins). For wide SCSI devices, the jumper set will have four sets (8 pins).

These sets of jumpers allow for settings between 0 and 7 for narrow devices and between 0 and 15 for wide devices. This range is possible because each jumper is a digit in a larger binary number. These numbers work just like the multidigit base 10 numbers that we use every day. Each digit to the left is multiplied by the base number times the number of positions to the left. For instance, the number 200 is 2 times 10 to the second power.

Binary numbers use powers of 2, not of 10. Thus, the digits are valued at 1, 2, 4, and 8, respectively. Table 11.1 shows the jumper settings and the resulting (base 10) numeric ID.

Table 11.1   Jumper Settings and Their SCSI IDs

Numeric ID	8	4	2	1
0	OFF	OFF	OFF	OFF
1	OFF	OFF	OFF	ON
2	OFF	OFF	ON	OFF
3	OFF	OFF	ON	ON
4	OFF	ON	OFF	OFF
5	OFF	ON	OFF	ON
6	OFF	ON	ON	OFF
7	OFF	ON	ON	ON
8	ON	OFF	OFF	OFF
9	ON	OFF	OFF	ON
10	ON	OFF	ON	OFF
11	ON	OFF	ON	ON
12	ON	ON	OFF	OFF
13	ON	ON	OFF	ON
14	ON	ON	ON	OFF
15	ON	ON	ON	ON

In addition to the ID-setting jumpers, SCSI devices also generally have jumpers for termination and termination power. Terminators, as you may remember from Chapter 3, Lesson 3, are required on both ends of a SCSI chain and should not be found in the middle of a chain. Applying a jumper to the termination jumper pins causes the disk or device to apply its own internal terminators to the SCSI chain. When possible, however, it's best to use external terminators just to eliminate the need to maintain the disks at the same locations on the cable.

Another jumper often found on SCSI devices controls termination power. Normally this jumper should not be used, since most controller cards provide termination power. Under certain circumstances, however, having a device provide termination power may make sense, particularly if the device isn't attached to the same power supply as the SCSI controller.

Some hard disks also have a jumper (or jumpers) that control when the disk starts to spin up. The choices are generally to spin the disk up when the controller initializes the device, after an interval of 10 seconds multiplied by the SCSI ID of the disk, or immediately when power is applied. The reason for this setting is to help spread out the startup process to avoid overloading the power supply. Disks require a relatively huge amount of power initially to break their inertia and reach their working speeds. If every drive were to try to spin up at the same time, the power supply might become overloaded. Delaying the startup of the disk motors distributes the load across a longer time, allowing it to be accomplished within the ability of the power supply.

Depending on the disk model, other options may be available as well. However, the options just discussed are relatively standard across all SCSI hard disks.

ATA/IDE Connectors, Cabling, and Settings

ATA/IDE drives are a bit simpler than SCSI drives. The cabling is simpler, and the number of jumpers is much smaller. This simplicity is due in part to the fact that ATA/IDE drives cannot be used externally; they must be installed inside the server case. These drives also lack many of the features that SCSI supports.

ATA/IDE Cabling and Connectors

Only one type of connector exists for ATA/IDE cables: a 40-pin connector that connects the disk and host adapter. There are two types of cables, however, that can attach to this 40-pin connector—a standard 40-conductor cable and the hybrid 80-conductor cable discussed in Chapter 3, Lesson 3. The hybrid 40-pin/80-conductor cables are required for Ultra ATA/66 or faster drives, but they can be used for drives of any speed.

ATA/IDE Operations and Settings

Generally speaking, every server has two ATA/IDE buses, each of which supports two attached devices, not including the controller (or host adapter). These buses, known as the primary and secondary buses, are usually attached through the PCI controller and support both the programmed I/O modes and the DMA modes. (Chapter 3, Lesson 3 discussed these modes of operation.) Sometimes, however, the ATA/IDE controller insists that all devices on the ATA/IDE bus operate in the same mode.

This restriction means that a hard disk capable of communicating via Ultra ATA/ 100 DMA might be slowed down to the programmed I/O mode 4 communications supported by the CD-ROM drive. Although this is becoming less and less of an issue as newer ATA/IDE controllers and BIOSs become available, you should consider it when deciding which devices to plug into which ATA/IDE buses.

In general, attach only hard disks to the primary ATA/IDE bus in a system, and place CD-ROM drives and other devices on the secondary controller. If four ATA/IDE devices are present, it may not possible to isolate the hard disks to the primary controller. When this is the case, attempt to attach the two fastest devices to the primary controller.

Settings on an ATA/IDE drive are also much simpler than their SCSI cousins. One reason for this is that there is no need to set termination on the ATA/IDE cables. In fact, each device partially terminates the ATA/IDE bus. This partial termination is done in such a way that the interference from reflected signals is minimized, so there's no need to be concerned about terminating the devices manually.

The only two settings that ATA/IDE drives support are a master/slave jumper and a cable select jumper. The master/slave jumper is simple in that only one master device and one slave device can be present on the bus. It doesn't matter where one device is plugged in in relation to the other, and any type of device can be assigned to either role. If you are connecting a hard disk and a nondisk device to the same bus, however, it's recommended that the hard disk be the master device and the other device be slave. Because the adapter and the master device control the bus, and hard disks generally support higher bus rates, this will help to ensure that the performance of a hard disk is not restricted by a slower nondisk device.

The cable select jumper on the drive is largely irrelevant in today's environment. It was historically used to determine which device should be considered the master and which should be considered the slave based on their positions on the cable, but the scarcity of special cable select cables and the relative ease of setting the drive as master or slave on the device itself have all but eliminated the use of cable select.

Fibre Channel Connectors, Cabling, and Settings

As you learned in Chapter 3, Lesson 3, Fibre Channel is a recent drive technology that is used for purposes other than just disk connectivity. Despite Fibre Channel's relatively recent entry into the hard disk marketplace, quite a variety of cables and connectors are available to connect Fibre Channel devices. Fibre

Channel can use either fiber optic or copper cables, and each type has its own connectors. Fiber optic cables are generally used to connect cabinets and storage area networks to the server. Copper cables are generally used for the distances inside the cabinet because of their lower cost.

Fiber Optic Cables and Connectors

Fiber optic cables come in two basic types: single-mode and multimode. Single-mode fiber optic cables are designed for transmission across longer distances, such as between buildings, and require higher-power transmitters. Multimode fiber optic cables require a smaller transmitter than the single-mode cables and work for distances of up to 200 meters. Multimode cables are the most common type of fiber optic cable used to connect Fibre Channel devices.

Two basic types of connectors are used for fiber optic cables: SC and ST. The ST type was historically used and consists of a bayonet-type locking mechanism in which an outer ring rotates around a post to hold the connector in place. The SC type is a square connector that is held in place with a plastic tab. Figure 11.6 shows what both types of connectors look like.

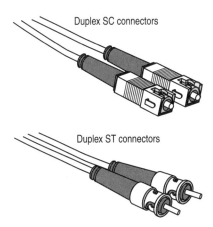

Figure 11.6 SC and ST fiber optic connectors

Copper Cables and Connectors

While only one type of copper cable is used to connect Fibre Channel devices, several different connectors are available. The two primary connectors used for Fibre Channel over copper are DB-9 and HSSDC (high-speed serial data connector). Each type of connector uses only four conductors. The DB-9 connector is larger than the HSSDC and is the same connector used for serial mice and Token Ring applications. It is also more rugged than the HSSDC. However, the HSSDC is sufficiently rugged for most applications.

Fibre Channel Settings

There are two addressing modes for Fibre Channel. One is a hardware mode that operates much like networks, in which the hardware address of the device is burned into a ROM chip on the device itself. The other addressing mode uses the physical port location that the device is plugged into to identify it. The nice thing about both of these addressing methods is that they provide a unique address to every device, meaning that you don't need to manually set the ID or configure a master/slave setting, as you do with other hard disk buses.

In addition to providing IDs automatically, Fibre Channel does not require any termination. Fiber optic cables don't have a problem with the signal being reflected off the end of the cable, and in copper cables this problem is addressed either by the switches and hubs or by the looping of cables between devices. In this way, each device terminates the signal from the preceding device.

Of all of the drive connectivity mechanisms described in this lesson, Fibre Channel is probably the easiest to set up because you can basically plug it in and get on with business.

Lesson Summary

In this lesson, you learned about the three types of hard disk connectivity: SCSI, ATA/IDE, and Fibre Channel. The lesson discussed the cabling and connectors used by each category of hard disk, as well as their requirements. It also covered the kinds of settings required for each bus type, as well as the methods for identifying orientation on the pin block connectors used in both narrow SCSI and ATA/IDE.

Lesson 2: Installing a Hard Disk

Although the actual process of installing a hard disk is straightforward in most cases, this lesson reviews that process and discusses potential issues so that the installation will go smoothly.

After this lesson, you will be able to

- Identify potential airflow issues within the server or external cabinet
- Install a hard disk in your server

Estimated lesson time: 20 minutes

Maintaining Airflow

Our discussion of environmental planning back in Chapter 2, Lesson 1 talked about the need to control both the humidity and temperature of a server's environment. That lesson indicated that temperatures in computer rooms are generally lower than in a standard office because of the need to leave a margin of safety and because the internal temperatures within a case can be far higher than the ambient room temperature.

Several factors influence the temperature inside the case, including the processor, the amount of memory, the number of hard disks, the capacity and number of fans, and finally obstructions to airflow. Although the processor and memory generate a fair amount of heat, most systems will have only a few processors (between one and four) and a few DIMMs' worth of memory. Conversely, a server may have several hard disks, which generate a significant amount of heat. For this reason, it is a good idea to review the airflow through a case when you're adding a hard disk.

The first step is to recognize the components that generate the most heat—the processor and hard disks, for the most part. If you maintain these two types of devices at an acceptable temperature, the internal temperature will more than likely be acceptable overall.

The most common cooling method in a server is *convective cooling,* in which air is passed over the components in order to produce a cooling effect. The effectiveness of convective cooling is related to three factors: the amount of air passing over the surface, the amount of surface area relative to the amount of heat generated, and the difference in temperature between the air and the component. The second factor in this list explains why a heat sink has lots of fins and spires. They give the heat sink a great deal of surface area for the air to flow over.

Unlike processors, however, disk drives don't have the luxury of massive heat sinks. They must make do with their own surface area and with the air flowing over it. Therefore, the best way to make cooling more effective for hard disks is to increase the amount of air flowing over the drive.

Most cases are designed to allow enough airflow over the hard disks to keep them sufficiently cool. However, the newer, faster drives generate more heat— heat that the case designers didn't plan on. Another potential problem is that cables aren't always routed well within the computer. This limits the ability of air to flow over the drives.

One simple way to improve airflow is to install fewer hard disks than the case has room for, and to spread out the ones you do install. Another simple solution is to route the cables, particularly the ribbon cables, in the server so that they don't obstruct the airflow as much. Many high-end servers have extensive cable routing assistance to ensure that airflow isn't obstructed.

Determining whether the airflow is effective in reducing the temperature is not a very easy process. For the processor, you can turn on the BIOS warning for CPU temperature. For the hard disks, no such warning exists. You can purchase devices that detect the internal temperature of a server case and sound a loud alarm when they detect a cooling problem. These devices are not a bad idea for "home-grown" systems that may not have adequate cooling. PC Power and Cooling (*http://www.pcpowerandcooling.com*) has a product called Alert 110 that indicates when the internal temperature of the case exceeds 110° F. It is a cheap and effective way to ensure that the internal temperature near the hard disks remains within a safe range.

If you've determined that the server is not able to cool the drives sufficiently, and you've already reworked the cable routing to ensure the best airflow across the drives, what else can you do? You basically have two options at this point. You can replace the power supply with one that has a higher-capacity fan, or you can add auxiliary fans to increase the airflow. Not all fans are created equal, even all fans of the same size. High-capacity fans spin faster and have better blade designs to increase the amount of air that they move. These high-capacity fans are not generally found in standard power supplies, but higher-end power supplies do have them.

Most vendors offer a variety of both high-capacity and standard-capacity auxiliary fans. One type of fan is mounted on the exterior of the case to help move air in and out of the case. This is probably the most effective additional fan that you can purchase because it helps the power supply exchange external (ambient room) air with the air inside the server. The quicker this air is exchanged, the more air will flow over the server's components and the lower the temperature of that air will be.

Caution Auxiliary fans can significantly improve airflow, but remember to mount them in the correct direction. If your power supply is an ATX power supply (as most are these days), its fan forces air into the case and allows the air to leak out. If you mount an auxiliary fan immediately below the power supply so that it blows air out of the case, the two fans will simply be exchanging air between themselves, and the air won't be flowing over all of the components of the server. You may want to mount fans on the lower front of a server and orient them to blow air out so that the power supply fan doesn't have to work as hard to get air into the case.

Other types of fans include ones that mount in the hard disk area and ones that mount in slots in the system. These types of fans help accelerate the airflow in the case. They are useful if a specific area of the case isn't getting enough airflow because of cards or cables, but they should generally be used only when there's a problem area that an auxiliary fan can't get air to.

One final note about airflow: Certain cases are not designed to maintain proper airflow when a large number of hard disks are installed. If you experience difficulty in maintaining appropriate airflow through the server case, you might consider replacing the case.

Installing a Hard Disk on a Sled

Servers today incorporate the same drive sleds that were previously used only for external drive cabinets. These sleds are designed to allow hard disks to be installed and removed quickly and easily. In addition, some sleds support hot swapping of disks into servers, allowing you to add disks without taking the server down.

Sleds are most often used for high-end servers or for hard disks that will be installed into external drive arrays. This limits their application to some SCSI and Fibre Channel operations. They are not used with ATA/IDE disks.

Two tasks are involved in installing a hard disk on a sled. The first task is to mount the hard disk on the sled itself. The second is to mount the sled in the cabinet.

Note Most server vendors allow you to purchase hard disks preinstalled on the sleds required for the server or external drive cabinet. It's recommended that you exercise this purchasing option if you can because it will ensure that the connectors are all installed in the correct order and in the correct locations.

▶   **To mount the hard disk on a sled**

1. Unpack the sled and hard disk on work surface. Use the same precautions discussed in Chapter 10 for eliminating the potential for ESD.

2. Set the hard disk on the sled to determine which mounting holes will be used to mount the hard disk. It's important to attach the disk to the sled with four screws, so determine the positioning that will allow this to happen.

3. Lightly tighten the screws to hold the disk on the sled. (You'll tighten them down the rest of the way later.)

4. Plug the data cable(s) into the back of the hard disk, and then connect the power.

5. If the hard disk sled controls the SCSI ID (as most SCSI sleds do), connect the ID leads (identified in the sled documentation) to the appropriate jumpers on the hard disk. Figure 11.7 shows SCSI ID leads from a hard disk sled connected to a hard drive.

Figure 11.7   SCSI ID leads from a hard disk sled

Note The process of connecting the ID leads can be tricky because most SCSI ID-setting cables use a pair of three-position or four-position cables that are meant to be installed over the pins on the disk. The second cable of the two generally has only one connector. This configuration creates two problems. The first is that the orientation for the first cable must match the disk's orientation so that the three positions on the disk's jumpers correspond to the wires on the cable. This generally means that the yellow wire must line up with the SCSI ID pin that controls the 4s place of the ID. The second problem is that the other cable should be installed on a common ground bus. This bus is generally on the bottom row of pins of the jumper, but it's difficult to determine for sure that the bottom row of pins on the jumper is the grounded side. Installing the cable with one connector on the signal side rather than the common side leads to interesting configuration problems.

6. If the hard disk sled has LED indicators for activity and errors, you'll need to connect these indicators. The pins for the remote indicators are generally located on the front of the disk. Because LEDs allow current to flow in only one direction, it's important to get the connection for the LEDs right. Failure to do so will not hamper drive performance, but it will make the activity and error indicators on the sled nonfunctional.

7. After you've plugged in all of the cables in the correct orientation, try to make sure they are routed within the sled so that they won't pull free or catch on anything. Disconnect and reroute the cables if necessary.

8. Tighten the screws that fasten the disk to the sled, but not so tight that you break the sled.

Once the disk is on the sled, the process of installing it is simple. Simply follow the manufacturer's instructions for installing the disk in the drive cabinet or server. This is generally done by pulling back arms or latches and inserting the disk. If the disks are mounted vertically (standing on their sides) as opposed to horizontally, the top of the disk is generally mounted to the right.

Installing a Hard Disk in a Server Case

In most moderate-size servers, and in servers that were built by local computer stores, the hard disks are mounted directly in the server without the use of a sled. This reduces the cost but means that you must shut the server down in order to install a hard disk.

▶ **To install a hard disk directly in a server**

1. Shut the server down normally.

2. Remove all cables from the back of the server, including power, network, keyboard, mouse, and video cables.

3. Move the server to your work area and remove the cover.

Caution Any time you open a server case, ESD is a consideration. If you don't remember how to protect your equipment from ESD, refer back to Chapter 10.

4. Locate an available bay for each hard disk being added, verify that a cable connector is available for each disk, and verify that there are sufficient power connectors.

Note Although you can use "Y" power adapters to make more power connectors available, you should be cautious when doing so. (A "Y" power adapter takes one power lead in and provides two power leads out.) Most power supplies have enough connectors for the number of devices they can support. You may find that the power supply isn't large enough to support all of the drives installed if you use "Y" adapters to get more power connectors.

5. Set all hard disk settings, using the jumpers provided with the hard disks.

6. Physically mount the hard disks into the available locations, and screw them into place with the screws provided with the hard disks.

7. Connect the data cable to each new disk.

8. Connect the power connector to each new disk.

9. For ATA/IDE or SCSI-based systems, power the system up on the bench and make sure that the new disks are detected. (Turn the server off before the operating system starts to load.)

10. Close the case.

11. Reinstall the server in the rack or computer room.

12. Reattach the network, video, mouse, keyboard, and any other cables, and turn the server on.

You've now physically installed the new disks. In the next lesson, you'll work on preparing them for the operating system by adding them into your RAID arrays.

Lesson Summary

In this lesson, you learned the importance of considering airflow when installing additional hard disks and how to improve the airflow if it's insufficient. You also learned how to install hard disks on sleds and directly in a server case.

Lesson 3: Adding to a RAID Array

Adding a disk to a RAID array is a little different from just adding a new hard disk to a server. The process of adding a new hard disk to a server is simple. You physically install the disk, partition it, and format the partitions, and you're done. Because with a RAID array you're working with existing data that must be reorganized and preserved, adding a hard disk to a RAID array is more dangerous.

After this lesson, you will be able to

- Identify the methods of expanding a RAID array
- Extend a RAID array to new physical drives

Estimated lesson time: 10 minutes

Options for Expanding a RAID Array

Someday every RAID controller and every server operating system will allow you to dynamically increase the size of RAID arrays without rebooting. For some high-end storage area networks and RAID controllers, the dream of seamless upgrades to hard disk space is already a reality. In these environments, disks can be dynamically added to the array, and the storage area network can add the new disks into the storage pool, reconfigure the RAID array, and provide the new space to the operating system dynamically. The operating system sees the additional drive space and allows you to extend the volume onto the new space.

This scenario is the ultimate in upgrading disk space: there's no downtime, and it's relatively easy to implement. However, not everyone can afford a storage area network or high-end RAID controllers, so we need to look at other alternatives. The complete range of options for expanding a RAID array is as follows:

- **Back up and restore.**   An option that is available to everyone is to back up the system, break the array, create a new array including the new disk(s), and restore the system. Although available for any operating system and storage configuration, this option is the most time-consuming alternative.

- **Resize and reboot.**   Some RAID controllers can dynamically resize the array. This is done on the controller while the server is running. When the process is complete (or in some cases when it starts), you reboot the server, at which point it sees the new space. The operating system can then be used to extend the volume. In this case, the downtime is limited to the time necessary to reboot.

- **Online expansion.**   This is the process described earlier, in which the RAID controller reconfigures the space and the operating system dynamically sees the space and allows it to be added to the volume. No downtime is necessary.

The sections that follow discuss each of these options in detail.

Back Up and Restore

Backing up and restoring the data is always an option, whether you have a high-priced storage area network or a few ATA/IDE drives. You can also use it with any operating system. In fact, it's the method that has historically been used to expand a RAID array. In more recent years, the significant amount of time required to perform a complete backup and restore of the data on a large RAID array has made this method intolerable for most large servers.

If your RAID software doesn't support online expansion, however, a backup and restore might be your only option. You may be using RAID software that is built into the operating system and that doesn't support online expansion, or you may have a hardware-based controller that doesn't provide this feature.

Even when you find yourself limited to a backup and restore as an expansion option, you may be able to use a hybrid technique if your server is using integrated software RAID. Although the RAID software built into operating systems doesn't include an option for online expansion, PowerQuest (*http://www.powerquest.com*) has a software product called ServerMagic that can be used to resize software-based RAID arrays on Microsoft Windows 2000 without losing data. Comparable products are a available from other companies. Utilities are also available for Linux that will resize software-based RAID arrays.

If you choose to use one of these utilities, it's still wise to have a valid backup before beginning. Although the utilities are generally well tested, there's always a chance that something will go wrong in the resizing process that will render the volume unusable.

▶   **To expand a RAID array using the back up and restore method**

1. Back up the server.
2. Shut down the server.
3. Install the new hard disk.
4. Break the existing RAID array.
5. Create a new RAID array that includes the new disk.
6. Partition and format the new RAID array.
7. Restore the backup to the new RAID array.

Resize and Reboot

If your RAID array uses a hardware-based RAID controller that supports online expansion, you can take advantage of this feature. It significantly reduces the amount of effort required to expand the RAID array. The only difference between a system that must use this resize and reboot option and one that can perform a full online expansion is whether the operating system supports dynamic changes in disk space. In today's environment, most systems require a reboot after resizing.

The only operating system that consistently supports dynamic changes in disk space is Windows 2000. Although some of the SCSI drivers for Linux are able to rescan the bus for new drives and changed parameters, this support isn't consistently available. Novell NetWare does not support rescanning for drive size changes.

The process of resizing the RAID array and adding that space to the server is relatively simple when your RAID controller supports online expansion. The following gives a basic overview of the steps involved:

1. Back up the server. (You've been warned!)
2. Install the new hard disk.
3. Use the RAID controller software to expand the RAID array.
4. Wait for the RAID controller to complete the RAID array rebuild.
5. Shut down and restart the server.
6. Add the additional space in the RAID array to the existing volume, using the operating system tools.

The first step of any drive expansion process is to make sure that you have a valid backup—even if you don't need it to complete the procedure. You never know when problems will occur that will render the volume unusable. If that happens, the backup may be your only way to recover.

Online Expansion

When the RAID controller supports online expansion, you can expand the RAID volume without rebooting the server. This method is quick and easy, but it requires some preparation.

For most operating systems, you'll need to enable the features on the RAID controller that allow it to report a higher capacity than actually exists in the array. This isn't necessary for Windows 2000, but for all other operating system it is. This process is sometimes called *virtual sizing*. Virtual sizing allows a RAID controller to report the size of the largest RAID array that it could create to the operating system. The operating system can then create a partition as large as the real available space in the array.

When new disks are added to the RAID array, new partitions can be created on the virtual drive, and the volume can be extended onto the new partition. The primary problem with using virtual sizing on hard disks is that the operating system may attempt to use more space than is really available. If your controller reports only the actual size of the array to the operating system, rather than an arbitrary maximum limit for the controller, you won't be able to do an online expansion, and you'll have to reboot to extend the RAID array.

If your RAID controller is capable of reporting a virtual size for the array, the process for extending the array is easy.

▶   **To extend an array when your RAID controller can report a virtual size for the array**

1. Back up the server. (You've been warned!)

2. Install the new hard disk on the RAID controller.

3. Use the RAID software to add the new disk to the disk array.

4. Add a new partition to the disk, and extend the existing volume onto it.

Lesson Summary

In this lesson, you learned the three different ways of expanding a RAID array: back up and restore, resize and reboot, and online expansion. You learned that the primary drawback of the back up and restore method is the amount of time it takes, and the primary requirement of the resize and reboot method is a RAID controller that supports online expansion. However, to fully utilize online expansion, your operating system must support requerying the drives to get new sizes or your RAID controller must be able to report a larger array than is available to the operating system.

Review

Here are some questions to help you determine whether you have learned enough to move on to the next chapter. If you have difficulty answering these questions, please go back and review the material in this chapter before beginning the next chapter. The answers for these questions are located in the appendix, "Questions and Answers."

1. What are the two types of cables used for ATA/IDE devices?

2. Why do ribbon cables present connector problems?

3. What three methods are used to identify how pin block connectors should be plugged in?

4. How many types of connectors and cables are there for internal SCSI connections?

5. Which disk drive buses need to be terminated?

6. What does the term "cable select" mean with respect to the ATA/IDE bus?

7. Which type of fiber optic cable is used most often with Fibre Channel?

8. How many addressing modes does Fibre Channel support?

9. What is the first thing you should do to address airflow issues?

10. What type of fan should be used first when an airflow issue is suspected?

11. Why are sleds used with hard disks?

12. What is the primary disadvantage of using the back up and restore method to expand a RAID array?

C H A P T E R   1 2

Adding and Upgrading Add-On Cards

About This Chapter

Chapters 10 and 11 talked about upgrades that can be made to a server to improve its performance or to add capacity. This chapter continues that discussion by covering add-on cards, including network cards, hard disk controllers, and other cards that you might add to a server to allow it to do its job. Add-on cards can substantially improve the performance of a system by reducing the load on the processor and on other add-on cards.

This chapter is our last stop for hardware upgrades in the server. Chapter 13 turns to a review of external devices and software that help to manage the server.

Note The process of adding a new card is basically the same as that of replacing an old card with another one. We focus our energy in this chapter on adding new cards because the process of removing a card is generally quite straightforward.

Before You Begin

To complete this chapter, you should have

- Your server documentation
- The parts to be installed

Lesson 1: Verifying Resource Availability

When you're looking to install a new processor, the question of availability is simple. If the motherboard has an open processor slot, there's room for another processor. This simplistic method doesn't work when you're looking at expansion slots for add-on cards in a computer, however. Just because there is physical space in the computer to add another card doesn't mean that the system will be able to use the new card. This lesson discusses issues related to the resources required by add-on cards and how the availability of those resources can affect your ability to install new cards.

After this lesson, you will be able to

- Identify the different types of slots used in a computer and determine whether any are available for additional cards
- Review available resources for add-on cards

Estimated lesson time: 5 minutes

Slots and Resources

Think of the slots on your computer as being like the electrical outlets in your home. An electrical outlet provides a place where you can plug a device in. It doesn't guarantee that you'll be able to use the device once it is plugged in. For example, you might have forgotten to pay your electric bill, or the circuit might be overloaded, tripping the circuit breaker. Similarly, slots are just access ports to the resources of the server; they don't guarantee that resources will be available to drive the cards that are installed in them.

Despite the fact that slots don't ensure the availability of resources, available slots are very important. Without an available slot, you can't install another add-on card, no matter how many resources are available. Further complicating the issue is the fact that there is more than one type of slot, and different motherboard designs may make some slots usable in one bus format (either ISA or PCI) but not both.

Installed servers today use two basic slot formats: ISA and PCI. Although the use of ISA cards in servers is strongly discouraged, and ISA slots in servers are being phased out, an ISA slot is still necessary—or at least appropriate—for some applications. It may not be long, however, before ISA slots in servers are a thing of the past.

At one time, one of the best examples of the usefulness of an ISA slot was for a remote access modem. Until sometime in the late 1990s, most modems were still ISA based, and the few PCI-based modems that were available were expensive and difficult to find. Having an ISA slot in a server meant that you could install an ISA modem for your remote access needs without paying the premium that PCI devices commanded.

I should mention here that the reason that ISA devices are suboptimal in a server is because they are so much slower than their PCI counterparts, and they can significantly decrease the overall performance of the server if the card is used actively. In the case of a modem for remote access, this slowness wasn't generally a problem because the remote access traffic was generally light and was confined to off-hours when the server wasn't heavily loaded.

In addition to ISA cards' slower performance, they sometimes share a single opening for a slot (the vertical backplane at the back of the server has several openings for slots) with the adjoining PCI slot. This overlap is due to the fact that ISA cards and PCI cards affix to opposite sides of their metal backing slats. If you're looking down on a server from the front, ISA cards are affixed to the left edge of the metal slat, and PCI cards are affixed to the right edge. This allows a single slot opening on the back to be used for either a PCI or ISA card, but it generally means that fewer total expansion slots are available because there aren't enough slot openings. Figure 12.1 shows a computer with mixed PCI and ISA expansion slots. When reviewing your server to determine whether additional slots are available, you'll want to ensure that the slot opening on the back of the server is available, too.

Unusable PCI slot (no slat opening available)

Usable PCI slot (slat opening available)

Figure 12.1   Intermingled PCI and ISA slots

No matter which slots you use, it's important to understand that the location of the slot doesn't control the resources that the add-on card can use. The resources are pooled and are available for all devices regardless of their position on the bus. There are some minor exceptions to this, in that some slots have features that others don't. Specifically, some slots may be capable of bus mastering. (PCI bus mastering was discussed in Chapter 1, Lesson 5 and will be reviewed in the upcoming section on DMA channels.)

Note Although it's not generally thought of as a resource, power can be a problem with add-on cards, just as it can when installing a hard disk. Consider whether the available output of the server's power supply will be enough to support the add-on card you're considering.

Interrupts

Chapter 1, Lesson 5 discussed interrupts, their function, and the various problems involved with them. Recall that interrupts are a mechanism for alerting the CPU that an add-on card needs attention. The biggest issues with interrupts are their consumption of CPU time and the fact that only a limited number are available within a server.

Historically, each device had its own interrupt, but today the PCI bridge allows PCI devices to share one or more interrupts (up to four). The CPU determines which card needs attention by querying the PCI bridge.

Not every device supports interrupt sharing, however. Some hardware drivers expect to have a direct interrupt to the card itself. Although this is rarely the case, and it isn't optimal, there's little you can do to avoid this situation because vendors generally won't tell you that the card or driver must be on its own interrupt until you call technical support with a problem.

When you're dealing with limited available interrupts, you'll want to minimize the number of interrupt request (IRQ) lines needed. One way to do this is to get "denser" add-on cards. For example, a single SCSI adapter might require one IRQ line. If you need three SCSI buses, three adapters might require three IRQ lines. However, a SCSI controller with four buses on it will generally require only one interrupt, saving precious IRQ lines for other cards. Therefore, when you're installing a new server or upgrading an existing server, consider how many cards of the same type you need. If you have a choice between a card that supports four SCSI buses and a card that supports only one, you may be better off with the card with four buses, even if you don't need all of them. It will be more efficient in terms of the number of IRQ lines it uses and, to some degree, in the number of interrupts that it generates. The same is true for network cards. Consider purchasing one faster network card instead of two or more teamed adapters to conserve IRQ lines as well as slots.

Another means of reducing the interrupt congestion is to remove or turn off devices that are not in use. For instance, if you don't use the second serial port on the server or the USB controller, you can turn it off in the BIOS so that the interrupt that it would normally use can be made available to other add-on cards.

DMA Channels

As you know from our discussion in Chapter 1, Lesson 5, PCI bus mastering is a mechanism to improve performance by allowing some transfers to occur without the intervention of the CPU. This technique isn't new to the PCI bus, however.

The ISA bus standard contains a mechanism to allow the same kind of CPU-independent transfers. This mechanism places a direct memory access (DMA) controller on the motherboard and allows the add-on card to request a channel on that DMA controller for its use.

As with IRQ lines, the number of DMA channels is limited. In fact, the total number available is only seven. When ISA devices were becoming more efficient, they started relying on DMA channels, sometimes causing the same sort of congestion on the DMA channels that was present in the IRQ lines. When the new buses were designed, the DMA controllers were placed on the add-on cards and were allowed to communicate directly with system memory. This change eliminated the need to use a fixed set of channels on the motherboard and made installing high-performance cards easier. If you're adding a high-performance ISA card, and not a card based on a newer bus, to a server, you'll need to make sure that you have enough available DMA channels. However, in most cases you won't be adding new ISA cards to a server, so it won't be an issue.

One final note on DMA channels: Even though the number of DMA channels is no longer limited by the motherboard, it's still sometimes the case that not every PCI slot supports bus mastering. Bus mastering is simply DMA through the use of controllers on the add-on card, instead of through the controller on the motherboard. For this reason, you'll want to be conscious of which PCI add-on cards require bus mastering support and which ones can function without it.

I/O Ports

In a welcome change from IRQ lines and DMA channels, the PC platform has more than 65,000 input/output (I/O) ports. Compared to the 15 IRQ lines and 7 DMA channels, the I/O ports are like wide-open country. The only real problem with them is the potential for two cards or devices to want the same port at the same time.

When installing non–Plug and Play ISA cards, you needed to set the I/O address manually. If two or more cards were set with the same I/O address, one or more of the cards would be unusable. This isn't a problem in today's servers because most of the cards are PCI based and fully support Plug and Play, allowing the motherboard BIOS and operating system to configure an available I/O range for the cards to use. Since most motherboard BIOSs and devices today are Plug and Play compatible, I/O port conflicts are quite rare.

Lesson Summary

In this lesson, you learned how to identify the available slots and slat openings in a server. You also learned that having physical space for a new add-on card doesn't mean that resources will be available for the card. The lesson reviewed IRQs, DMA channels, and I/O ports, and it explained that many of the issues associated with these resources are no longer of great concern because of the wide use of the PCI bus in servers.

Lesson 2: Verifying Compatibility

In Lesson 1, you ensured that you have sufficient slots and resources for a new card, but you're not ready to install the card yet. You still need to verify that the card is compatible with the operating system and with the server in which you'll be installing the card. This important step will help you avoid installing problematic add-on cards in the server. In this lesson, you'll verify compatibility and review other information sources to gain an awareness of potential problems.

After this lesson, you will be able to
- Verify that an add-on card is included on the compatibility lists
- Identify potential problems with an add-on card before they happen

Estimated lesson time: 10 minutes

Checking Compatibility Lists

Despite the fact that standards guide the development of the PC platform, there is no one true way of doing things. Some manufacturers or software vendors interpret the standards in one way, and other manufacturers interpret them in another way. These small differences in interpretation are not usually enough to cause problems, but sometimes these discrepancies can converge to cause severe stability issues.

Because of the potential for stability issues, Microsoft began maintaining a hardware compatibility list (HCL) for Windows NT back in the days of version 3.1. The list contained devices that Microsoft had tested and knew worked with Windows NT. Although it contained a few complete server systems, the bulk of the list consisted of add-on cards that Microsoft had certified to work with the operating system.

Were there add-on cards that would work that weren't on the hardware compatibility list? Sure. But if you chose hardware from the list, you were reasonably assured that it would work with the operating system. One of the primary reasons that the hardware compatibility list was needed was the development of so-called "clone" hardware.

Clone hardware is hardware that is supposed to work exactly like another piece of hardware. Sometimes, however, slight differences in the clone can wreak havoc. For instance, Novell had a standard network card called the NE2000. Microsoft wrote a Windows NT driver for that card. When the operating system began to be used in the field, there were many complaints about its stability with "NE2000" cards. On further investigation, Microsoft found that the cards the operating system was having trouble with weren't Novell NE2000 cards; they were third-party clones that were supposed to work exactly like the NE2000 card. When the drivers for Windows NT were rewritten, their means of interacting with the card changed slightly from the method used by the clients of the time.

When Microsoft tested the different method of access with the NE2000 cards, it worked, so Microsoft released the driver. However, some of the NE2000 clones couldn't handle the way the Windows NT driver was attempting to use them, and they would react by failing to initialize, locking up during use, or locking the whole server up. These problems obviously weren't conducive to Windows NT being considered a stable operating system.

As a result, the hardware compatibility list was born. It was designed to allow anyone to purchase and build a system that was verified to be compatible with Windows NT. By the way, this list doesn't ensure that all of the parts selected for the server will work with one another. It only means that each device has been tested individually to work with the operating system.

Today some Linux vendors, most notably Red Hat, have begun maintaining hardware compatibility lists for their version of Linux. These lists are very similar to the lists created by Microsoft, except that because there's no centralized control over the operating system, many of the entries in the list state that the product works based on "community knowledge." This indicates that others in the Linux community have been able to get the hardware to work. The lists also specify how easy or difficult it was to get the device to work.

Novell doesn't maintain a single hardware compatibility list; instead it relies on its YES program, which uses a "YES, Tested & Approved" logo to indicate to consumers that a particular product has been tested and approved for use with Novell NetWare. (It appears, based on information from Novell's Web site, that Novell is actively investigating expanding the YES program to include its non-NetWare products as well.) To determine whether a product has received the Novell YES program certification, review the product box or the vendor's Web site for the YES program logo.

In addition to the hardware compatibility list that Microsoft makes available, it also has a certification program for hardware that allows vendors to use a "Designed for Windows" logo to indicate products that have been tested to work with Windows. This is similar to Novell's YES program, except that Microsoft makes available a comprehensive compatibility list for all of these devices, whereas Novell does not, at this time, provide such information.

Checking compatibility lists or approval programs is a good first step in determining whether a product will work on a system. These certifications are not foolproof, however, so you should do some additional research to determine whether the add-on card will be supported if you can't find it on the compatibility list. For Microsoft, reviewing the hardware compatibility list is as easy as going to the Microsoft Web site at *http://www.microsoft.com/hcl*. For Linux distributions, you'll need to go to the distribution's Web site to find the hardware compatibility list, if one is available.

Finally, note that compatibility lists may not contain devices that work fine with the operating system. Because of the costs associated with receiving the certification (and logo), some companies opt not to have the testing performed. Although you must exercise extra caution with these devices, the fact that they are not included on the hardware compatibility list doesn't mean that they won't work, just that their operation hasn't been tested by a third party. You should check the vendor's Web site to determine their commitment to supporting their product on your operating system.

Verifying Hardware Compatibility

As was mentioned earlier, the fact that a device is included on a hardware compatibility list or in a certification program doesn't mean that it will function in your specific hardware environment. It only ensures that the device will work with the operating system. The job of determining whether an add-on card will work with your motherboard and with the other hardware in the system is your responsibility.

Admittedly, today's environment is much better than the one of only a few years ago. The nearly universal support of the PCI bus and the support for Plug and Play have made the process of installing new hardware relatively simple. They have also nearly eliminated all of the compatibility issues between devices. Intel did a good job of spelling out all of the details in the specification for the PCI bus.

The best way to ensure hardware compatibility is to review the vendor's FAQ and knowledge base for the product. You should also check for information in the Internet newsgroups. If you're not sure how to do this, review Chapter 1, Lesson 1.

Lesson Summary

In this lesson, you learned about hardware compatibility lists—what they do, who maintains them, and how to use them. You also learned about the marketing programs that are used to help consumers know which products have been certified to work with a given operating system, regardless of whether a hardware compatibility list is maintained. The lesson also discussed hardware compatibility and how to verify that a new add-on card will work with your hardware.

Lesson 3: Installing Add-On Cards

Installing a new add-on card is a relatively straightforward process, particularly when the operating system automatically detects the new hardware. The only challenges that sometimes arise involve the software driver needed to operate the hardware.

After this lesson, you will be able to

- Install new add-on cards

Estimated lesson time: 15 minutes

Installing a New Card

Once all of the preparations have been made, the actual installation of the add-on card is a simple process that takes only a few minutes.

▶ **To install a new add-on card**

1. Back up the server. (You've been warned.)

2. Shut down the server.

3. Remove all attached cables, and remove the server to your workbench.

Note Observe the ESD precautions described in Chapter 10 when you open the case.

4. Remove the server cover.

5. Remove the retaining screw for the slat where the card will be installed.

6. Remove the metal slat from the backplane of the server.

7. Remove the add-on card from its packaging and electrostatic bag.

8. Install the card in the server by inserting it directly in the slot. You may need to insert the back edge of the card just before the front of the card to help it fit into place. Additionally, you may need to reach outside the case and push the bottom of the metal slat attached to the new add-on card inward slightly so that it won't get caught on the back edge.

9. Once the card is in the slot, place both of your thumbs on the top of the card where the front and back of the slot are. Press the card firmly into the slot.

10. Replace the retaining screw you removed from the slat earlier, securing the new card. When the screw is tightened, the card should remain in the slot. If it doesn't it may be necessary to bend the top of the new card's slat slightly so that the screw holds the card in place.

11. Replace the server case.

12. Return the server to its location, and replace the cabling.

13. Boot up the server.

The installation of a new add-on card is generally trivial compared with the process of installing the correct driver for the card. We'll look at that process next.

Installing the Card's Software

The process for installing the software for the card you've just installed depends on the type of card and on the operating system you are using. However, there is a standard set of steps that you should follow whenever a new card is installed.

▶ **To install software for a card**

1. Ensure that the next bootup doesn't show any errors. Sometimes installing a new card will cause a conflict that is detectable by the motherboard BIOS or by the BIOS on the card. If an error is detected, refer to the documentation for the motherboard or the add-on card to determine the nature of the error.

2. If the add-on card has onboard BIOS, set all of the options for the card at the first bootup, before the device is detected by the operating system and before you install drivers for it. This will help eliminate any potential problems with devices whose behavior changes with different BIOS settings. Don't forget to document the BIOS version and the settings.

3. Install the device driver for the add-on card. Windows 2000 will probably detect the card automatically. In NetWare, you'll need to load the driver and set up the driver in the startup files. In Linux, you may need to install the module to support the device, depending upon whether the device support is compiled into the kernel or not.

4. Make sure that the device is working. The process for testing a new add-on card depends on the type of card. Here are some suggestions for testing different types of add-on cards:

   - **Hard disk (SCSI, Fibre Channel) controllers.** Attach a CD-ROM drive and look for it to show up on the server. Or connect a tape drive and attempt a backup to the tape drive. Or connect a hard drive and try to partition it.

   - **Network cards.** Connect the network card to a hub or a switch, and make sure that the link light turns on. Or give it a valid IP address, and use the server to ping another device on the local network.

   - **Multiport serial cards.** Most multiport serial cards come with loopback adapters and diagnostic software. Run the diagnostic software and make sure that the software finds the card and the ports.

   - **Multiport modem cards.** Use the diagnostic program that came with the card. Or use a terminal program to attach to one of the serial ports and send it an AT command, followed by a return. The modem should respond with "OK."

5. Reboot the server to make sure that the device continues to work. This will ensure that you have everything configured so that the device will initialize when the system boots.

Before you finish your installation of the new card, you'll want to make sure that its firmware is up to date (see Chapter 4), just as you did with all of the other server components when you installed them. Although this process takes a little time, it's generally better to do it while the server is already down for scheduled maintenance, rather than having to shut it down again later.

Lesson Summary

In this lesson, you learned the procedures for installing a new add-on card, installing the software driver, and testing the card.

Review

Here are some questions to help you determine whether you have learned enough to move on to the next chapter. If you have difficulty answering these questions, please go back and review the material in this chapter before beginning the next chapter. The answers for these questions are located in the appendix, "Questions and Answers."

1. Why might an open slot not be usable?

2. What techniques can you use to free additional interrupt request lines so that they can be used by new add-on cards?

3. What issues can be associated with I/O ports?

4. What information does a compatibility list convey?

5. What other sources, besides the hardware compatibility list, should you check when installing a new add-on card?

CHAPTER 13

Upgrading UPSs, Monitoring the System, and Choosing Service Tools

About This Chapter

The past several chapters have talked about upgrading the hardware within a server. This chapter finishes our discussion of upgrades by talking about upgrading the external equipment that most professionals forget about: the UPSs. It also describes the various software and hardware approaches to system monitoring. Finally, it lists a number of service tools that may help you maintain your existing systems and identify when an upgrade is necessary.

The lessons in this chapter will prepare you for the next few chapters, which focus on proactive maintenance of the system.

Before You Begin

To complete this chapter, you should have

- Your server documentation
- Any batteries or UPSs necessary to replace existing batteries and UPSs

Lesson 1: Upgrading UPSs

This lesson discusses the various ways of upgrading a UPS, including replacing existing batteries and adding new batteries to increase run time. It also discusses matrixed UPSs and how to upgrade the inverter units in addition to the batteries.

After this lesson, you will be able to

- Add or replace batteries on a UPS

- Install new inverter units on matrixed UPSs

Estimated lesson time: 20 minutes

Replacing UPS Batteries

UPS batteries have a fixed useful life, after which they are unable to provide the power the UPS inverter needs to support the attached load. Thus, all batteries eventually need to be replaced. Battery life is generally listed with the UPS but can range from 18 months to 5 years, depending upon the type, size, and usage of the battery. As you learned in Chapter 2, Lesson 2, there are three types of UPSs. The small UPSs have fixed batteries that aren't replaceable. In these UPSs, you must replace the UPS itself at the end of the batteries' life span. Mid-sized UPS have replaceable internal batteries, and large UPSs have external battery racks that house replaceable batteries.

This discussion focuses first on the mid-size UPSs that have replaceable batteries. Unless you have a large environment, you're likely to have this type of UPS, with batteries housed inside the unit.

Replacing a Battery in a Mid-Sized UPS

The primary challenge when replacing a battery in a mid-sized UPS is that you have to open the unit itself up to do so. In most cases, the UPS manufacturer will indicate that the unit is designed to allow hot swapping of the battery. That is, the UPS (and the servers it supports) need not be shut down to replace the battery.

However, the manufacturer will also generally include some strong cautions about doing a hot-swap upgrade because of the high voltages present inside the UPS. These cautions should be sufficient to convince you that it's best to plan to replace the UPS battery during scheduled maintenance. The risk of personal injury and the possibility that the UPS might shut down during this process are substantial enough to warrant replacing the battery while the connected servers are shut down.

Mid-sized UPSs use sealed lead-acid batteries similar to the ones used in cars. Unlike some car batteries, however, UPS batteries are completely maintenance free. The fact that these batteries are sealed helps ensure that no harmful acid leaks out inside the battery case.

Note The materials used in the construction of lead-acid batteries are harmful to the environment. Most UPS manufacturers will recycle old batteries for you. Because it's illegal to dispose of these batteries yourself in most locations, we recommend that you take advantage of these recycling programs.

A general process for replacing the batteries in a UPS appears below. This procedure is for reference only. Due to the potentially dangerous voltages present inside a UPS, please refer to the battery replacement instructions for your specific equipment.

▶ **To replace the batteries in a UPS**

1. Shut down all servers and equipment connected to the UPS.

2. Shut down the UPS.

3. Unplug the UPS from the wall outlet.

4. Remove the new battery from its packaging. (Save the packaging for returning the old battery.)

5. Remove the front cover or case as indicated in the battery replacement guidelines.

Caution Even though power is disconnected from the wall, the batteries and circuitry in the UPS still contain significant electrical energy. You may want to remove metal rings and bracelets and be cautious of contact with bare wires.

6. Remove the screws that hold the battery compartment door in place.

7. Slide the battery forward until both wires connecting the battery to the UPS are visible.

8. Disconnect the red, positive wire from the battery.

9. Disconnect the black, negative wire from the battery.

10. Slide the battery the rest of the way out.

11. Slide the new battery in a little, leaving both terminals exposed.

12. Connect the black, negative wire to the battery.

13. Connect the red, positive wire to the battery.

14. Ensure that no metal is exposed on the wire or the battery terminals.

15. Push the battery completely into the battery compartment.

16. Close and secure the battery door with the screws you removed earlier.

17. Replace the UPS cover.

18. Plug the UPS back into the wall outlet.

19. Turn on the UPS, and ensure that the bad battery indicator is not lit. If the bad battery indicator is lit, call the UPS manufacturer or follow the troubleshooting procedures in the UPS user manual.

20. Pack the old battery in the packaging you saved from the new battery, and seal it for return to the vendor's battery recycling program.

As you can see, the process of installing a replacement battery in an existing unit is relatively trivial. The only significant issue involves the need to exercise caution because of the potentially high voltages remaining in the UPS.

Replacing a Battery in a Large UPS

Once UPSs reach a certain size, the inverter—the part that converts the battery power to alternating current (AC)—is separated from the batteries. This separation allows you to replace the batteries without opening the inverter cabinet, helping to reduce the risk of shock when replacing batteries.

The size at which the inverter and batteries are separated varies by manufacturer and even by product line within a manufacturer. However, most of the time the change from internally sealed batteries to external batteries happens at around the 3 KVA threshold. UPSs that supply more than 3 KVA of power tend to have their inverter kept separate from the batteries, in part to keep the heat that the inverter generates away from the batteries, which don't respond well to heat.

For most larger UPSs, the procedure for replacing external batteries is simple. The following steps describe a typical UPS battery replacement when the UPS uses external battery packs supplied by the manufacturer. This type of arrangement is generally used in so-called matrixed UPSs (discussed in a later section) and in UPSs that are just large enough to warrant external battery cabinets but are too small to require a dedicated rack of batteries.

▶   **To replace a UPS battery when the UPS uses external battery packs supplied by the manufacturer**

1. Shut down the connected servers and devices (optional).

2. Shut down the UPS (optional).

3. Disconnect the battery cable from the UPS. You may have to remove a locking mechanism.

4. If you're removing more than one battery pack, disconnect each battery pack from the others.

5. Remove the battery pack(s).

6. Place the new battery pack(s) next to the UPS.

7. Connect the new battery pack(s) together, and lock the connectors in place (if a locking mechanism is provided).

8. Connect the first battery pack to the UPS, and lock the connector in place.

9. Verify that the battery failure indicator light on the UPS is off.

Larger UPSs require complete racks of batteries. Service technicians most often install these batteries to ensure that the wiring is done properly and that proper safety precautions are followed. If for some reason you decide to replace the batteries yourself, you'll follow a procedure similar to the following. As always, read the UPS documentation and follow the replacement instructions for the specific UPS.

▶ **To replace batteries in a large UPS**

1. Lock the UPS into line-conditioner-only mode, if possible. This will allow the UPS to continue using its transformers and MOVs to suppress power surges, along with preventing it from trying to transfer to battery power while the replacement is in progress.

2. Disconnect the batteries from the UPS by removing the main connector from the UPS to the batteries.

3. Disconnect each battery connecting cable, starting at the UPS and working backward. Place a protective plastic cap over the battery terminal after the cable is removed. Note the connection order, and be careful not to make contact between the positive lead of the battery and either the rack or a negative lead.

4. Remove each used battery from the rack.

5. Install each new battery into the rack.

6. Individually connect each battery, starting with the battery farthest from the UPS and moving forward. Be careful not to touch any positive terminal or cable with any negative terminal, cable, or the rack itself.

7. Once you've connected all of the individual cables, reconnect the battery racks to the UPS.

8. Verify that the UPS sees valid batteries attached and that it doesn't indicate any kind of an error.

Adding New UPS Batteries

Adding new batteries to a UPS is very similar to replacing the batteries in a UPS. However, there are some very important differences. The first difference is that not every UPS supports extra batteries. In these cases, you are limited to the batteries the UPS already has.

The second difference involves the need to make sure that the battery cables can handle the current they will carry. When you're simply replacing batteries, you know that the connecting cables are sufficient to carry the current from the batteries to the inverter. When you're adding batteries to an existing configuration, however, you need to verify that the battery cables connecting the batteries to the inverter are sufficient to carry the current.

There are guidelines for the size of cable required for a given voltage and amperage, but the best idea is to contact the UPS manufacturer and verify that the cables are sufficiently sized for the additional batteries.

Working with Matrixed UPSs

Somewhere in the middle ground between mid-sized and large UPSs exists a hybrid UPS that allows you to replace modules without taking down the entire system. These *matrixed* systems make expansion easy by allowing you to add inverter modules to support more load and battery modules to allow the load to be carried longer.

The fundamental difference between a matrixed UPS and a mid-sized UPS with replaceable batteries is that in a matrixed UPS the power generation and distribution components can be replaced independently. This means that it automatically supports a built-in fail-safe bypass mode of operation when the inverter is non-functional. In other words, the power will continue to be conditioned by the transformers and MOVs even if the inverter is not present.

This ability is certainly an advantage, but the sales of matrixed UPSs have not been significant, so similarly sized UPSs with replaceable batteries are usually a better deal than matrixed UPSs. (Due to economies of scale, devices that are sold in quantity are generally cheaper than those that cannot be made in similar quantities. This leads to matrixed UPSs being more expensive.)

Replacing an Entire UPS

With smaller to mid-sized UPSs, you're likely to just add a new UPS to handle new servers. However, if you have a large UPS, you'll generally replace it with a new, larger unit when you need to support greater loads. Using a single large UPS means that you have fewer units to monitor and maintain.

Replacing a large, hardwired UPS with a new one is a simple process. (Most large UPSs are hardwired into the electrical system of the building rather than being plugged in.) The new wiring is run for the new UPS, the supported systems are shut down, the old unit is shut down, the new unit is connected, and the new unit is started. The biggest catch to this whole procedure is the new wiring. Because the new UPS will support greater loads, it will require more power to run through it. As a result, the wires connecting the UPS to the outside utility and to the internal distribution panel often need to be upgraded. In addition, the internal distribution panel itself may need an upgrade. Take these electrical changes into account when you plan for the new UPS.

Lesson Summary

In this lesson, you learned the basic procedures for replacing batteries in mid-sized and large UPSs, as well as for adding batteries to a UPS. The lesson also discussed issues related to replacing a UPS in its entirety.

Lesson 2: Monitoring the System

Chapter 2, Lesson 4 provided a brief overview of system monitoring and the technologies used to monitor a system. This lesson revisits that topic, focusing on software and hardware specifically designed for system monitoring.

After this lesson, you will be able to

- Identify system monitoring tools and hardware
- Select appropriate tools for your environment

Estimated lesson time: 20 minutes

System Monitoring Hardware

System monitoring hardware comes in two basic categories: hardware that monitors a single server and hardware that monitors the environment in which the server is operating. I'll discuss the server monitoring hardware first.

Server Monitoring Hardware

No matter how reliable a server's hardware or operating system is, something will eventually fail. It's a simple fact of life. Server monitoring hardware is specifically designed to monitor the system and, if there are problems, provide notification and diagnostic tools to get the server back online quicker. The advantage that hardware-based tools have over software-based tools is that they can function regardless of whether the operating system is functioning.

Hardware-based tools provide their own processor, memory, and battery backup so that they can continue working even after the main processor and software have locked up. The battery backup on this hardware generally provides about 30 minutes of operation should the server power fail. This is generally enough time to send notifications to a numeric pager or to send SNMP traps to monitoring stations to ensure that someone is notified of the problem.

Intel has begun integrating server management into its motherboards, and other vendors, such as Compaq, HP, and Dell, offer add-on cards that provide enhanced functionality. Intel also offers a remote management card for non-Intel motherboards and for Intel motherboards produced before the integrated management tools were included on-board.

These add-on cards offer features that aren't possible in software, such as the ability to monitor failure events, provide outbound paging notification, add to system event logs while the operating system is not functional, and reboot the server. Having a hardware card that is able to create an event that can be set up as an SNMP trap eliminates the need to have a management console check the server continually to determine its status. It also decreases the amount of time necessary to determine that a problem has occurred. Because the SNMP trap is sent almost immediately to the management console, there's no delay due to the wait between polling intervals. Additionally, the server isn't burdened with having to respond to the SNMP management console queries associated with continual checking.

Outbound paging notification generally supports both numeric and alphanumeric pagers. The add-on cards generally support the Telocator Alphanumeric Protocol (TAP), meaning that they support virtually every alphanumeric paging device, including mobile phones with text messaging capabilities. Although the paging capabilities are not as sophisticated as those available in software-based system monitoring applications, they are generally a sufficient backup for sending SNMP traps to a management console.

Another important feature of the server monitoring hardware is its ability to log events that have occurred and to allow access to that information even if the server operating system isn't functioning. By using information obtained from the motherboard, the system monitor can indicate fan failures, disk failures, memory failures, and so on that may have led to the server's problems. Some system monitoring tools even allow for hardware-based remote control of the system. This feature allows you to control the server even if the operating system doesn't load. And finally, sometimes the system monitoring add-on cards allow you to see the last screen before the reboot. This lets you review the NetWare abend or the Microsoft Windows 2000 blue screen to review the diagnostic data.

The final capability that most of the hardware cards offer is the ability to reboot the server remotely. This is particularly useful if the server locks up and fails to restart properly or if the operating system fails and isn't set to reboot the server automatically.

Hardware-based server monitoring may be expensive (costing between $400 and $1,000 per server), but it's an incredibly effective way to manage servers remotely or to manage remote servers. These hardware tools can make remote access to a system as effective as local access to the system, providing almost exactly the same level of control.

Environment Monitoring Hardware

If you've got server monitoring hardware or software, you'll know when the server goes down or when it quits providing the services that it should. But you won't know when there are problems with the climate control or when the fire alarm goes off.

That is where environment monitoring hardware comes in. This hardware is designed specifically to monitor the status of the server's environment. Although some of the features that an environment monitoring device offers can be handled by an alarm monitoring system, others are unique to the environment monitoring devices.

These devices generally monitor the following environmental conditions:

- **AC electrical power.**   The device monitors its incoming power for failure. If the environmental monitor is connected to a UPS, it can monitor the status of the UPS.

- **Temperature.**   The system monitors the ambient room temperature and notifies you once a given threshold has been reached. If you set the threshold 4 degrees above the set point for the air conditioner, it can notify you of a potential climate control failure.

- **Sound levels.**   The unit can generally listen to the ambient noise in the room and notify you when it exceeds a certain level. This feature is useful to alert you when fire alarms go off or when other alarms in the computer room itself go off. It's a good indication that something is wrong in the computer room.

- **Battery.**   The device monitors the condition of its own battery. This alert is an internal warning to let you know that the unit will soon fail.

In addition to the internal monitoring that the unit performs by default, these devices often have connections for external inputs. These inputs, often called "dry contacts," are provided so that you can attach external devices and have them monitored by the system. This feature is useful for connecting flood sensors, UPS status indicators, and even motion detectors to detect movement in the server room.

Although server monitors are good for any server that requires remote control, environmental monitors are good primarily for situations in which the environment cannot be monitored continuously by humans. Most environment monitoring devices do not have network connectivity and can call only a small number of numbers, but they are useful because they can be deployed in remote locations or in locations where 24-hour support is not possible. These units can be programmed to call a central monitoring facility, where the support personnel can respond to the monitor. If your organization has no central facility that is monitored 24 hours a day, you can program the environment monitoring hardware to call one or more of the people responsible for maintaining the server room.

System Monitoring Software

Despite the advantages of hardware-based monitoring, it also has one major disadvantage: it's very expensive when compared to software-based alternatives. Because of the manufacturing costs associated with producing hardware, it is generally much more expensive than a software solution. In addition, most hardware-based solutions require the same software as a software-only solution. Software solutions, on the other hand, can be and often are used without hardware-based monitoring support. Software-based systems have three basic types: standards based, proprietary, and hybrid. The standards-based monitoring systems use the SNMP and DMI standards discussed in Chapter 2, Lesson 4, as well as other standards, such as the Self-Monitoring, Analysis and Reporting Technology (SMART) system used for monitoring hard disk drives. These standards-based monitoring systems generally serve as a warehouse for the performance and availability information collected.

Proprietary solutions gather data directly through operating system calls or through other methods of monitoring that are not standards based. Very few solutions are completely proprietary, but a relatively high number of hybrid software-based monitoring solutions exist, because most software with proprietary monitoring features also supports at least some standards-based monitoring.

The list of software-based monitoring solutions is seemingly endless. They vary from relatively simple utilities that graph performance to complex enterprise systems that monitor every server across an entire international organization. Most of these solutions support multiple levels of notification and notification distribution lists. This flexibility is unique to software-based solutions, and it means that notification of a problem can be routed to the appropriate person no matter what time of the day or night it is. Four basic methods are used to provide notification of a problem:

- **Console alert.**   This method displays an alert message on the monitoring console. It is useful only if you have the monitoring software up and running on the console and you're sitting there watching it. Console alerts are good for constantly monitored systems but are not practical for most environments.

- **E-mail.**   A Simple Mail Transport Protocol (SMTP) message is sent indicating a problem. This method is useful when you have an e-mail address that's tied to a portable electronic device such as a mobile phone with text messaging or a pager capable of receiving Internet mail messages. The disadvantage of this notification method is that it requires a lot of things to be functional in order to receive the message, including the Internet connection.

- **Numeric paging.**   This method of paging requires a modem attached to the monitoring console that is used to dial a pager number and then provide a series of numbers. This notification mechanism is very unreliable because there's no confirmation that the message was sent. You simply have to hope that the timing was set up right so that it worked. The cryptic messages are also often difficult to decipher.

- **Alphanumeric paging.**   This paging method allows for more descriptive alert messages, and it's more reliable due to the TAP used to communicate the message to the pager. This method also requires a modem attached to the monitoring system. It's probably the best way to receive alert notifications.

Of course, these notifications have to come from the monitoring mechanisms that the software supports. The following sections review the SNMP and DMI standards, so that you'll have the basic information you need to select a monitoring package.

SNMP

SNMP is a pervasive, cross-platform standard for network management. It was originally specified in the late 1980s and has been revised several times over the years to include new features. An SNMP environment has two basic components: the SNMP agent and the SNMP management console. The agent is responsible for communicating between the hardware or operating system and the SNMP management console. The SNMP management console performs three basic functions:

- Gets the status of a variable on a host

- Sets the status of a variable on a host

- Receives a trap from a host

From these fundamental building blocks, SNMP allows a management console to monitor the SNMP agent, control its configuration, and receive alerts. The primary purpose of SNMP is to monitor other devices and report problems. These two goals are accomplished via polling and in some cases via establishing traps to notify the management console that something is wrong.

Most of the SNMP activity occurs via *polling,* in which the management console periodically asks the remote device for the status of a series of variables. The management console then evaluates and sometimes records these variables. This process accomplishes two things: it allows the capture of performance data, and it ensures that the remote device is still connected and operational. Polling is relatively processor intensive for both the device and the management console. The more variables that are monitored and the more frequently they are polled, the greater the load is on both the device and the management console.

Increased overhead is a known effect of polling. The more polling you do and the more frequently you do it, the more resources are consumed. Imagine for a moment that you're the lone worker in an office that has both a front entryway, where you interact with customers, and a back room, where you do the work.

Imagine further that one day you're on your own. You need to get work done in the back, but you have to take care of customers too. You manage this by working for two minutes in the back and then walking up front to see if anyone is there.

What you're essentially doing, in continuously going between the back and the front, is polling. In addition to the time it takes you to look out front, you're spending time walking back and forth. You're also less efficient when in the back because you can't concentrate on what you're doing.

In the same scenario, if you added a bell in the front that customers could ring when they need assistance, you would no longer need to go back and forth just to see whether anyone is there. You could wait until the bell rang and then go take care of the customer. This is known as *event-driven* or *alert-driven* demand. It's very efficient from a processing standpoint.

Like the bell just described, SNMP *traps* are simply alerts that an event has occurred or a threshold has been exceeded. Traps are useful when a device needs to communicate information about a problem to a management console, but it doesn't make sense for the management console to continuously monitor the device. For example, a trap might be used when performance monitoring data isn't necessary. Not every device supports traps, however.

Let's return to our scenario. What happens if a customer won't ring the bell, or if you don't hear the bell when it is rung? Unfortunately, the customer may stand in the front for a long time until you happen to come out for something. This kind of problem occurs with SNMP traps. Sometimes the device can't send the alert because of internal problems, and sometimes the trap that the device does send doesn't make it to the management console.

For these reasons, traps are usually used in conjunction with regular polling to ensure that the management console discovers the state of the device at some point, even if the trap doesn't make it. This integrated method is used because of the failures that can occur with traps, and also to limit the amount of polling that must be done.

Another function of an SNMP management console is the ability to configure the remote device by setting the value of some parameters. This function allows the management console to change the configuration of the device, in the ways that the device has allowed through SNMP. Generally, the types of configuration that can be done via SNMP are relatively simple. This function is designed to facilitate simple changes rather than allowing for complete configuration of the system.

The parameters that can be configured are generally relatively detailed, such as the initial size of the maximum receive unit. This parameter is part of the Point-to-Point Protocol. Allowing a management console to change settings like this one permits it to adapt the configuration to changing conditions.

One of the other reasons for setting a variable is to perform actions on the remote device. For instance, with a device that can be rebooted remotely, the manufacturer might allow you to set an SNMP value (a variable) that specifies the number of seconds until reboot. This variable doesn't require that SNMP support a new reboot command; instead, the variable can use the standard facility built into SNMP to change the configuration of a device. However, it does allow other activities, such as a remote reboot, to be accomplished.

We haven't talked yet about how messages are communicated between the management console and the device. This communication occurs via a User Datagram Protocol (UDP) port. UDP is part of the TCP/IP protocol family and provides *datagram*, or nonguaranteed, delivery. That is, the protocol doesn't ensure that messages aren't lost or duplicated by the network. The software using the protocol must assume this responsibility.

This means that the SNMP management console must accept the possibility that its requests may get lost and will need to be resent. It also means that the SNMP management console may never see an SNMP trap sent by a device because it may be accidentally discarded by the network. This is one of the reasons that all trap-based monitoring should be backed up with at least some limited polling.

You now know how SNMP communication occurs. But how do the management console and the device know what to talk about? This is one of the most frustrating aspects of using SNMP. Although SNMP has built into it the ability to discover what parameters a device or agent exposes, simply getting the names and values of the remote parameters doesn't always make their purpose self-evident.

The job of communicating the meaning of the parameters exposed via SNMP is assigned to a file known as a management information base (MIB). This file contains detailed information about the information exposed by a device or agent and a description of what the exposed information means. MIBs are simple text files based on the Abstract Syntax Notation (ASN). They describe the hierarchy that the exposed information takes and indicate whether the information is readable, writable, or both.

For each object exposed by the device, the MIB contains a short section that lists the following:

- **Object.** The name of the object.
- **Syntax.** The type of data contained.
- **Status.** Whether the device must provide the information or has the option of not supporting the entry.
- **Access.** How the object can be used—for read or for read-write.

- **Definition.**   A text description that explains what the object is for and how it is used. This is the information displayed by the management console when you ask for help about an object.

The importance of these sections and of the ASN format is that they allow you to read the MIB yourself, without loading or installing a management console. Thus, you can review the MIB to determine whether the variables you want to monitor are available from the device or agent.

SNMP is an extremely flexible management framework that allows you to monitor and control a wide variety of devices, including routers, bridges, gateways, switches, and even servers. It should definitely be a part of your overall monitoring solution if your network involves the use of remote communications links, routers, and switches.

DMI

The Desktop Management Task Force (DMTF) developed the Desktop Management Interface (DMI) specification to help address the growing need to be able to control PCs throughout an organization. As mentioned in Chapter 2, DMI and SNMP are similar but different, and they're not yet interoperable. The DMTF document on the topic of DMI-to-SNMP integration doesn't paint a good picture for interoperability between the two standards anytime in the future.

One of the fundamental differences between DMI and SNMP is that SNMP is generally implemented on a fixed piece of hardware that doesn't vary much from one device to another, whereas DMI is focused on PCs, in which hardware is added, removed, and changed frequently. As a result, DMI defines three layers of software instead of the two present in SNMP. They are

- **Component interface.**   Communicates between the hardware and the service provider.
- **Service provider.**   Bundles communication with various components and provides the standardized code for supporting queries and information storage.
- **Management interface.**   Provides a user-level interface to manage and review systems via the DMI architectures.

This three-tier design is more flexible than the two-tier design in use by SNMP, but it is implemented in only a small number of management applications, so it's not widely used.

Practice: Select an Appropriate Monitoring Solution

In this practice, you'll review a corporate environment and choose an appropriate monitoring solution.

For the purposes of this practice, let's examine a firm called Compression Engineering. Compression does rapid product development. It has seven offices throughout the United States. None of these offices have information technology support, but all of them have a Windows 2000 server. The servers are connected together via virtual private networks. The connectivity is relatively stable but has been known to fail from time to time.

The support for the network is handled by two individuals at the central office. Both cover the network in tandem and work well with each other to coordinate activity. Both individuals wear alphanumeric pagers.

What kind of monitoring solution should be implemented?

A hardware-based and software-based solution should be used. Because the remote servers don't have any support, there needs to be a mechanism to control the server remotely, preferably one that doesn't depend upon the operating system running. Another reason for hardware-based monitoring is that network connectivity is sometimes not functional, and so it's important to provide an alternative method for remote support.

Although it would be possible to get by with just hardware-based monitoring, coupling this with software-based monitoring will allow more of the events to be filtered out and, in some cases, handled automatically. This is important because two support personnel supporting seven sites can use all the help they can get.

Lesson Summary

In this lesson, you learned about the different ways in which a system can be monitored, including hardware-based and software-based monitoring. You learned that hardware-based monitoring can be used to monitor servers or the environment that the servers are in.

Next you learned that there are a variety of ways for monitoring software to alert you of a problem, including via direct console messages, e-mail, alphanumeric paging, and numeric paging. You also learned when each of these methods may be appropriate and the problems with each.

Finally, you learned some details of the SNMP and DMI management architectures, including how they work, when they are appropriate, and how they differ.

Lesson 3: Selecting Service Tools

This lesson discusses tools that can help you maintain servers and diagnose problems. Although there are no silver bullets for solving problems, having the right tools with you can make the difference between a day-long project and a simple solution.

After this lesson, you will be able to

- Select the hardware tools to maintain the server and network
- Select the software tools to maintain the server and network

Estimated lesson time: 20 minutes

Essential Hardware Tools

When selecting hardware tools, you need to decide which ones you want and need. More tools are available than you can efficiently use or afford. This section helps you choose the right tools for your needs.

LAN Cable Scanner

One of the essential tools has nothing to do with the server at all. It's a device that's specifically designed to evaluate the performance of a LAN cable, measuring the resistance and capacitance of the cable. In some cases, the cable scanner will be able to review the current network traffic as well as evaluating the cable itself.

Most people don't realize that one of the things a cable scanner does is to verify that the pairs of the cable are aligned correctly. Ethernet cables use a wiring configuration that splits some of the pairs of the cable, instead of using them side by side. Figure 13.1 shows a wiring configuration for an Ethernet cable.

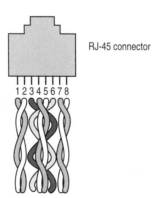

Figure 13.1   Ethernet wiring configuration, showing a split across pins 3 and 6

A LAN cable scanner is an important tool because it can help you eliminate the possibility that cable problems are preventing the server from communicating with the clients. It can verify new cables that you create, identify problems that are causing performance issues, and test existing cables.

Multimeter

A multimeter measures voltage, amperage, and resistances. This is one of the lightest and best devices for performing quick checks. You can use a multimeter to check the voltages being output by a power supply. By checking the power of a free drive lead (power connector) like the one shown in Figure 13.2, you can often determine whether a power supply is working properly. The yellow lead should have 12 volts when compared to either of the black wires. The red lead should have 5 volts when compared to either of the black wires.

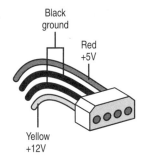

Figure 13.2   Drive power supply lead

The actual voltage may be plus or minus 10 percent of these values, so the yellow lead may have between 11 and 13 volts, and the red lead may have between 4.5 and 5.5 volts. However, most power supplies maintain voltages much closer than the 10 percent allowed by the specification. Low voltages are often a cause for mysterious lockups. High voltages may be a reason for parts going bad or burning out at a higher than normal rate.

Multimeters can also be used to test the continuity of a cable. This function is useful when you're installing cables, both internally and externally, and are having trouble with the connected devices but can't determine why. You can use this tool to ensure that every connector runs through the cable as it should.

ATX Power Supply Tester

An ATX power supply tester has a single, simple purpose: to test an ATX power supply to ensure that it's working properly. This testing can't be done with a multimeter if an ATX power supply won't power up via a motherboard, because the multimeter can't control the necessary lines in the motherboard connector to instruct the power supply to start to carry the load. This type of power supply tester is generally constructed with some large resistors and an LED. It's a cheap and effective tool.

POST Card

A power-on self test (POST) card is useful for determining the cause of problems when the system won't boot. The card is inserted in a free slot in the computer and generally has a few multisegment LED modules that indicate a numeric error code that you can look up in the card's manual. It's a quick way to diagnose problems that prevent the system from booting up. Although expensive, this type of card can be valuable if you have many machines that don't complete the boot cycle when powered on and you're having difficulty finding the source of the problem.

RS-232 Breakout Box

An RS-232 breakout box is particularly helpful when you're trying to attach a UPS or other serial device and you're having trouble getting the communications correct. The breakout box allows you to see the signals on the serial line. It also allows you to reroute signals from one conductor to another until you have a working configuration. Once you have a working configuration, you can make a custom cable to replicate the changes that you made to the breakout box. Figure 13.3 shows a breakout box.

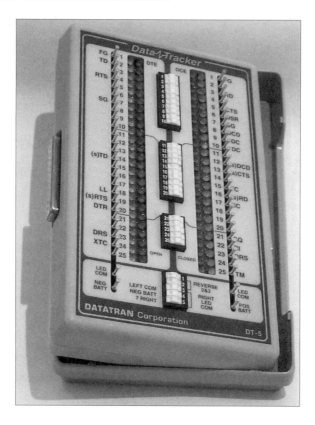

Figure 13.3 Breakout box

Serial Port Tester

A serial port tester is a mini-breakout box that shows the state of only some of the basic signals and doesn't allow the signals to be remapped to different pins. It's lightweight and cheap, and it's often a good way to perform an initial diagnosis of a problem. The device uses dual-state LEDs to show the status of each line, rather than the two separate LEDs that most breakout boxes use.

RJ-45/RJ-11 Crimp Tool

An RJ-45 crimp tool allows you to replace broken RJ-45 connectors on the end of Ethernet cables. The lack of strength in an RJ-45 connector makes this tool a necessity if you don't maintain a ready supply of replacement cables. The plastic clip that holds an RJ-45 connector in place breaks often, and once broken, the connector won't stay connected.

RJ-45 crimp tools are cheap and are relatively easy to learn to use, but they can sometimes be frustrating when you're initially getting used to them. Shoving eight tiny wires into the little space in an RJ-45 connector isn't easy.

PC Toolkit

It should go without saying, but a standard PC toolkit with a hex driver as well as Phillips and flat-blade screwdrivers should be an essential part of your equipment. These kits may also include other tools, such as soldering irons, that can be useful when you've accidentally disconnected a wire or you need to make your own cable.

Software Tools

Hardware-based tools generally bring with them a certain amount of weight. That is, they are heavy to carry around. However, software is very light. In some circumstances you can fit all of the tools that you need on a single CD and a few floppies. Even better, most of the software-based tools you need are built into the operating system and thus don't require that you carry anything. For that reason, most people have a much larger variety of software-based tools than hardware tools. This section describes some of the software tools you'll find most useful.

Fsck/VREPAIR/SCANDISK

The first software tool that you should have is the disk repair/scanning utility of the operating system you're using on the server. You should know how to run it, when to run it, and the options that allow you to perform intensive scans of the disks and volumes attached to the server. Every operating system has some sort of a disk-scanning tool. Sometimes third-party offerings have additional features, such as enhanced file recovery or more in-depth analysis of problems, that may be worth their cost.

Disk Defragmenter

Because servers have many things going on at once and many users trying to write to the volumes at one time, they are more prone to fragmentation of files than a standard system. That is, when the files are written to the volume they are not written in one contiguous string; instead, they are written in a series of small, scattered blocks.

A defragmentation utility rearranges the storage on the drive so that all of the pieces of a file are consolidated in one place, allowing the file to be accessed quicker. Defragmenting can thus give your server a performance boost. A defragmentation run should be scheduled weekly as a part of your preventive maintenance plan. If weekly defragmentation is not practical, you should schedule it as often as is feasible.

Some operating systems, such as Windows 2000, come with disk defragmenting tools built in. Other operating systems, such as NetWare, require the purchase of third-party disk defragmentation software.

Hardware Diagnostics

Hardware diagnostic programs are a great way to exercise a system before installing the operating system or before moving the server into production. These programs can test components sequentially or at random, over a fixed number of loops or until interrupted. The ability of a hardware diagnostic program to repeatedly test hardware components makes it ideal for a burn-in. (*Burning in* is a process that involves running a computer and exercising it to help identify failures before it is put into service.) These programs do have the limitation that they rarely test add-on cards; they're normally limited to testing standard components. Most operating systems do not have built-in hardware diagnostics. This is a utility you'll need to buy.

ARP

TCP/IP uses an Address Resolution Protocol (ARP) to convert IP addresses to media access control (MAC), or hardware, addresses. The ARP utility queries and controls the functions of the cached addresses that the ARP protocol has previously resolved. ARP is included with all server operating systems. Reviewing the ARP cache is useful when you're trying to determine the hardware addresses of machines with the same IP address, as well as when you're trying to determine whether the subnet mask and default gateway have been configured correctly.

If you attempt to communicate with a machine that's not on the local network, the ARP cache should contain the MAC address of the default gateway. This is because the default gateway's MAC address is the address that the packet should be sent to when the destination network address isn't on the same network.

ifconfig/BIND/IPConfig/winipcfg

The IP configuration information for UNIX/Linux, Netware, Windows NT/2000, and Windows 95/98 can be retrieved by ifconfig, BIND, IPConfig, and winipcfg, respectively. These commands all tell you the current IP address, subnet mask, and default gateway of the network cards installed in the server. This information is useful for verifying that the DHCP server has provided IP address information to the computer. It can also be helpful when reviewing statically assigned information that you suspect may contain errors.

PING

PING, short for Packet Internet Groper, is a utility that uses the base-level functionality of the TCP/IP protocol suite to verify end-to-end connectivity between two devices. It is built into every server operating system. The command takes one mandatory parameter, the IP address or name of the remote host. PING then attempts to communicate with the other device and indicates success or failure.

Note that when using PING you should try to use the IP address first because this is a more specific connectivity test. By using an Internet name for the device, you're forcing PING to look up the name at a DNS server before testing the connectivity. It's possible that PING will report a connectivity problem even if you can communicate with the device, due to DNS errors or problems.

Note PING works great internally within your network, but it uses mechanisms that are sometimes shut down by firewalls. As a result, you may or may not be able to ping hosts on the Internet.

Traceroute

Traceroute is a utility that uses the same basic technique as PING to determine the path that a packet takes through the network. By manipulating a time-to-live field within the TCP/IP packet, traceroute can force routers to progressively report their addresses. This utility is quite useful for identifying where a routing error or disconnection exists. A routing error will result in a loop, which can be seen as the same routers coming up again and again in the same sequence. A disconnection will be seen as a final router reporting that the destination host isn't available. Traceroute is available as a part of UNIX/Linux and Windows NT/2000. The Windows NT/2000 utility is named tracert.

Nslookup

Nslookup is a DNS lookup utility that allows you to control the type of information retrieved and the servers from which the information is retrieved. This utility helps in the identification of bad name system information that may prevent users from reaching the information they want and need. The redundant nature of the

DNS system leads to occasions when some information is correct and other information is incorrect. Depending upon which server responds faster, the user may receive bad information. Nslookup is valid in both Windows NT/2000 and UNIX/Linux, but it isn't supported on Novell NetWare.

Lesson Summary

In this lesson, you learned about the hardware and software tools that you should at least be familiar with when working on servers. The hardware tools run the gamut from expensive, heavy tools that can be used to solve a variety of problems to small, inexpensive testing tools that have a single purpose.

Software tools are often included with the operating system and are invaluable for troubleshooting connectivity problems. Other tools that aren't installed with the operating system can be quite useful as well.

Review

Here are some questions to help you determine whether you have learned enough to move on to the next chapter. If you have difficulty answering these questions, please go back and review the material in this chapter before beginning the next chapter. The answers for these questions are located in the appendix, "Questions and Answers."

1. What types of batteries are used in most UPSs?

2. What factor do you need to consider when adding additional batteries to a UPS that you don't need to worry about when simply replacing batteries that have reached the end of their life span?

3. Why is it advisable to shut down the servers attached to a UPS when replacing the batteries?

4. What is the line-conditioner-only mode of a UPS?

5. What advantages does hardware-based server monitoring have over software-based server monitoring?

6. What conditions in a server's environment do most environmental monitoring systems monitor?

7. What are the four ways that software-based monitoring systems can notify you of a problem?

8. What are the three functions within SNMP?

9. What are the disadvantages of polling?

10. What are the disadvantages of event-driven or alert-driven notification?

11. How does DMI differ from SNMP?

12. What function does an MIB serve?

13. What problems can a multimeter help you diagnose?

14. What is ARP, and what does it do?

15. Why would someone use nslookup?

Performing Proactive Maintenance

CHAPTER 14

Establishing a Backup Plan

About This Chapter

The previous chapters have described how to install and configure your server, as well as how to upgrade it and monitor its performance—tasks that you'll generally perform only once, or at fairly long intervals. The process we discuss in this chapter is one that must be attended to daily. In fact, backups are the single most important activity that you'll perform on a server.

The critical importance of a good, well-maintained backup plan cannot be overemphasized. This chapter expands the discussion begun in Chapter 2 of the various types of backup plans. It helps you work through the issues involved in implementing your plan and addresses common problems you'll need to resolve to keep the backups running.

Before You Begin

To complete this chapter, you should have

- Your backup software selected
- Identified the people or group responsible for implementing and maintaining the backup plan (even if that is you)

Lesson 1: Types of Backup Plans

All the way back in Chapter 2, Lesson 4 we talked briefly about backups and some of the different rotations that you can use to back up a system. This lesson expands that discussion by describing backups for databases and other transactional systems. It also covers some more-complicated backup plans.

After this lesson, you will be able to

- Explain how tape rotations work
- Set appropriate options for databases and transaction-based systems

Estimated lesson time: 15 minutes

Types of Backups

Chapter 2 discussed the three basic types of backups used for files systems and databases. You'll recall that they are

- **Full backup.**   All files are backed up.
- **Incremental backup.**   Only files that have changed since the last full or incremental backup are backed up.
- **Differential backup.**   Only files that have changed since the last full (or incremental) backup are backed up.

However, that discussion didn't go into the details of how these different types of backups work on a file system or how they work with databases and transactional systems. The following sections provide these details, because the mechanism by which backups are performed on both file systems and transactional systems, including databases, can be useful in allowing you to verify correct backup operation.

Backing Up File Systems

The FAT and FAT32 file systems have a bit, known as the *archive bit,* that indicates whether a file has changed since the last time it was backed up. The operating system sets this bit whenever the file is modified. Backup software then uses the archive bit to determine which files to back up during an incremental or differential backup.

After a full backup is completed, the backup software resets the archive bit for each file that it backed up, so that the bit indicates that there has been no change to the file since the last backup. When the backup software performs an incremental backup, it generates a list of files that have their archive bits set and backs up only those files. When the backup is complete, the backup software resets all of the archive bits for the files it just backed up, just as it did with the files backed up during the full backup.

Differential backups are fundamentally different, however. The backup software performs the same review of the archive bit to see if the file has changed, but it does not change the status of the archive bit after making the backup. This means that differential backups don't leave behind any signs that they were done. It still appears that the files haven't been backed up. As a result, the next differential backup that is run backs up all of the files from the previous backup as well as any new files that have changed.

As you can see, you could run into problems by performing a full backup followed by an incremental backup and then a differential backup. The full backup would reset all of the archive bits. When the incremental backup ran, it too would reset the archive bits. When the differential backup ran, it would see only those files that had changed since the incremental backup, not all of the files that had changed since the full backup. As a result, restoring the server would require you to restore the full backup, the incremental backup, and the differential backup, because the differential backup wouldn't have backed up any of the files stored on the intervening incremental backup.

This runs counter to the expectation that you should need to restore only the full backup and the differential backup. After all, the reason for using differential backups is to minimize the number of restoration processes you'll have to go through to get the system back online.

NTFS supports the same archive bit as FAT. However, other file systems, such as NetWare's file system and Linux's ext2 file system, handle things differently. NetWare's file system provides perhaps the best backup support by recording the date and time a file was last backed up. Linux's default file system, ext2, doesn't support archive bits, and therefore backup software needs to determine which files have been updated on its own. Other file systems available for Linux do support information on whether the file has been backed up, and some indicate when the file was last backed up.

In file systems that record when a file was last backed up, the process of determining whether a file has been backed up is not as simple as reviewing a flag, although it is simple enough. The time of the last backup is compared with the time of the last modification. If the modification time is more recent than the backup time, the file has been modified.

Backing Up Transactional Systems

Until this point, our discussion has used a single file as the smallest unit of measure. If you change the capitalization of a single letter in a large document, the document is listed as having changed and thus needs to be backed up again. While this method works for many systems, it's not effective for backing up most transactional systems, including databases. That is because transactional systems store a large amount of information in a single file or in a few files. The amount of information that actually changes in these files from one backup to the next is generally relatively small compared to the size of the file.

Transactional systems are so named because their operations take place as *transactions*—discrete events that perform specific changes to the system's data files. Transactional systems have one common characteristic: a transaction log file. This file contains a record of every transaction since the last time it was cleared. The transaction log and the information files from the time the transaction logs were reset can be used to regenerate the information up to the point of the most recent transaction in the log. (We'll use the term "information file" to refer to the file or files containing the information for the system. In a database, this would be the tables and records of data. In an e-mail system, this would be the e-mail messages.)

Having a transaction log means that you can back up a transactional system by backing up the information files and clearing the transaction log. This is, in effect, a full backup. You can then perform an incremental backup by backing up the transaction log and then clearing it. Differential backups are the same as incremental backups, except that you don't clear the transaction log.

The restoration process is the same as in a file system. You restore the full backup and then each incremental backup or the last differential backup. However, one of the advantages of differential backups does not apply to transactional systems. The discussion of incremental vs. differential backups in Chapter 2 recommended differential backups, both because they use fewer tapes and because files that have been updated multiple times don't have to be restored multiple times. Both of these factors speed up the restoration process.

When restoring transactional systems, such as databases and mail servers, you have to run every transaction again, even if successive changes to the same information have rendered a transaction out of date. Therefore, the only difference between incremental and differential backups in a transactional system is that differential backups take longer to perform and require fewer tapes. The difference in the total restore time is negligible and is due to the additional time required to switch tapes for incremental backups.

One of the most common problems with performing incremental and differential backups on transactional systems involves how the log files are set up. Databases often allow the transaction log to be truncated, or cleared, when a checkpoint occurs. A checkpoint is a logical event that happens periodically within the server. It places the transaction log in a consistent state to which the system can be rolled back in the event that the server is shut down abnormally. Checkpoints can also be forced to occur by a command issued to the server. Other transactional systems sometimes permit circular logs. These logs use the same space over and over again.

Neither of the cases just described supports incremental or differential backups. If the server is automatically clearing the transaction log periodically when checkpoints occur, some of the transactions needed for an incremental or differential backup will be missing. Similarly, when circular logging is enabled, there's no way to guarantee that all of the transactions occurring since the last backup can be backed up.

If you decide to perform incremental or differential backups on a transactional system, you'll need to ensure that the transaction logs are valid. They must not be set to clear themselves automatically, nor to allow transactions to be overwritten before a backup.

Backup Rotations

Chapter 2, Lesson 4 covered two types of backup rotation:

- Sets
- Grandfather-father-son (GFS)

There's one more type of rotation that, although not widely used, is well known and is supported by some backup software. This backup rotation is called the Tower of Hanoi. It is significant because it tends to wear the tapes more evenly and because it allows you to reduce the number of tapes you must use. Because of the complexity involved with implementing this backup rotation, you should use it only when there is support for it in your backup software.

The Tower of Hanoi backup rotation is based on a puzzle created by a French mathematician. In it there are three pegs. On one of these pegs is a series of progressively smaller rings—in other words, a tower. The goal is to move the entire tower of rings from the first to the third peg, one at a time. The complicating factor is that at no time should a larger ring be placed over a smaller one. Figure 14.1 shows the puzzle and the steps for moving a four-ring tower from the peg on the left to the peg on the right.

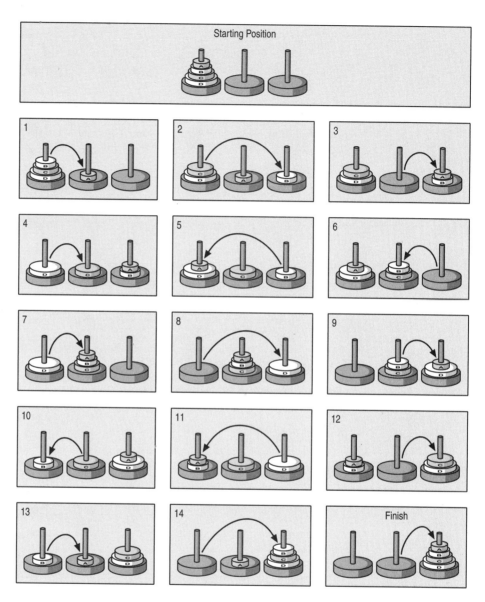

Figure 14.1 The classic Tower of Hanoi puzzle

The interesting thing about the Tower of Hanoi puzzle is that for each ring you add, you double the number of moves required to complete the puzzle. The example with four rings shown in Figure 14.1 takes 15 steps to complete (16 if you count the starting position). In other words, if you raise 2 to the power of the number of rings (and subtract 1 if you don't want to count the starting position), you have the number of moves it takes to solve the puzzle. Table 14.1 shows the number of moves required to complete the puzzle for various numbers of rings.

Table 14.1   Number of Moves to Complete the Tower of Hanoi Puzzle

Number of Rings	Number of Moves
1	1
2	3
3	7
4	15
5	31
6	63

When implementing the Tower of Hanoi in a backup schedule, you use one backup set for each ring. (Let's say that you use four sets labeled A, B, C, and D, to match Figure 14.1.) Each time you would move a ring in the Tower of Hanoi, you use the backup set corresponding to that ring. At the end of a cycle, set C is moved to set B, set B is moved to set A, and so on. This slow rotation of tapes between rings allows the tapes to be used in a way that will wear them evenly.

In the Tower of Hanoi backup rotation, each backup is a full backup. One of the benefits of this system is that it tends to produce a large number of complete backups. Thus, if an individual tape or backup turns out to be bad, there's generally a recent tape backup that will have a complete backup on it. It also helps for situations, discussed later, in which the problem with a file is not immediately evident. The drawback, however, is that you need a large enough backup window every evening to back up the entire system.

Alternate Backup Methods

Before leaving the topic of backup rotations, it bears mentioning that some less frequently used backup methods exist for specialized applications. Most of these are designed to back up the server continuously so that the server can be recovered to the point of failure.

Some database servers allow you to write a copy of the transaction log file to tape every time a transaction completes. In the event of a disk failure, the tape log of transactions and the last full backup can be used to regenerate the database. This technique isn't used often, but it is useful in environments in which the failure to recover a single transaction is not acceptable.

The technique just described for databases has, on occasion, been applied to file systems as well. The backup software detects a change in a file immediately (usually through security auditing) and marks the file as needing to be backed up.

As soon as everyone who might have been using the file closes it, the file is backed up to tape. This technique, which might be considered an extreme form of incremental backups, can be quite effective for restoring files. However, it is subject to the same multiplying effect as incremental backups. Because the file is backed up every time it changes, multiple copies of the file end up on the tape.

The continuous backup systems have largely been replaced by clustered systems, in which the failure of a single server will not prevent a transaction from being completed.

Tip It may help to think of the multiplying effect of making instant tape backups in this way. Suppose that every time you save a file in an application such as Microsoft Excel, Word, PowerPoint, and so on, you essentially create a new version of the file on the tape. Although tape storage is generally relatively cheap, the continual storage of different versions of the file takes a lot of room. This is particularly true if the file is large. Conversely, you've always got a series of backups of your work should the file become corrupted at some point.

Neither of the methods described here is generally used to replace normal backups; they normally augment the already existing backup system to allow it to recover more transactions. They can often even recover transactions that occurred in the hour or minutes just before the failure.

Tape Wear

One of the other factors to consider when planning a tape backup rotation is tape wear. Tape wear is measured by the number of times the tape passes under the read-write heads. The number of times it can do so before the tape is no longer able to store information varies by tape type and somewhat by tape construction. Table 14.2 shows various tape media and their expected life.

Table 14.2   Tape Media with Expected Life

Type	Rated Passes	Passes per Backup	Number of Full Backups
AIT	20,000	2	10,000
DAT/DDS (4 mm)	2,000	20	100
8 mm (Advanced Metal Evaporated Tapes)	20,000	2	10,000
DLT (DLT 4000)	1,000,000	64	10,000
DLT (DLT 7000)	1,000,000	52	10,000

The more a tape is used, the closer it comes to the maximum number of passes it can take underneath the read-write heads. Although this is rarely an issue with tapes that are used monthly or less frequently, it's often a concern with tapes that are used each week, such as those in a set rotation, or the daily tapes for a grandfather-father-son rotation. Because these tapes are used so frequently, they eventually wear out. The verification feature of a tape backup drive can be useful because it can report media problems before you attempt a restore.

Other factors, such as the tape drive having to stop and restart, can significantly reduce a tape's life. All of the numbers you'll see related to tape life assume that the system can supply the tape drive with sufficient information to keep the tape moving. Any time the tape drive doesn't have enough information, it has to stop the tape and back it up, using two tape passes. Obviously, the more times the system isn't able to keep up with the tape drive, the more passes the drive will make on the tape, and the more quickly the tape will wear out. As you are implementing your system, it is important to try to optimize it to allow the tape drive to run continuously.

Unless you're running a particularly fast tape drive, you can normally keep it more than busy. However, backups across slow networks or on slow systems can sometimes cause the system to drop below the tape drive's throughput, resulting in excessive tape wear. The easiest way to determine whether the tape drive is having to start and stop is to listen to the unit during a backup. If you hear a continuous whizzing sound, chances are that the system is keeping up with the tape drive. If, on the other hand, you hear periodic clicking, the system isn't keeping up with the tape drive, and access should be optimized.

Tape Failure and Tape Rotations

Earlier I mentioned that the Tower of Hanoi is a good backup rotation because it makes a full backup each night. This means that, should the most recent backup tape fail, you can restore from the previous night's full backup. Having full backups provides an extra layer of protection for a tape failure.

The sets tape rotation method is similar to the Tower of Hanoi in that it involves making nightly full backups and gives you one day-old full backup to restore from should the most recent backup happen to fail. Although it may seem that the most recent backup tapes will rarely fail, it happens all too frequently.

Tip If you haven't had a media failure in your career yet, rest assured that you will. I have seen two cases in which the most recent backup was at least partially defective, and we were forced to revert to previous backups for some information. It's a scary experience that you'll want to plan for before it happens.

Delayed Identification

When most of us think about the reasons for a backup and the need for a restore, we think about critical system errors that will immediately be apparent, calling for the entire system to be restored immediately. However, some of the problems that we need to back up for aren't noticed immediately.

In cases where a single file is accidentally overwritten, or a file becomes corrupted, it may be days or weeks before you realize that there is a problem. This is another reason why selecting a rotation scheme that maintains several versions of every file is so important. The more flexibility you can provide in the age of useful backups, the more effective you can be at resolving problems that the server's users are having. Maintaining various versions of a file can mean the difference between the user having to re-create a few hours' worth of work, or several days' worth.

Tip It's all too common in most organizations for someone to need to restore a file that he or she accidentally overwrote three weeks ago. Having older backups is of great use in these situations.

Lesson Summary

In this lesson, you learned the details behind full, incremental, and differential backups, and how the various types work both on file systems and on transactional systems such as database servers. The lesson also took you through the complicated Tower of Hanoi backup rotation so that you could see its ability to provide a good backup solution when the tape backup software supports this type of rotation.

At the close of this lesson, you learned about tape wear as well as the importance of keeping multiple versions of your backups. Having multiple backups can protect you against the failure of a backup tape and can also allow you to resolve problems that don't come to light immediately.

Lesson 2: Establishing a Backup Plan

The process of establishing a backup plan looks simple on paper. You establish the schedule in the backup software, set up notification, and finally start rotating the tapes. In reality, however, it's rarely that simple. In this lesson you'll work through the issues associated with establishing a tape backup plan, including assigning primary and secondary responsibility for monitoring the backups, locating appropriate places to store the tapes, and identifying a tape drive cleaning schedule.

After this lesson, you will be able to

- Make informed decisions regarding media storage
- Implement a tape backup plan

Estimated lesson time: 15 minutes

Understanding the Procedural Components

As was mentioned in the chapter introduction, backups are different from almost every other task we've discussed because they must be done every day once a server is installed. They are also different because you will normally turn them over to other individuals.

Because you won't be performing the backup tasks yourself, you need to do more than just decide on a rotation schedule and plug it into the backup software. You must also develop procedural instructions for the activities to be performed. These instructions should include procedures for reviewing the tape logs for success or failure as well as procedures for changing the tape.

These procedures are vitally important because they will release you from having to monitor the backup forever. They will provide a simple method by which new people can be trained to maintain the backup system. Without these procedures, you'll find yourself having to retrain people in the process every time the person who is primarily responsible for the activity moves on or goes on vacation.

You'll also find backup procedures quite helpful after you've been away from the day-to-day operation of the tape backup for a while. The simple parts of the procedure regarding cleaning the tape drive, storing the tapes, and managing the backup logs will come in quite handy if you need to fill in while the person responsible is on vacation.

Figure 14.2 shows a sample form that you can use to keep track of whether a backup has been performed and what other actions related to backups have been performed. This worksheet is helpful in that it allows you to see the cleaning

frequency and error rates at a glance to determine whether any action, such as
ordering more cleaning tapes, is necessary, and whether cleaning should be performed before the tape drive indicates it needs cleaning, due to errors. You'll find
a copy of this worksheet, including specific suggestions regarding how to implement it in your environment, on the CD that accompanies this book.

Month: March		Sun	Mon	Tues	Wed	Thur	Fri	Sat
Week 1	Day of Month					1	2	3
	Cleaned							
	New Set					D	3	
	Error							
Week 2	Day of Month	4	5	6	7	8	9	10
	Cleaned		✓				✓	
	New Set		A	B	C	D	4	
	Error				✓			
Week 3	Day of Month	11	12	13	14	15	16	17
	Cleaned							
	New Set		A	B	C	D	5	
	Error							
Week 4	Day of Month	18	19	20	21	22	23	24
	Cleaned							
	New Set							
	Error							
Week 5	Day of Month	25	26	27	28	29	30	31
	Cleaned							
	New Set							
	Error							
Week 6	Day of Month							
	Cleaned							
	New Set							
	Error							

Figure 14.2 A sample worksheet for keeping track of backup activity

Of course, you might be able to handle the backups yourself and thus avoid having
a written procedure. I'd recommend, however, that you find someone else who
can take on the responsibility. Most technicians don't follow the same pattern in
their day. One day they're building a new server, the next day they are doing support, and the next day they're doing something entirely different. This variation
in schedule tends to make remembering things that must be done every day, such
as changing backup tapes and checking the backup log, difficult. The best candidates for monitoring the tape backup system are people who do the same thing
every day.

Assigning a Responsible Party

Many technicians don't have the luxury of being able to choose who will watch
the backups of their server. Often, people in their organization are already assigned
to perform this task. If you don't already have someone assigned, you should try
to find someone to take responsibility for the daily changing of tapes.

Ideally, you'll want to choose someone who has a stake in making sure that the activity is done correctly. In other words, if possible you'll want to find someone whose activities are computer based and who thus would feel the negative effect if the backup didn't run and the system needed to be restored. This is an important motivational factor for ensuring that the backups are checked each day.

In addition, the person you choose should follow a relatively routine pattern each day. This helps because the person can get into the habit of checking the tape backup every day at a certain time and won't have to rely so much on a specific reminder.

The final consideration is that whoever you choose needs to be reasonably trustworthy. The person will have access to the backups for the systems and physical access to the systems themselves and could cause significant damage if he or she wanted to be malicious.

Choosing Sites for Tape Storage

One of the logistical issues for any backup solution involves deciding where to store the tapes containing the backups. You have two basic options: on-site storage or off-site storage. The decision as to which of these is more appropriate for your organization is based on a variety of factors, not the least of which is the risk tolerance of the organization.

On-Site Storage

If it's assumed that the company will cease to exist if a natural disaster wipes out the building, the choice is easy. Keep the media on-site, since there's no need to recover from the kind of catastrophic disaster that would destroy the backup tapes and the server at the same time. However, most organizations aren't clear as to whether a catastrophic natural disaster would mean the end of the organization.

Whether you decide you need off-site storage or not, you'll need some on-site storage space available to hold the tapes until you can get them off-site. This on-site storage should be in a media-rated fireproof safe. A media-rated fireproof safe is different from a regular fireproof safe.

Fireproof safes are designed for paper, which spontaneously combusts at 457 degrees Fahrenheit. As a result, the goal of a fireproof safe is to keep the internal temperature below 457 degrees for a period of time. Computer media can't sustain anywhere near this level of heat. Their maximum storage temperature is around 100 degrees—substantially lower than the temperature at which paper spontaneously combusts. Thus, fireproof safes used to store computer media must be designed specifically for this type of storage.

Media-rated fireproof safes come in all shapes, sizes, and varieties. Some are even sold as inserts for standard fireproof file cabinets. These inserts are very convenient when the media you need to store take up a relatively small space and you already have fireproof file cabinets for your important documents.

Media-rated fireproof safes are, obviously, good protection against fires, but they also protect your backups against other natural disasters. In parts of the country that are prone to earthquakes, hurricanes, or tornados (that should cover just about everyone), media-rated fireproof safes provide additional weight around the tapes, helping to keep them in place even if the other equipment is blown away. These safes are also good protection against water damage because they are reasonably, if not completely, airtight. This helps to minimize water damage from sprinklers or from rain coming through a hole in the roof.

Tip If you need a short-term storage place for tapes until a media-rated fireproof safe arrives, you can place them in their cases, put them in a zipper-top bag, and place them in the bottom of the company refrigerator. Refrigerators are heavy, fairly airtight, and relatively impervious to fire. If you do this, however, make sure to pull the tapes out a few hours before you intend to place them in the tape drive to allow them to reach room temperature.

Off-Site Storage

If your organization would continue to exist after a catastrophic natural disaster, or if it wants the added safety that off-site storage provides, there are several options to consider. You could have an employee take a set of backups home, hire an off-site storage company, or rotate the backups among multiple sites, if the organization has more than one site.

The first option, which is used primarily by very small organizations, is to have one or more members of the staff take home a backup set. The theory is that doing so physically separates the backups from the building, and the chances of a natural disaster taking out both the employee's home and the company location are slim.

This is a great idea, and it provides some additional level of protection against natural disasters, but it is prone to problems, not the least of which is remembering to rotate the tapes. Remembering to take a tape set home each week and return another set at the right time is more than most people are up for. Some people put the backups in their cars and leave them there, the idea being that if a natural disaster destroys the building, the person is not likely to be there—a questionable assumption. In addition, tapes require a fixed temperature and humidity range for storage. It's not likely that the conditions within an automobile are always within those storage guidelines. In the warm climates and during the summer, it gets too hot for the tapes. In colder climates and during the winter, it gets too cold.

If you have the opportunity to hire an outside organization to handle off-site storage for you, you should consider doing so. These firms offer the same type of protection as you get by having an employee taking home a tape set, but without the negatives. Because the organization is specifically contracted to perform a service, its staff arrive at approximately the same time each day or each week. This ensures that the rotation happens as planned. Additionally, when the tapes are removed they are stored in a climate-controlled environment that is conducive to tape storage, not someone's car.

The only disadvantage to off-site media storage organizations is that you don't have immediate access to the tapes. However, most of these firms give you the ability to pick up your tapes with very little notice, and you generally maintain the most recent tapes, which you are most likely to need for restoration, on-site. For these reasons, having immediate access to the tapes is usually not a large concern.

The final way to accomplish off-site storage is generally only for larger organizations with multiple facilities in a region. This option involves swapping the backup tapes between the two facilities on a regular schedule. It allows you to have the advantages of an off-site storage company without the expense. Because the space on both ends is corporate controlled, you can provide media-rated fireproof safes on each end for the tapes to go into. Generally, a single person is assigned to move intracompany mail between the two facilities. That person is the logical one to be responsible for transporting the tapes from one facility to the other.

Scheduling Tape Drive Cleanings

One of the details that tends to get lost in the hustle to get the backup system on-line is the need to establish a cleaning schedule or, for that matter, the need to order cleaning tapes. Tape drives work by passing a large amount of tape under the read-write head, and as they do so the tape often leaves deposits. These deposits can build up to a point that it becomes difficult or impossible to write to or read from any tape.

For this reason, every tape drive has special cleaning tapes that are specifically designed to remove the buildup on the read-write head and other components, restoring the system to full efficiency. These tapes are, necessarily, different from the tapes that data is backed up onto. They are generally inserted into the tape drive, and the drive ejects them between 20 seconds and a minute later. The tape drive automatically detects that a cleaning tape was inserted and runs a cleaning cycle on itself. Each cleaning cartridge has a fixed number of times that it can be used before it must be discarded. Generally, a cleaning cartridge is good for about 20 cleanings.

One of the biggest challenges for the person responsible for changing tapes used to be knowing when a drive needed cleaning. Because a cleaning cartridge is necessarily abrasive, using one on a read-write head that doesn't need to be cleaned induces unnecessary wear on the head. That is why most drives today have an indicator on the tape drive itself that signals when a cleaning tape is necessary. This helps to minimize the cleanings.

For those drives that don't have a cleaning indicator, you must know how many hours of use the tape drive gets during each backup. The drive itself will be rated for a number of hours of operation between cleanings. All that is necessary is to divide the total hours between cleanings by the number of backup hours each night to determine how frequently the tape drive should be cleaned. From there it's best to make up a calendar that indicates the days on which the tape drive should be cleaned.

If your drive does have a light that indicates when cleaning is necessary, it's best to follow the indication from the tape drive, rather than a fixed schedule. This is because the rate at which harmful deposits are added to the tape drive depends on the tapes being used, how long they've been used, how they are stored, and a variety of other factors. The tape drive's internal sensors can take some of these factors into account and recommend the cleaning at the appropriate time.

Solving Startup Problems and Testing the Backups

When you start trying to get backups of the server, don't expect things to go smoothly right out of the box. In fact, if they do go smoothly from the start, you may want to make sure you test everything. Backups are notorious for taking a few times to get right. There are always last-minute driver problems, or security issues, or tape drive problems.

Some of the common problems you'll see when you're trying to get the backup software up and running are as follows:

- **No media (tape) available.**   This problem can occur when the backup software doesn't accept tapes it doesn't know. You may have to "import" all of the tapes so that the backup software knows it can use them. It can also happen if you have the media retention feature set to protect tapes from being overwritten for a long period of time.

- **SCSI bus timeout.**   Generally, this problem means that your SCSI controller is trying to communicate with the tape drive at a faster rate than it supports. You need to go into the SCSI BIOS and slow down communication with the SCSI ID of the tape drive. If the tape drive is on the same bus as the hard disks, move it to its own SCSI bus, if possible.

- **Unable to connect to a remote server.**   If you're planning on backing up remote servers, you may need to ensure that the account running the backup software has access to the appropriate shares and files on the remote system. Most of the time it is the service account for the backup software that is used for backups, not the user who is logged on.

- **Unable to locate the tape drive.**   Sometimes the operating system may try to install a driver for the tape drive that is incompatible with the backup software. In such cases it's necessary to disable the device to the operating system by disabling the driver.

- **Unable to open a file.** Most of the time this problem means that the file is in use when the backup software tries to back it up. If you have an open file option in the backup software, it can sometimes back up the data even if the file is open during the backup. You'll want to see if there is a way to back up open files from within the software.

- **Backup takes too long.** In most cases, this problem simply means that you need to optimize the system. Agents may be available that can speed operations, or you may be able to make other optimizations to improve performance. Often, resolving these kinds of issues requires the assistance of the backup software vendor (and sometimes the tape drive vendor).

Because of these problems, you should expect to baby-sit the backup process for the first two weeks, even if you are being shadowed by the person who will eventually have responsibility for monitoring the backups. This implementation time is often one of the most frustrating periods because there's no good way to speed it up, and it's something that's vitally important to the long-term maintenance and support of the server.

I mentioned earlier that having the backup software perform a verification of the backup is a good first line of defense against tape wear. It also instills a little more confidence in the backup process. However, this doesn't eliminate your responsibility to perform test restorations from the backup. Test restorations should be done at a minimum of once a year, but performing them at least quarterly is recommended.

Test restorations are often a difficult proposition. You don't want to restore the entire system because of the amount of time it would take, but conversely you need to make sure that you can do so when necessary. It's generally recommended that you try to rebuild at least one server, using the backup software and a recent backup, so you know the process before you have to perform it for real. However, most people don't recommend completely rebuilding every server with backups if you're using the same software.

Instead, the usual recommendation is to restore the system to an alternate directory on the server or to a directory on another server that has sufficient space. This will ensure that the tape drive can restore the data from the tapes without problems. It's recommended that you use a large data set for the restoration process, rather than a single directory.

Note I have had an unpleasant experience after testing backup software by restoring only a relatively small directory. That restoration worked, so the backup was put into production. When we finally had a failure and tried to restore the whole system, we started getting firmware errors from the tape drive. A call to technical support yielded the answer that there was a bug in the drive's firmware that prevented large restores, but that small restores worked fine. That bug cost us a day of additional downtime to get the new firmware in and then restore the data. If at all possible, try to restore the entire data set.

Other suggestions for tests you may want to consider are as follows:

- **Attempt a restoration on another tape drive of the same make.**   Tape drives occasionally become so misaligned that no other tape drive will read their tapes. This is a problem if the drive dies or is destroyed. You can use another server in your organization, or perhaps work with an associate at another organization to attempt a restoration on its system.

- **Turn the power off to the tape drive and turn it back on.**   If you are using an external tape drive and it isn't attached to the UPS, it may get turned off and then back on during a single boot cycle of the server. Test this to see if it will be a problem for the backup software. You may want to consider doing this while the tape drive is writing.

- **Turn on the write-protect tab and attempt a backup onto the tape.**   This will ensure that the write-protect tab is working and will let you know what happens if the write-protect tab is accidentally left on, so that you can reference it in your procedures. Some drives, for instance, automatically eject tapes that are write-protected when you attempt to write to them.

Practice: Select a Person to Implement Backups

In this practice, you'll get a chance to choose appropriate people to administer a backup rotation for a small office.

In a small sales and marketing office, you have five people who are potential candidates for administering the backup system. Because there's a high turnover within the organization, you want to select two administrators: a primary and a secondary. You're given the following people:

- **Tom.**   Tom is the top-producing salesperson for the organization. He is often out of town "wining and dining" clients. His desk is a mess. He has an office plant that looks like a fossil because he's forgotten to water it—since the day he bought it.

- **Susan.**   As the accountant, Susan is organized. Her office is always orderly, even when she's going through the middle of an audit. Nothing seems to rattle Susan, not even the IRS.

- **Kathy.**   An efficient receptionist, Kathy arrives at the same time almost every morning. She has a series of duties that she performs when she gets in, including disarming the alarm system and setting the phones up to be answered. She also starts the coffee. When she leaves, she consistently resets the phone system to go to the automated attendant and turns on the dishwasher to wash the glasses used that day.

- **Carl.**   As the "big boss," Carl gets to saunter in when he feels like it, take customers out to golf outings, and do whatever he would like most of the day. He oftentimes is prone to periods of extremely brilliant thinking followed by days of absence from the office.

- **Sam.**   Sam does odd jobs around the office, mostly as a gofer to go get things from businesses in the area. Sam was hired quickly and doesn't have a key to the front door, or a code for the alarm system. He is reliable and shows up and leaves at the same time each day.

Which members of the office are best suited to being primary and secondary backup administrators? Let's review each person individually.

- **Tom.**   Because Tom is often gone "wining and dining" clients, he's not a good choice. You need someone who will be available. In addition, forgetting to water a plant is a sign that he can't remember to do things at periodic intervals. Finally, he probably has little information on the system, so he doesn't have a true vested interest in making sure the backups work.
- **Susan.**   Susan is a good choice. She's organized and likes everything in its place. In addition, because Susan is the accountant she probably has a vested interest in making sure that the systems are backed up. However, as the accountant she may have other more pressing matters to attend to and distractions that would cause her to forget about the backup.
- **Kathy.**   Kathy seems to be an ideal candidate. She's expected to be present most days (because she's the receptionist). Her schedule is routine and varies little from day to day. Because Kathy is most often going to be at her desk, it's reasonable to assume that a fair amount of her work is done on the computer system. She'll probably have a vested interest in the backup succeeding.
- **Carl.**   As with Tom, Carl's erratic schedule will probably present a problem. Also, even though he has a vested interest in the backups being done, he'll probably consider that a detail that is beneath him and that should be handled by someone else.
- **Sam.**   Although Sam has a reasonable schedule, his lack of a key and alarm code indicate that there's a trust issue with him, and so he's probably a bad choice for a backup administrator. In addition, none of his work appears to be on the computer systems, giving him no vested interest.

In summary, Kathy is probably the best candidate as a primary administrator, with Susan looking good as a secondary administrator.

Lesson Summary

In this lesson, you learned the procedural issues involved with establishing a backup plan and how to create a backup procedure to ensure consistent implementation. You also learned how to find the right person in the organization to maintain the backups. Finally, you learned about media storage and how to provide safe storage both on-site and off.

Lesson 3: Maintaining Backups .

Maintaining backups so that they are available when they are needed requires a dedication to the reasons for doing backups in the first place. Often, problems that are minor develop into larger problems because of a lack of persistence. This lesson talks about the problems that can occur in backup routines once they are implemented.

After this lesson, you will be able to

- Identify issues that may develop into problems
- Develop plans for resolving failures

Estimated lesson time: 15 minutes

Establishing Notification

As we discussed in Chapter 2, Lesson 4, monitoring of all systems is important. In the case of backups, monitoring needs to be done consistently. Reporting only when a backup fails doesn't help, because it doesn't tell you whether the backup was successful, only that it didn't complete in error.

One of the most important things about setting up notification is not how you do it—via e-mail or pager or by printing the log. The most important thing is not to condition yourself to expect that the backup will always complete, so that you no longer bother to look at the results of the backup and just blindly insert the next tape.

I mentioned earlier that it's best to find another person to actually administer the backup process—someone who has a fixed schedule and who does the same kinds of things every day. No matter how good a candidate you find, you should set up the system to help that person succeed in maintaining the backup. Here are some ideas that can help:

- **Eject the tape after backup.**   If your backup software supports ejecting the tape after a backup, turn this feature on. Having the tape sticking out of the drive provides a clear visual reminder, and if the tape isn't sticking out of the drive, it's a clear sign that something is wrong.

- **Print the backup log to the responsible person's printer.**   At some point in the day, the person handling the backups will probably print something, or at least look at the printer. Having the printout sitting there provides a physical reminder of the backup and that it needs to be tended to.

- **Create a file for the printed backup logs.**   Having a file for the printed backup reports means that the printed paper must be moved from the printer to the place where the log is kept, making it more difficult for the responsible person to neglect to change the tape because the printed report will be in the way until he or she moves it. It's best to have the backup log live in the server room near the tape backup unit itself. Using a three-ring binder for the log also helps because the pages have to be punched and inserted into the book. This tends to give more opportunities to discover problems.

- **Make sure you're notified too.**   Be a backup for the person who's responsible for the backup. Establish e-mail or paging notification to yourself, and watch the subject line to ensure that the backups are completing successfully.

- **Check the backup logs periodically.**   Every now and then, check the backup log to make sure that the backups are completing successfully. This is a good time to review the log line by line and ensure that all of the devices are being backed up.

The goal of these efforts is to ensure that backups are happening correctly, every day. Sometimes, however, there's some small problem. Perhaps a server is taken offline and the backup software can no longer find it. Instead of the normal success messages, all of a sudden you start getting failure messages. A quick check confirms that it is due to the server that was taken offline. There's a strong temptation to continue about the day, rather than modifying the backup setup.

That's a dangerous temptation. Eventually, you quit looking at the logs because you know why they failed. You begin to ignore messages that tell you something is wrong with the backup process. This is when problems tend to occur. That is, you know, Murphy's Law.

Note Some of you may be thinking that no one would ignore a failure message from the backup system and allow it to continue. I can tell you that it most certainly does happen. I've seen it personally. I've also been involved in trying to change the culture to prevent this kind of indifference to backup problems from continuing.

Addressing Problems

Most backup problems appear with little or no warning, and they often seem to appear at the most inopportune times. Backups require the coordination of a series of complicated components, so it's no wonder that from time to time the process breaks down. This section takes a look at some of the common problems with backup systems and discusses how to identify and resolve them.

Security Failure

One of the most frequent reasons that a backup will fail is a security failure. The cause usually is that the password that the backup software is using has either changed or expired. It may also be caused by a trust relationship failing between the backup server and the server it's trying to back up.

No matter what the cause, the normal symptom is that the backup software indicates that it doesn't have access to the files or directories that you're trying to back up.

The resolution is simple. Check the user name and password being used to access the remote system. Try logging on to the remote system with the user name and password yourself. If it appears to work, reset the user name and password in the backup software's connection information. If you're still having trouble, make sure that the system you're backing up, and all of the intervening security information, is synchronized.

Tape Failure

Tapes are remarkably durable, given that most of them are less than a centimeter wide and are very thin. However, tapes are subjected to stretching due to sudden starts and stops. Eventually the tape will break under the strain. A tape can also be broken or shredded if it happens to fall off the rollers inside the tape case, or if the tape drive itself is misaligned or damaged.

If the tape breaks, the backup software no longer recognizes that a tape is installed. When this occurs, some but not all tape drives will automatically try to eject the tape. If the tape ejects, you've got a quick indication that something's wrong. If it doesn't, you'll probably have to wait until the next morning to discover that there was no backup because there was no report.

The best thing to do if you suspect that a tape has been broken is to visually inspect it. Although most tapes are protected by a plastic door that closes when the tape is ejected, a little bit of work should find the release for the door, which you can then move out of the way to see the tape itself. If no tape is visible when you open the safety door, you know it's been broken.

The other kind of problem that can occur is that the tape may no longer be capable of holding information. You will most often notice this problem by performing verification after a backup. However, some tape drives keep track of errors, often called soft errors, and may quit backing up on a tape if the soft error rate exceeds a predetermined threshold.

The resolution to this problem is no mystery: replace the tape. You may want to clean the tape drive as a precaution, even if the tape drive's cleaning indicator is not lit. It's possible that the tape drive is causing the soft errors or that the drive caused the tape to break because of an internal problem. A cleaning tape should remove buildup from the read-write heads that may have been causing soft errors. However, it may break if the tape drive broke the previous tape.

Tape Drive Failure

The failure of a tape is not a big problem. You replace the tape and move on. Most environments have dozens of tapes. However, when the tape drive itself goes bad, there are some real concerns. In most environments, losing a tape drive means that backups can't be performed.

There are three basic ways that a tape drive can fail. First, it may just quit responding. In other words, the electronics or motors of the tape drive may stop working, rendering the tape drive itself unusable. Second, a tape drive may no longer read or write to the tape. The drive responds to software commands but doesn't store information to or read information from the tape. Finally, a tape drive can start breaking tapes. This happens when something breaks or becomes severely misaligned in the drive itself, and it starts breaking tapes when it attempts to read from or write to a tape.

The priority for a tape drive failure is getting the drive fixed or replaced. Most tape drive vendors offer on-site support or at least one-day cross-shipping. You'll have to contact the vendor and often provide a credit card for the cross-shipment, if you didn't purchase a service contract ahead of time. Sometimes technical support can help by forcing resets and reloading the firmware code on the drive itself or by reviewing the tape drive's error log.

In the meantime, you should consider finding alternative ways to back up the server, or at least the critical files, until the new tape drive arrives. You can do this by copying files to other servers that have additional space, or you can piggyback the backup normally performed by the server with the failed tape drive onto the tape backup for another server, thereby backing up the same files, even if it takes longer.

Planning Tape Retirement

Earlier you learned that tapes have a finite lifetime. You also learned about the different tape backup rotations. With these two pieces of information, you can determine when a set of tapes will reach the end of their usable life. Since you know when the tapes will fail, you should plan to retire them when they near that point. The planned retirement of tape helps to ensure that tapes are not used beyond their useful life. This in turn helps reduce problems with the backup.

If you've already installed your tape backup system and haven't planned a time to retire the tapes you have, you can often take a look at the backup software's media log. The media log will generally tell you how many times the tape has been backed up on. From that you can project the end of the useful life of the tapes.

Lesson Summary

In this lesson, you learned about issues that may cause backups to fail and what to do about them. The lesson also identified techniques for monitoring the status of backups so that you can identify problems and address them quickly.

Review

Here are some questions to help you determine whether you have learned enough to move on to the next chapter. If you have difficulty answering these questions, please go back and review the material in this chapter before beginning the next chapter. The answers for these questions are located in the appendix, "Questions and Answers."

1. How do incremental and differential backups work for transactional systems?

2. What is an archive bit, and what does it do?

3. Where did the Tower of Hanoi backup scheme get its name?

4. What is a continuous backup?

5. What is tape wear?

6. What factor during a backup can significantly affect tape life?

7. What are important characteristics in the party responsible for monitoring the backups?

8. What kind of on-site storage should be provided for tape backups?

9. What are the three options for off-site storage?

10. What is the best way to determine whether a tape drive needs cleaning? What can you do if this isn't an option?

11. Why shouldn't the notification for the backups be set up to notify only on failure?

C H A P T E R   1 5

Performing Physical Housekeeping and Verification

About This Chapter

In the previous chapter, you learned how to make backups a part of your overall maintenance routine for the server. This chapter takes you through all of the other miscellaneous tasks you'll have to perform to maintain a server properly. To make the list more manageable, I've broken these tasks into two categories: physical housekeeping and hardware verification.

The next chapter moves into a discussion of troubleshooting, tying together all of the previous chapters.

Tip Most physical housekeeping and verification can be addressed by different monitoring systems. Although these systems are a great idea, you'll still want to make periodic checks to ensure that the monitoring systems haven't missed something.

Before You Begin

To complete this chapter, you should have

- Your server documentation
- Patience

Lesson 1: Performing Physical Housekeeping

If the world were perfect, you would set up a server and never have to worry about it again. Unfortunately, in the real world preventive maintenance is required. In this lesson you'll learn about the various inspections and tests you need to perform for proper maintenance of the server.

After this lesson, you will be able to
- Verify that proper power protection is functioning
- Verify that the environmental controls are still functioning

Estimated lesson time: 15 minutes

Making a Visual Inspection

Your first and best tool for diagnosing physical problems with a server or its environment is your own senses. You can identify most such problems by performing a simple visual inspection of the environment. Other problems can be identified by your sense of temperature or of hearing. The key is to be observant and to pay attention to what is going on around the server.

Obvious Inspections

Some of the inspections you need to perform can be done easily and are fairly obvious. These inspections, which should be performed at least once a week, include the following:

- **Climate.** When you enter the server area, do the temperature and humidity feel correct? When you verify the temperature and humidity at the climate control center, are they within the limits you've established? If not, the climate control system may need to be repaired.

- **Air conditioning filters.** When you look at the filters in the air conditioning system, do you see any visible standing dust? Are the filters obscured by dirt? If so, they should be replaced.

- **Roof leaks.** Are any leaks visible on the ceiling? Obviously, such leaks should be investigated and resolved.

- **Water in the subfloor.** Is there water beneath the raised floor? If you have a raised floor, remove a few of the tiles in various places to verify that no water is standing underneath it. If you see standing water, investigate to determine where it came from.

- **Papers on top of a monitor.** Have papers been left on top of a monitor? This is a fire hazard because the monitor generates a great deal of heat and needs the vents on the top of the monitor to cool itself.

These inspections interfere very little with normal operations and don't require a great deal of investigative effort.

In-Depth Inspections

Beyond the quick inspections just discussed, you should perform other more in-depth inspections on a regular basis—preferably monthly, but at least quarterly. Some of these are as follows:

- **Rack fans.** To ensure proper cooling of servers in a rack, the rack fans must be functional. A quick inspection to see that the rack fans are turning will help you prevent potential heat damage to your servers.

- **Hardware error log.** Most high-end servers have an LCD panel on the front that you can use to review errors, including soft errors detected by ECC memory. It's a good idea to review these logs periodically.

- **Card access system.** If you have a card access system to limit access to the computer room, you'll want to periodically review who has access to the room and verify that they still need access. It's not uncommon to find that many people who are no longer with a company still have access to the computer room. Obviously, this isn't a good idea.

- **Cables.** Cables sometimes work themselves free, particularly ones that aren't secured with a clip or with screws. While you're inspecting the racks and computers, make sure that all cables are plugged in securely.

Of course, you should also be looking for anything out of the ordinary while you're going through the computer room. If you see something that is different than you remember it, check it out. The thing you don't check will be the one that bites you.

Performing Proactive Testing

Sometimes observation isn't enough. You need to take action to test the equipment you have to ensure that it's working correctly. Here is some of the equipment you should test periodically:

- **UPS.** Most UPSs are capable of doing internal testing. However, you should test them periodically to ensure that the batteries are still working. Consider shutting down the devices attached to the UPS when you do this, as they may shut down unexpectedly if a severe UPS failure occurs during the test.

- **Generator.** If you have a backup generator connected for extended power outages, power it on and make sure that it is able to run for 5 to 10 minutes and support the load.

- **Emergency lighting.** Most computer rooms have emergency lighting packs on the walls that are supposed to turn on when the power goes out. Unfortunately, they don't always light up. Check the emergency lighting to ensure that it will light in the event of a power loss.

- **Flashlight batteries.** It's always helpful to have flashlights around in case the power goes out. But flashlights are useless without working batteries. Note that you should leave the flashlight on for two or three minutes to make sure that the batteries will hold up to extended use.

- **Remote access.** If you have remote access set up specifically for problems and remote administration, you'll want to test it periodically. This is particularly true of hardware-based remote access cards because they are used so infrequently. You'll want to take a few minutes to connect to each server to ensure that the modems are working.

Proactive testing takes time. However, if it saves you from a problem down the road, it's time well spent.

Lesson Summary

In this lesson, you learned some of the common inspections and tests you need to perform to make sure that the server is properly cared for. Some of these tasks might seem obvious, such as looking for water leaks on the ceiling. The lesson also discussed inspections that require a bit more effort, such as checking the status of rack fans. Finally, it reviewed tests that are more proactive, such as testing the emergency lighting.

Lesson 2: Performing Hardware Verification

With all of the redundancy options available today, it's important to physically verify that the hardware you have is functioning correctly and that the fault-tolerant options aren't being used, preventing you from seeing a failure.

After this lesson, you will be able to

- Identify individual faults in fault-tolerant components
- Review potential operational performance issues

Estimated lesson time: 15 minutes

Verifying Fault-Tolerant Components

The purpose of fault tolerance is to prevent the users from noticing a failure. Unfortunately, all too often a fault occurs and no one notices it until the next fault occurs, bringing down the system. This sometimes happens because notification of the fault wasn't received or was ignored. This section discusses the different fault-tolerance options and describes how to make sure all of the devices are functional.

RAID Arrays

The most popular type of fault tolerance in use is the RAID array. This popularity is due to the fact that a hard disk is much more likely to fail than any other component of the server. Yet most people don't actively monitor their RAID arrays for a disk failure. As a result, it can be days, weeks, months, or even years before a disk failure is detected.

There are three very simple ways of detecting a RAID failure. The first one is painfully simple: Look at the drives that make up the RAID array. If one of them has a consistently flashing activity light, or the online light isn't illuminated at all, there's clearly some problem. Although most problems will cause the online drive indicator light to go off, other problems will cause it to flash with a consistent frequency. The second way is to open the RAID array software and look at the status of the array. RAID controller software (or BIOS) isn't shy about reporting failed drives. The final way of detecting a failure is to review the error log of the server to see if the RAID software reported a drive failure.

Some argue that failures are what hot-spare drives are for: to become an immediate part of the RAID array, removing the need for any observation of the system. There are a few reasons why this isn't true. First, hot spares don't always work as they should. For example, something might prevent them from becoming properly integrated into the array. Second, what happens when the second drive in the array fails?

Make it a habit to check the status of the RAID array and promptly address any issues, even if you have hot spares in the array.

Note One of my close friends had an experience in which a drive failed in the RAID array and the hot spare wasn't activated because of a problem in the RAID controller BIOS. No one noticed the problem until a few weeks later, when a second drive failed, taking the server down. These things do happen.

Network Adapters

Another case in which fault tolerance can obscure the fact that a failure has occurred involves redundant network adapters. Making it worse, the performance impact of a failed network adapter isn't as significant as it is with a drive failure in a RAID array, so it may go unnoticed for longer.

As with RAID arrays, you can check the error log for messages indicating that a network adapter has failed. You can also check the indicator lights on the backs of the network cards. If one of the cards doesn't even have a link light lit, chances are that it's been disabled because of problems and should be replaced. You can always double-check your findings by going into the driver for the network cards and running a test on the cards to verify whether they are working or not.

Power Supplies

Most high-end servers support multiple power supplies. This redundancy allows the server to continue to function after the failure of a single power supply. Having multiple power supplies eliminates yet another potential problem with servers, but it introduces another component that you need to check.

Most servers with redundant power supplies have LED indicator lights on the power supply itself that indicate whether the power supply is working. However, even if the power supply doesn't have an indicator light, you can always check its fan. If the power supply is working, its fan should be working also. If the fan isn't working, the power supply should be replaced anyway.

Verifying Component Operation

Not every component that isn't working is indicated as a potential fault. Sometimes the devices that are present just to prevent potential problems quit working. These devices aren't generally monitored, and their failure doesn't have any immediate, direct impact on the operation of the server. This section discusses some of these components.

Power Supply Fan

The fan on a power supply is designed to help prevent potential heat damage to the server because of rising temperatures. The failure of a power supply fan doesn't indicate any instant danger, but it can mean that the server will become unreliable. That is why it's important to replace power supplies in which the fan has failed.

Most power supply fans, even those found in servers, are manufactured inexpensively, and they often wear out before the power supply itself. For this reason, you should check the power supply fans in a server to ensure that they are working properly.

Tip Although it's technically possible to replace just the fan in a power supply, it's usually not worth it. The cost of a new power supply isn't that much compared to the amount of time necessary to replace the fan.

CPU Fan

The hottest component in the server is the CPU. It generates the most heat and consumes the most power. However, most CPUs use tiny fans that frequently fail.

The failure of a CPU fan can significantly reduce the life of a server. Every server should have its case removed and the CPU fan reviewed periodically to ensure that it's still functional.

Replacing a defective CPU fan may be difficult, depending on the processor and how the fan is attached or used to cool the CPU. When in doubt as to how to resolve CPU fan failures, contact the server manufacturer or the CPU manufacturer.

Surge Suppressors

The discussion of power in Chapter 2 mentioned that most surge suppressors use MOVs. MOVs have a limited lifetime and die after they have suppressed a certain number of surges. To help you determine when the MOVs are no longer functioning, most modern surge suppressors have an indicator light. If the light is not lit, the MOVs are no longer protecting the server and other attached equipment. Surge suppressors whose MOVs have been exhausted should be replaced as soon as possible to help maintain the life of the server and equipment.

Removing Dust in the Case

One of the side effects of having large amounts of electricity flowing through a server is that it creates a big magnetic field, attracting dust. It doesn't help that the fans pull a great deal of air through the case.

Dust buildup is a natural occurrence. It happens because the conditions in a server are so right for dust to collect. Unfortunately, dust is an enemy to electronic components because it helps retain the heat that the air flowing through the case is supposed to remove.

Periodically examine and, if appropriate, blow dust out of the server case. However, don't use compressed air from an air compressor, and don't use excessive amounts of pressure. The air from an air compressor can be so high in humidity that it can actually deposit small amounts of water on the server. As we discussed in Chapter 2, servers and water don't get along.

Excessive pressure can sometimes dislodge cards, memory, and cables that are necessary for proper operation. The goal is to remove only the dust in the case, not the components of the server itself.

Special cans of compressed air can be used to dislodge the dirt, or a small vacuum, specifically designed for removing dust from a PC, can be used. Neither of these methods for removing dirt will use excessive pressure or deposit condensation on the components.

Checking for Theft

Although it may seem strange or silly to think that someone might steal from a server without the theft being noticed, it does happen. One of the important hardware verifications you should perform is to check that the correct number of processors is installed in a multiprocessor system and that the correct amount of memory is installed in every server.

In systems with only one processor, you'll obviously know that no one has removed the processor, because otherwise the server wouldn't work. However, in multiprocessor systems, it is possible for a processor to be removed without being missed. It's also possible for someone to replace a single processor with a slower processor that may go unnoticed.

The virtual memory functions of most network operating systems can even hide the theft of memory from immediate attention. Because of this, a periodic review of the RAM installed in a server is prudent.

Note Not every environment will need to be concerned about theft of server components. However, there are certainly environments where this is a valid concern. I've heard stories from close friends who have had these kinds of problems with servers at remote locations.

Lesson Summary

In this lesson, you learned about the activities that are necessary to verify that the server hardware and other devices are working properly. These activities include inspecting the fault-tolerant hardware and associated error logs and verifying the operational status of various other devices intended to maintain the long-term well-being of the server. The lesson ended with a short discussion of the need to monitor the servers for potential theft of components.

Review

Here are some questions to help you determine whether you have learned enough to move on to the next chapter. If you have difficulty answering these questions, please go back and review the material in this chapter before beginning the next chapter. The answers for these questions are located in the appendix, "Questions and Answers."

1. Why are physical housekeeping and verification important, even if the proper monitoring systems are in place?

2. Why is it important to verify climate control and the operational status of fans?

3. When should you specifically test remote access?

4. Why is it important to check fault-tolerant systems?

5. Why should surge suppressors be checked?

P A R T   5

Troubleshooting

CHAPTER 16

Understanding the Troubleshooting Process

About This Chapter

This chapter is somewhat different from the others you've read. It's much like the transition you needed to make from your other high school classes to your chemistry class. All the rules have changed. In this chapter, instead of learning facts and figures, you'll be learning about the processes you'll use to solve a wide variety of problems.

Because this chapter is different, you'll want to work on understanding the process it discusses, rather than just comprehending each step on its own. Although most of the things you learned in the rest of the book weren't tightly coupled and didn't have an inherent order, the material in this chapter does need to be understood in the order it's presented.

The next and final chapter takes you through a series of troubleshooting scenarios, using what you'll learn here to further solidify your understanding of these processes and how to use them.

Before You Begin

To complete this chapter, you should have

- Some quiet time in a place where you won't be interrupted
- A notebook

Lesson 1: Applying the Scientific Method to Troubleshooting

In this lesson, you will learn or relearn about the scientific method and how to apply it to troubleshooting problems. This simple, time-honored method has real value today for troubleshooting computer problems.

After this lesson, you will be able to

- Identify the major components of the scientific method and their application in troubleshooting
- Develop plans to troubleshoot problems using the scientific method

Estimated lesson time: 30 minutes

The Learning Process

Before you begin learning about the scientific method and how it applies to troubleshooting computer problems, it's important to take a moment to review how the learning you're doing here is different from the learning in the rest of the chapters thus far.

An author by the name of Benjamin Bloom and his colleagues wrote a book that explained what he called a taxonomy of educational objectives. These objectives were organized into three different hierarchies. There were domains for cognitive skills, emotional skills, and motor skills. The cognitive hierarchy was established in such a way as to represent the cognitive levels at which people can acquire knowledge. Figure 16.1 shows an overview of Bloom's cognitive domain, followed by a list explaining each of the levels in the hierarchy.

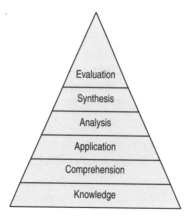

Figure 16.1   Bloom's cognitive domain

- **Knowledge.**   This is the simple recall of information. For instance, the sentence "In 1492 Columbus sailed the ocean blue" represents knowledge. Once you have memorized this sentence, you can probably recall when Columbus sailed fairly easily, when asked. In doing so, you would demonstrate the knowledge level within Bloom's cognitive domain.

- **Comprehension.**   At this level, you understand the meaning of something and can translate or interpret it. For instance, if you were to listen to a lecture on the conditions surrounding Columbus's journey and summarize it, you would demonstrate the comprehension level within Bloom's cognitive domain.

- **Application.**   This level involves applying what you've learned to a topic or situation that isn't directly related. For instance, you might predict the state of mind of the first astronauts to explore space, based on what you had learned from the discussion of Columbus's journey. Although the two types of exploration are different, they are similar in that they involve explorers who are headed into uncharted territory.

- **Analysis.**   When you break learning down into component parts that can be separated from one another, you are demonstrating the analysis level of the cognitive domain. For instance, you might compare the astronauts to the crew of Columbus's ships, describing how they are similar and how they are different. In doing so, you would dissect the emotional component from the socio-economic factors.

- **Synthesis.**   This level involves building a new understanding or system based on loosely related knowledge. For instance, you might synthesize your knowledge of kites, gasoline motors, and wind to create an airplane.

- **Evaluation.**   At this level, you make judgments regarding the value or appropriateness of ideas or materials. An example of evaluation would be selecting the right candidate to be an astronaut based on the person's ability to fly aircraft, operate scientific equipment, and work under extreme conditions.

The reason we're discussing this model is that most of your work in this book has involved developing cognitive abilities to the second level, comprehension. The goal has been for you to know enough to translate the information here into something useful in your environment.

In this chapter, however, you must jump up a level or two to the application and analysis levels of Bloom's cognitive domain. This is because troubleshooting is a process that involves applying the scientific method to different problems and breaking a problem into its parts.

Scientific Method

If you're like me, you were introduced to the scientific method in about the seventh grade. At first, it didn't mean much to me. It was just a short series of steps. However, the more science I was exposed to, the more I began to respect the elegance of the scientific method. Just in case you've forgotten how it goes, here's a summary:

1. Observe, identify, and understand the problem.
2. Hypothesize a solution.
3. Test the hypothesis.
4. Repeat as necessary. If the test fails, go back to step 1.

As I mentioned, it's elegantly simple: only four basic steps. In these four steps, however, is a process that has been used throughout the last several centuries to discover new truths about science. And it can be used to discover the source of server problems. The next few sections explore each step and how it applies to troubleshooting your environment.

Observe, Identify, and Understand the Problem

The first step in solving a problem is to understand that the problem exists. In this step you work to identify the problem and quantify what the problem is and isn't. The goal is to gather as much information as possible about the problem, not necessarily to try to resolve it.

Most of the time, this process takes the form of a series of questions that explore what does and does not work, as well as the solutions that the user or other technician has already tried. For large problems, the answers to these questions are often written down into a personal log, to help with memory after several solutions have been attempted.

Identifying what the problem isn't is as important as identifying what it is. It helps set limits on what the cause can be. If your definition of a problem with your car is that it won't go, you've got a pretty broad definition. However, if you say that the problem isn't in the engine, because the engine is running fine, you eliminate more than half of the potential problems. You can then focus your efforts on the transmission and beyond. The same kind of identification is important in troubleshooting.

Sometimes identifying the problem includes actively testing various parts of the system. For instance, Figure 16.2 depicts the process of printing from a DOS client through a NetWare server to a network-attached printer. When printing problems occur, it's often necessary to review the various parts of the system to determine where the print job might be getting stuck or rejected.

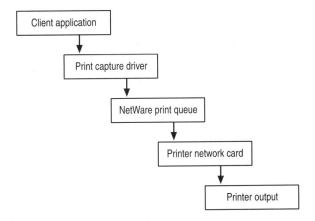

Figure 16.2   NetWare printing from a DOS client

As you can see, what may seem like a simple process from the client actually has several steps. (I chose this example both because of the number of steps involved and because it's a process I've had to teach to more than one technician over the years.) Part of identifying the problem involves isolating the cause of the problem.

In the specific case I'm thinking of, a technician walked into my office to tell me that one of our internal customers was having trouble printing and he didn't know what to do. The information I received from him was limited to the fact that the printout wasn't being printed on the printer.

Because we hadn't identified the problem well enough, we couldn't proceed to the next step to test any hypotheses. We needed to actively identify the root cause of the problem. To that end, I asked the technician to stop, or pause, the print queue so that any print jobs that got placed in the queue would stay there and not go further in the process. He could then try again to print from the workstation and see if it showed up in the print queue.

He found that the print job wasn't making it to the print queue. We now knew that the problem was earlier in the process. As a result, all we needed to check was the client application and the capture driver. In this case, the capture driver was pointed to the wrong printer queue.

Being able to identify and quantify the problem is so important that it is the subject of Lesson 2. For now, you simply need to know that identifying the problem involves determining both what the problem is and what it isn't.

Hypothesize a Solution

It sounds simple: come up with a potential solution to the problem. Despite this seeming simplicity, devising a potential solution can be difficult. The one good thing about the scientific method is that it doesn't require that this step be right the first time. You can come up with a series of thoughts on what the problem might be and develop solutions to those problems. You can try the solutions one at a time until you find the exact cause of the problem.

The two tricks in applying the scientific method to troubleshooting are in developing hypotheses and in selecting the hypothesis that either has the greatest likelihood of solving the problem or requires the least effort.

To develop hypotheses, you must understand the processes involved with or surrounding the problem. That is why we exposed the process for printing from a DOS client to a NetWare server in our earlier example. By exposing the process and understanding the potential problems, you can form one or more hypotheses as to which potential problem is likely to be occurring. These hypotheses can be based on further identification or isolation of the problem, as described earlier, or by knowing which problems occur most frequently in your environment.

Deciding which hypothesis to test first involves the analysis level of the cognitive domain. At this level you're making a decision based on several factors and trying to break the problem apart to determine which hypothesis to test or whether to perform more evaluation first.

The two primary factors to consider when choosing between hypotheses are the ease of testing and the probability of success. These two factors will determine which hypothesis is the better one to test first. In the example of the printing problem given earlier, we noted that there were two areas where the problem could be occurring: the client application and the capture driver.

We determined which one to test first based on both probability and ease of testing. The most frequent printing problem in that environment at the time was that the capture driver was configured or operating incorrectly, indicating a need to test the capture driver. In this case, the ease of testing neither backed up nor contradicted this factor. Although it would be simple enough to query the capture driver as to its current configuration and reset any configuration problems, we could also easily test another application on the same computer to see if the problem still occurred. Because the probability favored checking the capture driver, that was what we did, and it resolved the problem.

Test the Hypothesis

Testing the hypothesis is the simplest part of the process. You simply follow the procedure to fix the component you believe is broken. In the case of software, this might involve reinstalling the software, reconfiguring the software, or applying updates. In the case of hardware, it almost universally means attempting to replace the component.

The key to testing the hypothesis is to try not to introduce other potential problems into the process. Back in Chapter 1, I relayed a story about a developer who became hung up on a problem, in part because he had accidentally introduced another problem into the environment by upgrading his development environment. If a hypothesis fails, the environment should most often be rolled back to the environment that existed before the test.

This point applies to hardware as well as software. If you are having a problem and you decide to swap out the network interface card to test whether it is the cause of the problem, you should replace the original card if the new card fails to resolve the problem. That way, you will avoid introducing other problems into the environment.

Tip You may get through your entire career without introducing new problems into an environment by testing different hypotheses. However, it is much more likely that you'll eventually do so. I can guarantee that the time you spend backing out of a change will be several orders of magnitude smaller than the time you spend resolving the original problem in the altered environment.

Repeat as Necessary

Failing to get the hypothesis right the first time is to be expected. Problem solving is an iterative process that requires patience and organization. You eventually overcome the problem by sticking to it and trying new things.

The value of repeating the process is that each time you do so you have new information as an input to the process. At the beginning of this discussion, I talked about the importance of learning what the problem isn't as well as what the problem is. When a hypothesis fails, you have clearly identified something that isn't causing the problem, and in doing so you have gained more information about the process.

Lesson Summary

In this lesson, you learned about the basis for the scientific method and how it applies to the process of troubleshooting server problems. You learned that the identification step is the most important phase and that the hypothesis step is a natural outgrowth of this step.

Lesson 2: Quantifying the Problem

The most difficult part of troubleshooting a problem is understanding the problem. As we discussed earlier, generating a hypothesis regarding what the problem might be requires a thorough understanding of the problem and the processes surrounding the problem. This lesson describes how to localize and isolate problems in order to gain a better understanding of them.

After this lesson, you will be able to

- Explain the need to localize problems
- Describe how to localize problems
- Explain the need to isolate problems

Estimated lesson time: 20 minutes

Localizing the Problem

In the preceding lesson, you learned that knowing what a problem isn't is just as important as knowing what it is. Whether you're dealing with printers or automobiles, it's important to limit your focus to as small an area as possible.

This is largely because the bigger the problem appears to be, the more potential hypotheses you will have as to the real root cause. And the more hypotheses you have, the longer it will take to test them all. Going back to the car analogy from Lesson 1 for a moment, if you don't localize the problem to something other than the engine, you will be faced with thousands of potential causes in the engine alone.

By determining that the problem is not the engine, you localize it, removing a whole series of potential problems. You can now focus on those components in the car that are involved with motion but that aren't the engine. These components would include the transmission, the drive shaft, and the wheels. So your hypotheses might be that the transmission is broken, the drive shaft is broken, or the wheels are seized up. These hypotheses, while not simple, can be tested quickly to help you further localize the problem.

In order to localize a problem, you must understand the processes that the system uses that may have broken and the components that the system uses that may have failed. A good example of a complicated system that can cause problems is the network. The components of the network include the protocol software on the server, the network interface card driver on the server, the network interface card hardware in the server, the hub or switch to which the server is attached, all of the intervening routers and switches, the network interface card hardware in the client computer, the network interface card driver on the client computer, and the protocol software on the client. And that just gets you basic communication between the two devices; it doesn't even provide for file sharing or printing services. It also doesn't provide for any protocol-specific services that may need to be installed on the network.

The first step in troubleshooting a problem is to localize it. For example, if you can't establish connectivity between a server and a client, it's important to localize the cause of the problem. In this case there are several approaches that you can take, but in general the first step is to verify that the protocol configuration information is correct. For the purposes of this discussion, let's assume that we're using TCP/IP. This means that the configuration for each system and all of the intervening routers must have the appropriate IP address, subnet mask, and default gateway. (The default gateway is required only if the server and client are separated by a router.)

If the configuration appears correct on the client and server, you can use the diagnostic tools to test the network to see if there is connectivity between the server and the client. By using the PING command from the client to the server's IP address, you can test end-to-end connectivity. If the PING command succeeds, you know that there isn't a problem with the network or the TCP/IP configuration information. Conversely, if the PING doesn't work, you know that more diagnosis is necessary to determine where the connectivity problem is within the network.

Assuming that the PING worked, you still have naming services to check to make sure that the client can resolve the server's name to an IP address. If the client can't resolve the name to an address, it won't be able to connect to the server by name. The NSLOOKUP tool can be used to test name resolution, if that is the problem.

If you still haven't been able to localize the problem, you can test the client with another server or test the server with another client to try to determine whether the server or the client is the source of the problem. This process continues until you have pinpointed the source of the problem, which you can then test with different hypotheses of what might have gone wrong.

In this case, a knowledge of how TCP/IP functions and how the network is put together will allow you to slowly ferret out the problem by getting closer and closer to it. For the most part, the problems you'll address will have only a few potential components and will take only a few attempts until you've localized the problem to a single part or a small set of parts that may be broken.

At other times, however, localizing the problem will be difficult if not impossible, particularly when you don't have the tools necessary to perform the localization tests. For instance, if your server is refusing to boot up but doesn't report any errors, you may be able to check the power supply to ensure that power is making it to the motherboard, but it may be difficult to determine the cause of the failure if you don't have a memory tester, a spare motherboard, a spare processor, or other tools and components that you could use to localize the problem.

To a certain extent, there's no need to localize the problem beyond a certain point, because you won't be able to fix the problem anyway. For instance, if you localize a problem to a motherboard, it's pointless to try to identify which integrated circuit on the motherboard is bad, because you won't repair that circuit anyway. You'll just replace the motherboard. Therefore, you may not need very specialized tools; instead, it may make sense to have only the tools and parts necessary to perform the basic localization, and from there determine how to replace the defective unit.

Isolating the Problem

If localization is about finding the core of the problem, isolation is about keeping other problems away from your core problem so that they don't gang up on you. Isolation prevents other potential problems from causing problems during the testing. For instance, if you are having a connectivity problem with all of the remote locations for an organization, you'll want to use the remote location that has the most reliable communications link while troubleshooting, so that a communications problem doesn't compound the existing problem or confuse the process.

Most problems that become overwhelming do so because they really involve several issues that are occurring simultaneously. These clusters of problems can make it appear that none of the solutions work, and as a result they tend to require more and more isolation, well below the level that is normally necessary.

Localizing a Problem vs. Testing a Hypothesis

At this point, you may be wondering what the difference is between performing tests in order to localize a problem and testing a hypothesis as part of the scientific method. You can probably make your own decision about where to draw that line. When you perform a test for localization or you review a configuration, you're testing a specific component to see whether it's functioning or not.

The primary difference is that you don't expect that a test for localization will resolve the problem; you're just looking for new information about the source of the problem. Strictly speaking, these tests to determine where a problem is centered, or localized, are a cycle of the scientific method. You hypothesize that the process is broken before or after that component and then test that assumption. In practice, however, the distinction is immaterial. The key is learning more about the problem so that you will eventually get to a resolution.

Dividing the Process in Half

One final note about working on problems. When dealing with processes and components that make up a system, you should generally start in the middle of the process and determine whether the problem is occurring before or after that stage or component. Then pick a point in the middle of the remaining part of the process to test. Keep doing this until you've found the source of the problem.

This method of searching for the problem is called a binary search, because the answer you get is that the problem occurs either after the point you tested or before it. This type of search can significantly reduce the number of tests you have to perform.

However, remember that this type of division should be done only if all other things are equal. If a particular step is difficult to test, you'll probably want to avoid it when trying to locate the problem. Likewise, if there are easy tests that can be performed on certain areas of the process, it may make sense to try them first.

Lesson Summary

In this lesson, you learned some techniques you can use to make solving problems more manageable. Localization allows you to pinpoint the source of a problem so that it is small enough to hypothesize solutions for. Isolation keeps other problems from creeping in and disturbing your analysis of the problem.

Lesson 3: Knowing Who to Call and What to Do

Until this point, this chapter has assumed that you're solving problems on your own, without any resources. However, that's rarely the case in today's world. Technical support is available to answer questions, and there are other technicians to consult. This lesson expands our previous discussion to include the appropriate use of external resources.

After this lesson, you will be able to

- Identify who to call in various situations
- Resolve issues preventing problem resolution

Estimated lesson time: 15 minutes

Who to Call

Once you've exhausted your resources in trying to resolve a problem, it's time to pick up the phone. But who do you call? This section talks about who to call and when, so that your problem can be resolved quickly.

Tip Before you call any technical support, make sure you have all of your server documentation together so that you'll be able to answer questions quickly. If you need help, refer back to Chapter 9, which covered documenting the installation.

Hardware or Software?

One of the first decisions you need to make before calling for help is whether you believe the problem is related to hardware or software. Hardware problems, or problems with hardware drivers, need to be directed to the hardware vendor. Software problems should be directed to the software vendor for assistance. Of course, some problems appear to be operating system problems, and in those cases you should contact the operating system vendor for assistance. (An operating system is just a special kind of software.)

When it's not clear where the problem lies, such as when a complete system lockup occurs, you should generally contact the software vendor. Its technical support may be able to help you determine where the problem is. On the other hand, you may have better luck with the hardware vendor, depending on the level of support available.

Costs Associated with Calls

Sometimes technicians worry about the cost of long-distance phone calls for technical support or, more often, about the cost the vendor charges for the call. While these costs can indeed be nontrivial, if the calls save even a few hours of troubleshooting on your part they will quickly make up for their cost.

Think back to our discussion in Chapter 1 of the cost of lost opportunity. The cost of a call to technical support is generally not very expensive relative to the amount of money the organization is losing while a server is down. If you need to get help to resolve the problem, do so. Don't worry about spending a few dollars.

Note Some managers have a hard time understanding the need to pay for technical support. Before you make the call, be sure to consult with your manager to convey the importance of obtaining timely technical support.

Practice: Solve a Software Copy Protection Problem

This practice explores a hypothetical problem with a software copyright protection device known as a "dongle" and discusses who you would call for help in resolving the issue.

Your organization has just bought the LMM (Lose My Money) accounting system. It requires you to place a hardware key device, called a dongle, on the parallel printer port of the server to prevent the software from being copied. Unfortunately for you, the LMM software doesn't detect the dongle. You've already checked the README file included with the software, as well as the user manual, without results. Who should you call for support?

You should call the LMM accounting system vendor. Its technical support staff can tell you what testing tools it has for testing the dongle and can help determine whether the hardware key you have attached doesn't match the key the software is looking for. Finally, it can confirm that the message about the dongle not being detected is truly the error you are having, and not a problem from some other part of the system that is being misreported.

Alternatively, you could call the dongle manufacturer, but it would be able to provide only basic utilities to detect the presence of the dongle, not potential mismatches in the software or problems in which the software is reporting the wrong error.

It's also possible to contact your operating system or hardware vendor, but neither is likely to have much experience with hardware dongles, and they will probably just refer you to the software vendor.

Practice: Troubleshoot an Adaptec SCSI Controller

This practice looks at a hypothetical problem in which an Adaptec SCSI controller mysteriously generates SCSI bus reset errors in the operating system's event log. These events seem to correspond to performance issues that the clients are having.

You're running a Dell computer with Microsoft Windows 2000 on it. The SCSI adapter has three Seagate hard disks and a Quantum DLT-7000 tape drive attached. All of the devices are internal, and the termination on the SCSI card has been turned on. There's also a stand-alone terminator on the end of the cable internally. You've exhausted your thoughts as to what the problem might be, having checked everything that you can think might be causing the SCSI bus reset errors. Who should you call about the problem?

The best candidate to call is Adaptec, the SCSI card manufacturer, because it is most likely to know what conditions or devices may generate this kind of problem. Although it's possible to contact Seagate and Quantum, they will be able to give you suggestions only for how their devices should be configured, and they probably won't be able to assist much with general SCSI issues.

You could, of course, contact the operating system vendor, Microsoft, or the server hardware vendor, Dell, but those parties will probably not have first-hand information about how to resolve hardware-based SCSI errors. (The error is hardware based as evidenced by the fact that the message is generated by the controller, and it says that the bus was reset.)

What to Do When Nothing Makes Sense

Perhaps the hardest part of working with computers is encountering a problem that just won't seem to go away. Eventually, everyone encounters a problem that is so big or so tangled that resolving it seems impossible. The techniques you've seen up to this point will get you only so far. Beyond that, you need to use different techniques and approaches. (And we're not talking about throwing the server out the window.)

Most of the time, people work on a problem until they become stuck. They believe they've tested, replaced, or verified everything that could possibly be causing the problem. Sometimes, however, they've made a simple error in the testing that led a test to come back negative when it should have been positive.

Tip Sometimes just walking away from the problem helps. Thomas Edison was having a difficult time getting his incandescent light bulb to work. Time after time, it would burn up. Working frantically, he repeated the procedure he had done dozens of times and removed all of the air from the inside of the light bulb. Then he walked away. When he came back he again removed all of the air from the inside of the light bulb. This time his invention worked, because the second time he removed the air he had evacuated the last oxygen molecules that had adhered to the glass and the filament because of atmospheric pressure. Take a step back from the problem when things don't make sense. Then come back to it.

Verify Assumptions

The first step in working through a seemingly endless problem is to verify all of the assumptions that you've made. We all make assumptions when we try to solve a problem. That is how we simplify things to the point that we feel we can resolve the problem. For instance, if our car fails to start in the morning, we often assume that nothing has changed since we left it the previous evening. It may have been driven by our spouse or child, but we assume that it's just as we left it. We wouldn't immediately check to see whether a spark plug wire has been removed. Instead, we'd assume that our car won't start for a more common reason, such as a dead battery.

While these assumptions are helpful and allow us to solve problems more rapidly, they can also be a barrier because we generally won't test things that we assume are working normally, or we'll test them only when we have no other options left. When you run out of obvious possible causes of a failure, start looking for the obscure ones.

For instance, during the course of writing this book, I had problems with my digital subscriber line (DSL) Internet connection. It would intermittently stop responding. The odd thing was that the last time it broke, the modem quit responding to pings from the firewall.

The technical support person I spoke with saw that the modem wasn't responding to pings across the line itself and assumed that I must have a line problem. Admittedly, more than 90 percent of the problems the company deals with are probably of this type. However, that hypothesis couldn't explain my problems with the modem. If the line had been the problem, the firewall should have been able to ping the modem. So while I was convincing technical support that there must be a different explanation to the problem, I tested something that most people just assume is correct: the power pack from the wall. It was supposed to be outputting 6 volts at 2 amps to the modem. When I tested it, I got 8.79 volts. I replaced the power pack with an adjustable transformer that I set for 6 volts, and the problems went away.

Of course, I had previously replaced the whole modem because I thought it was defective. The problem went away for a while but then came back. Most people wouldn't have checked the power supply, and I'll admit that I didn't change it when the new modem arrived, because I assumed that it was good. The moral, of course, is to examine the assumptions that you're making about what is or isn't going to affect the operation of a device.

Tip My favorite assumption is that the power is OK. Replacing a cheap power supply in a computer with a quality power supply has often led mysterious problems to disappear. Don't underestimate the impact that flaky power can have on your electronic devices, and on your server.

Check the Unlikely

A favorite quote of mine is from Sir Arthur Conan Doyle's *The Adventure of the Beryl Coronet,* in which his character Sherlock Holmes says, "It is an old maxim of mine that when you have excluded the impossible, whatever remains, however improbable, must be the truth." It's a favorite because it reminds me that just because something is unlikely, or improbable, doesn't mean that it can't be the cause.

Here are just a few examples of problems I've come across and their solutions, to get you thinking of improbable but possible causes of problems you are having:

- **An add-in I/O card that wasn't working.**   The motherboard ports, although disabled, didn't fully release the resources, and the I/O card wouldn't function unless all of the resources were available to it exclusively.

- **An erratic mouse pointer on a notebook.**   The internal trackpad and an external wheel-type mouse could not be used together if power management was turned on. Turning off either power management or the internal mouse port made the problem go away.

- **IBM 5250 terminals that were burning out.**   The terminals were located in a building across the street that was powered by a different transformer. A 2-volt difference in the grounding of the two buildings would eventually burn out terminals connected to the other end. The solution was to use fiber optic cables to connect the two buildings. These cables use light, rather than electrical signals, to communicate information, so they are immune to the voltage differential problems that were causing the terminals to burn out.

- **A T1 communications line that wouldn't stay connected.**   The phone company replaced every repeater between the two buildings connecting the T1. Eventually, the problem was found to be a piece of copper in one connector that had broken but was being held into position by the weight of the cable. When the cable was moved or brushed against, it would open up until the weight of the cable pulled the cable back into a position where the wire made contact again.

- **A conversion from a System/38 to an AS/400 that kept losing the workstation controller.**   When converting from a System/38 to an AS/400, we moved all of the workstations over from the System/38 to the AS/400. The AS/400 had the same Twinax type controller as the System/38. The resolution to the problem was to remove the older Twinax emulation cards from the workstation controller. (This solution was found after IBM replaced the workstation controller.)

These are all problems whose resolution I was personally involved in, to some extent. The point is that sometimes what seems to be a common problem can have an unlikely resolution.

Recheck Previous Tests

One of the final actions to take when you're stuck is to retrace your steps. This process is never fun, but it's sometimes necessary to solve the problem. When you're reviewing your notes, look for a few things. You want to expose assumptions you've made that may have been incorrect, and you want to expose changes that you may have made during testing that you didn't back out of after finding out that they didn't work.

Looking for assumptions that you've made is a particularly difficult process because you're likely to make the same assumptions when reviewing your notes. It is often helpful to get someone else from your organization to review your notes with you. That person can be a junior technician to whom you have to explain everything, or it can be another technician who is familiar with the problem. A less experienced technician will ask a lot of questions about how things work that may spur you to other thoughts as to what the cause might be. Additionally, having to teach someone else the processes will cause you to think about the inner workings of the process more deeply than before.

An experienced technician will likely bring a different set of experiences to the process and will be able to share with you similar problems that he or she has solved and their causes. This may be helpful in identifying tests that you haven't performed.

If you've reviewed your notes and can't find any assumptions or things that you may have changed to perform a test, it's time to start from scratch and start re-testing everything. Although definitely a last resort because it means duplicating all of your earlier effort, it's sometimes necessary.

When running the tests again, pay particular attention to behavior that has changed between the first and second runs of the test. Such changes often indicate the source of the problem, or that an underlying assumption is invalid.

Lesson Summary

In this lesson, you learned who you should call when you get stuck, and what you can do to get unstuck. You learned that the primary decision as to who to call relates to whether the problem is hardware or software related. You also learned that resolving a stubborn problem can be as easy, and as boring, as reviewing your previous assumptions and tests.

Review

Here are some questions to help you determine whether you have learned enough to move on to the next chapter. If you have difficulty answering these questions, please go back and review the material in this chapter before beginning the next chapter. The answers for these questions are located in the appendix, "Questions and Answers."

1. What is Bloom's cognitive domain?

2. Why is troubleshooting different from most other learning?

3. What is the first step in the scientific method?

4. Why doesn't the hypothesis being tested have to be right?

5. Why is localization of a problem so important?

6. Why is isolation of a problem important?

7. Who should you call if a hardware driver is responsible for locking up the computer?

C H A P T E R   1 7

Troubleshooting Common Problems

About This Chapter

This chapter finishes our journey together by discussing common problems and how to resolve them. It allows you to reinforce the skills you learned in the previous chapter and apply your new troubleshooting skills to common problems.

Before You Begin

To complete this chapter, you should have

- A notebook

Lesson 1: Bootup Problems

One of the largest categories of common problems relates to booting the system. The size of this category is due in part to the multitude of things that can go wrong with the bootup process and to the relatively small amount of error-handling code that can be loaded to detect and correct problems.

As you know from Chapter 16, the key to solving a problem is to understand it. Therefore, this lesson begins with a review of the bootup process before delving into specific bootup problems and resolutions.

After this lesson, you will be able to

- Explain the bootup process
- Identify the cause of missing hard disks
- Identify and eradicate boot sector viruses
- Localize a failure in the bootup processes

Estimated lesson time: 20 minutes

Understanding the Bootup Process

The bootup process starts with one painfully simple step. All Intel 80x86 and compatible processors execute the instruction found at system memory address FFFF0h. This is exactly 16 bytes below 1 MB. The instruction found at this location is generally a jump instruction telling the processor to go to some other place in memory.

This initial instruction, and the point to which the processor is directed, are in the ROM (read-only memory) on the motherboard. This ROM contains the basic input/output system (BIOS) and power-on self test (POST) instructions. During bootup, the processor is directed to execute the instructions for a POST.

Note Most motherboards today use a FlashROM, a user-updatable version of ROM. Regardless of the type of ROM, however, the result is the same: a set of software that instructs the computer how to boot up is installed on the motherboard.

The POST process tests the basic functions of the system and sets the parameters that were recorded in the ROM BIOS, as discussed in Chapter 4. It also initializes all of the add-on cards that have firmware on them and allows them to run their own diagnostic tests.

After all of the tests have been completed, including tests such as SCSI device detection initiated by the SCSI controller(s), the POST attempts to locate an operating system that can be booted from the devices that were specified in the

BIOS setup screens. These devices can be the CD-ROM drive, a floppy drive, or a hard disk.

When booting from a floppy disk, the POST reads the first sector of the floppy into memory and executes it. When booting from a hard disk, the POST reads in and executes the portion of the first sector that doesn't contain the partition table. On a hard disk, this initial code is called the master boot record (MBR). The MBR is written automatically by the operating system when it initially prepares a hard disk for use.

The MBR contains the instructions that the operating system vendor wants to have performed. For instance, in MS-DOS, Microsoft Windows 95, and Windows 98, it causes the MSDOS.SYS and IO.SYS files to be loaded. These in turn execute COMMAND.COM, which processes the CONFIG.SYS and AUTOEXEC.BAT startup files.

In Linux, Microsoft Windows NT, or Windows 2000, the MBR may contain or reference a menu loader. These boot menus then transfer control to a copy of the MBR that they copied for the operating system when it was selected.

As you can see, although the bootup process starts with a simple instruction, it doesn't stay simple. Because the process has so many different links and very little facility for error handling, a multitude of things can go wrong. The next few sections talk about what can happen to disrupt this process.

Troubleshooting Missing Hard Disks

One of the problems that can occur during bootup is that the BIOS or SCSI BIOS does not detect the drive containing the MBR during the POST. This obviously means that the system won't be able to boot up the installed operating system. There are basically three potential reasons why a hard disk might not be detected:

- The hard disk has failed
- The bus that the disk is on has a problem
- The bus isn't being scanned or is being scanned incorrectly by the BIOS

The cause of a disk failure is pretty obvious, but problems on the bus or with the scanning of the bus can have more than one cause. Although you can generally assume a disk failure if the missing hard disk is on a bus with other devices and that disk is the only one missing, it's still a good idea to review the other two options to ensure that the disk really has failed.

Note While problems with IDE hard disks do occur, their frequency is substantially less than the problems with SCSI devices, partially due to the additional complexities of SCSI and partially due to the sheer number of SCSI devices used in servers today. You'll probably notice that this discussion is taking a distinctly SCSI turn.

Generally, when a problem on the bus is the cause of a hard disk not being detected, it's because either the termination is wrong or there are conflicting SCSI IDs. If a device was recently removed from the system, termination may have been set on the device itself and not replaced on that end of the cable after the device was removed. If a new device was added, it may have internal termination set when it shouldn't, or it may have the same ID as the hard disk that is not being detected properly. In any case, a verification check of SCSI IDs and termination is warranted. If no devices have been added to or removed from the device chain recently, you should still double-check the settings on the bus, although it's unlikely that the problems are related to the bus itself.

Note If you didn't install the system and you are being asked to troubleshoot a bootup problem in which a SCSI hard disk is not being detected, you should definitely verify all of the devices and settings on the SCSI chain. Although SCSI is generally sensitive, I've seen systems that have had either no termination or termination on every drive work for a while before failing.

Sometimes bus problems occur on IDE devices as well, but they are normally caused by a cable being unplugged or a drive failing. Since an IDE bus can have only two devices connected, conflicting devices are rare, and termination isn't an issue.

The other potential cause of hard disk detection problems is the bus not being scanned correctly. This can happen when the system is not detecting the SCSI card, resulting in the SCSI card's BIOS not being loaded, or when the SCSI card's BIOS has been disabled. If the SCSI card isn't being detected by the motherboard ROM, either it is not plugged in firmly or it has become defective. You can quickly check whether the SCSI BIOS has been disabled by going into the SCSI BIOS setup and seeing whether the missing device is detected on the SCSI bus. If the device is detected but isn't showing up for booting purposes, it's likely that a SCSI BIOS setting is preventing the SCSI BIOS from loading. Checking to make sure that the SCSI BIOS installed itself is usually a good first step if there haven't been major changes to the devices on the SCSI bus.

Eliminating Boot Sector Viruses

It used to be that the only infection you needed to worry about was the possibility of getting a cold from one of the users you were helping. That time is long since past. In today's environment, a variety of viruses can cause havoc on a server or on an entire computer network. Before delving into how boot sector viruses infect servers and what to do about them, a basic primer on viruses is appropriate.

You need to understand three important points about computer viruses. The first is that a virus is a program. It is a piece of software written by a programmer for purposes other than the ones the owner of the hardware has in mind. The second point is that viruses have two cousins that you may also run into. They are

- **Worms.**   Software whose primary purpose is to reproduce. Worms reproduce to the point that they clog systems and cause havoc by slowing things down. A virus without any purpose other than replication is a worm.

- **Trojan horse.**   A program that appears to have a purpose and is run knowingly by the computer operator. Only after a user has run the program does he or she determine that the program has other effects. Trojan horse programs are typically designed to steal passwords for the program's author or authors.

The third and final point to understand about viruses is that they use three basic infection types:

- **Boot sector infectors.**   These viruses infect the master boot record of a hard disk or the boot sector of a floppy disk and spread the infection through the sharing of floppies. They stay in memory from the time the system is started until it is shut down.

- **Extenders/replacers.**   These viruses extend an application to include their code or replace a program with their code (storing the original somewhere else). These viruses run whenever the infected program runs.

- **Scripts/macros.**   These relatively new viruses live in simple text-based scripts or macros and are executed when the script or macro is executed.

Our focus here is on boot sector infector viruses. This type of virus has all but been eradicated through the conscientious use of virus scanners and the decreased reliance on floppy disks as a medium. Table 17.1 shows the top 10 variations of known viruses based on Trend Micro's virus encyclopedia on February 20, 2001.

Table 17.1 Top 10 Known Viruses by Variation

Number of Known Viruses	Virus Variation
19,763	File infector virus (extenders/replacers)
3,474	Macro virus
2,345	Trojan horse program
674	Boot sector infector virus
332	VBScript virus
124	Joke virus
79	HTML virus
51	Java applet virus
16	IRC script virus
13	Batch file virus

As you can see, boot sector viruses are currently number 4 on Trend Micro's list of the most numerous viruses, and their rank is falling.

Boot sector infector viruses used to be prevalent because simply booting from an infected floppy disk would cause a system to become infected, and every new floppy disk that was inserted into an infected system would become infected as well. Back when floppy disks were used frequently on servers, this was a real issue. However, since most servers are now updated via the network rather than via floppy disks, the problem has all but disappeared.

Note It's important to know that because viruses are programs, they cannot become active unless they are run. Therefore, simply inserting an infected floppy disk into a drive cannot cause the server to become infected. The code in the boot sector of the floppy must be run, which happens only at bootup. If you don't boot with an infected floppy disk in the drive, the machine cannot be infected.

Boot sector infector viruses often prevent the server from booting, because for the virus to infect the system it needs to move the existing boot sector code out of the way and load it when it is done. This worked fine when the only operating system in widespread use was MS-DOS. The virus would know exactly what to expect in the boot sector. However, as operating systems such as OS/2, Windows NT, and Linux came on the scene, the viruses would unknowingly break the bootup code for these operating systems when they tried to move it. As a result, the system wouldn't boot at all.

The technique for fixing a boot sector infector virus is simple. You need to reinstall the master boot record on an infected hard disk or the boot sector on an infected floppy disk. Some virus tools can do this automatically, and others require a manual process for recovering the boot sector.

Lesson Summary

In this lesson, you learned the steps in the bootup process as well as some of the common causes of bootup problems and how to localize and resolve them.

Lesson 2: Network Problems

Although our focus here, and the focus of the Server+ exam, is not on networks and the problems associated with them, a server can't operate without some sort of network. As a result, the Server+ exam includes questions relating to the resolution of network problems. This lesson reviews basic network connectivity and discusses problems that can interfere with network connectivity.

After this lesson, you will be able to

- Identify the components of network communication
- Identify and resolve DHCP issues
- Identify and resolve name resolution issues
- Identify faulty network interface cards

Estimated lesson time: 35 minutes

Understanding How Protocols Interact

Communication is difficult no matter how it's done. Whether you're trying to send smoke signals or an e-mail message, the process of communication is inherently tricky. Before we explore how networks communicate, let's go through an exercise that will help you understand some of the issues involved.

Suppose that you work in a manufacturing company in China, and you're shipping a container full of plastic soldiers with parachutes to your customer in the United States. Your customer has asked to be notified when the container is actually underway. You've just received a note, handwritten in Mandarin Chinese, that the container has been loaded and the ship has sailed. You need to communicate this to your customer in the United States.

The first step in communicating this information is deciding what language to use. You are a native speaker of Mandarin Chinese, and your customer is a native speaker of English. You speak and write some English. Your customer speaks but doesn't read Mandarin Chinese. For this reason, you decide that you'll have to notify the customer in English.

The next step is determining how you'll communicate the information. In this case you're going to use a fax machine. This means that you need to write a letter encapsulating the message into a format that your customer is expecting. In other words, you'll have to add a greeting, such as "Dear Customer," to the beginning of the message, as well as a closing, such as "Thank you," to the end of the message.

After you've added some more information in the letter itself to make it look right, you have to work up a fax cover page. This page contains more information than the letter, but it still doesn't contain the message. It basically contains the routing information indicating who the recipient of the letter should be.

Finally, you fax the cover page and the letter to your customer and pull the delivery confirmation report from the fax machine. You staple the fax cover sheet, letter, and delivery confirmation receipt together, completing the packet, and file it away.

A similar process has to happen with network communications. The message gets wrapped up into more and more layers, each communicating slightly more information, but the information in these layers is not the message itself. Years ago, when networking was in its infancy and many protocols were competing for market acceptance, the International Organization for Standardization (ISO) produced a reference model, known as the Open Systems Interconnection, or OSI, model, that could be used to describe how this packaging might occur within a network. Figure 17.1 shows this reference model alongside a Microsoft Windows 2000 implementation of file and print services over TCP/IP. (These services are implemented with server message block, or SMB.) ISO also produced an actual open standards protocol, but the industry never embraced it.

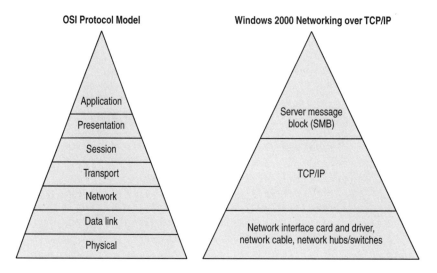

Figure 17.1   OSI reference protocol model compared with Windows 2000 over TCP/IP

As you can see, the OSI reference protocol model defines seven layers. Each layer encapsulates the information on the layer below it and adds new information. The following is a brief overview of the seven layers of this model:

- **Physical.**   This layer is concerned with encoding the message onto the medium. On a 10BaseT Ethernet network, it would control the electrical signals that indicated the binary bits of information. In a 1000BaseF card, the physical layer is responsible for encoding pulses of light to communicate bits of information. For instance, 10BaseT, 100BaseT, and 1000BaseF define different physical interfaces for the Ethernet standard.

- **Data link.**   This layer defines the format of the information as it is transmitted over the local network. It has error detection codes in it and defines where in the packets information should appear. Ethernet defines the data link layer.

- **Network.**   The network layer is concerned with the routing of information from one local network to another network. The network layer loosely corresponds to the Internet Protocol (IP) portion of the TCP/IP protocol suite. Other helper protocols, such the Address Resolution Protocol (ARP), are used at this level to translate between data link, or hardware, addresses and network addresses.

- **Transport.**   This layer is responsible for communicating information over the network layer. It packages the message to be communicated in the protocol specified by the network layer for delivery. The User Datagram Protocol (UDP) part of the TCP/IP protocol suite roughly corresponds to this layer.

- **Session.**   This layer is responsible for guaranteeing delivery of a message. It is concerned with acknowledging the receipt of information on the remote end. The Transmission Control Protocol (TCP) part of the TCP/IP protocol suite roughly corresponds to this level of the OSI reference model.

- **Presentation.**   This layer is responsible for preparing data for the application layer. It is not directly implemented in the TCP/IP suite of protocols or in any other protocol suite in common use today.

- **Application.**   This layer allows actual, meaningful information to be exchanged. An example of an application-level protocol in Windows 2000 is server message block (SMB), which is used to authenticate users and then to allow them access to file- and print-based resources.

Although these layers are rarely exposed in this exact way in systems any longer, some correlations remain between the current implementation and the layers defined by the OSI model, as you can see in Figure 17.1. The greatest difference between the OSI reference model and current implementations is that many of the OSI reference model's original layers have been merged into larger layers.

You need to understand the OSI reference model so that you can conceptualize the way in which the different pieces of a network interact. This understanding is the foundation from which you can make your troubleshooting decisions. Even if the layers don't exist separately within modern network protocol implementations, they must still perform the same functions.

Diagnosing Physical or Data Link Problems

The starting point for diagnosing network problems in today's environment is the physical and data link layers of the OSI reference model. You can diagnose problems at these levels by reviewing the connectivity of the network cables, network interface cards, and network hubs or switches. In most environments, the network interface cards will verify this connectivity for you. Most modern network interface cards have a "link" light that indicates the status of their physical link to the network.

Although historically the link light didn't become active until the network card was initialized by the network card driver, these lights are now most often initialized by firmware on the network card, so the link light should illuminate shortly after all of the cables have been connected. If you're not sure how your card will react, load the driver before worrying about a link light that isn't illuminated.

Network hubs and switches have the same link indicator light that network interface cards have, and this light should be lit whenever the card on the other end is connected and ready to be communicated with. Take particular care to ensure that the link lights on both ends of the wire are lit, because some cabling problems can cause one or the other of these link lights to illuminate even if problems exist in the physical cabling.

Diagnosing TCP/IP Problems

The next few levels of diagnosis are centered on TCP/IP. There are three basic problems that can occur with TCP/IP:

- Local connectivity problems
- Remote connectivity problems
- Name resolution problems

The sections that follow discuss each type of problem in turn.

Note If the material in this section looks familiar, it's because there was a brief discussion of network troubleshooting in the section on localization in the previous chapter. This section goes into much greater detail.

Local Connectivity Problems

The first step in testing for TCP/IP connectivity involves testing a device on the local network. This is because many of the problems that can occur when more than one network is involved won't happen in a single network; the default gateway doesn't need to be used, and the potential problems with routers having invalid or incomplete routing tables aren't an issue.

Use the PING command to test connectivity in the local network. This command tests some of the most basic TCP/IP services by using internal checks in the protocol. If the machines that you can't get to communicate happen to be on different physical networks, your starting point is to see if each machine can ping its default gateway. This will verify that both machines can establish basic connectivity on their local networks.

If the machines aren't able to ping on the local network, either there is a cabling problem or the IP address and subnet mask are not set correctly. The key to setting up TCP/IP on a machine is the subnet mask. This piece of information helps the system determine whether an address that the system is communicating with is local or remote. If the subnet mask is set incorrectly, it can prevent all communication.

The process for determining whether an IP address is local or not is quite simple. An IP address is really two addresses concatenated together: the network address, or the identifier for the network to which the computer is connected, and the host address, or the unique identifier for the machine. The local IP address is logically ANDed with the subnet mask to produce an address that contains only the network portion of the original IP address. This is because the subnet mask is a binary 1 digit whenever the associated bit in the address is a part of the network address and is a binary 0 digit when the associated bit is a part of the host address. When a logical AND is performed, only those bits that are binary 1s in both the subnet mask and the IP address are 1s in the result. The result is only the network portion of the IP address.

Once the local network address has been determined, the same process is performed on the destination IP address. The resulting destination network address is compared with the local network address. If they are the same, control is passed to ARP to resolve the physical address of the destination on the local network. If they are different, ARP is requested to resolve the physical address of the default gateway, if it's not already in its cache. Figure 17.2 shows this process for both the local network and a remote network.

ARP first checks its cache to make sure that the IP address isn't there. If it doesn't find the address in the cache, ARP sends a broadcast message out to all computers on the local network, asking them if they are the destination IP address. The computer that is the IP address in question responds to the ARP request of the originating computer. ARP then adds the IP address to the hardware address mapping information in its cache, based on the information received from the other network card. It doesn't matter whether the IP address that ARP is resolving is for the ultimate destination or just for the default gateway.

```
                        Local ARP Example
                   Local IP Information    Known Remote IP Information
      IP Address    10.1.1.3               10.1.1.2
      Subnet Mask   255.255.255.0

              00001010.00000001.00000001.00000011 (10.1.1.3)
      AND     11111111.11111111.11111111.00000000 (255.255.255.0)
              00001010.00000001.00000001.00000000 (10.1.1.0) Local network

              00001010.00000001.00000001.00000010 (10.1.1.2)
      AND     11111111.11111111.11111111.00000000 (255.255.255.0)
              00001010.00000001.00000001.00000000 (10.1.1.0) Remote network

          Local Network = Remote Network -> Local Address
```

```
                        Remote ARP Example
                   Local IP Information    Known Remote IP Information
      IP Address    10.1.1.3               10.1.2.2
      Subnet Mask   255.255.255.0

              00001010.00000001.00000001.00000011 (10.1.1.3)
      AND     11111111.11111111.11111111.00000000 (255.255.255.0)
              00001010.00000001.00000001.00000000 (10.1.1.0) Local network

              00001010.00000001.00000010.00000010 (10.1.2.2)
      AND     11111111.11111111.11111111.00000000 (255.255.255.0)
              00001010.00000001.00000010.00000000 (10.1.2.0) Remote network

          Local Network ≠ Remote Network -> Remote Address
```

Figure 17.2   Determining whether an address is local or remote

Note ARP must broadcast a message asking for the other system being communicated with to respond with its hardware address. For this reason, it's impossible to completely eliminate all broadcasts on a TCP/IP network.

If ARP doesn't receive a response to its broadcast asking the machine owning the IP address to identify itself, it reports to the rest of the TCP/IP stack that the host was unreachable. Most of the time this ARP error gets communicated back to the user as a general communications error.

Problems with subnet masks can occur when ARP tries to resolve an address of a machine that's really on a remote network, when ARP believes that an IP address on the local network is on another network, or when ARP believes that the default gateway isn't on the local network.

When a subnet mask is set so that an address that is really remote seems to be local, ARP's attempts to resolve the address will, obviously, fail, and connectivity with the remote host won't be possible.

When a subnet mask is set so that a local address seems to be remote, the packet will be sent to the default gateway. The default gateway (router) will detect that the destination address is on the same interface that the packet came from and will reject the packet as being invalid.

When the subnet mask is set so that the default gateway seems to be remote, ARP will invalidate it. This will cause any communication that isn't directed to a local address to be rejected.

A discussion of ways to set subnet masks appropriately for your network is beyond our scope here. If you want more information, refer to the *Microsoft Network + Certification Training Kit* (Microsoft Press, 2001).

Remote Connectivity Problems

Once you've established that local connectivity works (or you've found out why it didn't), you can continue testing by pinging a host on a remote network. If the machines you're having problems with are on different networks, you can ping the other host directly. If not, you may want to check a remote host anyway, to verify that the setup is correct. The best candidates for pinging on a remote network are a server or router. These devices are generally going to be up more than any other device, and they are most often able to respond to pings.

If the remote host does not respond to a ping, the most likely cause is a router misconfiguration or a communications link failure. The best way to track down which router is misconfigured or which communications link is down is to use the traceroute utility. When you use traceroute with the same IP address, you'll be shown the path that a network packet takes before it is discarded or returned. If a communications link is down or there is a problem with a router, the last router you see will be the one that the packet arrived at before it was discarded.

Name Resolution Issues

Once you've established remote network connectivity, it's time to test name resolution. It's important to understand that the name resolution we're talking about here is the kind used to resolve TCP/IP names. It doesn't always match up with the name resolution mechanism that the operating system uses at a higher level of the protocol model to resolve addresses.

Windows 2000 specifically uses NetBIOS names to refer to remote computers when using SMB. While the NetBIOS name and the TCP/IP name of every machine should be the same, they don't have to be, and the method for resolving the two types of names is different. We'll look first at the name resolution process for TCP/IP and then review the process for resolving NetBIOS names and NetWare IPX/SPX names.

TCP/IP Name Resolution

TCP/IP has two basic methods for resolving host names: a special file called a *hosts file* on the local machine, containing the host name to IP address translation, and the Domain Name System (DNS). The hosts file is a simple text file that contains a line for each name and its associated IP address. These files were historically used for all name resolution on the Internet. However, the management effort required to synchronize this file across every machine rapidly became overwhelming. As a result, the DNS, a distributed system, was adopted.

The DNS uses a network of name servers, each of which has some of the information for translating TCP/IP names to IP addresses. All of the name servers in the system know the addresses of the root name servers. These root name servers know the addresses of every name server for the second-level domains, such as microsoft.com, yahoo.com, thorprojects.com, and so on.

Note DNS provides other types of information besides IP addresses. The most common of these is mail hosts for a domain. This kind of resolution is done through a different type of record in the DNS zones.

The process of resolving a name using DNS servers is simple. The client sends a message to the local DNS server, asking it for the IP address for a TCP/IP name. That DNS server determines whether it can answer the request itself by checking the domains or, in DNS server terms, zones that the server hosts. If it cannot find the answer there, it checks its cache of recently requested information. If the information requested isn't in the cache, the DNS server contacts one of the root servers to locate the server that has the information for the domain that the TCP/IP name is a part of. The DNS server then contacts this server on behalf of the client, retrieves the information, stores it in its cache, and reports the answer to the client. Figure 17.3 shows the DNS resolution process for an address that is not in the local DNS server's cache.

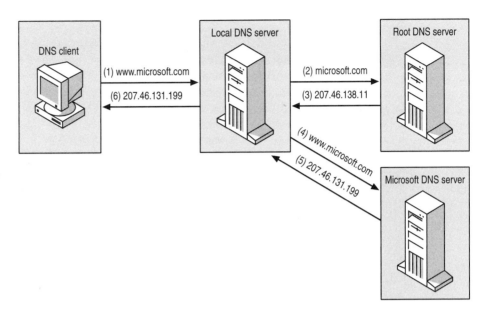

Figure 17.3 How a local DNS server resolves an address

If the machine is buried way down within the domain hierarchy, as the machine xyz.abc.myloc.mycount.microsoft.com might be, it's possible that the domain name server for microsoft.com may further delegate the answer to another DNS name server, which the local DNS name server would contact to get the answer.

To test name resolution, you can ping by name instead of by IP address. If the PING command is successful in resolving the name, you'll see it contact the remote device. If it is unsuccessful you'll see a response that says "bad IP address." One of the first things to check, if name resolution is failing, is that the domain name setting for the client machine is correct. If the domain name of the remote machine doesn't match the domain name of the client, a fully qualified domain name will be required, and the host name of the remote machine will not be able to be resolved. In other words, if you attempt to ping the host adatum, and adatum is in the blueyonderairlines.com domain, but the client computer is set up for the microsoft.com domain, adatum will not be found. However, if you attempt to ping adatum.blueyonderairlines.com, the name resolution will be able to translate the name to an IP address.

If the name resolution is still unsuccessful, you'll need to decide how the IP address should be resolved. If the name is in the local hosts file, it's possible that the file is in the wrong location or that the system needs to reread the hosts file.

More than likely, however, DNS is being used for name resolution. In this case you can use a special tool to interrogate the DNS servers to determine whether they are returning the correct information. Typing the command **nslookup** connects you to the default DNS server. You will see an NSLOOKUP prompt that consists of a single greater-than (>) sign.

At this prompt, you can type the TCP/IP name you want to resolve, and NSLOOKUP will query the server to which you're connected to try to resolve the information. NSLOOKUP is particularly useful if you have multiple DNS servers for internal use or different DNS servers for internal and external use. By issuing a **server** command to NSLOOKUP, you can switch between DNS servers. For example, if you wanted to switch to the DNS server at 10.1.1.254, you could type the command **server 10.1.1.254**. NSLOOKUP would then start issuing queries specifically against the DNS server at 10.1.1.254.

By testing the name resolution capabilities of each server individually, you can identify which server is reporting incorrect information or doesn't have the information for all of the hosts.

Note The new Dynamic Domain Name System (DDNS) allows machines to register their name with the DNS server when they start up. This system is useful in environments that use DHCP, in which the machines may not always have the same addresses. If you're using a dynamic method of translating host names to IP addresses in your DNS server, you'll want to make sure that this dynamic addition of addresses is working. Microsoft's DNS server included with Windows NT 4 and later supports getting names from a WINS server (explained momentarily) to supplement the static information in the DNS server. However, the feature must be specifically turned on.

NetBIOS Name Resolution

Above the TCP/IP connectivity layer are the application services that can have their own method of name identification. As I mentioned earlier, Windows 2000 uses a NetBIOS name to refer to other computers on the network. NetWare uses the Service Advertising Protocol (SAP) to broadcast the names of all of the servers on the network.

NetBIOS names are very similar to TCP/IP names in that they can be resolved through a local hosts file, called LMHOSTS, or via a server-based mechanism, but unlike TCP/IP names, NetBIOS names can also be resolved through the use of broadcasts across the network. The server for NetBIOS name resolution is called Windows Internet Name Service (WINS). When a NetBIOS system that is using server-based name resolution starts, it contacts the server and registers itself. The WINS server places the NetBIOS name, name type, and IP address in its database, along with information that has been entered manually and information received from other WINS servers. When a client needs to resolve a name, it contacts the WINS server and gives it the name that it wants to resolve as well as the name type. The WINS server responds with the IP address, if it knows it.

Tip Don't get hung up on the name type that WINS holds. WINS, like DNS, provides more than just simple name resolution services, but the other features of WINS are not required for basic name resolution.

If the WINS server doesn't know the IP address for a given name, the client generally sends a broadcast announcing that it is looking for a computer with the name attached. If the machine with that name sees the broadcast, it responds, thus giving its IP address to the client requesting it.

Although the process just described is the one most often used by NetBIOS clients when a name server is present, it is also possible for the client to perform the lookups in a different order. This order is controlled by a setting called the NetBIOS node type.

NetWare Name Resolution

NetWare's architecture is slightly different from that of Windows 2000 because NetWare requires names only for machines that are providing services, and most NetWare clients don't provide services. Although NetWare servers have names, the services they provide may have the same name or an alternative name. The client accesses the service, not the server, so the names that NetWare maintains are service names. Recall that NetWare communicates service names through the use of a Service Advertising Protocol (SAP), which periodically broadcasts the services that a server knows about. These broadcasts allow other servers to add the services to their SAP broadcasts as well.

This method of name resolution works, but it generates a fairly large amount of traffic for a relatively small number of name requests. Still, it's the method that NetWare uses over the IPX/SPX protocol, and it has the advantage of not requiring any special server setups.

Diagnosing Problems with DHCP

The Dynamic Host Configuration Protocol (DHCP) grew out of a need to manage the growing amount of configuration information that each machine on a TCP/IP network needs to be able to communicate. A typical Windows-based PC needs the following information to function in a large network:

- IP address
- Subnet mask
- Default gateway
- WINS server(s)
- NetBIOS node type
- DNS server(s)

And in a mixed environment that contains UNIX-based systems, an additional set of parameters can be configured. Because of this, a method was developed by which a computer without an IP address could get its configuration information from a server.

The method of giving a client its IP address information was adapted from an earlier technology, BOOTP (Boot Protocol), which was used to allow UNIX-based X terminals to boot from the network. This protocol allowed the terminal to download not only the configuration information but a complete operating system image as well.

DHCP uses a series of messages to assign an IP address, as depicted in Figure 17.4. The figure shows the order in which the messages are sent, from the start of the process to the finish. The numbers followed by the letter "B" are broadcast messages that go to every computer on the network.

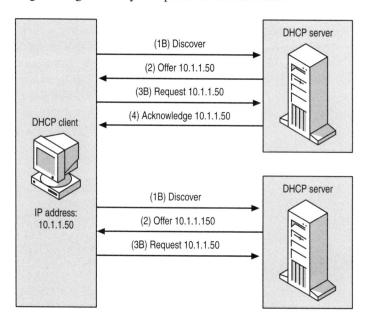

Figure 17.4   Process by which an IP address is assigned under DHCP

The process of receiving a DHCP-assigned address involves four basic messages:

- **Discover.**   This broadcast message is sent by the DHCP client seeking an IP address. The message is used to discover DHCP servers.

- **Offer.**   This directed message from the DHCP server offers an IP address to the DHCP client.

- **Request.**   This broadcast message is sent from the DHCP client to a DHCP server requesting an offered address. Because this is a broadcast message, every DHCP server that responded to the original discover message sees the address being requested. If it's not the address the server offered, the server cancels the offer.

- **Acknowledge.**   This directed message is sent from the DHCP server to the DHCP client.

Figure 17.4 shows two DHCP servers on the same network responding to the same DHCP request. In practice, this rarely happens because maintaining two servers is more difficult than maintaining just one. The redundancy is also unnecessary, because once a DHCP server has leased an address to a client, the client will start trying to renew the address with the DHCP server when 50 percent of the lease period has expired. This means that a DHCP server can be offline for 50 percent of the lease period without preventing a DHCP client from communicating. In practice, most DHCP leases are set to three days. This means that a DHCP server could be down for 36 hours before it would start affecting the network. That's more than enough time to put another DHCP server on the network if necessary.

A more common situation is for the main DHCP server to be located on the local network with the DHCP client, and to back it up with a remote DHCP server that has a small number of reserve addresses that it can lease to new clients if the primary DHCP server happens to be down. This scheme works because DHCP clients generally accept the first offer they receive, rather than waiting for one they "like."

When a backup server is located on another network, the routers connecting the two networks must be configured to pass BOOTP packets, so that the remote DHCP server can see the client attempting the discovery. The remote DHCP server then sends the offer packet back through the router. The delay caused by the router transitions generally means that the DHCP client will request the address offered by the local server first.

A few basic problems can occur when assigning IP addresses based on DHCP information:

- Physical connectivity issues may exist in the network.

- Conflicting IP information might have been manually entered into the workstation.

- No DHCP server found on the local network or connected networks may be leasing addresses.

- A DHCP client might not attempt a full discovery after being moved from one network to another.

Some of these are the same kinds of problems you would have if you were configuring the DHCP client manually. For instance, the physical connectivity issues are the same whether you're using hard-coded IP addresses or DHCP-assigned addresses. Likewise, a configuration error entered in hard-coded information will occur even if DHCP is not being used.

However, not finding a DHCP server on the local network or via a connected network is a problem specific to DHCP-based configuration. Obviously, a server needs to be present on the local network or on a remote network that is reachable. If you're trying to get DHCP addresses from a remote network, you'll need to make sure either that there is a DHCP proxy on the local network or that the routers are configured to pass BOOTP packets between the local network and the remote network containing the DHCP server. If neither of these is true, the DHCP discover packets won't be transmitted to the remote network, and therefore the DHCP server won't be able to respond.

Another potential problem for DHCP servers that are not being seen involves the scopes that contain the addresses on the DHCP server. If all of the scopes are in an inactive state, the server cannot generate any more leases. The obvious solution is to activate a scope. If, however, the DHCP server has leased all of the addresses it has, it will be unable to offer an address to the client. If this is the case, you'll have to review your DHCP structure to determine a way to ensure that the scope doesn't run out of addresses.

DHCP-related problems with clients include situations in which the client may not attempt to lease an address from any DHCP server other than the one it received an address from the last time. In other words, it doesn't attempt a DHCP full discovery. This used to be a problem with Windows 3.11 and Windows 95. Once they got an address, they kept it until the lease expired. However, later versions of Windows attempt to lease an address from any available DHCP server when it boots up. This change has basically eliminated the problem of Windows machines needing to have their DHCP-assigned addresses manually released and renewed.

Finally, problems can occur when DHCP clients have information manually entered into their configuration. In Windows, DHCP information is overridden by manually entered TCP/IP information in the client. This can have the effect of breaking name resolution because the client has manually set the domain name or DNS servers. If a specific DHCP client is having problems that the other DHCP clients don't have, release and renew the configuration and then verify that all of the manual configuration information has been removed from the TCP/IP Properties dialog box.

Practice: Review TCP/IP Settings in Windows 2000

In this practice, you'll review the TCP/IP settings on your Windows 2000 server. (The same procedure also applies to Windows 2000 Professional workstations.)

▶ **To review TCP/IP settings**

1. Select Start, Settings, Network And Dial-Up Connections.
2. Right-click the Local Area Connection icon, and select Properties.
3. In the Local Area Connection Properties dialog box (Figure 17.5), double-click the Internet Protocol (TCP/IP) entry.

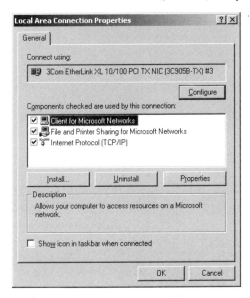

Figure 17.5 Local Area Connection Properties dialog box

4. The Internet Protocol (TCP/IP) Properties dialog box shows the IP address information and DNS server information, or it will be set to obtain the IP address automatically (from a DHCP server). Figure 17.6 shows this dialog box, set for automatically assigned addresses. If the information you need is not in this dialog box, click the Advanced button to display the Advanced TCP/IP Settings dialog box (Figure 17.7).

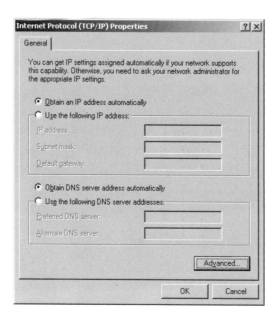

Figure 17.6   Internet Protocol (TCP/IP) Properties dialog box

5. Display the DNS, WINS, and Options tabs in sequence to reveal detailed information about DNS, WINS, and technical TCP/IP settings. When you're done, click OK.

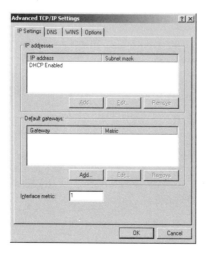

Figure 17.7   Advanced TCP/IP Settings dialog box

Of course, if the computer you're investigating is set up to use DHCP, like the one shown in the figures, these pages will contain very little information. All of the information about the IP address and related settings must be fetched using the IPCONFIG command. Using the command without parameters will cause the information displayed in the Internet Protocol (TCP/IP) Properties dialog box to be displayed in text format in the command window. By using the /ALL command-line switch, you'll receive most of the information that can be found in the Advanced TCP/IP Settings dialog box. Figure 17.8 shows an example of a response to an IPCONFIG/ALL command.

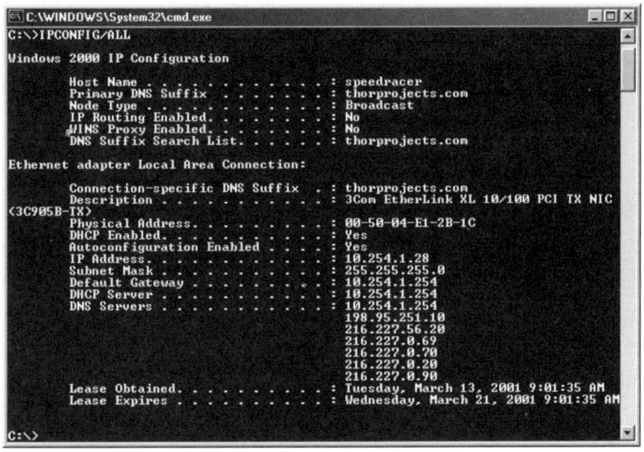

Figure 17.8   TCP/IP setting information, retrieved with the IPCONFIG/ALL command

Lesson Summary

In this lesson, you learned how network connectivity is established, how to troubleshoot connectivity problems, and how DHCP works. This lesson is a good foundation for TCP/IP network troubleshooting.

Lesson 3: Other Common Problems

In this last lesson of the last chapter, you'll learn about two other common issues involving troubleshooting. First, you'll learn what options you have for working with the core dumps generated by the operating system after a critical error, and then you'll learn what causes hard disk vibration and how to minimize it.

After this lesson, you will be able to

- Identify uses for a core dump file
- Identify ways to limit hard disk vibration

Estimated lesson time: 10 minutes

Working with Core Dump Files

Most operating systems are capable of producing a reasonable amount of trouble-shooting information when problems occur. This information is usually written to the system log, as described in Chapter 7, Lesson 1. However, there are some times when an operating system problem is so severe that it can't write a nice, succinct message to the log. In those cases, it writes a complete copy of memory, known as a *dump file*, to the file system. Most operating systems generate some kind of dump file, or at least have the ability to generate such a file.

Two different kinds of dump files can be generated: those centered on the user's memory space and those that affect the system as a whole. Problems with the memory space of a user aren't generally that critical. In Windows 2000, the file created when this type of problem occurs is called USER.DMP. In Linux, these files simply have the name "core." System faults are a little more serious. In Windows 2000, the dump files resulting from system faults are named MEMORY.DMP, and in Linux the name of the dump file can be determined when the operating system is set up to write the dump file. Novell NetWare doesn't support the creation of a dump file.

No matter what type of dump you receive or what operating system you're running, these files can be valuable to technical support personnel in identifying the source of the problem. They may be useful to you as well, as utilities are available to help you identify what was happening when the problem occurred. These utilities expand the structures contained in the file and turn them into a human-readable format that you can use to dissect every process that was running on the system at the time.

For the most part, you won't need to explore dump files. Unless a problem is recurring and you have some insane desire to review the dump file yourself, you'll probably just forward it to technical support.

Minimizing Hard Disk Vibration

Describing hard disk vibration as a common problem might be a slight overstatement, since vibrational issues that aren't compensated for in the drive itself are somewhat rare. However, it is helpful to understand the impact of vibration on the reliability of hard disks when planning your installation and when installing hard disks.

The primary cause of vibration within a hard disk itself is a slight offset in the center of mass of the disk medium itself. This slight variation means that the spindle on which the hard disk is mounted is not at the exact center of the disk, and as a result it is tugged slightly in the direction of the center of the mass of the hard disk. While the amount of force exerted in that direction will be slight, hard disks spinning at 10,000 rpm can generate a powerful vibration.

To understand how this vibration occurs, try a very simple experiment (or think back to when you did this as a child). Take a bucket of water in one or both hands and start spinning around. As you spin faster and faster, the bucket of water will start lifting up due to centrifugal forces. The water will be held in the bucket by the same centrifugal forces. Keep spinning for a moment and then notice what is happening to you as you spin. The bucket of water is tugging on you, pulling you out of the center of the circle.

The amount by which the bucket of water displaces you is based on your weight, the weight of the bucket, your strength in fighting the forces, and the speed at which you're spinning the bucket. In this experiment, you're a very off-balance cylinder, but you're also spinning at a much lower speed. The same forces that cause you to be moved out of the center of the circle traced by the bucket are the same forces that are pulling on the hard disk spindle.

Because the hard disk spindle is attached to the hard disk shell, the hard disk itself starts to move. The hard disk is in turn attached to a hard disk case or to the server chassis. While the additional weight of the hard disk shell and the case or chassis will tend to minimize the vibration caused by the disk, the forces that are pulling on the spindle will still be there.

The forces of a single hard disk are generally not sufficient to cause problems with vibration. However, if multiple hard disks start exhibiting the same kind of vibration, or if they begin to vibrate in a way that naturally resonates within the case, problems can occur because of the buildup of vibrational forces.

Resonance happens when the natural characteristics of an object tend to line up the amplitude of a previous force with the force that is being produced. This amplification has the effect of generating progressively larger force, until the resonance is disrupted or until the material creating the resonance is destroyed.

Since the vibration caused by a hard disk can be destructive to its own existence, most hard disks are designed so as to minimize the potential for resonance. However, there are still factors to consider when mounting hard disks to prevent harmful resonance in the disks' internal vibration.

One of the best ways to prevent resonance is to isolate the vibration. You can do this by using rubber washers between the hard disk and the material to which it is being mounted. This helps to isolate the vibrations of the disk from the mounting chassis, significantly reducing the apparent effects of the vibration and making it more difficult for a resonance to build.

Another, less effective way to address this issue is to ensure that the mounting material is rigid enough to directly translate any vibration. Resonance happens more often in materials that flex, because when a material flexes it stores energy for later release. When that energy is released in the same phase as the source vibrational energy, it causes resonance.

If you're using a rigid mounting material, you'll want to ensure that the disk is secured firmly to the case. This helps eliminate any resonances that can occur when the disk can move within its mounting system.

Lesson Summary

In this lesson, you learned about two somewhat common occurrences. Core dumps provide information that can help your operating system vendor diagnose the cause of a problem. Hard disk vibration can cause disks to fail rapidly, but you can avoid this problem by using the techniques given in this lesson.

Review

The following questions reinforce key information presented in this chapter. If you're unable to answer a question, review the appropriate lesson and then try again. The answers for these questions are located in the appendix, "Questions and Answers."

1. What is the first step in the bootup process?

2. Where is the POST stored?

3. What is the first thing you should check when SCSI drives are missing from the bootup process?

4. Why are boot sector viruses not a significant issue in today's environment?

5. What is the most prevalent type of virus today (based on the number of different viruses)?

6. What is the first step in resolving a network connectivity problem?

7. Once you've verified the physical layer of connectivity, what steps should you use to diagnose a TCP/IP problem?

8. Why is DHCP used?

9. What is a core dump?

10. Why do hard disks vibrate?

Appendix

A P P E N D I X

Questions and Answers

Page 3

Chapter 1
Laying the Groundwork

Review Questions

Page 33

1. You've just received a new product that you ordered. Your boss walks by with someone from another division who's considering the same product. He wants to know whether the product has a particular feature. How would you go about finding out for sure?

   The best place to start is probably to log on to the vendor's Web site and search for the name of the feature. If that's not effective, you might try skimming the documentation for a mention of that feature or a similar feature. If you don't find it there, you could call technical support.

2. You're evaluating three different products with similar features and similar costs. You're concerned about making the right decision. How should you determine which is the best product?

   The information you need at this point is not available in the spec sheets or from the sales reps. You need to see what the experience of other users has been. The best way to do this is to search the Internet newsgroups for feedback.

3. You've been on vacation for a week, and you get in early your first day back to read your e-mail and get settled. As you're walking in, however, a user stops you and says that she can't log on. After a quick check at her computer, you determine that you can't log on either. What should you do to figure out what is going on?

   The first step is to try to log on at your workstation. That will determine whether it's a problem with the user's computer or with the entire network. Assuming that it's not a network-wide problem, check the network activity log to determine what changes were made while you were gone.

4. You've done the necessary analysis for a new server. You've taken into consideration the needs of the organization and have quantified the issues around the need. However, management doesn't seem pleased with the solution. What might have you forgotten?

   Perception is reality. Even though you may be able to quantify the cost of downtime and the expenses that you've included in your solution to address risks, management may have a different perception of what is risky and what isn't.

5. Your company is planning a phase of rapid growth. You're trying to determine the best course of action for purchasing servers. What options should you consider?

   There are a few approaches that you may need to pursue in parallel. The first is trying to purchase a server that will accommodate the projected load. Another approach is to set up a small clustered environment and then add servers to the cluster as the load increases. Finally, you could consider adding a single server now to handle all services and then slowly shift services to new servers as the load increases.

6. You're getting ready to add a new server. What method might you use to choose the operating system to run on that new server?

   You can choose it based on what you know or based on what is popular. However, the best technique would involve factoring in the benefits and weaknesses of each operating system.

7. Which will perform better, hierarchical PCI buses or peer PCI buses?

   Hierarchical PCI buses use a root PCI bus for all transfers, while peer PCI buses allow for concurrent communications on different buses. Because of this, peer PCI will have a performance advantage over hierarchical PCI bus designs.

8. When is hot-swappable PCI important?

   When availability is paramount. A server with hot-swap PCI slots is generally more expensive, but it does allow you to remove and replace some PCI cards without powering down the server. This can be a great advantage in 24-hour operations.

Page 35

Chapter 2
Planning a Server's Environment

Lesson 2: Addressing Power Needs
Practice: Size a UPS System for a Small Environment

Page 54

1. What is the total number of volt-amps that are necessary?

   A 1680 VA UPS is necessary to carry the load.

2. If you require 30 minutes of run time, which UPS is necessary?

To run for at least 30 minutes, the 3 KVA UPS is necessary.

3. If you require 60 minutes of run time, which UPS is necessary?

To run for 60 minutes, the 6 KVA UPS is necessary.

Practice: Size a UPS System for a Larger Environment

Page 55

1. What is the total number of volt-amps that are necessary?

A 3960 VA UPS is necessary to carry the load.

2. If you require 30 minutes of run time, which UPS is necessary?

To run for at least 30 minutes, a 6 KVA UPS is necessary.

3. If you require 60 minutes of run time, which UPS is necessary?

To run for 60 minutes, two 6 KVA UPSs would be necessary.

Review Questions

Page 76

1. Why is climate control important? What impact does it have on performance or availability?

Climate control ensures that components of the server are not damaged or prematurely aged by excessive heat. It also ensures that the contacts don't corrode due to excessive humidity, leading to long-term reliability problems. The impact of climate control is solely on availability or reliability. Controlling the climate into which the server is placed has no impact on performance.

2. Your organization's business offices are located on the Florida Keys, where hurricanes are a real concern. The organization wants to make sure that if a natural disaster strikes it will be able to get back up and running right away. What is the best disaster recovery solution?

A hot backup site is the most effective solution because it offers the quickest recovery time in a natural disaster situation. Having exact duplicates of the systems means that all you need to do is load the systems from the latest backup.

3. Your organization is an application service provider (ASP), hosting applications for companies across the United States. One of the biggest concerns that customers express to the sales people is the potential for your systems to be down, preventing them from getting their work done. What power precautions should you take to minimize the risk that a power failure could keep your systems from operating?

The obvious power protection involves having surge suppressors and UPSs. You would probably also need a generator because you may need to keep the systems up for several hours while the local utility resolves a problem.

4. Your organization has a computer room with a raised floor. Some people in the organization say you shouldn't be worried about flooding because the computer room is 12 inches above the floors in the rest of the building. Why isn't this true?

Although it's true that the computer room floor is 12 inches above the rest of the building flooring, there are power cables running on the subfloor of the computer room, which is the same height as the rest of the building floors. Those power cables can short out and cause problems or fires if they come into contact with water.

5. You're installing a new server and you don't have any new circuits available to you, so you have to use an existing circuit. What should you do before plugging in the new server?

Evaluate the load on the circuit. Remember that the circuit is connected with a circuit breaker or fuse that will shut down power to everything on that circuit if too much power is drawn at one time. If you're not sure how much power is on a circuit, have an electrician give you an idea; this can be done without disrupting the power to the existing devices.

6. Your organization has just hired a new director of information technology, and as a part of his initiation to the organization he wants to know what everyone does and has asked to see any materials that you have to show the processes you go through. You're responsible for monitoring backups. When you show him the five failed backup reports over the last six months, he seems concerned. What might be concerning the new director of information technology?

The new director may be concerned that you're monitoring backups only for failures and not for successes and thus wouldn't notice if the process never finished and therefore didn't generate an error message. Monitoring for success, not just failure, is particularly important when the system that might be failing is not tested frequently.

7. You're installing a new server in a new rack, complete with a very heavy rack-mount UPS. Your boss likes the fact that the UPS has LEDs on it indicating load and battery availability and wants the UPS mounted at the top of the rack where everyone will be able to see these LEDs. Why is this a bad idea?

Rack installation guidelines require that the heaviest items be placed at the bottom to help stabilize the rack. By placing the UPS on the top of the rack, you risk having the rack tip over and harm someone. If there's some doubt about the need to mount the UPS at the bottom of the rack, refer to the documentation provided by the rack manufacturer.

8. Your organization is in the pharmaceutical industry and must maintain records of clinical studies for several years. Although most clinical study information is archived on optical media, you're concerned about the ability to restore the study data from the regular tape backup and archive mechanisms. What consideration should you give to tape backup systems?

You should consider the life of the medium that the drive uses. Although most server-class tape backup systems have long life spans, some don't. Because you might need to recover information from a tape, you should give special consideration to tape life.

Page 79

Chapter 3
Planning the System

Review Questions

Page 108

1. You're working for a medium-sized organization that needs a new terminal server. What kind of server should you select?

   When trying to select hardware for a terminal server, the priority should be squarely on processor and memory. A multiprocessor AMD Athlon system with a gigabyte or so of RAM would be a good start. Although SCSI would be preferred, you could probably get by with an IDE drive in a pinch. By using a multiprocessor AMD Athlon system and ample memory, you can get high performance without paying the premium for the fastest machine.

2. You're putting together a file and print server for an organization with a few hundred users. You're trying to determine how much cache to order for the processor. What guidelines should you use?

   The guidelines for selecting a cache size are based on the amount of memory that will be used and the relative dependence on the processor. Since memory isn't specified, the rule of thumb that file and print servers don't traditionally have large amounts of memory, and the knowledge that file and print servers are rarely processor limited, should lead you to choose a smaller processor cache size.

3. A soft memory error has been recorded on a server. What should be done?

   A soft memory error indicates that an ECC memory module detected and corrected a failed bit of memory. The memory module should be replaced as soon as is practical. Although ECC memory can correct single-bit errors, it cannot correct multiple-bit errors.

4. You're putting together a server to be a firewall. What kind of hard disk is appropriate?

   Since firewalls don't access their disks frequently or in response to user requests, an IDE hard disk makes sense for this server. It's cheap and fast, and the multiuser performance implications don't apply.

5. Your organization has grown and has just built a huge new data center. It wants to standardize on a set of high-performance drives in one cabinet. What kind of bus is appropriate?

   Fibre Channel is appropriate for this kind of connectivity because the organization is obviously large (because of the new data center) and therefore has the potential need for very powerful servers. Also, because

the drives are going to be kept in one area, the additional cable length that fiber optic cable provides may be necessary.

6. Your organization recently upgraded the backbone to support additional growth and has given you the task of selecting a new file and print server. You've settled on CPUs, memory, and hard disks. What kind of network connectivity should be provided?

Given the size and growth of the organization in the question, a Gigabit Ethernet connection is probably warranted. Additionally, because the server will be the primary file and print server, a redundant, or fault-tolerant, NIC might be appropriate.

Page 111

Chapter 4
Gathering and Configuring Firmware and Drivers

Review Questions

Page 130

1. What is the greatest risk when installing new firmware?

The greatest danger is that the power will go off during the programming phase of the firmware installation. This can render a card unusable.

2. What precautions should you take when installing new firmware?

You should minimize the system configuration and test the power. You should also save the previous version of the software and take any additional precautions recommended in the README file.

3. When should firmware updates be performed?

When the system is initially installed. After that, they should be performed only when you need to address problems or performance issues. Firmware updates are inherently risky and should be performed only when there's a specific reason.

4. What kind of a reboot should be performed after a firmware installation?

Unless you're specifically directed otherwise in the firmware utility documentation or installation procedures, all reboots during a firmware reload should be cold reboots. That is, the power should be removed for a period of not less than five seconds and then reapplied.

5. What BIOS settings should never be changed?

Those options pertaining to clock cycles, wait states, or memory speeds. These settings are set by the manufacturer and should not be changed unless technical support specifically directs you to do so.

6. Several options deal with video settings. How should the video settings be set up for a server?

In general, a server has little need for advanced video features and enhanced video performance. The server is better off conserving resources for operations other than video display. Video BIOS can be cached, but

the memory aperture size should be set to its smallest size, and an IRQ should not be assigned for the video card.

7. You are installing Novell NetWare as your server operating system. How should the PnP/PCI settings be set?

    As of this writing, Novell NetWare is not Plug and Play compatible, so the BIOS should be set to indicate that a PnP operating system is not present. Configuration should be done manually via the BIOS and through PnP utilities provided by the manufacturers of the cards installed in the system.

8. You've added a new hard disk to a RAID controller and want it to be used as a hot spare. What must you do to accomplish this?

    You must flag the drive as a hot spare drive in the RAID controller's BIOS or in the RAID controller's configuration utility.

Page 131

Chapter 5
Installing and Configuring the Network Operating System

Review Questions

Page 162

1. What are some of the benefits of installing an operating system across the network?

    The primary benefit is that there is no chance of a media error. Additionally, the system will always try to locate the files at the original installation location when additional features are installed. Finally, network installations can be scaled to dozens of machines without creating or locating a large number of installation CD-ROMs.

2. Why do in-place upgrades take so long?

    In-place upgrades take a long time because of the need to back up the system and make changes slowly and deliberately. Sometimes they take longer because the server hardware is older and less compatible with the new operating system. When doing an in-place upgrade, you need to preserve the data that already exists on the system. In a new installation, there isn't any data to worry about backing up.

3. You're a busy professional who needs to maximize the effectiveness of your time. You're planning on loading a new server over the course of two days. What steps should be completed the first day?

    At the very least, you should establish the RAID arrays in the RAID controller BIOS. Because building the RAID array can be the most time-consuming process, you should start it and allow it to run. It might make sense to try to get to the drive formatting step before quitting for the day, because the RAID array build and the drive formatting could run simultaneously and be complete by the time you return in the morning.

4. What is the first step in installing most operating systems?

The first step for most operating system installations is a basic hardware scan to make sure that the installation program will be able to complete and that the operating system will work on the hardware. This step generally finishes quite quickly.

5. What partitions are required for a Windows 2000 installation?

A boot and system partition, although a single partition can be both the boot and system partition.

6. Why is the correct setting of the date, time, and time zone so important?

In today's environment of unified security systems such as Novell's NetWare Directory Services (NDS) and Microsoft's Active Directory, a great deal of synchronization of data occurs. To reduce the number of problems with data synchronization, it's important to keep the dates, times, and time zones correct and synchronized with one another.

7. What unique partition is used to boot a Novell server?

A DOS partition is used to boot a Novell server. The server starts from a DOS partition of no less than 50 MB and continues booting by using the NetWare SYS volume.

8. What NetWare volume is required for a NetWare server?

SYS, short for system. This volume contains the system and public utilities, in addition to various other components. It is required for any NetWare 5 installation.

9. Will a .DSK module work with NetWare 5?

No, NetWare 5 requires the NetWare Peripheral Architecture that uses Host Adapter Modules (HAMs) and Custom Device Modules (CDMs). .DSK modules were used in prior versions of NetWare.

10. What kinds of partitions are required for a Linux installation?

Linux requires a boot partition to boot from, a swap partition to use for virtual memory space, and a root partition for the system. You can omit the boot partition, in which case the system will boot from the root partition, but this configuration is not recommended. Additional partitions can be created but are not required.

11. What is a service pack?

A service pack is a collection of previously released patches that are assembled into a single package for installation on computers. Service packs are useful because they are extensively tested for potential interaction in various environments, whereas individual patches get less attention.

12. When should a patch be applied?

When there's a clear indication that the problem that the patch solves may occur or has occurred in the environment. In general, patches that

fix problems that are unlikely to occur in the environment or that will not cause harm if they do occur should not be installed unless thoroughly tested.

13. A user name and password are used to determine what?

Identity. The identity of the user is assumed once a user name and password combination is received. Security or authorization is based on the access control lists to which the user belongs.

14. What is CRUD?

CRUD is an acronym for create, read, update, and delete. These are the basic accesses supported by all server operating systems except for Linux and other varieties of UNIX.

Page 165

Chapter 6
Installing Hardware and Peripheral Drivers

Review Questions

Page 181

1. Which message is generally used to initiate automated shutdown of a server?

The "low battery" message is generally the one used to start the unattended shutdown. This is because the "on battery" message may occur frequently.

2. How can a UPS be connected to a server for notification of events?

Either by serial cable or via a TCP/IP-based network. Almost all UPSs support serial communications natively. The TCP/IP-based network option generally requires an add-on card or external device.

3. What might cause the input amperage to be higher than the output amperage in a UPS?

A slight difference may be caused by the UPS electronics themselves, but most frequently this is due to the UPS charging its batteries.

4. What does an "emergency power-off" message in the event log mean?

A user initiated an emergency power-off, via either direct keypad entry or a remote power-off switch. This message should not occur during normal operation. The emergency power-off option should be used only when there's potential for damage to the servers or injury to people.

5. Why is battery temperature important?

Battery life is directly affected by the temperature of the battery. Batteries are heated when being charged as well as when being discharged. The charging of the batteries is regulated so that they don't overheat.

6. Drive cabinets generally have three connections to them. What are they?

Power, drive bus, and monitoring. The need for power is obvious. The drive bus allows the server to communicate with the disk drives contained in the

enclosure. The monitoring connection allows the server to keep track of the condition of the cabinet itself, including the power supplies and fans.

7. In Linux, how can you determine the version of a driver?

If you have the C source file, you can review the first few lines of the driver. Otherwise, the console log is the best place to look for the driver's version. Forcing the driver to reload, if it's a dynamically linked module, can generate console messages that might contain version information. These messages will appear at the bottom of the console window.

Page 183

Chapter 7
Performing Routine Tasks

Review Questions

Page 195

1. What is the name and location of the Novell NetWare log file that records critical errors?

SYS:SYSTEM\ABEND.LOG. This file contains the dump information created each time the server reboots due to an abnormal end.

2. What is the file that Linux records when an abnormal process termination occurs?

Abnormal process terminations in Linux generate core dumps.

3. How does the procedure for resolving progressive errors differ from that for resolving critical errors?

Critical errors require immediate resolution. The procedure for resolving critical errors is aggressive and focused. The procedure for resolving a progressive error involves a slow, calculated effort designed to identify the root cause and eliminate it.

4. What are the two different signs of a progressive error?

Increasing severity and increasing frequency. Increasing severity of errors means that the errors themselves are getting more severe. Increasing frequency means that the same error is occurring more often.

5. Why is it important to review the log files of a server?

To identify progressive errors and to manage the size of the log files.

6. What is the shutdown procedure for a Novell NetWare server?

You shut down a NetWare server by issuing the DOWN and EXIT commands in sequence.

7. How can Linux be shut down?

Linux can be shut down in a variety of ways, including the reboot, shutdown, and init commands.

8. What two settings should be established for unattended shutdowns to be completely effective?

The UPS should be set to restart a few minutes after utility line power is restored. The server should be set to boot when the UPS resumes supplying power to it.

Page 197

Chapter 8
Monitoring a Server's Performance

Review Questions

Page 229

1. What is performance monitoring?

Performance monitoring is the act of collecting performance-related statistics so that decisions regarding performance and capacity planning can be made.

2. What are the four basic categories of counters?

Memory, processor, disk, network.

3. What is SNMP?

SNMP, short for Simple Network Management Protocol, is a protocol that can be used, among other things, to monitor the performance of computers running Linux, Windows 2000, NetWare, and network devices such as switches and routers.

4. Why is the amount of memory being used for a disk cache important?

Disk caching reduces the number of times that the server must access the disk. In general, the more physical memory being used for disk caching, the better the overall performance will be. (However, beyond a certain point additional memory will not be used for cache and will not be helpful.)

5. What size disks are appropriate for database servers?

Smaller disks are generally appropriate for database servers because the smaller capacity will require more disks to reach the necessary total capacity. Each additional disk in an array improves the maximum throughput. Database servers generally require more disk access for the same amount of disk space, so higher throughput is desirable.

6. Why shouldn't you use the monitoring tools on the server to determine whether the network is the bottleneck?

Network performance monitoring shows only the traffic seen by the server. When switches and routers are used in the network environment, it's impossible for the server to show the complete traffic pattern on the network. Appropriate tools for network monitoring are an SNMP management console capable of reading the routers and switches on the network and/or a packet sniffer.

7. What are non-unicast packets?

   Unicast packets are packets directed to a single destination. Non-unicast packets are packets destined for more than one machine. Typically these are packets that were broadcast from a machine to all other machines on the same network. Limiting non-unicast packets is a good idea, particularly when switches are present in the network.

8. What is the most common cause of inbound network errors?

   Collisions. Ethernet uses Carrier Sense Multiple Access/Collision Detection (CSMA/CD). This method of access will generate a small number of collisions that are read by the network adapter as inbound errors.

9. What mechanisms can you use to control the size of a performance log?

   To control the size of performance logs, select only the counters that are necessary for analysis, and change the frequency at which the performance data is captured to a longer interval.

10. What is a baseline?

    A baseline is a meaningful reference point for performance data. It serves as a basis for comparison with later data. Baselines are always run on the same server and should be run under the same initial production load that subsequent performance data will reflect.

11. Why should you review performance data in a specific order when identifying bottlenecks?

    Some areas of performance can mask other areas. By analyzing and assessing the performance data in an orderly way, you can ensure that you're looking at the root cause of an issue.

Page 231

Chapter 9
Documenting the Installation

Review Questions

Page 245

1. Why do we document a server's installation?

   To make it easier for us and others to do capacity planning, maintain the server, and provide support.

2. Why can't we document every detail?

   There are too many options to document every one. The goal of this type of documentation is to describe the framework for the installation, along with details that are difficult to determine or get. It is not the intention of documentation to take the place of interactive investigation of the operating system.

3. Why do we make copies of invoices and purchase orders relating to the server?

To ensure that we can provide proof of purchase if the vendor requires it for technical support, even after the accounting department has archived the information pertaining to the purchase.

Page 249

Chapter 10
Upgrading Processors and Memory

Review Questions

Page 267

1. What is a thread?

A thread is the smallest unit of execution within an operating system. Threads, not applications, are scheduled to run within the operating system.

2. What is processor affinity?

Processor affinity is an operating system setting that controls how the operating system schedules threads to be run. A higher processor affinity means a greater chance that a thread will be scheduled to run on the same processor as the last time.

3. What is thread binding?

Thread binding is a processor affinity setting that requires the operating system to run a task on one of the processors. This setting can be used for applications that do not run well on multiple-processor systems and thus need to run on only one processor. The use of thread binding is generally not recommended because it doesn't allow the operating system to optimize itself.

4. What are the requirements for adding an additional processor to the system?

You need operating system support, the same or similar processor stepping levels, and a processor slot that can have a processor inserted in it without interfering with any add-on cards. Not all operating systems support multiprocessor systems, and those that do support them sometimes require different installations or licenses. Maintaining similar processor stepping levels ensures that the timings within the system won't vary so much as to be a problem. A power supply capable of driving the additional processor is also required.

5. What are the three concerns you need to address when upgrading an existing processor to a faster one?

Memory speed, core voltages, and clock rates. As the processor speed increases, so must the speed of the memory. As processors get faster, they generally require less voltage to power their core, and higher voltages will cause damage. Clock rates are controlled by the motherboard, so if a faster processor is installed on a motherboard that won't support the higher speed, there won't be any speed improvements.

6. After you've physically installed the memory and verified it in the BIOS, what is left to do?

Verify that the memory is detected by the operating system, or register the memory with the operating system. You may also need to resize the virtual memory files and partitions.

Page 269

Chapter 11
Adding Hard Disks

Review Questions

Page 291

1. What are the two types of cables used for ATA/IDE devices?

ATA/IDE devices use either a 40-conductor cable with a 40-pin connector or an 80-conductor cable with a 40-pin connector. The hybrid 80/40 cable is required for IDE devices operating at Ultra/66 or higher speeds.

2. Why do ribbon cables present connector problems?

Ribbon cables themselves don't cause problems. However, the pin block connector type that is frequently used with ribbon cables doesn't have an inherent method for orienting the connector the right way.

3. What three methods are used to identify how pin block connectors should be plugged in?

Pin 1 identification, blocked pins, and keyed connectors. Pin 1 identification is present on almost every cable. Blocked pins are rarely used any longer. Keyed connectors are often used with ribbon cables today.

4. How many types of connectors and cables are there for internal SCSI connections?

There are two types of connector and two types of cable for internal SCSI connections: a 50-conductor cable with a pin block connector and a 68-conductor cable with a high-density D-shaped connector.

5. Which disk drive buses need to be terminated?

Only SCSI buses require manual termination. Every bus has terminators; however, with ATA/IDE and Fibre Channel the termination is automatic.

6. What does the term "cable select" mean with respect to the ATA/IDE bus?

Cable select is an older mechanism that identifies which device on an IDE bus is the master and which is the slave, based on the location of the device on the cable. However, it's rarely used anymore because most ATA/IDE cables do not support cable select.

7. Which type of fiber optic cable is used most often with Fibre Channel?

Multimode fiber optic cable. Multimode cables use lower power transmitters and have a maximum length of approximately 200 meters.

8. How many addressing modes does Fibre Channel support?

Two: Hardware addressing, in which internally burned IDs are used to reference the device, and physical addressing. Physical addressing identifies a device by its physical location on the Fibre Channel network. Hardware addressing is similar to the type of addressing used by networks.

9. What is the first thing you should do to address airflow issues?

Check the cable routings and try to reduce their interference with airflow through the server. Drives should also be spaced out if possible.

10. What type of fan should be used first when an airflow issue is suspected?

An auxiliary fan that pulls air out of a server (in the front) or that pushes air into a server. The goal is to move more air through the server, rather than moving the air in the server across more components.

11. Why are sleds used with hard disks?

They are used to simplify the installation and removal of disks. Most sleds allow drives to be inserted and removed without removing power (called hot swapping). Once a drive is installed on a sled, it can be inserted quickly.

12. What is the primary disadvantage of using the back up and restore method to expand a RAID array?

Time. The process requires a huge amount of time to implement. However, the method is available to anyone who needs to expand a RAID array, regardless of the operating system or RAID controller being used.

Page 293

Chapter 12
Adding and Upgrading Add-On Cards

Review Questions

Page 304

1. Why might an open slot not be usable?

It could be that the adjoining slot is in use. In some systems with both ISA and PCI slots, the two types share one common slat on the back, so if one slot is in use, the other isn't available. Another reason might be that the power supply is insufficient.

2. What techniques can you use to free additional interrupt request lines so that they can be used by new add-on cards?

Consolidate add-on cards so that you have fewer of them. For example, get SCSI controllers with multiple buses instead of one per controller. You can also disable unused ports and devices on the computer. For example, you can disable an unused USB controller or serial port, freeing its interrupt request line.

3. What issues can be associated with I/O ports?

More than 65,000 I/O ports are available, so running out isn't an issue. However, problems can occur when more than one device tries to use the same I/O port. Fortunately, this is rare in today's environment because of the use of Plug and Play.

4. What information does a compatibility list convey?

A compatibility list indicates only that the operating system vendor or its agents have tested the device to certify that it works with the operating system. It does not indicate whether the hardware will work with any other hardware. In the case of Linux, the hardware compatibility list may indicate only that there are reports from users of the device working or not working.

5. What other sources, besides the hardware compatibility list, should you check when installing a new add-on card?

You should check the vendor's knowledge base and FAQs, as well as the Internet newsgroups. As you learned in Chapter 1, Lesson 1, these alternatives to the documentation are invaluable because they can help identify potential installation problems.

Page 305

Chapter 13
Upgrading UPSs, Monitoring the System, and Choosing Service Tools

Review Questions

Page 327

1. What types of batteries are used in most UPSs?

Most UPSs use sealed lead-acid batteries. They are similar to the ones used in your car, except that they are always sealed and never require maintenance. Like the battery in your car, however, they have a fixed useful life.

2. What factor do you need to consider when adding additional batteries to a UPS that you don't need to worry about when simply replacing batteries that have reached the end of their life span?

When adding new batteries, you're changing the potential total output of the batteries. For that reason, you need to confirm that the cables connecting the batteries to the UPS are sufficiently large to conduct all of the current.

3. Why is it advisable to shut down the servers attached to a UPS when replacing the batteries?

The first reason to shut everything down is to limit the amount of power that is flowing through the UPS, thus limiting the amount of power that you can come into contact with. The second reason is that you may accidentally disconnect power during the operation, and it's better to have shut down the servers normally.

4. What is the line-conditioner-only mode of a UPS?

UPSs have transformers and MOVs designed to condition the power most of the time. Line-conditioner-only mode limits the UPS to using the transformers and MOVs, and thus prevents it from attempting to transfer the load to the inverter and batteries. This mode is used when you know that the batteries or inverter are incapable of supporting the load.

5. What advantages does hardware-based server monitoring have over software-based server monitoring?

Hardware-based monitoring can continue to function and report even after the motherboard or operating system has failed. The on-board battery backup and separate network connection allow hardware-based monitoring cards to report errors that software-based systems can't report.

6. What conditions in a server's environment do most environmental monitoring systems monitor?

Environmental monitoring systems generally monitor power, temperature, and noise. They also generally have contacts that allow them to monitor up to three other devices.

7. What are the four ways that software-based monitoring systems can notify you of a problem?

Console alert, e-mail, numeric pager, and alphanumeric pager. Each has its own advantages, but no matter what your environment is there is a solution to help you become aware of problems on the network.

8. What are the three functions within SNMP?

SNMP management consoles can read values from an SNMP agent, set values on an SNMP agent, and receive trap messages from SNMP agents. These three functions allow SNMP to perform a variety of functions.

9. What are the disadvantages of polling?

Polling incurs overhead. The more values you poll and the more frequently you poll for them, the more overhead you create on both the device doing the polling and the device being polled. Polling also means that there is a delay between when an event occurs and when it is discovered. This delay is inversely related to polling frequency.

10. What are the disadvantages of event-driven or alert-driven notification?

Event-driven notification requires greater complexity on the remote end, but its primary disadvantage is the potential for the event to get lost.

11. How does DMI differ from SNMP?

SNMP is designed for the management of network devices. DMI is designed to manage PCs. SNMP devices are generally fixed, while PCs change with new additions and removals. Because of this, DMI uses a three-tier architecture that uses separate component-based modules that plug into an agent and a third management layer.

12. What function does an MIB serve?

An MIB, or management information base, is a text-based file that identifies all of the objects and values that an SNMP agent supports. It's the roadmap to the SNMP agent.

13. What problems can a multimeter help you diagnose?

A multimeter can help you diagnose problems with the power supply in a server and can also verify end-to-end connectivity within a cable.

14. What is ARP, and what does it do?

Address Resolution Protocol (ARP) resolves TCP/IP addresses to hardware addresses. The ARP command allows you to view and control the cache of addresses translated by the ARP protocol.

15. Why would someone use nslookup?

Nslookup is a command to interactively query Domain Name System (DNS) servers. It is used to diagnose problems with the Domain Name System.

Page 331

Chapter 14
Establishing a Backup Plan

Review Questions

Page 354

1. How do incremental and differential backups work for transactional systems?

Transactional systems maintain transaction logs. These logs are backed up during either a differential or an incremental backup on a transactional system. An incremental backup clears the log once it's been backed up. A differential backup does not clear the transaction log.

2. What is an archive bit, and what does it do?

The archive bit is an attribute of a file in a FAT or NTFS-based file system that is used to determine whether the file has been backed up. This bit is set automatically whenever the file is modified. The backup software clears the archive bit after it completes a full or incremental backup. Other file systems support different mechanisms to identify files that may have been backed up.

3. Where did the Tower of Hanoi backup scheme get its name?

The Tower of Hanoi is a puzzle created by a French mathematician. The tape rotation is based on the same recursive, revolving solution required to solve the Tower of Hanoi puzzle.

4. What is a continuous backup?

A continuous backup is a special type of backup that backs up the system after every file change or completed transaction. It's used most often in environments where not even a single transaction can be lost. It has largely been replaced by clustered systems.

5. What is tape wear?

The tape medium eventually wears out. Tapes can be run underneath a tape drive read-write head only so many times. When a tape has been passed underneath the read-write heads enough times, it becomes unstable. A tape shouldn't be used after it has passed underneath the heads the rated number of times.

6. What factor during a backup can significantly affect tape life?

If a tape drive is not able to maintain motion, the continuous starts, stops, and restarts of the tape drive will wear out the tape quicker. The tape gets stressed when the tape drive stops and restarts. For the tape drive to maintain continuous motion, the system must feed it sufficient information. That is, the server should be able to provide the tape drive with enough information to keep the tape moving. This rate varies if hardware encryption is being used, but it is generally twice the uncompressed data rate.

7. What are important characteristics in the party responsible for monitoring the backups?

The person responsible for the backups should have a relatively routine schedule that doesn't change. The more stable the schedule, the more likely it is that the person will remember to monitor the backups.

8. What kind of on-site storage should be provided for tape backups?

A media-rated fireproof safe should be provided for the on-site storage of tapes. Media-rated fireproof safes keep the tapes safe from excessive heat; a regular fireproof safe doesn't offer enough protection against heat.

9. What are the three options for off-site storage?

Having an employee take tapes home, hiring a professional off-site storage service, and cross-rotating tapes among different organization sites.

10. What is the best way to determine whether a tape drive needs cleaning? What can you do if this isn't an option?

The best method for determining when a tape drive should be cleaned is to look for the cleaning indicator on the drive itself. If no indicator is present on the drive, you can estimate the number of hours between cleanings from the tape drive documentation and establish a regular rotation based on that information.

11. Why shouldn't the notification for the backups be set up to notify only on failure?

Because if the backup routine gets stuck and doesn't complete, you won't know there is a problem. If you perform notification only on failures, you won't know that the backup completed successfully, only that it didn't end in failure. It may not have completed at all.

Page 357

Chapter 15
Performing Physical Housekeeping and Verification

Review Questions

Page 365

1. Why are physical housekeeping and verification important, even if the proper monitoring systems are in place?

   Not every potential problem can be monitored. In addition, monitoring systems can fail. Nothing is more reliable than a physical review of the systems.

2. Why is it important to verify climate control and the operational status of fans?

   Servers must be maintained within a specific operating environment. When this range isn't maintained, the useful life of the server is reduced. The climate control equipment establishes this environment. The fans ensure that this environment exists inside the server as well as outside it.

3. When should you specifically test remote access?

   When remote access is limited to providing support for the servers and isn't used by the general user population, it should be tested periodically to ensure that it is still functional.

4. Why is it important to check fault-tolerant systems?

   Because fault-tolerant systems such as RAID arrays, redundant power supplies, and redundant network adapters are designed to hide failures from the users, they are often not noticed by the administrator. The key is for the server administrator to notice the problem before the next failure happens.

5. Why should surge suppressors be checked?

   Surge suppressors have a finite amount of protection they can offer to the connected equipment, based on the MOVs that are at their core. After the MOVs have been exhausted, they should be replaced.

Page 369

Chapter 16
Understanding the Troubleshooting Process

Review Questions

Page 386

1. What is Bloom's cognitive domain?

   It's a representation of the levels at which information can be learned. By progressing from the lower levels to the higher levels, Bloom believed, you achieved a deeper understanding of the material.

2. Why is troubleshooting different from most other learning?

   Troubleshooting requires a deeper understanding of the material and the ability to apply your learning toward a solution. It's the exercise of a process using the information you know to solve a problem.

3. What is the first step in the scientific method?

To understand the problem. Before you can solve the problem, you must understand it in detail. The first step deals with the collection of information to define the problem.

4. Why doesn't the hypothesis being tested have to be right?

The scientific method is an iterative process. It requires only that something be learned in each iteration. In the next iteration of the process, you use that new information in conjunction with the previous information to come up with another hypothesis.

5. Why is localization of a problem so important?

Localization is important because it helps to contain the possible problems, and thus the possible solutions, at a manageable level.

6. Why is isolation of a problem important?

It keeps problems from ganging up on you. Finding two problems at the same time is exponentially harder than finding one problem. Isolation ensures that you're trying to solve only one problem.

7. Who should you call if a hardware driver is responsible for locking up the computer?

The hardware vendor that provided the device for which the driver was written. The operating system vendor can't help with third-party hardware drivers.

Page 387

Chapter 17
Troubleshooting Common Problems

Review Questions

Page 413

1. What is the first step in the bootup process?

The CPU executes the instruction at system memory address FFFF0h. This leads to a jump instruction that points to the location of the POST.

2. Where is the POST stored?

In the ROM on the motherboard. The POST routine also executes POST routines contained in the ROM of add-on cards.

3. What is the first thing you should check when SCSI drives are missing from the bootup process?

If no devices have been changed, you should check the SCSI BIOS to make sure that the drive is being located and that the BIOS itself is being installed in memory. If any bus configuration changes have been made, it's important to check termination and ID settings.

4. Why are boot sector viruses not a significant issue in today's environment?

Most software installations today are not done from floppy disks. Boot sector infector viruses require floppy disks in order to spread.

5. What is the most prevalent type of virus today (based on the number of different viruses)?

The most prevalent type of virus is the file infector virus, one that extends or replaces an executable to include itself. Admittedly, script/macro viruses are catching up at an alarming rate.

6. What is the first step in resolving a network connectivity problem?

Review the physical layer. Make sure that the cables and hubs are connected so that the link indicators on the network cards and on the hubs themselves are lit. If the physical layer isn't working, nothing will work.

7. Once you've verified the physical layer of connectivity, what steps should you use to diagnose a TCP/IP problem?

Test the local network, test a remote network, and finally test name resolution.

8. Why is DHCP used?

DHCP simplifies the task of maintaining a TCP/IP network. The DHCP server can give out not only IP addresses but also other TCP/IP configuration information as well.

9. What is a core dump?

It's an operating system response to a critical error that couldn't be logged in the system log. Core dumps can be either dumps of user information space caused by an error that doesn't generally affect overall system performance, or system dumps, which are generally produced following errors that result in the system being rebooted, affecting everyone using the system.

10. Why do hard disks vibrate?

Because the disk is set slightly off center and is spinning at a high rate of speed.

Glossary

10Base2 An Ethernet physical media type that runs on a thin coaxial cable for distances of up to 185 meters. Characterized by the use of BNC connectors.

10Base5 An Ethernet physical media type that runs on thick coaxial cable for distances of up to 500 meters. Generally used only for Ethernet backbones. No longer in common use.

10BaseT An Ethernet physical media type that runs on twisted pairs of wire. Good for distances of up to 100 meters. The most common Ethernet physical medium in use today.

A

AC *see* alternating current

Accelerated Graphics Port (AGP) An Intel-designed port used for graphics adapters because of the need for high-speed communication between the processor, memory, and video card. AGP ports should not be a consideration for servers because servers do not need high-performance communication between the video card and the rest of the system.

access The ability to use a resource.

access license A license to use the services provided by the server. Access licenses are required for all clients connecting to both Novell NetWare and Microsoft Windows 2000.

access permissions The rules by which access is granted to a resource. Generally, access permissions specify the type of access being granted and the users who are permitted this access. The user's access permissions are the sum of those permissions explicitly granted to the user and those permissions inherited from their membership in groups.

access violation error An error caused when a program attempts to access memory in a way that is not authorized, such as attempting to write to memory for which only read-only access has been granted.

ACPI *see* Advanced Configuration and Power Interface

Active Directory Windows 2000's network security and information system.

active terminator A terminator that uses a series of capacitors and resistors to actively terminate signals on the end of the line so that the signal reflected back on the bus is greatly reduced.

activity log A record, electronic or written, of activity. Used during problems to identify recent activities that may have led to the problem.

Address Resolution Protocol (ARP) A component of TCP/IP that performs the translation of IP addresses to MAC addresses. Also the name of a command that can be used to interrogate the ARP component of TCP/IP.

Advanced Configuration and Power Interface (ACPI) A BIOS feature that allows an operating system to interact with the power management features of the motherboard.

AGP *see* Accelerated Graphics Port

AGP aperture The size of the opening for memory on an AGP attached video card.

airflow The flow of air through a case or a rack. Proper routing of airflow is necessary for proper cooling.

alarm system A system designed to generate a loud notification tone and/or notify a remote facility when unauthorized access is gained to a facility.

alternating current (AC) The type of current that comes out of a standard wall outlet. The flow of electrons is reversed several times a second. AC power can be transmitted over long distances with little loss of current.

ambient room noise The average noise in a room. Not the noise measured at a specific point, such as near a power supply fan.

ambient room temperature The average temperature of the room. Not the temperature measured at a specific point, such as inside a server case.

amp Short for ampere. A unit of measure for electrical current.

ampere *see* amp

antivirus software Software designed to help prevent infections from computer viruses. Frequent updates are required to maintain antivirus software and allow it to prevent infection by the latest viruses.

API *see* Application Programming Interface

application programming interface (API) An interface designed to allow programmers to integrate or use the services of an application or operating system. It may consist of simple function calls, or objects.

archive bit A bit recorded for each file on FAT, FAT32, and NTFS file systems. When set, the bit indicates that the file needs to be backed up. It is fundamental in helping backup software perform differential and incremental backups.

arcing Electrical current jumping a gap in a circuit, usually generating visible light. Lightning is the largest example of arcing.

ARP *see* Address Resolution Protocol

AS/400 Application System/400. An IBM midrange computer product.

ATA *see* AT Attachment

ATAPI *see* AT Attachment Packet Interface

AT Attachment (ATA) The official name for a series of standards for drive connectivity that is more commonly known as Integrated Drive Electronics (IDE).

AT Attachment Packet Interface (ATAPI) An extension of the AT Attachment standard that allows devices other than hard disks to be attached to the AT Attachment interface.

AT power supply A power supply characterized by two single-row motherboard power connectors and a mechanical on/off switch. Not in common use any longer.

ATX power supply The type of power supply used in most systems today, characterized by a single motherboard power connector with two rows and an electronic on/off switch.

audit To verify activities. Generally results in the creation of an audit trail.

audit trail An accounting of actions, generally involving resource access. A security measure used to investigate activities after the fact.

AUTOEXEC.BAT One of the two primary configuration files for MS-DOS. The other is CONFIG.SYS.

autoloader A tape drive that has a mechanism for swapping a small number of tapes. Used when a higher capacity, but not faster speeds of backup, is necessary.

availability The ability to get access to a system. High availability is accomplished through the use of fault-tolerant subsystems.

B

backbone The main connecting point for a network.

backup domain controller A Microsoft Windows NT server that maintains a read-only copy of the domain security database for the purpose of distributing the load of the primary domain controller.

baseline A reference point to which future observations can be compared.

basic input/output system (BIOS) The programs contained on motherboard ROMs that provide basic control of and interaction with the motherboard.

BBS *see* bulletin board system

Berkeley DNS server *see* Berkeley Internet Name Domain

Berkeley Internet Name Domain (BIND) The most popular DNS server for UNIX-based systems. Sometimes known as Berkeley DNS server.

best fit line A line representing the best fit of the given data points. The resulting line indicates the relative growth of a value when the value is growing in a linear or nearly linear way. Used to reveal a trend within a large series of data points.

BIND *see* Berkeley Internet Name Domain

BIOS *see* basic input/output system

bit A single piece of information that can have only two states, on and off. A bit is typically signified as being a 1 or a 0.

blackout A period when no utility power is available. The primary reason for having SPS and UPS devices.

blocked pins A method of identifying the correct orientation of a pin block cable by use of a blocked hole in the block side of the connector and a missing pin on the pin side of the connector. Rarely used today because it requires an unused connector and because the component must support the method if the cable supports it.

BNC *see* British Naval Connector

BogoMIPS A measure of a CPU's processing speed, used by Linux to calibrate internal timing loops. "Bogo" is from bogus—that is, fake—emphasizing the limited value of such measurements for comparison purposes.

boot The process of starting a computer.

BOOTP Short for Boot Protocol. A TCP/IP protocol used for downloading an operating system to a terminal or other network-attached device. Used as the basis of the Dynamic Host Configuration Protocol (DHCP).

boot sector virus A virus that infects the boot sector of floppy disks and the master boot records of hard disks.

bridge A network device that operates at the physical layer, deciding whether to forward packets between two or more connected networks by determining whether the physical (MAC) address is remote or local to the sender.

British Naval Connector (BNC) The type of connector used for 10Base2 cabling. It's a circular connector that uses two metal bars on either side of a cylinder. The matching connector uses a rotating collar to grab the two metal bars.

broadcasts Network communications intended for all network devices attached to the local network. Broadcasts have a negative performance impact on switched networks because the fact that they are sent to every port eliminates the performance benefits of the switch.

broadcast storm A period of activity characterized by extremely high utilization that causes packets to be retransmitted. This happens in protocols that use Carrier Sense Media Access/Collision Detection (CSMA/CD) as an access method. Eventually, broadcast storms will cause connectivity failure until the storm is over.

brownout A sustained period of reduced voltage from a power utility. Extreme brownouts cause incandescent light bulbs to dim and turn more brown than white; hence the name "brownout."

bug A failure or defect. Named for a moth that was the cause of one of the first failures of the first computer.

bulletin board system (BBS) An electronic system by which messages and files can be exchanged. BBSs were historically accessed via dial-up analog modems and were used by vendors to provide a way of downloading updated drivers and information. No longer in popular use, BBSs have been replaced in large part by the Internet.

bus mastering A technique used by add-on cards to directly access memory and other resources without the intervention of the CPU. The card itself takes responsibility for communicating on the bus.

bypass To go around a device, usually temporarily. In a UPS, you will bypass the UPS circuitry when working on or replacing it.

byte A grouping of 8 bits.

C

cable scanner A tool designed to test cables and identify faults. Useful in identifying physical layer faults that will prevent communications or cause problems.

cache A fast buffer used to limit the number of accesses to a slower medium. Memory caches use high-speed memory on the CPU to reduce the need to access slower main memory (RAM). Disk caches use RAM to reduce the number of accesses to slower hard disks.

capacitance A property of conductors that allows them to store a charge. Capacitance is detrimental to signals because it has the effect of reducing the high signals and increasing the low signals on the wire until they are indistinguishable.

capacity planning The process of planning for growth by determining the additional capacity that will be necessary to support future needs.

card access system A physical access system in which the user must insert a card to gain access to a room. This type of system is different from a key and lock system in that the accesses are generally logged.

carrier A device in which multiple tapes are installed. Carriers are used for both autoloaders and libraries.

Carrier Sense Multiple Access/Collision Detection (CSMA/CD) A network access method in which each member of the network listens before seizing control of the medium. Should a collision occur between two network devices, they detect it, and each device waits a random time before reattempting the transmission. CSMA/CD is similar to the method used in citizens band (CB) communications.

Category 5 A type of cabling that is certified for communications up to 100 MHz. This type of cable is the minimum recommended for installation today and is required for Fast Ethernet.

CDM *see* Custom Device Module

center of gravity The point at which the entire mass of an object is perceived to be centered.

central processing unit (CPU) The primary, or central, processor within a computer. The CPU is commonly referred to as the processor. Intel, AMD, and Cyrix make central processing units.

centrifugal force The force that acts on a mass that is in circular motion, attempting to pull it into a straight line.

charge The process of adding electrical energy to a device, most frequently a battery.

checkpoint A point at which the system records the current state of all transactions. Used in databases and other transactional systems to indicate that the transaction log can be truncated.

circuit breaker A device used to limit the amount of current that can be drawn by a circuit. Different from a fuse in that the process of limiting the current doesn't destroy the circuit breaker. A circuit breaker can be reset shortly after it disconnects to restore the circuit.

cleaning tape A tape that is specifically designed to clean a tape drive. It cannot be used for data storage.

client/server A division of processing in which the client performs validation and the server applies business rules, such as limiting transaction amount, requiring a particular credit rating for transactions over a given amount, or requiring additional approvals for transactions over a certain amount. Depending upon the implementation, processing can be either very server-intensive or very client-intensive, or both.

climate control system A system that controls temperature and humidity through the use of air conditioning and humidification. Designed to maintain the ambient temperature and humidity within optimal ranges for servers.

Clock cycle The smallest unit of time within a processor. No operation can complete in less than one clock cycle.

clock speed The base unit for timing. The speed of the clock indicates the speed of the operations. Note that the clock speed is not directly equivalent to the overall speed. Other factors, including the number of clock cycles an operation takes to complete, affect overall operating speed.

cluster A group of servers acting as a single unit. Clusters are used to improve scalability by dividing the work among several machines.

coaxial cable A cable characterized by two conductors centered around the same axis. It most frequently has one conductor at the core and another that doubles as a shielding layer around it.

cold backup site A remote location that has been secured for use should a disaster wipe out the primary site. A cold backup site does not have duplicate systems installed and operational, as is the case in a hot backup site, but these can usually be obtained rapidly.

compiler A program that translates the source code of a language into an executable file.

condensation Water that appears on surfaces when relative humidity is high.

CONFIG.SYS One of the two primary configuration files for MS-DOS. The other primary configuration file is AUTOEXEC.BAT.

contingency planning The process of planning for potential problems. This type of planning generally includes identifying problems that should be planned for. It is part of disaster recovery planning.

core dump A file generated by an operating system containing the contents of memory when a critical error occurred. Depending on the type, a core dump can consist either of all system memory or of user memory only.

core voltages The voltages used for internal CPU operation. These voltages vary among processor types, and even among different processors within a type. Incorrect core voltage can damage or destroy the CPU.

CPU *see* central processing unit

CRC *see* cyclic redundancy check

CSMA/CD *see* Carrier Sense Multiple Access/ Collision Detection

Custom Device Module (CDM) A Novell NetWare module that supports devices on a bus. Part of NetWare Peripheral Architecture (NWPA).

cyclic redundancy check (CRC) A method of calculating a mathematical checksum that is used by the receiver to determine whether the data was corrupted during storage or transmission.

D

database A structured set of data. Used for rapid retrieval of information.

DC *see* direct current

DDNS *see* Dynamic Domain Name System

DDR SDRAM *see* double data rate synchronous dynamic random-access memory.

density The amount of information that can be contained in a given amount of space. Used in reference to memory and hard disks.

Desktop Management Interface (DMI) An initiative and API for managing PC systems. Includes configuration and inventory.

Desktop Management Task Force (DMTF) An organization dedicated to improving desktop PC management. Responsible for the DMI initiative.

Device Manager A component of Windows 2000 responsible for managing the server hardware. Includes resource settings, driver version, and operational status of all devices.

DHCP *see* Dynamic Host Configuration Protocol

differential backup A backup that backs up all files that have changed since the last full or incremental backup. It uses the archive bit, or a similar mechanism, to determine which files need to be backed up. Differential backups don't reset the archive bit or similar mechanisms.

digital versatile disc (DVD) A high-capacity storage medium used for digitally compressed movies and for distribution of digital data that is too large to fit on a CD-ROM. *Also called* digital video disc.

digital video disc *see* digital versatile disc

DIMM *see* dual in-line memory module

DIP switch Short for dual in-line package switch. Used on older add-on cards and some motherboards to control settings. An alternative to jumpers.

direct current (DC) A type of current in which the electrons all flow in a single direction. It is produced by batteries and is the type of current used in the internal circuitry of computers.

direct memory access (DMA) The ability of an add-on card to access memory directly without the intervention of the CPU. A DMA controller on the motherboard coordinates the exchange of information.

disaster recovery The process of recovering from a disaster. A disaster can be defined as an equipment failure, an act of nature, or another problem that causes interruption of service or potential interruption of service.

discrete event An event that cannot be broken down into smaller parts. Also known as an atomic event. Used in transactional systems such as databases.

disk queue length The number of commands currently pending for a hard disk drive, or the number of commands pending to a hard disk at the end of a polling interval. Used to determine how busy a hard disk is.

distribution list A recipient list to which messages are distributed. This type of list is typically associated with electronic mail programs and notification lists for systems monitoring software and hardware.

DMA *see* direct memory access

DMA channel A logical conduit over which an add-on card can communicate directly with main memory. It is provided by a DMA controller located on the motherboard.

DMI *see* Desktop Management Interface

DMTF *see* Desktop Management Task Force

DNS *see* Domain Name System

domain controller A keeper of security information for Windows NT's domain architecture. Domain controllers come in two varieties: primary domain controllers and backup domain controllers.

Domain Name System (DNS) The system for the distributed management and distribution of information used to translate TCP/IP names to IP addresses. Also supports special queries to return information not directly related to name translation. Characterized by a hierarchy of DNS servers that communicate with one another to solve DNS client requests.

DOS Short for Disk Operating System. Typically used to refer to Microsoft's version of DOS, MS-DOS. An out-of-date operating system that Novell NetWare still uses to boot.

double data rate synchronous dynamic random-access memory (DDR SDRAM) SDRAM that returns twice the amount of memory by returning data twice in a single clock cycle. Used for extremely high-performance servers to improve memory performance.

download A file transfer from a remote machine to the local machine.

DRAM *see* dynamic random-access memory

driver A small piece of software that allows an operating system or other software to use installed hardware. A driver is required for the use of add-on hardware.

dual in-line memory module (DIMM) A memory packaging format in which memory is installed on a 168-pin memory module. "Dual" refers to a dual 32-bit word. DIMM modules present memory as a 64-bit double word.

DVD *see* digital versatile disc

Dynamic Domain Name System (DDNS) An extension to DNS that allows for dynamic updates to the information used to translate names to IP addresses. DDNS is used to improve name resolution when DHCP is in use.

Dynamic Host Configuration Protocol (DHCP) A protocol that is used to simplify the administration of TCP/IP networks by leasing IP addresses and associated information to client computers for a fixed period of time. DHCP dramatically reduces the effort involved in managing a TCP/IP network.

dynamic random-access memory (DRAM) A volatile memory technology that requires constant refreshing to maintain information. The basis for memory technologies used today.

E

ECC *see* error checking and correcting

ECP *see* Enhanced Communications Port

EIDE *see* Enhanced Integrated Drive Electronics

EISA *see* Extended Industry Standard Architecture

electrostatic discharge (ESD) The rapid release of energy stored in an electrostatic field, with potential arcing and damage to electrical components.

emergency power-off A mechanism whereby all power in a room, or running through a UPS, can be immediately turned off. It is designed as a safety precaution for situations in which power flowing through a circuit would be hazardous to people or equipment. Emergency power-off mechanisms are generally connected remotely to UPSs and circuit breakers so they can be executed without going near the dangerous area.

encrypted Encoded or translated in a way that is not readily decipherable without decryption. The process of encoding is called encryption. The process of decoding is called decryption.

Encrypting File System (EFS) An extension to the NTFS file system that allows files to be encrypted before they are stored, for extra security.

Enhanced Communications Port (ECP) A new and current standard for parallel ports. Parallel ports, often called printer ports, are used to connect printers and, historically, other devices needing higher performance than was available through the serial ports. ECP defines higher bidirectional transfer speeds than were available in the bidirectional parallel port standard, which it replaced.

Enhanced Integrated Drive Electronics (EIDE) A marketing term used to refer to certain features within the AT Attachment interface.

enhanced parallel port (EPP) An IBM-supported standard that improved the communication speed of parallel ports. Released at around the same time as ECP, EPP is largely supported in today's environment but is rarely used because of the advanced features available in ECP ports. Most parallel ports on a computer can be configured to operate in EPP mode.

EPP *see* enhanced parallel port

errata sheets Pages included with a product at the last minute that indicate errors discovered in the hardware, drivers, manual, or installation. These sheets usually contain important information and should be reviewed prior to installation.

error checking and correcting (ECC) A method of memory organization that uses additional bits of information to detect and correct single-bit memory errors.

ESD *see* electrostatic discharge

Ethernet A networking topology that uses Carrier Sense Multiple Access/Collision Detection (CSMA/CD) to determine when it is OK to transmit. It was originally defined as a 10-megabits-per-second (Mbps) baseband transmission but extended to 100-Mbps and 1-gigabit per second (Gbps) implementations. Ethernet is the most prominent network topology in use today.

Ethernet switch A network device that improves performance by selectively sending packets to remote locations by reading the destination MAC address. Only broadcast packets and packets specifically destined for a port are sent to that port. An Ethernet switch can dramatically improve performance when multiple servers are being used by a pool of users.

event log A record of events. The term generally refers to logs kept by the operating system to indicate events that have occurred on that server. Sometimes event logs are separated by type.

ext2 file system The default file system used with Linux.

Extended Industry Standard Architecture (EISA) An extension to the Industry Standard Architecture that is easier to configure and provides better performance.

F

fail over *see* hot spare

FAQ *see* frequently asked questions

Fast Ethernet A 100-megabits-per-second (Mbps) variation of the Ethernet network topology.

FAT file system Short for file allocation table. The file system used by MS-DOS, Microsoft Windows 95, and Windows 98. Readable by most operating systems, the FAT format is limited to 2-GB partitions.

FAT32 file system A 32-bit variation of the popular FAT file system that removed the 2-GB barrier. It is supported by Windows 95 OSR-2 and later, as well as Windows 2000.

fault tolerance The ability to accept a fault within one component of a subsystem and still maintain services to the user. The term is generally used in reference to redundant components or in architectures such as RAID-5 that can continue to function after the failure of a single hard disk.

fax server A server that provides inbound and outbound fax capability to clients. Performance for this kind of server varies widely, depending upon how the communication is accomplished. Dedicated fax cards can significantly reduce the amount of processing required by the server.

FC *see* Fibre Channel

fiber A clear, slender conductor of light. It is used for high-speed communications over long distances.

Fibre Channel (FC) A standard for communications over fiber and copper at high speeds that supports the use of LAN and storage-based protocols over the same medium.

file and print server A server designed to provide both file and printing resources to clients. File and print servers are the basis for most networks.

File Transfer Protocol (FTP) A session-based, simple protocol for the exchange of files that runs on top of TCP/IP. FTP servers are common on the Internet for the purpose of sharing files.

fire alarm A system designed to monitor for the presence of fire. It generally provides both an on-site indication of the problem and off-site notification.

firewall A device or software designed to prevent unauthorized access to internal systems.

firmware The software designed to run hardware that is on the ROM on the hardware.

FlashROM ROM that is reprogrammable without the use of special equipment. Once the new code is loaded to the ROM, it stays there until removed or replaced.

forced perfect termination A type of SCSI terminator with active circuitry to force the termination to be perfect. Used for high-end applications that cannot tolerate SCSI bus issues.

formatting The process of creating the root data structures of a disk so that a partition can be used for the storage of information. Sometimes this process includes verifying every sector of the partition.

frequency The number of actions per unit of time.

frequently asked questions (FAQ) A popular type of file designed to contain the questions most frequently asked about a particular subject so that they are not asked repeatedly. FAQs initially started with Internet newsgroups but later were adapted to vendor-based technical support.

FTP *see* File Transfer Protocol

full backup A backup that includes every file, or all of the data.

fuse A device that limits the maximum amount of current a circuit can consume. The process of fusing (disconnecting the circuit) destroys the fuse so that it must be replaced.

G

gateway A device or server that converts one application protocol to another. Most frequently used to allow a PC access to a minicomputer or mainframe.

GFS *see* grandfather-father-son

Gigabit Ethernet A revision of the original Ethernet standard that transfers data at 1 gigabit per second (Gbps).

grandfather-father-son (GFS) A tape rotation scheme characterized by three different sets of tapes: those used daily, those used weekly, and those used monthly.

ground The electrically neutral state to which other signals and energy are referenced.

H

HAL *see* hardware abstraction layer

HAM *see* Host Adapter Module

hard disk controller The device to which hard disks are attached. It translates the communication from the hard disk into a format the host computer can understand.

hard disk medium The magnetic medium that spins inside a hard disk and holds the information.

hard disk sled A carrier for hard disks that allows them to be quickly and easily inserted into drive cabinets or server cases. They frequently provide hot-swap support.

hardware abstraction layer (HAL) A device driver that allows Microsoft Windows 2000 to use and take advantages of motherboard features.

hardware compatibility list (HCL) A list of devices that were tested and found to be compatible with the operating system in question. This list is maintained by the operating system vendor.

HCL *see* hardware compatibility list

hertz (Hz) A unit of frequency equal to one cycle per second.

hierarchical PCI bus A type of PCI bus that connects through PCI-to-PCI bridges to a master PCI bus. This bus type is less expensive but slightly slower than peer PCI buses.

High Performance File System (HPFS) The native file system of OS/2. It provides for extended attributes that are not available in FAT. HPFS was supported in Microsoft Windows NT until version 3.51.

high-speed serial data connector (HSSDC) The copper-based connector used for some Fibre Channel implementations.

high-voltage differential SCSI (HVD SCSI) A version of SCSI that uses differential signaling and a higher voltage than single-ended SCSI. It is incompatible with and potentially destructive to single-ended SCSI devices but uses the same connectors.

Host Adapter Module (HAM) A disk controller driver for Novell NetWare. It is part of the NetWare Peripheral Architecture.

hot backup site A remote location that has been secured for operation should a disaster strike the primary site. A hot backup site maintains an operational copy of the systems at the primary site to minimize the amount of time necessary to get back online after a disaster.

hot plug *see* hot swap

hot spare A device that is installed in the system but is inactive until a failure occurs, when it is automatically activated and used. Hot spares are most frequently used to provide additional redundancy in a RAID-5 array cabinet.

hot swap The ability to remove and replace a component during operation of the system. Used in reference to hard disks in a hard disk array and to PCI-based cards in a server.

HPFS *see* High Performance File System

HSSDC *see* high-speed serial data connector

HTML *see* Hypertext Markup Language

HTTP *see* Hypertext Transfer Protocol

humidity The amount of water vapor in the air. It is almost always expressed as a percentage, or as relative humidity. Relative humidity is the amount of water vapor in the air compared with the maximum amount of water vapor the air can hold.

HVD SCSI *see* high-voltage differential SCSI

Hypertext Markup Language (HTML) The definition language used to create Web pages.

Hypertext Transfer Protocol (HTTP) The protocol used to transmit HTML pages and other information from one computer to another. The transfer protocol for the World Wide Web.

hypothesis An explanation as to the cause of a problem, subject to further proof. An untested theory.

hypothesize The act of creating or asserting a hypothesis.

Hz *see* hertz

I

I2O *see* Intelligent Input/Output

IDE *see* Integrated Drive Electronics

incremental backup A backup consisting of files or data that has changed since the last full or incremental backup.

induction The electromagnetic process whereby electrical current is induced onto a conductor located close and parallel to a conductor carrying electrical energy or signals.

Industry Standard Architecture (ISA) The original add-on card bus for the IBM PC. Although it has fallen out of favor recently, it was the primary bus used in PCs for 15 years.

inheritance Something received from another, generally of earlier lineage, such as one's parents or grandparents

inherited rights The transmission of access rights from the parent container structure to objects contained within it.

init state The type of run environment being provided by a UNIX operating system. Init states include single-user, text-only, and graphical modes. The individual run states are semistandard, with the basic single-user, text-only, and graphical run states being common across most flavors of UNIX.

input/output (I/O) Information coming into the computer, such as from a keyboard, mouse, or communications line, and information being sent out of the computer, such as through a monitor, printer, or communications line.

Integrated Drive Electronics (IDE) Computer industry jargon that refers to hard disks which use the AT Attachment standard for connectivity.

Intelligent Input/Output (I2O) An initiative designed to help reduce the processor utilization of servers and to reduce the complexity of driver development for hardware vendors.

interleave The process of using more than one bank of memory in an alternating fashion to improve access speed.

International Organization for Standardization (ISO) An organization responsible for the creation of international standards, including the OSI protocol reference model.

Internet A large network consisting of tens of thousands of interconnected computers through which access to information and software is available. An outgrowth of the network sponsored by the Defense Advanced Research Projects Agency (DARPA), which developed TCP/IP.

Internet newsgroups Also called Usenet, a collection of servers running the Network News Transport Protocol (NNTP) for the collaborative exchange of information. Unlike e-mail, messages sent to newsgroups are available for all to view.

Internet Protocol (IP) The network protocol responsible for the routing of messages. It is part of the TCP/IP suite of protocols.

Internetwork Package Exchange (IPX) The Novell protocol that is the preferred protocol for installation on Novell NetWare servers. It is based on the work of Xerox at its Palo Alto Research Center.

Interpreted language A computer programming language that is translated into machine instructions on the fly rather than ahead of time.

interrupt A signal to the CPU that attention is required to respond to an add-on card or user action.

interrupt request line (IRQ) A specific indicator line used to signal an interrupt to the CPU. Fifteen usable interrupts exist in a PC.

interval The amount of time between two events.

inverter An electrical device that converts DC electricity to AC electricity.

I/O *see* input/output

ionize To convert into ions by causing the atoms to gain a charge through the gain or loss of electrons.

I/O ports A provision in the CPU architecture that allows the CPU to communicate with nonmemory devices such as add-on cards. Information can be written to or read from any port.

IP *see* Internet Protocol

IPX *see* Internetwork Packet Exchange

IPX/SPX *see* Internetwork Packet Exchange and Sequenced Packet Exchange

IRQ *see* interrupt request line

ISA *see* Industry Standard Architecture

ISO *see* International Organization for Standardization

isolation The process of eliminating potential interference caused by outside factors. Isolation is used in troubleshooting to eliminate outside causes.

J

joule A measurement of energy.

jumper A small plastic block with metal conductors used to connect two pins on a motherboard or add-on card for the purposes of configuring the device or causing a device reset.

K

keyed connectors A cable orientation method in widespread use today because of its ability to positively identify the orientation for a pin block connector and because either side of the connector can fail to support it without preventing correct installation.

KVA One thousand volt-amps.

KVM switch Short for keyboard-video-mouse switch. A switch designed to allow a single keyboard, monitor, and mouse to be used with multiple machines.

L

LAT *see* Local Area Transport

latency The time it takes for the disk to rotate such that the heads are positioned over a sector of data.

lead-acid battery A type of battery based on lead and acid materials, used in automobiles and UPSs, among other applications.

library A tape backup device containing one or more tape drives and one or more carriers. Libraries are used when needed backup capacity exceeds the capacity available on a single tape, and when there's a need or potential need for the performance enhancement gained by running multiple drives simultaneously.

link light An indicator light on most network interface cards and hubs that indicates physical network connectivity.

Linux An open-source operating system based on UNIX.

Local Area Transport (LAT) A Digital Equipment Corporation protocol for communicating between VAX servers and terminal servers.

localization A process whereby the source of a problem is narrowed down to a portion of the process rather than the whole process. Localization is used to limit the number of potential hypotheses.

lock-on connectors Connectors that have a mechanism for staying connected. Typical mechanisms include screws, pinch clips, and other latching devices.

logical storage Storage that doesn't directly correspond to physical disks. Examples include RAID-5 array storage and partitions. This type of storage is typically thought of as drive letters in Microsoft Windows 2000 and volumes within Novell NetWare.

lost opportunity Potential revenue that is lost due to some abnormal cause such as a server failure.

low-voltage differential SCSI (LVD SCSI) A SCSI bus that uses low-voltage differential signaling. Attaching an LVD SCSI device on a bus with a single-ended SCSI device will not work but will not cause damage.

LVD SCSI *see* low-voltage differential SCSI

M

MAC *see* media access control

magnet A device that attracts iron and produces a magnetic field.

magnetic poles Two spots of opposite magnetic field on a magnet. Opposite magnetic poles attract; similar magnetic poles repel.

management information base (MIB) The information database used by SNMP consoles to determine what values are available from an SNMP agent and what those values mean.

master boot record (MBR) A portion of the first sector on a hard disk that the BIOS loads and tries to execute at boot time.

matrixed UPS A UPS that has modular batteries and electronics that can be replaced while the unit is online. This type of UPS generally falls in the power midrange of UPS devices.

MAU *see* Multistation Access Unit

MBR *see* master boot record

media access control (MAC) The hardware or physical address for a network card on the network.

media failure An inability of magnetic media to retain information. It is caused by use beyond the rated lifetime of the media or by a physical defect.

media lifetime The maximum amount of time that can elapse between the data being written to a medium and when the data is retrieved from the medium.

media wear The tendency for media of different types, particularly tape, to wear out after use.

memory A device for the storage and retrieval of information. The term is generally used to refer to volatile memory—that is, memory that loses the stored information when power is no longer applied.

memory bus The communications mechanism through which information is exchanged between memory and other parts of the system, most notably the processor.

metal-oxide varistor (MOV) A device used in the construction of surge suppressors that has an extremely high resistance to current until a particular voltage is reached, at which point it develops an extremely low resistance. The result is that these devices can clamp voltage at a certain level.

MFM *see* modified frequency modulation

MIB *see* management information base

millisecond One thousandth of a second.

modem Short for MOdulator/DEModulator. Modems are used to convert digital information into an analog signal and vice versa.

modified frequency modulation (MFM) A method of storing information on hard disks that is no longer in widespread use.

motion detector A device that detects the presence of motion. Motion detectors are most often used in alarm systems to detect unauthorized access to a location.

MOV *see* metal-oxide varistor

MPS *see* MultiProcessor Specification

MSAU *see* Multistation Access Unit

multicast A single packet of information that is sent to multiple destination addresses at the same time. Multicasts are most often used to limit the amount of network traffic.

multimeter A device designed to measure voltage and amperage of circuits, most frequently for both DC and AC. It is useful in diagnosing power problems.

MultiProcessor Specification (MPS) An Intel specification for multiple processors installed in the same machine.

Multistation Access Unit (MAU or MSAU) Equivalent to an Ethernet hub, these devices serve as the connection point linking Token Ring computers to the network. Connectivity between MAUs is redundant. This allows the Token Ring network to continue to operate if a single MAU-to-MAU cable is cut.

N

nanosecond One billionth of a second.

NAT *see* network address translation

NCP *see* NetWare Core Protocol

NDS *see* NetWare Directory Services

NetBEUI Short for NetBIOS Enhanced User Interface. A low-level protocol designed specifically for the transport of NetBIOS.

NetBIOS A set of application-level protocols for providing services, such as file and print services.

NetBIOS node type A NetBIOS configuration option that controls how the computer attempts to resolve names.

NetBIOS over TCP/IP (NetBT) Defined by RFC 1001 and RFC 1002. The transportation of NetBIOS services over TCP/IP networks.

NetWare A series of Novell operating system products that provide file and print services.

NetWare Core Protocol (NCP) The application-level protocol that Novell NetWare uses to provide file and print services to clients. It is equivalent to Microsoft's use of server message block.

NetWare Directory Services (NDS) Novell's unified security and information database. It is used to simplify the administration of large networks.

NetWare Loadable Module (NLM) An application compiled to be run on Novell's NetWare operating systems.

NetWare Peripheral Architecture (NWPA) Novell's new architecture for disk controllers and disk controller–attached devices. It splits the old .DSK driver format into. CDM and .HAM modules.

network address translation (NAT) A translation between internal, private network addresses and external network addresses.

Network File System (NFS) A standard for file sharing services that is used primarily by UNIX-based systems.

Network Information System (NIS) A UNIX standard for a security and information database used to simplify the administration of large networks.

network interface card (NIC) The electronic circuitry that connects a computer to a network.

network operating system An operating system specifically designed for providing network services. Only Novell NetWare would be considered a popular network operating system today. Microsoft Windows 2000, OS/2, and Linux would be more appropriately described as operating systems because they can be run on desktop computers.

NFS *see* Network File System

NIC *see* network interface card

NIS *see* Network Information System

NLM *see* NetWare Loadable Module

Novell Storage Services (NSS) A new type of NetWare volume that supports additional features over NetWare's standard volume type.

NSS *see* Novell Storage Services

NTFS file system Originally short for New Technology File System. The file system introduced with Microsoft Windows NT and used by both Windows NT and Windows 2000. NTFS supports large partition sizes, alternate data streams, file-by-file compression, file-by-file encryption, and other features not found in FAT or FAT32 file systems.

NWPA *see* NetWare Peripheral Architecture

O

off-site storage Storage that is accomplished at a remote location from the one where the information or backup was generated.

on-site storage Storage that is accomplished at the same location as the one where the information or backup was generated.

operating system The basic software that controls the hardware and arbitrates between other software applications.

opportunity loss *see* lost opportunity

OSI protocol reference model A seven-layer model for how network protocols should be inter-related. Although not widely implemented, it's still the basis for most training on network protocols. Most popular implementations of protocols diverge from the OSI protocol reference model by merging the services provided by two or more layers of the OSI reference model.

outer shielding A layer of aluminum, metallized Mylar, or sometimes aluminum braid that eliminates interference from outside interference.

outer and inner shielding Shielding that consists of an outer layer that eliminates interference from external signals and an inner layer around each pair of conductors that eliminates interference between the pairs of wires.

oxidation The addition of oxygen to a compound, most notably the process of rusting iron.

P

packet A small unit of data that contains a header designed to verify successful transmission and to indicate the destination for the information.

paging The process of using virtual memory. Reading memory from or writing memory to disk.

paging file A file used as virtual memory.

palette A color range used by video cards to allow a smaller number of colors to be selected out of a wider range. A typical palette would select 256 colors out of 16 million.

parity A technique for determining, through the use of an additional bit of memory, whether a single bit within a byte or larger set of memory has failed.

partitioning The act of indicating which sections of a hard disk are to be used for which formats. Partitioning selects the space to be used on a hard disk for a logical volume.

passive terminator A simple bus terminator consisting simply of resistors. It was replaced by active terminators due to the enhanced rejection of errant signals.

password A string used to indicate authorization. A password is used in conjunction with a user name to indicate identity.

password-cracking program A program that attempts to guess passwords based on brute force. These programs are run continuously against a system or file for the purpose of finding a successful password or user name and password combination.

patches Fixes to an operating system or application designed to address specific issues reported by customers. Patches are generally, but not always, collected into service packs.

PC board A board on which electrical components are mounted. For instance, the motherboard of a personal computer is a PC board.

PCI *see* Peripheral Component Interconnect

peer PCI bus Multiple PCI buses connected directly to the CPU, not to one another as in a hierarchical PCI bus. Peer PCI buses offer better performance but have a higher cost.

Peripheral Component Interconnect (PCI) An Intel specification for a PC bus architecture in current use. PCI bus connectors on a motherboard are generally white.

Perl An interpreted scripting/programming language.

physical security The prevention of unauthorized access by means of physical barriers and access systems. Physical security is distinct from software-based security.

physical storage The physical devices on which data storage is accomplished, most commonly hard disks. Physical storage is distinct from logical storage.

PING Short for Packet Internet Groper. A utility that uses low-level TCP/IP functions to verify basic connectivity to a host.

ping To contact a host via the PING utility.

PIO *see* programmed I/O

Platform Support Module (PSM) A device driver for Novell NetWare that provides access to hardware-specific functionality. It is equivalent to the Microsoft Windows 2000 hardware abstraction layer (HAL).

Plug and Play (PnP) A technology for ISA-based add-on cards and PCI-based add-on cards that allows the card to be configured by the BIOS or by a Plug and Play operating system rather than requiring you to physically set DIP switches or jumpers on the card.

PnP *see* Plug and Play

Polling The process of repeatedly checking for an event or activity.

POST *see* power-on self test

power-on self test (POST) The process that occurs when a computer is first turned on. This process tests components to ensure that they are functioning correctly and then hands control over to a boot device.

power sag A brief decrease in voltage.

power spike A momentary dramatic increase in voltage.

power surge A brief increase in voltage.

primary domain controller The read-write copy of the security and computer information database in Microsoft Windows NT. Backup domain controllers are used to distribute the workload involved in maintaining this security database.

processor affinity A setting that causes processes or threads to be run more frequently on one processor in a multiprocessor system. This setting optimizes on-board processor caches. Affinity can be set to hold a thread to a processor, to prevent a thread from running on certain processors, or to require that a thread be run on a specific processor.

programmed I/O (PIO) A method of interaction between the operating system and an add-on device that requires the use of I/O ports. This method of interaction is very processor-intensive and should be avoided when possible.

proxy server A server that accesses a service or network on behalf of its clients. Proxy servers are frequently used for access to the Internet from corporate computers.

PSM *see* Platform Support Module

Q, R

RAID *see* redundant array of inexpensive disks

RAID-0 Disk striping. The interleaving of two or more disks to combine the storage capacity of all of the disks. This type of RAID is not fault tolerant.

RAID-1 Disk mirroring or, when used with two controllers, disk duplexing. A mechanism of providing fault tolerance by means of making an identical copy of the data.

RAID-5 A mechanism of providing fault tolerance and extended capacity by means of generating parity information. This type of RAID requires a minimum of three disks.

Rambus dynamic random access memory (RDRAM) A form of memory that operates at high speed. RDRAM is the most expensive form of memory available today.

RAS *see* remote access server

RDRAM *see* Rambus dynamic random access memory

README A file included with software distributions and drivers that indicates late-breaking or important news about the installation. README files can come in several formats.

read-only memory (ROM) Nonvolatile memory. ROM does not lose its contents when power is removed, and it cannot be written to or changed.

redundant array of inexpensive disks (RAID) Also known as redundant array of independent disks. A series of mechanisms for using multiple smaller drives as if they were one large drive. All of the original RAID levels provide for fault tolerance. The addition of RAID-0 provided a non-fault-tolerant solution.

registry A database of configuration information used in Microsoft Windows 95, Windows 98, Windows 2000, Windows Me, and Windows NT.

relative humidity The amount of water vapor in the air compared to the maximum amount of water vapor the air can hold. Relative humidity is based on temperature. *See also* humidity.

remote access server (RAS) A server whose purpose is to provide remote access to the network through the use of modems or encrypted communications channels.

request for comments (RFC) The mechanism by which Internet standards are proposed. Request for comments documents are published and comments are received.

resistance Any opposition to current flowing. Resistance reduces the voltage and converts the energy into heat.

resonance An increase in amplitude of energy caused by the natural frequency of a material matching the phase and frequency of the input energy in the system.

reverse DNS lookup Resolution of a TCP/IP name from an IP address.

RFC *see* request for comments

RLL *see* run-length limited

ROM *see* read-only memory

rotational speed The speed at which something is turning or rotating. This term most frequently refers to hard disk speeds, which may be 3600 rpm, 5400 rpm, 7200 rpm, 10,000 rpm, 14,000 rpm, or greater.

round-robin DNS A method of balancing the load among servers by providing different IP addresses, and thus different servers, in series for the same TCP/IP name.

router A device that operates at the network level. It routes packets to the appropriate destination based on the destination information in the packet.

RS-232 A serial communications standard used in PCs.

RS-232 breakout box A device that allows the signals on an RS-232 serial connection to be visualized through a series of LEDs. It also allows for the connection between two devices to be rewired to correct any connectivity problems.

run-length limited (RLL) A method of encoding information on a hard disk that is no longer in common use.

S

Samba An application for Linux that allows it to provide SMB-based file and print services.

SAP *see* Service Advertising Protocol

SCA *see* single connection attachment

scalability The ability to expand to handle dramatically greater loads than originally anticipated.

SC connector A square type of connector used for fiber optic connectivity.

scientific method A process by which unknowns can become known. A useful technique for troubleshooting computer problems.

SCSI *see* Small Computer System Interface

SDRAM *see* synchronous dynamic random-access memory

Sector A small region of space on a hard drive capable of holding a fixed amount of data.

Secure Sockets Layer (SSL) An encryption layer applied to HTTP communication channels.

Self-Monitoring, Analysis and Reporting Technology (SMART) A technology built into some hard disks that monitors the number of hard and soft errors encountered by a hard disk to provide a proactive identification of potential critical failures.

Sequenced Packet Exchange (SPX) A connection-based guaranteed delivery protocol that is part of the IPX/SPX protocol suite made popular by Novell NetWare.

server message block (SMB) An application-level protocol for file and print services used by Microsoft servers and clients. It is similar to Novell NetWare's NCP.

Service Advertising Protocol (SAP) A protocol used by Novell NetWare and IPX/SPX to announce the availability of services to clients.

service pack A collection of patches that are retested and repackaged for widespread implementation.

SE SCSI *see* single-ended SCSI

shell script A relatively inflexible programming language that does not get compiled but is interpreted by the command shell.

shorting The process by which a circuit is unintentionally created, usually without the limits of resistors, causing a large amount of current to flow through the circuit very rapidly. Normally this results in a fusing of the circuit itself, leading to damage.

SIMM *see* single inline memory module

Simple Mail Transport Protocol (SMTP) The server-to-server communications protocol used to transport e-mail messages across the Internet.

Simple Network Management Protocol (SNMP) A protocol for monitoring, configuring, and identifying problems with network-attached devices, including servers with SNMP agents installed. SNMP comprises two components: the SNMP agent that runs on the device and an SNMP management console that collects information and communicates with the user.

single connection attachment (SCA) A connector for SCSI hard disks that combines signaling, configuration, and power connectors into a single unified connector to simplify installation.

single-ended SCSI (SE SCSI) The most common type of SCSI in use today. Although high-end implementations are now starting to switch to LVD SCSI, a large number of SE SCSI devices are already installed. SE SCSI manipulates only one of the pair of wires involved in communication, unlike differential versions, which drive both lines.

single inline memory module (SIMM) An arrangement of memory on memory cards that organizes memory in 16-bit-wide or 32-bit-wide chunks. SIMMs come in 36-pin and 72-pin varieties. They are not largely used in servers or newer workstations but may exist in some environments.

Small Computer System Interface (SCSI) A connection bus designed for connecting hard disks and other devices to a computer. SCSI performs better than the AT Attachment bus in multiuser environments. Several revisions of SCSI exist.

SMART *see* Self-Monitoring, Analysis and Reporting Technology

SMB *see* server message block

SMP *see* symmetric multiprocessing

SMTP *see* Simple Mail Transport Protocol

SNA *see* Systems Network Architecture

SNMP *see* Simple Network Management Protocol.

SNMP trap A notification generated by an SNMP agent for the purpose of indicating to the management console that an event has occurred. This type of trap allows the management console to reduce the polling frequency for some devices.

software-based security The prevention of unauthorized access to information or resources through the use of software. The term generally refers to the software-based identification of users and authorizations associated with those users.

software metering A type of monitoring involving software designed to indicate the number of copies of a particular application that are in use at any given time and sometimes to prevent more copies of the application from being used than are currently licensed. Software metering is often used in larger organizations to contain software costs.

solder A metallic compound with a relatively low melting point, used to connect two pieces of metal.

solder traces Thin lines of solder used to connect components on a PC board.

SPS *see* standby power supply

SPX *see* Sequenced Packet Exchange

SQL *see* structured query language

SSL *see* Secure Sockets Layer

standby power supply (SPS) The most common type of power protection in use today. An SPS differs from a UPS because of the momentary (brief) switching time required to transfer to the power supply.

static electric field An electromagnetic field kept in stasis by the electrical charges until disrupted.

ST connector A connector used with fiber optic cables that has a latching mechanism similar to a BNC connector. The connector itself is a cylinder with a rotating collar that attaches around posts on the other side.

stepping level The indication of the specific manufacturing process and internal circuit design used in the manufacture of a CPU. The stepping level is important because of potential timing differences that may result in small changes in the design. Most multiprocessor systems should use only CPUs with the same or similar processor stepping levels.

string A variable that contains a collection of alphanumeric digits.

structured query language (SQL) A language developed to standardize and simplify queries submitted to different database engines. ANSI (American National Standards Institute) has defined several different revisions of SQL that are supported in varying degrees by the different database engine providers.

subfloor The flooring underneath the surface that is walked on. The term is generally used to refer to the space underneath raised flooring.

Super Video Graphics Adapter (SVGA) An old pseudo-standard for video cards supporting higher resolutions and higher color depths than VGA supported.

sustained throughput The maximum speed or transfer rate that can be continuously maintained.

SVGA *see* Super Video Graphics Adapter

symmetric multiprocessing (SMP) A multiprocessor architecture in which no one master processor assigns work. All of the processors cooperatively determine which threads of execution to use.

synchronous dynamic random-access memory (SDRAM) A faster version of DRAM that is in common use today.

Systems Network Architecture (SNA) IBM's application and network infrastructure for mainframe and midrange computers.

T

TAP *see* Telocator Alphanumeric Protocol

tape backup window The amount of time available for a tape backup to be completed. This window is based on the organization's tolerance for scheduled downtime or reduced performance.

tape wear *see* media wear

taxonomy Classification in an ordered system of natural relationships.

TCP/IP *see* Transmission Control Protocol/Internet Protocol.

Telocator Alphanumeric Protocol (TAP) An interface to digital alphanumeric paging systems that is accomplished through the use of a modem and a specific sequence of communications. It is supported by almost every alphanumeric paging and messaging system.

termination The act of preventing something from continuing. With respect to computers, termination stops signals from reflecting off of the end of an electrical conductor.

thread A portion of a program that follows its own execution order independently of other parts of the program.

throughput The amount of output occurring in a given unit of time.

time synchronization The process of synchronizing clocks to a single source. It is often done through atomic clocks available via radio transmission, Web sites, or Network Time Protocol (NTP).

time zone A geographic area that observes a particular time offset from the Universal Time Coordinate (UTC) at Greenwich, England. The continental United States has four time zones within its boundaries.

token ring An IEEE 802.5 standard that defines physical and data link layers of communication for a token-passing topology. It defines speeds of 4 megabits per second (Mbps) and 16 Mbps. Token ring is still supported but is no longer widely implemented.

topology The medium (cable) and connecting devices used to connect computers to a network.

Tower of Hanoi A puzzle created by a French mathematician, adopted as a backup rotation scheme.

transactional systems Systems based on discrete events that are either completed as a unit or rejected as a unit. Most transactional systems are databases.

Transmission Control Protocol/Internet Protocol (TCP/IP) A suite of protocols that are used for the Internet and in large corporate environments. The TCP/IP suite of protocols encompasses all layers, beginning at the network layer, of the OSI protocol reference model.

U

U A vertical unit of space in an industry-standard 19-inch rack that is equal to 1.75 inches.

UDP *see* User Datagram Protocol

uninterruptible power supply (UPS) A power supply that converts incoming energy into storable energy or motion and separately converts that stored energy or motion into output power. True UPSs are used for environments that cannot accept even the momentary loss of power that occurs in SPSs when they switch over.

unicast Data packets sent to a specific hardware address, as opposed to multicast or broadcast packets.

Universal Serial Bus (USB) A bus designed for connectivity with devices external to the computer. Automatic configuration of devices is supported. Often used for input devices and devices needing a bus capable of moderate data speeds.

UNIX A powerful operating system originally developed at Bell Laboratories and since extended into several variations, including Linux.

UPS *see* uninterruptible power supply

USB *see* Universal Serial Bus

Usenet *see* Internet newsgroups

User Datagram Protocol (UDP) A protocol within the TCP/IP protocol suite responsible for unverified, connectionless communication.

V

VA *see* volt-amp.

Variable A place in memory that holds a value or series of values. Used in computer programs.

VESA *see* Video Electronic Standards Association

VGA *see* Video Graphics Adapter

Video Electronic Standards Association (VESA) An organization formed to help define standards for video adapters and access to them. VESA endorsed a Video Local Bus (VLB) standard of connectivity for video cards that was popular due to its low cost at the time when 80486 processors were popular.

Video Graphics Adapter (VGA) A video adapter standard that most advanced video adapters now support that allows for a selection of modes, including a resolution of 640x480. Almost every video card in use today in PCs is at least VGA compatible.

virtual memory The ability for an operating system to give the appearance of more physical memory (RAM) to the applications that are running by storing some information that would normally be stored in main memory on disk.

virus A malicious program that is self-replicating.

volt A standard unit of measure for electrical potential.

volt-amp (VA) A measurement of electrical power used in the sizing of UPSs.

W

Web server A server designed to provide HTML files through the use of the HTTP protocol.

Windows 2000 A Microsoft operating system designed for commercial installation providing robust security features.

Windows Internet Name Service (WINS) A naming server for NetBIOS running over TCP/IP (NetBT). WINS provides a centralized name database to limit the amount of IP address discovery that must be performed via broadcasts.

WINS *see* Windows Internet Name Service

World Wide Web A hyperlinked set of HTML documents referring to one another on the Internet. It is accessed via the HTTP protocol.

WORM *see* write once, read many

write once, read many (WORM) A type of medium that can be written to only once but read many times. Standard CD-R discs are a WORM medium in that any given sector of the CD can be written only once.

write-protect tab A safety device located on tapes that signals the tape drive that writing should not be permitted to the tape. This tab is often set during a restore to prevent accidental erasure of the information that is being restored.

X

X Window System A graphical user interface used on UNIX-based systems.

Y

"Y" power adapter An adapter that takes one drive power lead in and provides two new drive power leads. It is used when the power supply does not provide a sufficient number of leads.

Z

zero insertion force (ZIF) A type of pin grid array (PGA) socket in which the processor is set into position without any pressure and locked into place by a locking arm on the side of the socket. ZIF sockets are implemented in most motherboards using 80486 processors and later.

ZIF *see* zero insertion force

Index

Note: Italicized page references indicate figures, tables, or code listings.

Colophon

The manuscript for this book was prepared using Microsoft Word 2000 and submitted to Microsoft Press in electronic form. Pages were composed using Adobe PageMaker 6.52 for Windows, with text in Times and display type in Helvetica-Narrow. Composed pages were delivered to the printer as electronic prepress files.

Cover Graphic Designer
Landor

Interior Graphic Designer
Jim Kramer

Principal Graphic Artist
Michael Kloepfer

Screen Capture and Graphic Conversion Specialist
Bill Teel

Manuscript Editor
Rebecca Pepper

Principal Copy Editor
Lisa Pawlewicz

Principal Compositor
Gina Cassill

Indexer
Richard Shrout

Ready solutions *for the*
IT administrator

Keep your IT systems up and running with the ADMINISTRATOR'S COMPANION series from Microsoft. These expert guides serve as both tutorials and references for critical deployment and maintenance of Microsoft products and technologies. Packed with real-world expertise, hands-on numbered procedures, and handy workarounds, ADMINISTRATOR'S COMPANIONS deliver ready answers for on-the-job results.

In-depth. Focused. *And* ready for work.

Get the technical drilldown you need to deploy and support Microsoft products more effectively with the MICROSOFT TECHNICAL REFERENCE series. Each guide focuses on a specific aspect of the technology—weaving in-depth detail with on-the-job scenarios and practical how-to information for the IT professional. Get focused—and take technology to its limits—with MICROSOFT TECHNICAL REFERENCES.

Data Warehousing with Microsoft® SQL Server™ 7.0 Technical Reference
U.S.A. $49.99
Canada $76.99
ISBN 0-7356-0859-8

Microsoft SQL Server 7.0 Performance Tuning Technical Reference
U.S.A. $49.99
Canada $76.99
ISBN 0-7356-0909-8

Building Applications with Microsoft Outlook® 2000 Technical Reference
U.S.A. $49.99
Canada $72.99
ISBN 0-7356-0581-5

Microsoft Windows NT® Server 4.0 Terminal Server Edition Technical Reference
U.S.A. $49.99
Canada $72.99
ISBN 0-7356-0645-5

Microsoft Windows® 2000 TCP/IP Protocols and Services Technical Reference
U.S.A. $49.99
Canada $76.99
ISBN 0-7356-0556-4

Active Directory™ Services for Microsoft Windows 2000 Technical Reference
U.S.A. $49.99
Canada $76.99
ISBN 0-7356-0624-2

Microsoft Windows 2000 Security Technical Reference
U.S.A. $49.99
Canada $72.99
ISBN 0-7356-0858-X

Microsoft Windows 2000 Performance Tuning Technical Reference
U.S.A. $49.99
Canada $72.99
ISBN 0-7356-0633-1

mspress.microsoft.com

Microsoft® Resource Kits—
powerhouse resources
to minimize costs while
maximizing performance

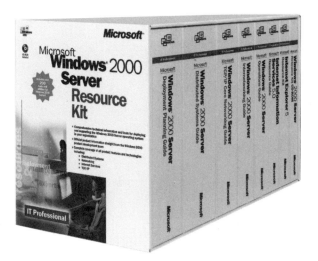

Deploy and support your enterprise business systems using the expertise and tools of those who know the technology best—the Microsoft product groups. Each RESOURCE KIT packs precise technical reference, installation and rollout tactics, planning guides, upgrade strategies, and essential utilities on CD-ROM. They're everything you need to help maximize system performance as you reduce ownership and support costs!

Microsoft® Windows® 2000 Server Resource Kit
ISBN 1-57231-805-8
U.S.A. $299.99
U.K.   £189.99 [V.A.T. included]
Canada $460.99

Microsoft Windows 2000 Professional Resource Kit
ISBN 1-57231-808-2
U.S.A. $69.99
U.K.   £45.99 [V.A.T. included]
Canada $107.99

Microsoft BackOffice® 4.5 Resource Kit
ISBN 0-7356-0583-1
U.S.A. $249.99
U.K.   £161.99 [V.A.T. included]
Canada $374.99

Microsoft Internet Explorer 5 Resource Kit
ISBN 0-7356-0587-4
U.S.A. $59.99
U.K.   £38.99 [V.A.T. included]
Canada $89.99

Microsoft Office 2000 Resource Kit
ISBN 0-7356-0555-6
U.S.A. $59.99
U.K.   £38.99 [V.A.T. included]
Canada $89.99

Microsoft Windows NT® Server 4.0 Resource Kit
ISBN 1-57231-344-7
U.S.A. $149.95
U.K.   £96.99 [V.A.T. included]
Canada $199.95

Microsoft Windows NT Workstation 4.0 Resource Kit
ISBN 1-57231-343-9
U.S.A. $69.95
U.K.   £45.99 [V.A.T. included]
Canada $94.95

mspress.microsoft.com

Get a **Free**
e-mail newsletter, updates,
special offers, links to related books,
and more when you

register on line!

Register your Microsoft Press® title on our Web site and you'll get a FREE subscription to our e-mail newsletter, Microsoft Press Book Connections. You'll find out about newly released and upcoming books and learning tools, online events, software downloads, special offers and coupons for Microsoft Press customers, and information about major Microsoft® product releases. You can also read useful additional information about all the titles we publish, such as detailed book descriptions, tables of contents and indexes, sample chapters, links to related books and book series, author biographies, and reviews by other customers.

Registration is easy. Just visit this Web page and fill in your information:

http://mspress.microsoft.com/register

Microsoft®

Proof of Purchase

Server+ Certification Training Kit
0-7356-1272-2

CUSTOMER NAME

Microsoft Press, PO Box 97017, Redmond, WA 98073-9830

MICROSOFT LICENSE AGREEMENT

Book Companion CD

IMPORTANT—READ CAREFULLY: This Microsoft End-User License Agreement ("EULA") is a legal agreement between you (either an individual or an entity) and Microsoft Corporation for the Microsoft product identified above, which includes computer software and may include associated media, printed materials, and "online" or electronic documentation ("SOFTWARE PRODUCT"). Any component included within the SOFTWARE PRODUCT that is accompanied by a separate End-User License Agreement shall be governed by such agreement and not the terms set forth below. By installing, copying, or otherwise using the SOFTWARE PRODUCT, you agree to be bound by the terms of this EULA. If you do not agree to the terms of this EULA, you are not authorized to install, copy, or otherwise use the SOFTWARE PRODUCT; you may, however, return the SOFTWARE PRODUCT, along with all printed materials and other items that form a part of the Microsoft product that includes the SOFTWARE PRODUCT, to the place you obtained them for a full refund.

SOFTWARE PRODUCT LICENSE

The SOFTWARE PRODUCT is protected by United States copyright laws and international copyright treaties, as well as other intellectual property laws and treaties. The SOFTWARE PRODUCT is licensed, not sold.

1. **GRANT OF LICENSE.** This EULA grants you the following rights:

   a. **Software Product.** You may install and use one copy of the SOFTWARE PRODUCT on a single computer. The primary user of the computer on which the SOFTWARE PRODUCT is installed may make a second copy for his or her exclusive use on a portable computer.

   b. **Storage/Network Use.** You may also store or install a copy of the SOFTWARE PRODUCT on a storage device, such as a network server, used only to install or run the SOFTWARE PRODUCT on your other computers over an internal network; however, you must acquire and dedicate a license for each separate computer on which the SOFTWARE PRODUCT is installed or run from the storage device. A license for the SOFTWARE PRODUCT may not be shared or used concurrently on different computers.

   c. **License Pak.** If you have acquired this EULA in a Microsoft License Pak, you may make the number of additional copies of the computer software portion of the SOFTWARE PRODUCT authorized on the printed copy of this EULA, and you may use each copy in the manner specified above. You are also entitled to make a corresponding number of secondary copies for portable computer use as specified above.

   d. **Sample Code.** Solely with respect to portions, if any, of the SOFTWARE PRODUCT that are identified within the SOFTWARE PRODUCT as sample code (the "SAMPLE CODE"):

      i. **Use and Modification.** Microsoft grants you the right to use and modify the source code version of the SAMPLE CODE, *provided* you comply with subsection (d)(iii) below. You may not distribute the SAMPLE CODE, or any modified version of the SAMPLE CODE, in source code form.

      ii. **Redistributable Files.** Provided you comply with subsection (d)(iii) below, Microsoft grants you a nonexclusive, royalty-free right to reproduce and distribute the object code version of the SAMPLE CODE and of any modified SAMPLE CODE, other than SAMPLE CODE, or any modified version thereof, designated as not redistributable in the Readme file that forms a part of the SOFTWARE PRODUCT (the "Non-Redistributable Sample Code"). All SAMPLE CODE other than the Non-Redistributable Sample Code is collectively referred to as the "REDISTRIBUTABLES."

      iii. **Redistribution Requirements.** If you redistribute the REDISTRIBUTABLES, you agree to: (i) distribute the REDISTRIBUTABLES in object code form only in conjunction with and as a part of your software application product; (ii) not use Microsoft's name, logo, or trademarks to market your software application product; (iii) include a valid copyright notice on your software application product; (iv) indemnify, hold harmless, and defend Microsoft from and against any claims or lawsuits, including attorney's fees, that arise or result from the use or distribution of your software application product; and (v) not permit further distribution of the REDISTRIBUTABLES by your end user. Contact Microsoft for the applicable royalties due and other licensing terms for all other uses and/or distribution of the REDISTRIBUTABLES.

2. **DESCRIPTION OF OTHER RIGHTS AND LIMITATIONS.**

   - **Limitations on Reverse Engineering, Decompilation, and Disassembly.** You may not reverse engineer, decompile, or disassemble the SOFTWARE PRODUCT, except and only to the extent that such activity is expressly permitted by applicable law notwithstanding this limitation.

   - **Separation of Components.** The SOFTWARE PRODUCT is licensed as a single product. Its component parts may not be separated for use on more than one computer.

   - **Rental.** You may not rent, lease, or lend the SOFTWARE PRODUCT.

- **Support Services.** Microsoft may, but is not obligated to, provide you with support services related to the SOFTWARE PRODUCT ("Support Services"). Use of Support Services is governed by the Microsoft policies and programs described in the user manual, in "online" documentation, and/or in other Microsoft-provided materials. Any supplemental software code provided to you as part of the Support Services shall be considered part of the SOFTWARE PRODUCT and subject to the terms and conditions of this EULA. With respect to technical information you provide to Microsoft as part of the Support Services, Microsoft may use such information for its business purposes, including for product support and development. Microsoft will not utilize such technical information in a form that personally identifies you.

- **Software Transfer.** You may permanently transfer all of your rights under this EULA, provided you retain no copies, you transfer all of the SOFTWARE PRODUCT (including all component parts, the media and printed materials, any upgrades, this EULA, and, if applicable, the Certificate of Authenticity), **and** the recipient agrees to the terms of this EULA.

- **Termination.** Without prejudice to any other rights, Microsoft may terminate this EULA if you fail to comply with the terms and conditions of this EULA. In such event, you must destroy all copies of the SOFTWARE PRODUCT and all of its component parts.

3. COPYRIGHT. All title and copyrights in and to the SOFTWARE PRODUCT (including but not limited to any images, photographs, animations, video, audio, music, text, SAMPLE CODE, REDISTRIBUTABLES, and "applets" incorporated into the SOFTWARE PRODUCT) and any copies of the SOFTWARE PRODUCT are owned by Microsoft or its suppliers. The SOFT-WARE PRODUCT is protected by copyright laws and international treaty provisions. Therefore, you must treat the SOFTWARE PRODUCT like any other copyrighted material **except** that you may install the SOFTWARE PRODUCT on a single computer provided you keep the original solely for backup or archival purposes. You may not copy the printed materials accompanying the SOFTWARE PRODUCT.

4. U.S. GOVERNMENT RESTRICTED RIGHTS. The SOFTWARE PRODUCT and documentation are provided with RESTRICTED RIGHTS. Use, duplication, or disclosure by the Government is subject to restrictions as set forth in subparagraph (c)(1)(ii) of the Rights in Technical Data and Computer Software clause at DFARS 252.227-7013 or subparagraphs (c)(1) and (2) of the Commercial Computer Software—Restricted Rights at 48 CFR 52.227-19, as applicable. Manufacturer is Microsoft Corporation/One Microsoft Way/Redmond, WA 98052-6399.

5. EXPORT RESTRICTIONS. You agree that you will not export or re-export the SOFTWARE PRODUCT, any part thereof, or any process or service that is the direct product of the SOFTWARE PRODUCT (the foregoing collectively referred to as the "Restricted Components"), to any country, person, entity, or end user subject to U.S. export restrictions. You specifically agree not to export or re-export any of the Restricted Components (i) to any country to which the U.S. has embargoed or restricted the export of goods or services, which currently include, but are not necessarily limited to, Cuba, Iran, Iraq, Libya, North Korea, Sudan, and Syria, or to any national of any such country, wherever located, who intends to transmit or transport the Restricted Components back to such country; (ii) to any end user who you know or have reason to know will utilize the Restricted Components in the design, development, or production of nuclear, chemical, or biological weapons; or (iii) to any end user who has been prohibited from participating in U.S. export transactions by any federal agency of the U.S. government. You warrant and represent that neither the BXA nor any other U.S. federal agency has suspended, revoked, or denied your export privileges.

DISCLAIMER OF WARRANTY

NO WARRANTIES OR CONDITIONS. MICROSOFT EXPRESSLY DISCLAIMS ANY WARRANTY OR CONDITION FOR THE SOFTWARE PRODUCT. THE SOFTWARE PRODUCT AND ANY RELATED DOCUMENTATION ARE PROVIDED "AS IS" WITHOUT WARRANTY OR CONDITION OF ANY KIND, EITHER EXPRESS OR IMPLIED, INCLUDING, WITHOUT LIMITA-TION, THE IMPLIED WARRANTIES OF MERCHANTABILITY, FITNESS FOR A PARTICULAR PURPOSE, OR NONINFRINGEMENT. THE ENTIRE RISK ARISING OUT OF USE OR PERFORMANCE OF THE SOFTWARE PRODUCT REMAINS WITH YOU.

LIMITATION OF LIABILITY. TO THE MAXIMUM EXTENT PERMITTED BY APPLICABLE LAW, IN NO EVENT SHALL MICROSOFT OR ITS SUPPLIERS BE LIABLE FOR ANY SPECIAL, INCIDENTAL, INDIRECT, OR CONSEQUENTIAL DAM-AGES WHATSOEVER (INCLUDING, WITHOUT LIMITATION, DAMAGES FOR LOSS OF BUSINESS PROFITS, BUSINESS INTERRUPTION, LOSS OF BUSINESS INFORMATION, OR ANY OTHER PECUNIARY LOSS) ARISING OUT OF THE USE OF OR INABILITY TO USE THE SOFTWARE PRODUCT OR THE PROVISION OF OR FAILURE TO PROVIDE SUPPORT SERVICES, EVEN IF MICROSOFT HAS BEEN ADVISED OF THE POSSIBILITY OF SUCH DAMAGES. IN ANY CASE, MICROSOFT'S ENTIRE LIABILITY UNDER ANY PROVISION OF THIS EULA SHALL BE LIMITED TO THE GREATER OF THE AMOUNT ACTUALLY PAID BY YOU FOR THE SOFTWARE PRODUCT OR US$5.00; PROVIDED, HOWEVER, IF YOU HAVE ENTERED INTO A MICROSOFT SUPPORT SERVICES AGREEMENT, MICROSOFT'S ENTIRE LIABILITY REGARDING SUPPORT SERVICES SHALL BE GOVERNED BY THE TERMS OF THAT AGREEMENT. BECAUSE SOME STATES AND JURISDICTIONS DO NOT ALLOW THE EXCLUSION OR LIMITATION OF LIABILITY, THE ABOVE LIMITATION MAY NOT APPLY TO YOU.

MISCELLANEOUS

This EULA is governed by the laws of the State of Washington USA, except and only to the extent that applicable law mandates governing law of a different jurisdiction.

Should you have any questions concerning this EULA, or if you desire to contact Microsoft for any reason, please contact the Microsoft subsidiary serving your country, or write: Microsoft Sales Information Center/One Microsoft Way/Redmond, WA 98052-6399.

System Requirements

To use the *Server+ Training Kit* compact disc, you need a computer equipped with the following minimum configuration:

- 486 or higher processor
- Microsoft Windows 95, Windows 98, Microsoft Windows NT4 SP3 or later, or Windows 2000
- CD-ROM drive
- Microsoft Mouse or other pointing device (recommended)

For the Chapter 9 worksheets:

- 4 MB RAM
- 5 MB hard disk space
- Microsoft Word 97 or later, or Microsoft Word Viewer (included on this CD)

For Word Viewer:

- 4 MB RAM for Windows 95, 16 MB RAM for Windows 98, 12 MB RAM for Windows NT Workstation, 64 MB RAM for Windows 2000
- 7 MB of hard disk space (9 MB free for installation only)
- VGA or higher-resolution video adaptor
- Microsoft Mouse or compatible pointing device

For each eBook:

- 12 MB RAM with Windows 95; 16 MB RAM with Windows 98; 16 MB RAM with Windows NT4 SP3; 64 MB RAM with Windows 2000
- 10 MB disk space to install and run from a network (network installation); 20–31 MB disk space to install to the hard drive (local installation)
- 110 MB disk space to install Microsoft Internet Explorer to the hard drive (local installation) and install and run an eBook from a network (network installation)
- 120–131 MB disk space to install Microsoft Internet Explorer to the hard drive (local installation) and install and run the eBook from a hard drive (local installation)
- Internet Explorer 5.0 or later. Microsoft Internet Explorer 5.01 is included on the CD and will be installed on the user's machine automatically if necessary. The Internet Explorer setup has been configured to install the minimum necessary files and will not change the user's current settings or associations.